Undue Burden

Undue Burden

———

LIFE-AND-DEATH DECISIONS
IN POST-*ROE* AMERICA

Shefali Luthra

DOUBLEDAY   NEW YORK

Front-of-jacket photographs: Jackson Women's Health
Organization, Jackson, Mississippi © Rory Doyle/Reuters;
sky © Max play/Shutterstock
Jacket design by Emily Mahon

A cataloging-in-publication record has been established
for this book by the Library of Congress.
LCCN: 2024933781
ISBN: 978-0-385-55008-6 (hardcover)
ISBN: 978-0-385-55009-3 (ebook)

MANUFACTURED IN THE UNITED STATES OF AMERICA
1 3 5 7 9 10 8 6 4 2
First Edition

For Mom, for Mummy, and for all the aunties

Whatever the exact scope of the coming laws, one result of today's decision is certain: the curtailment of women's rights, and of their status as free and equal citizens.

—JUSTICES STEPHEN BREYER,

SONIA SOTOMAYOR,

AND

ELENA KAGAN,
Dobbs v. Jackson Women's Health Organization

Contents

Introduction

It's difficult to think of a public health crisis more inevitable than the impending end of *Roe v. Wade*. And yet, on June 24, 2022, the country was profoundly unprepared.

Roe, one of the U.S. Supreme Court's most consequential decisions, had been on the chopping block since it was first decided, and the protection it promised was long treated as expendable. In 1973, the very year the U.S. Supreme Court ruled that the Constitution guaranteed the right to an abortion up until the third trimester of pregnancy, statehouses across the country passed more than eighty different restrictions on the procedure, according to the nonpartisan Guttmacher Institute, which supports abortion rights but whose data are cited across the political spectrum. It didn't matter if these laws wouldn't pass constitutional muster. More important was what they signified: the energy that would galvanize the anti-abortion movement for the next fifty years, ensuring that *Roe* would someday fall. In 1976, only three years after *Roe,* the U.S. Congress effectively siloed abortion from any other form of health care, passing a law that prohibited the use of federal money to pay for abortions. It was a choice that would help cement in the national consciousness the idea that abortion could and should be treated as a niche concern, separate from normal medical care. Barely two decades later, in 1992, the Supreme Court issued a ruling that, while preserving *Roe*'s protections, fundamentally weakened it, ruling on a case challenging the constitutionality of a series of abortion restrictions passed in the state of Pennsylvania. In that case, *Planned Parenthood v. Casey,* the court held that states could indeed limit access to abortion before viability—the point at which the fetus can live independently outside the womb—as long as they didn't impose what the court called "an undue burden." The court never defined what exactly that meant. It was a step back from what *Roe* had originally promised: an abortion protection continuing throughout the first two-thirds of pregnancy, without threat of legislative interference. The ruling was monumental and would eventually open the door for states to pass and enforce laws that would make abortion increasingly difficult if not impossible to access.

Casey's significance wouldn't fully materialize for another twenty years, until the 2010s, when the Tea Party, whose endorsed candidates strongly opposed abortion, won control of legislatures across the country. Abortion rights, treated by the court as a federal issue, would now be fundamentally undercut by statehouses. Republican-led states passed abortion restriction after restriction, imposing new limits on when people could terminate a pregnancy, adding new barriers and requirements for both patients seeking care and health care providers offering it, and in some cases passing regulations so onerous—and, critically, without proven medical benefit—that they would force clinics to shut down. The laws were challenges; state lawmakers were daring the Supreme Court to weaken *Roe* and to someday overturn it. The eventual evisceration of *Roe* is perhaps one of the Tea Party's greatest successes and most potent legacies.

Then came 2016, when Donald Trump was elected to the White House after campaigning in no small part on a promise to appoint Supreme Court justices who would vote to undo *Roe*. Candidate Trump had even argued that there must be "some form of punishment" for the people who sought to end their pregnancies—a statement more overtly threatening than what major anti-abortion activists had previously said out loud. Trump's election was a turning point in the nation's history and was arguably the last nail in the coffin, leading to *Roe's* demise. Yet despite all the evidence illustrating where we must be heading, it remained difficult to truly fathom that the United States would soon enter a world without abortion rights—let alone internalize what that meant.

. . .

The right to end a pregnancy is at least as old as the country itself;
through the 1700s and up until the late 1800s, common law held
that abortions were generally permissible as long as the pregnant
person hadn't yet begun to feel the fetus moving—known as the
"quickening"—and even major Catholic institutions didn't oppose
abortion up to this point. It wasn't until 1880 that every state had
passed laws criminalizing abortion, a shift less about religion and
more the product of a campaign orchestrated by a male-dominated
medical establishment. Historians have written at length about
how physicians promoted the regulation and restriction of abortion in part to consolidate power and weaken the credibility of the
midwives—typically women—who often helped people terminate
their pregnancies. One of the era's leading anti-abortion crusaders,
Dr. Horatio Storer, proselytized another explicitly racist argument:
banning abortion was necessary to ensure that White Anglo-Saxon
Protestant women kept giving birth in order to prevent American
demographics from shifting to become too Irish, too Italian, too
Jewish, or too Black. Around the same time, the 1873 Comstock
Act—an effort to police American morality—targeted reproductive health, outlawing the mailing of information regarding contraception or "unlawful abortion" as "obscene." Still, abortion never
went away. Through the Great Depression, some physicians helped
people terminate pregnancies, understanding just how many could
not afford to feed and care for another child. A small number of
physicians even began to argue for the first time that abortion
should be made explicitly legal, reflecting a new understanding
that economic well-being influenced one's health—and that abortion access shaped both. But illegal abortions remained a public
health concern: 2,700 pregnancy-related deaths, or nearly one out
of every five recorded in 1930, were because of illegal abortion; the
figure fell to just under 1,700 by 1940 largely because of the advent
of antibiotics.

It was around the same time that the nation's anti-abortion
movement began developing ties to a specific religious group:
American Catholics. Their vocal opposition to abortion coincided
with improved access to care in the Depression. Religious leaders
wrote frequently that access to abortion would weaken the nation's

moral character, including in periodicals circulated among Catholic physicians. When in the late 1950s and early 1960s state legislatures first began to consider passing laws that might loosen abortion restrictions, Catholic organizers entered the nation's political battle over the procedure, campaigning effectively for even that brief period to weaken or prevent states' efforts to allow at least some form of access.

White evangelical Protestants, who are now a major voice in anti-abortion politics, came to the movement later. Starting in the 1960s, evangelicals began to organize against abortion and were vocal in their opposition to the practice, with leaders like the televangelist Billy Graham describing abortion as an unequivocal sin. But the movement remained led by Catholics. Critically, Catholic and evangelical organizers united in 1972 to defeat a Michigan campaign that would have legalized abortion—one of the first meaningful tests of just how potent a religiously affiliated anti-abortion movement could be. *Roe,* by making abortion more available, and accessible in cases beyond a life-threatening pregnancy, upped the stakes for the anti-abortion movement. The heightened anti-abortion energy came at the same time that many evangelicals and conservative Catholics alike had felt threatened by the proposed Equal Rights Amendment. The same people—including often anti-feminist women—who campaigned against the Equal Rights Amendment were now energized and politically engaged to fight against abortion. By 1978, the anti-abortion religious movement was poised to exert a far greater influence over American conservative politics.

In this same period, the health imperative of abortion access had become more obvious. Changing cultural norms in the 1950s and '60s—in particular, the post–World War II idealization of the American nuclear family and the subsequent heightened stigma surrounding choosing an abortion—had made the procedure harder to come by than it had been earlier. The consequences were immediate. By 1965, almost one in five reported pregnancy-related deaths were attributed to illegal abortion. Although the consequences were devastating for all racial groups, the mortality rates varied dramatically. Between 1972 and 1975, the death rate resulting from illegal abortion was twelve times higher for non-White women, to say nothing of all the deaths and health risks never captured by this data. There were cases in which pregnant people died because they thought taking extra sleeping pills might help them end a pregnancy, or whose efforts to end a pregnancy by blowing air into the cervix killed them through a lethal embolism. Physicians and nurses old enough to remember the pre-*Roe* era carry these memories with them to this day: the desperation and fear they saw in their patients seeking abortions under any circumstances possible, and how little they could do to help. One doctor recalled a woman who shot herself in the uterus, hoping it would end her pregnancy.

With *Roe v. Wade* gone, this history matters all the more. Before 1973, people lost their lives because they could not access abortion, a right that had in fact been taken for granted at the time of the nation's own establishment, and whose promise of self-determination and physical autonomy felt impossible to extricate from its founding principles of life and, critically, liberty. Others did not die but went to extreme lengths—seeking out underground abortion providers, or self-inducing by ingesting poisons and using instruments such as the infamous coat hanger—because they knew that, for whatever reason, they could not have a child at that point in their lives, if ever. Their names and stories are lost to us. Now, in a post-*Roe* world, the past is eerily reminiscent of the present.

Technically, *Roe* fell on June 24, 2022, the day the Supreme Court ruled in a case known as *Dobbs v. Jackson Women's Health Organization*. But it had been on the verge of collapse for decades, even more so in recent months. In Texas, *Roe* effectively fell in September 2021, the night that federal courts allowed a six-week abortion ban to take effect—before many people know that they are pregnant, and a direct contradiction of *Roe*'s promise to federally protect the right to an abortion—even without explicitly overturning the 1973 decision. *Roe* fell again in Oklahoma, when a similar ban took effect the following spring. And then there was June 24, the day Americans read the final decision authored by Justice Samuel Alito explicitly eviscerating any shred of federal abortion protections. That the nation had literally seen this moment coming—an early version of the opinion had leaked to the public almost two months before—did not soften the blow. Neither did that forewarning prepare lawmakers in Washington to issue the kind of all-hands response that other health disasters or human rights crises might elicit. Weeks after the decision came down, officials in President Joe Biden's administration continued to protest that they needed more time to figure out what came next, arguing that a ruling overturning *Roe* had been impossible to foresee.

Over the past several years, I have traversed the country to speak to abortion providers, medical experts, and, most critically, patients who face unwanted or medically complex pregnancies and who seek abortions. The end of *Roe v. Wade*—and the subsequent elimination or significant reduction of legalized abortion in more than twenty states—has drastically reshaped the lives of Americans across the country, from all backgrounds. It has for decades been easy for individuals to cast abortion bans and restrictions as policies that affected other people, but that left one's own life untouched. If that was ever true, it certainly is no longer. An abortion ban in Texas radiates to New York or Maine. Restrictions in Florida affect those living in California. People traveling from out of state make appointments wherever they can, resulting in a bottleneck that limits everyone's access to abortion care, contraceptive counseling, and other sexual and reproductive health care. The system is simply too fragile to hold. Data collected over the first year after *Roe*'s fall suggested that in the decision's immediate aftermath the number of abortions across the country held steady, a testament to the resilience of health care professionals in states where the procedure remains legal. But the same numbers tell a deeper truth: since the *Dobbs* decision, patients have surmounted tremendous obstacles to access care, and abortion providers have been stretching themselves to the breaking point to attempt to meet demand. Universally, they have described this level of labor as unsustainable. As restrictions to abortion increase, it will grow more difficult—even impossible—to meet patients' need for care.

There have been efforts to speak about abortion in only the starkest terms—highlighting the most horrific cases of unwanted pregnancy, focusing on the people who would die without an immediate abortion, or, on the flip side, characterizing every abortion as a mistake people regret forever. This book is an effort to correct that narrative. People of all circumstances get abortions for all sorts of reasons. They relate to those experiences differently, and those different stories are all equally valid and deserving of our attention.

The coming years will be pivotal for abortion rights, and in turn for shaping our understanding of gender equality in America. Even before *Roe* fell, the nation's pregnancy-related death rate had been on the rise—the United States ranks the worst of all wealthy nations on this metric—and states with abortion bans have higher death rates than those without them. We know that more people will lose their lives because they cannot legally end their pregnancies; pregnancy-related deaths are simply more common in countries that limit access to abortion. Across the globe, as many as 13.2 percent of all pregnancy-related deaths are the result of unsafe abortions, occurring largely in countries where the practice is outlawed or where access is precarious, and where people who seek abortions face discrimination and stigma. Even in countries where abortion is technically legal, people die because the burdens associated with accessing care—including long, expensive journeys and the price of medication or a procedure—are insurmountable. Now the United States represents the rare country to be going backward, to be enacting more restrictions while other nations are largely expanding legal abortion access; the near-total bans being enforced in many states are among some of the most restrictive in the world.

Abortion access is a high-stakes story, but lawmakers, politicians, and many news outlets have long treated it like a footnote, merely a niche culture war struggle or a "women's issue" instead of a serious health crisis worthy of our collective attention. That framing could not be more misguided.

In these pages, you'll meet the people for whom abortion access would have been transformative and essential. There are young girls like Tiff, a sixteen-year-old from outside Houston, Texas, who became pregnant well before she intended to—and for whom the barriers to getting an abortion were simply too much to overcome. Angela, a twenty-one-year-old mother from San Antonio, traveled hundreds of miles in secret to access care in another state, spending money she could ill afford because she knew that she needed an abortion if she wanted to continue supporting the son she already had. Darlene Schneider, forty-two, desperately wanted to carry her pregnancy to term, but her doctors feared that doing so might threaten her own life, and her home state's abortion bans made it impossible for her to access comprehensive reproductive health care. And Jasper, a transgender man who was nineteen when he discovered that he was almost fifteen weeks pregnant, struggled to access care in Florida, the abortion network of which was overwhelmed in the first year after *Roe* was overturned as abortion bans radiated across the American South.

Their stories reinforce what should be obvious: abortion access is a story of racial and economic inequality, a story of health care, and a story of human rights. Denying people abortions can entrench them in poverty. It treats the people who seek abortions—women, nonbinary people, and trans men—as second-class citizens, unable to make their own medical decisions without the approval and guidance of the state. It denies them ownership over their own bodies.

The arguments used to silo and marginalize the discussion of abortion rights—to treat this as a cultural issue, rather than one of human rights, health care access, bodily autonomy, and basic equality—have been extended to conversations about LGBTQ equality, and in particular to protections against anti-trans discrimination. It is no accident that conservative lawmakers have lined up attacks on these different civil rights concerns at the same time; they are inherently connected. The end of *Roe* is the first time we have seen a major civil rights protection taken away, but it is likely not the last.

Rather than focusing on the political battles over *Roe,* the reporting in these pages concentrates on the human stories of abortion access, from the perspectives of doctors, activists, lawmakers, providers, and most of all patients. The landscape of abortion rights will undoubtedly keep changing well after this book is published. But the experiences of these patients—those who had to cross state lines to seek lifesaving care, who risked everything they had in pursuit of their own bodily autonomy, and those who were unable to plan their reproductive future in the way that they deserved—will always remain meaningful.

—February 2024

PART I

Tiffany

LOSING *ROE*

———

CHAPTER 1

Where It Started, Where It Ends

Texas

By Texas standards, it had been a cool morning in Dayton, a tiny town lying just under an hour outside Houston and half an hour from the beach. Tiffany woke up late that morning. She had good reason: it was January 1, and she had been out late last night at a party with some friends. They'd stayed up past midnight, toasting to the new year, 2022.

For sixteen-year-old Tiffany—Tiff to her friends—things were looking up. She'd been feeling optimistic lately about her relationship with Manuel. If they were being technical, he was her ex; they'd been broken up for a few years now. But functionally, she knew, the story was more complicated than that. They had never really stopped being together. She still spent weeks sleeping at his house, and they talked and texted constantly. Maybe, she told herself, this was the year they were officially going to get back together.

By her own assessment, Tiff was an ordinary teenager. She spent her days mostly goofing around on the internet, cuddling with the cat and the three dogs she loved fiercely. She liked playing video games, going to the beach, passing time with her friends, and hanging out with her cousin from down the street, one of her best friends and so close in age that sometimes they felt like twins. And, like so many teenage girls, she'd had pregnancy scares and near misses before—always with Manuel, whom she'd known since seventh grade. Now her period was a few days late, and she was starting to worry.

So she did what she'd always done. She went to the bathroom. She peed on her test, and she waited just a few minutes, hoping to put her mind at ease. One pink stripe appeared. That was good. It was just a sign the test worked, and that she'd taken it correctly.

But then came the second one—the one that meant her luck had finally run out.

Oh my god, she thought. *This is it.*

Her mind flashed to her parents, an older couple who'd adopted her and her brother when they were just babies. She knew they would never approve of this. How could she tell them? Would they kick her out of the house? Where was she going to go? She was only sixteen.

And then there was Manuel. How was she supposed to tell him? How would he take it? And what would all of this mean for their relationship?

Tiff knew she wanted an abortion. Ever since she was little, she had promised herself that if she ever became a parent it wouldn't be like this. She wanted to give her child a better life than what she had known. They'd live in a nicer house than the one she was raised in. There wouldn't be the regular exposure to her parents' cigarette smoke, a constant Tiff had lived with since childhood and one that, she would ruefully admit, had encouraged her to pick up smoking as a teenager. And they wouldn't live with someone who drank like her father.

It wasn't the right time for her—far from it. Some days, it felt like she could barely take care of herself. She wasn't healthy enough, mature enough, or responsible enough to be a mom; Tiff was supposed to finish her own childhood first, finish school, get a job. When she was younger, she thought maybe she'd become a surgeon when she grew up. But lately she'd been thinking more about nursing. Either way, she'd need to finish high school, get a college education of some sort first. If she had a baby, how was she supposed to do any of this?

The thought stayed with her. *I'm going to be a single mom.* There wasn't any way to change it, was there?

Tiff had every reason to worry. She lived in Texas, in the year 2022. If she lived anywhere else, or, really, if this had happened even a few months earlier, things could have been different. She might have had options. But in Texas in 2022, as would soon be the case in almost half the country, people like Tiff no longer had choices. She had the right to an abortion, but in name only—and even that wouldn't hold for much longer.

———

In Texas, abortions had been exceptionally difficult to access for years, the result of a decades-long project by lawmakers to shut down clinics and pass laws that would limit people's ability to terminate a pregnancy. Sometimes the courts struck down those laws, citing the protections conferred by *Roe v. Wade,* arguably among the most famous Supreme Court cases in American history, and the one that guaranteed the right to an abortion. Other times, though, the courts let some of the restrictions in Texas stand.

But, only a few months before Tiff's positive pregnancy test, the state had gone even further. It had become the first state to functionally overturn *Roe*'s protections, or, at the very least, find a way to work around them.

That Tuesday, August 31, 2021, Marva Sadler, a veteran of abortion care and longtime employee at one of the state's largest clinic networks, was waiting for good news to come. But Sadler, a no-nonsense mother of six who usually strove for optimism, was finally starting to worry that time might be running out. There was now one day left before the new law was supposed to kick in, twenty-four hours before Texas would start enforcing an abortion ban unlike any ever seen before. Starting Wednesday, September 1, the law—a soon-to-be-infamous piece of Texas legislation known as Senate Bill 8—would ban abortions for any pregnancy in which "fetal cardiac activity" could be detected. Anyone caught "aiding or abetting" the provision of such an abortion could be sued in civil court, for a minimum of ten thousand dollars.

The practical implications were clear. If the law took effect, anyone at about six weeks of pregnancy—early enough that many people didn't even know they were pregnant—could not legally get an abortion in the state of Texas, the second-largest state in the country, and where about fifty-five thousand abortions took place each year. Abortion opponents marketed the law as a "heartbeat ban." It was at best a misnomer, and at worst actively deceitful. That early in pregnancy, the fetus is about as big as a single lentil, and there is no properly developed cardiac system, let alone a "heartbeat."

For Sadler, abortion restrictions were nothing new. She'd worked at abortion clinics for about a dozen years, starting at Planned Parenthood before joining Whole Woman's Health, then Texas's biggest network of independent abortion clinics. Well before she became an abortion-rights advocate, Texas lawmakers had been positioning the state as a leader in the far-right movement's quest to limit—if not outright eliminate—access to abortion. As Sadler was fond of saying, hers wasn't the kind of work people did because it was easy, and they certainly weren't in it for the money. Reproductive health care, and abortion specifically, drew people who believed they were providing a public service, and who were prepared to do battle with state lawmakers to continue that work.

It was the last day of August, the hottest month in Texas, and the air was thick with humidity in Fort Worth. For Sadler, at the time the director of clinical services at Whole Woman's Health, that morning was supposed to be a day of relief. Senate Bill 8, like every abortion ban passed in Texas, had been challenged in court almost as soon as Governor Greg Abbott signed it into law. Whole Woman's Health was one of the organizations arguing for the law to be blocked. A hearing had been scheduled for the day before, in a federal court based in Austin. And the judge, a man named Robert Pitman appointed by former president Barack Obama, was one they trusted to make a fair assessment.

The case seemed straightforward. *Roe* said that the U.S. Constitution guaranteed the right to an abortion up until the third trimester of pregnancy. A 1992 sequel case, *Planned Parenthood v. Casey*, had scaled back the line, but only somewhat. Under *Casey*, states couldn't ban abortions for people before the fetus could live independently outside the uterus—what's known as viability, which typically occurs between twenty-two and twenty-five weeks. States could regulate pre-viability abortions, as long as those restrictions didn't pose an "undue burden" on the person seeking an abortion. But they couldn't outright ban them.

There was a tremendous difference between six weeks and twenty-two. If you looked at *Roe* and you looked at *Casey,* it was clear the Texas abortion ban didn't comply. Pitman would hear arguments on Monday and could issue a decision that day, or even the next, if he wanted a bit more time. The assumption was that of course he would block the law. This shouldn't be a complex case. But in recent days, things had begun to unravel.

Four days earlier, on Friday night, the hearing scheduled for Monday had been canceled. The change hadn't come from Pitman. A higher authority—the Fifth Circuit Court of Appeals, based in Louisiana—had made the decision with no explanation. The clinic's lawyers had worked through the weekend; on Saturday, they asked the Fifth Circuit's justices to hear the case themselves, or at the very least to block the abortion ban while it was being challenged. When they were denied, they appealed to the only body they had left: the U.S. Supreme Court, more than a thousand miles away. It was a Hail Mary. There was no telling when they would hear back, or even if they would. And that meant today could be the last day that Texas protected abortion rights—and the last day *Roe* truly existed in Texas.

In Texas, anyone seeking an abortion was required to make two visits to the clinic, separated by twenty-four hours. At the first, they received an ultrasound and written information about the procedure, and at the second, they could terminate their pregnancy. So, early in the morning of August 31, Sadler, who lived in San Antonio, drove in from her hotel to the Whole Woman's Health clinic in Fort Worth. They were opening at seven thirty a.m., with about seventy patients scheduled for the day. All had come previously for their ultrasounds and were now seeking abortions. It was a tall order, but if the clinic staff worked until midnight, Sadler hoped, maybe they could provide care for all of them.

Fourteen hours in, around nine thirty p.m., Sadler was growing concerned. Midnight was closer than she'd like, and she couldn't count how many women were left in the clinic, how many medical charts they still had to review. She began brainstorming ways they could speed things up or otherwise give themselves more time. Could they bring another doctor in? Would one be willing to come in at ten that night? And what if they started some patients' abortions now, but the procedures were finished after midnight? By nine forty-five, Sadler was panicking. There were too many patients left, and the lawyers had told them every procedure had to be done by midnight. It wasn't clear how they were going to make it, but they had no choice but to keep going. Then two hours later—at 11:49 p.m.—Sadler looked around the room. They'd done it: with ten minutes to spare, every last patient had gotten an abortion.

The tension was gone, displaced by a short-lived sense of triumph and accomplishment. Employees high-fived each other. Somehow, they had done the impossible. For ten minutes, they let themselves bask in the moment, thinking of every patient who had come through the door. They didn't know when—if ever—they'd feel like this again.

And then at midnight, the new reality started to sink in.

In the rest of America, *Roe v. Wade* was law. But in Texas, it was already gone.

———

Roe was functionally overturned in Texas, and in a twisted way, there was no place more fitting. The landmark decision would die in the state where it was born. Norma McCorvey, the apocryphal Jane Roe, was a waitress from Dallas who became pregnant in 1969 and sought an abortion, which was then illegal in Texas. The case wouldn't bring McCorvey an abortion—it took so long to argue that, by the time a decision came, she had given birth to a daughter, an outcome even her attorneys had expected. Sarah Weddington and Linda Coffee, the two lawyers who agreed to take up her case—and who while still in their twenties argued it to victory in front of the Supreme Court—were born in Abilene and Houston, respectively. Weddington was practicing in Austin when she first met McCorvey; Coffee was working in Dallas. Henry Wade, the man who gave the case its other name, was a district attorney in Dallas.

The pre-*Roe* days were a different world. When Donna Howard, who would in her later years become one of the state's loudest voices for abortion rights, started college at the University of Texas, the procedure was still outlawed. Howard worked to put herself through school and was financially independent; even so, her father still had to cosign for her credit card. As a woman, her money wasn't good enough on its own. The health care she could access was severely limited, too. Once, as a young student, she tried to obtain a prescription for birth control pills from the university's health center and the physician laughed at her. Only married couples were allowed to get the pill, he told her. But then he handed her a business card; if she came to his office after hours, he'd help her get what she needed.

Like birth control, abortion in the mid-1960s was an open secret. Howard knew people, including some of her own family members, who had become pregnant and left the state to obtain abortions elsewhere. Her family minister, working in concert with other religious leaders, was often the one helping them figure out how to make the journey; she recalled one case when he helped pay for someone's travel to get her out of Texas for an abortion—to a place where, even if the practice wasn't legal, he knew of a provider he trusted who could safely terminate her pregnancy. It was a well-known arrangement in the churches that lined the main drag of campus, which were religious institutions that largely preached a more progressive form of politics, and that hadn't been co-opted by any anti-abortion movement. In fact, underground church support systems were a fairly common mechanism for people seeking abortions across the country. In the years leading up to *Roe*, a network known as the Clergy Consultation Service united liberal Catholic, Protestant, and Jewish faith leaders—among others—to help thousands of Americans find abortions. They viewed the work, in the words of one historian, as an extension of their pastoral responsibility: their directive from God was to care for their congregants, without judgment. That work meant helping them get the health care they needed, including abortion.

Howard was fortunate. Nobody she knew had lost their lives trying to terminate a pregnancy, but many friends of friends knew someone who had. She was always just a few degrees of separation away from someone who died because abortions weren't legal.

Everything changed after *Roe*. For the first time, you could control when you became pregnant. The decision, Howard said, opened the world up to people like her, giving women the power of self-determination. It helped them feel as if they were finally full participants in society like never before. Howard became a nurse and later got involved in local politics. In 2006, she became a state legislator, representing Austin in the state house. She'd held the position ever since.

Texas's history made the fall that much harder. For decades, state Republicans had been eager to bring about *Roe*'s end as a way to almost erase the past. "They wanted Texas to be the place that resulted in overturning *Roe v. Wade*," Howard said. "There was a strong sense of, since this is where it started, this is where it ends."

By the 2000s, the state had become a laboratory for developing new abortion restrictions, often to sharp criticism from its own residents. In 2003, the state legislature passed the law enacting its twenty-four-hour waiting period for people seeking abortions, and also requiring anyone in their second trimester to get their procedure done at an ambulatory surgical center or hospital. It was an impractical and unnecessary stipulation. Most second-trimester abortions are relatively simple procedures that do not require a surgical center or hospital care; hospitals often did not have abortion-providing physicians on staff and, given the stigma surrounding such care, along with restrictions imposed by religiously affiliated hospitals, many were reluctant to offer it. In fact, less than 5 percent of abortions nationwide are performed in hospitals. Two years later, the next time the legislature met, it passed two more abortion laws: one requiring that minors get parental consent before they receive an abortion, and another banning the procedure for people beyond twenty-four weeks of pregnancy. In 2011, buoyed by the rising Tea Party, Texas passed a law requiring that patients be given sonograms before their abortions. And in 2013, the state passed what was, at the time, one of the most restrictive abortion bills in the country: House Bill 2 banned abortions for pregnant people who were more than twenty weeks past fertilization, and it imposed strict new limitations on how abortion clinics could operate and how medication abortions—which can be safely accomplished in a patient's home—could be administered.

The bill sparked an all-night filibuster by State Senator Wendy Davis, who spent hours on the statehouse floor, clad in bright pink Mizuno shoes and reading testimony from people across the state who shared why they had received abortions. Dressed in Longhorn burnt orange, women from across Texas flooded Austin to declare why the right to abortion was sacrosanct. Lubbock-born Natalie Maines, the lead singer of the band then known as the Dixie Chicks, performed at a rally outside the capitol building, famous in Austin for its dome of pink granite. But the backlash didn't change the outcome. Weeks later, in mid-July, the state's governor, Rick Perry—only two years out from launching his second failed presidential campaign—signed the House Bill 2 ban into law.

That Halloween, in 2013, Sadler was working in the clinic dressed as Rosie the Riveter. It was the last night Whole Woman's Health would be open; the next day, the clinic would have to close. They couldn't afford to operate under the strict new requirements, which stipulated that all abortions be performed in ambulatory surgical centers and that physicians providing abortions have admitting privileges at a hospital within thirty miles. The restrictions, which were taking effect the next day, had little medical justification, given abortion's incredibly low complication rate—lower, in fact, than the complication rate for giving birth—as well as hospitals' general resistance toward granting such privileges to outpatient doctors. (One study found that childbirth is fourteen times more likely to result in death than is a legal abortion.) Only once the bill was blocked—in late 2014, after about a year—would they be able to resume providing abortions.

Some abortion clinics in Texas were forced to close entirely after House Bill 2 took effect. The restrictions were too onerous to comply with, and any reprieve that came was too late; they didn't have the staff or resources to reopen. But other health centers, like Sadler's, could hold out hope that eventually the 2013 law would be struck down—it had to be, if *Roe* meant anything. And when that happened, they'd be able to provide care without fear. Their faith was warranted; in 2016, the Supreme Court ruled against House Bill 2, in a case that bore the name of Sadler's employer, *Whole Woman's Health v. Hellerstedt*. Critically, the case reaffirmed the right to an abortion and once again rejected laws like Texas's that had made it harder to access one.

But when Senate Bill 8 took effect in 2021, five years after the 2016 ruling, that sort of hope no longer felt reasonable. It was a different world, thanks in no small part to the recently defeated former president, Donald Trump. As a candidate, Trump had vowed to fill the court with justices who would overturn *Roe v. Wade*. It was a promise generally understood as an effort to win over White evangelical Christian voters, the religious group most likely to oppose abortion rights. Soon after assuming office, Trump began that task in earnest: in 2017, he appointed the conservative Neil Gorsuch to an open seat on the bench, one that had opened under Obama but that Senate Republicans had previously refused to fill. The next year came Brett Kavanaugh, who was confirmed despite being accused by multiple women of sexual assault. And then, just two years later, in 2020, following the death of liberal justice Ruth Bader Ginsburg, Trump nominated Amy Coney Barrett, a former law professor from Notre Dame who had long expressed her distaste for the *Roe* precedent. Not even a month after Coney Barrett's confirmation, Trump lost his campaign for reelection. But he'd accomplished his goal: only three liberals remained on the court, against six justices who opposed abortion rights to varying degrees. Months prior to Senate Bill 8 taking effect, the court, with its new conservative supermajority, had agreed to hear a case about a Mississippi law banning abortion at fifteen weeks. In that case, known as *Dobbs v. Jackson Women's Health Organization,* the plaintiffs directly argued that *Roe* was wrongly decided and should be overturned in full.

Abortion rights had perhaps never looked more tenuous. And in Texas lay the first clues to what this might mean. The night of August 31, 2021, Sadler was the last to leave the clinic. By the time she got to her Fort Worth hotel, it was two a.m., and she had accepted that a proper night's sleep was a lost cause.

Two hours later, Sadler, a morning person by nature, was awake and getting ready to head back to work. If yesterday was tough, she knew today would be even worse. Today was the day they had to start turning people away. Even running on fumes and coffee, Sadler's mind kept going back to a woman who had come to the clinic the previous day around four p.m. She was twelve weeks pregnant and, Sadler recalled, set to begin a prison sentence the next week. Her sentence, she had told them, was five years. If she couldn't get an abortion that day, she'd give birth while incarcerated. This was her only option. It was a desperate situation, and yet they hadn't been able to help her. The woman hadn't come for a previous visit, she hadn't had the state-mandated sonogram or waited the required twenty-four hours between two appointments. She begged them for an abortion. Still, Sadler had to turn her away. She would spend the next years of her life wondering what had happened to her.

Dating a pregnancy is imprecise at best, but gestational age is based roughly on when someone got their last menstrual period. By the time someone misses a period—often the first clue that they might be pregnant—their pregnancy is technically already at a gestational age of four weeks. Menstrual cycles typically last twenty-eight days, but they can be highly irregular, influenced by any number of factors including stress, diet, birth control, and depression. By the time someone knows to take a test, and by the time it shows up positive, there is a good chance that they're already five weeks into the pregnancy.

More than twenty people came to the clinic on September 1, hoping they were within the six-week cutoff. The staff performed ultrasounds for each of them to figure out just how far along they were. Some were still early enough that they could undergo the state-directed counseling today and then get scheduled for an abortion tomorrow. But others were too late, forcing the staff to turn them away. The phone calls kept coming in. People from across the Fort Worth area had heard about the new law, but they still didn't quite grasp what it meant—could they still get an abortion? Was the clinic open? If they couldn't get an abortion in Texas, where else could they go?

In previous years, every time a new abortion law was passed, Sadler had worried about what it meant for the patients she saw at the clinic, and how they would lose access to care. This was the first time she worried almost equally about her staff. Overnight, they had become not just abortion providers, but also grief counselors. The people on the phone were desperate, often crying. But they had to keep telling them no.

In the background, there was still a glimmer of hope. The Supreme Court hadn't blocked the law and brought legal abortion back to Texas. But they hadn't said they wouldn't do so later. It was still a possibility; maybe they were just taking their time.

Overwhelmed by what was going on at work, Sadler had

stopped watching the news. When the update finally came—late Wednesday night, just before the morning of Thursday, September 2, 2021—she was asleep. It wasn't until her four a.m. wake-up that she checked her phone and learned that, in the dead of night, hidden from the public eye, the Supreme Court had refused to help. Later that day, reactions would start pouring in from Washington. President Joe Biden would condemn the court's decision as well as Senate Bill 8. He would direct his government to see how they could "ensure that women in Texas have access to safe and legal abortion." A week later, the Department of Justice would sue the State of Texas in federal court, arguing that Senate Bill 8 violated *Roe*'s protections and should be blocked immediately. National news outlets would, at least for the next few weeks, descend on Texas, seemingly caught off guard by the notion that, even with *Roe* still standing, a state could in fact effectively ban most abortions.

But at four a.m. on Thursday, all Sadler could see was the court's refusal to step in and what it would mean for her patients. She knew that tomorrow, and the day after, and for weeks and months to come, she'd have to keep turning people away. Within a year, she realized, *Roe* was going to fall. In Texas, it already had.

———

Just a few months later, Tiff was realizing what it meant to live in a state where abortion rights no longer existed. After the pregnancy test came back positive, she called her best friend. "Oh my god," she remembered saying. "What am I going to do?" And did she really have to tell Manuel? Her friend talked her down as much as he could. Yes, Tiff, he told her. You know you have to.

Heart pounding, she snapped a picture of the pregnancy test, texting him the image. When she broke the news, he wasn't as shocked as she'd imagined, she said. Somehow, he told her, he'd had a feeling this might happen. Even though Tiff knew she wanted an abortion, she didn't discuss it with Manuel—it was too private, something she wanted to figure out herself, on her own. If she was able to find a way to terminate her pregnancy, she'd find a way to explain it to everyone. Right now, though, she needed to tell people what was happening. It wasn't quite logical, but in the moment everything just felt too overwhelming, too confusing for her to keep this news a secret.

Tiffany and Manuel decided that they'd tell his parents first about the pregnancy, and after that, she'd tell her mom. The first conversation was easy. No matter what happened, Manuel's parents said, they'd be supportive. But Tiff's mom posed a bigger problem.

Tiff took her time to muster up the courage. A week later, when she finally felt ready, she walked into her mom's room. She took a deep breath.

"Mom? You love me no matter what, right?"

Her mom looked confused. Yes, of course she did.

"I don't know how to say this . . ." Tiff trailed off. She waited for the right words to come.

Her mom finished the sentence. "You're pregnant, aren't you?"

Tiff nodded. But instead of the anger and disappointment she'd expected, her mom was calm—even supportive. Everything was going to be okay, she told Tiff. They were going to get through this together. She'd make an appointment for Tiff at the ob-gyn, and they'd find out how far along she was, and if she was in good health. Tiff's parents would help her raise the baby.

It was a reaction far better than Tiff had imagined—but still, there was a world of difference between what her mom expected and what she hoped for herself. Tiff wanted an abortion, but she could never tell her parents that—or Manuel, for that matter. In retrospect, she'd think later, maybe her dad would have supported her if she had indicated what she wanted. But there was no way her mother would've felt the same. And without her mom's approval, her dad would never get on board.

Practically, though, Tiff's preferences wouldn't really matter. A few days later, she went to her first prenatal gynecologist visit. By medical standards, she found out, she was still early in her pregnancy: five weeks and five days. But under the rules of Texas she was right on the edge, and if she wanted an abortion in her home state, she would need it done within two days. It was an impossible timeline. On top of the six-week limit and the twenty-four-hour waiting period, Texas state law said minors like Tiff also needed a parent to consent to the procedure. She could try to appeal through state court; if she convinced a judge that she was mature enough to make the decision on her own, she could be granted what's called "judicial bypass"—an override of the parental consent requirement to let her get an abortion. That would work as long as, by the time the bypass was granted, she was still within six weeks. There were advocacy groups that did their best to help girls like Tiff, though getting a judge's sign-off often took weeks, meaning that beating the six-week deadline was functionally impossible.

Tiff didn't know about any of this. All she knew was that an abortion wasn't happening within the bounds of the law.

She spent the next two months secretly trying to find a way to end her pregnancy. She turned to her friends. There had to be something she could try, some way they could help her. But they knew as little as she did. One offered her mugwort, an herbal supplement the two of them hoped might induce an abortion. She brewed it in tea, drank it, and waited, but nothing happened. Someone else had told her about a website where Tiff might be able to find pills for a medication abortion—mifepristone and misoprostol, which can end a pregnancy within the first trimester and which are safe to take at home. But Tiff couldn't recall the name of the website, and, despite repeated searching online, she couldn't find any place that might send her the medication she needed. Everywhere she looked, it seemed, was dead end after dead end.

———•———

"Abortion care is a bubble," Sadler said, almost a year after Senate Bill 8 took effect. "And it's a bubble that most people don't enter until you realize you need it."

In the weeks that followed September 1, the interview requests were almost nonstop. Major news networks devoted segments to the loss of abortion rights in Texas. The story made the front page of *The New York Times* and the home page of *The Washington Post*. Across the country, the focus on Texas was inescapable.

Politicians were paying attention, too. Howard flew to Washington to testify before the Senate Judiciary Committee. She told them what she was hearing: about the doctors who were afraid to provide basic medical care because they were no longer sure what violated the law—a chilling effect that constrained access to abortions but also to prenatal care for wanted pregnancies and to miscarriage management. She told them about the pregnant Texans who were leaving the state in droves to seek abortions elsewhere. She told them about her fears for the people who wouldn't be able to leave, who would have no legal options for abortions. The senators were attentive, Howard recalled. Democrats Cory Booker and Amy Klobuchar—former presidential candidates—asked her detailed questions about the law's impact. But the partisan lines were already clear. Texans needed help from the federal government, but Democrats had a razor-thin majority in Congress, and no Republicans were interested in helping.

When Howard flew back to Austin that afternoon, she'd already given up hope that the federal government might help. She'd come to Washington before, meeting the vice president earlier in the summer to discuss a different Texas law restricting voting rights. The administration had expressed concern but done nothing. Now Democrats nationwide said they wanted to talk to her about abortion. But unless they were creative, or somehow changed the rules of how the Senate worked, there was nothing they could do. And indeed, Howard never received any follow-up—a call, a visit, or even an email—from the senators who claimed they cared about what was happening to the people in her state.

The national attention dissipated quickly. Senate Bill 8 took effect around the same time as the U.S. withdrawal from Afghanistan, a story that continued to dominate headlines. So did the COVID-19 pandemic, along with debates in Congress over whether to pass President Biden's social spending agenda. Soon enough, it seemed like hardly anybody was concerned about abortion access in Texas.

The Supreme Court, despite its refusal to block the law, agreed to hear two cases challenging Senate Bill 8. There was the one launched by the Biden administration, and Sadler's employer, Whole Woman's Health, was leading the other. But the court still refused to discuss how the case against Texas's law affected *Roe* specifically. All they would weigh in on, the justices said, were technical matters: the questions of how this law worked and who, if anyone, the state's abortion providers were allowed to sue in response. Oral arguments would take place on November 1, 2021, precisely a month before *Dobbs,* the other big abortion case. It felt in a way like everything was happening at once. The nine justices would effectively rule on whether Texas was allowed to ban abortion so early in pregnancy—a clear violation of *Roe*'s protections—while also weighing whether to overturn *Roe* itself. The two cases together would signal whether the reality in Texas might soon become true across the country: whether states could and would soon ban abortion, potentially entirely.

Five weeks later, on December 10, 2021, the court issued its decision, refusing to block the Texas law. It was a confusing ruling, but consequential: Whole Woman's Health was allowed to challenge the law in court, but it could sue only a narrow collection of state officials. And, critically, the conservative justices said the case would now be sent back to the same appeals court—the Fifth Circuit—that had initially allowed the law to take effect. Senate Bill 8 would remain the law of Texas. When the case went back to the federal appeals court, the judges continued to punt on making any kind of decision, still choosing not to halt enforcement of the six-week abortion ban. After all, one appeals judge mused, *Roe* might not be law much longer anyway—and if it was overturned, states would be able to ban abortion.

The unsaid implication was, What did it matter, really, if Texas got a head start?

———

By late February 2022—week thirteen, the start of her second trimester—Tiff was growing increasingly desperate. Pregnancy was physically so hard. Her breasts hurt, she was tired, and her food cravings were so overwhelming. She was throwing up almost every day. The pregnancy felt like a nightmare, like something that couldn't really be happening to her. She wasn't actually going to be a mom, she told herself. This wasn't real.

Tiff's parents, on the other hand, were thrilled. They'd been in their forties when they brought her and her brother home, and they were now approaching retirement age. Still, they promised to help her with the new baby, and she noticed her dad was even drinking less than he used to; maybe, she told herself, it was because he was so excited to be a grandparent.

But Tiff still didn't want any of this. She wanted to grow up, to finish her high school education, go to college, get a job. But there was little she could do. If she were only a few years older, if she had her own car and money and didn't live with her parents, maybe she could have driven across state lines. People were going to New Mexico, Oklahoma, and even Florida to get their abortions. Others were going to Mexico, where you could buy misoprostol over the counter. But instead, Tiff, who had a history of severe depression and self-harm, felt like she was spending more and more time alone in her room, posting on internet forums in case someone might know how to help her. Maybe they could give her advice on how to induce her own abortion. Tiff's inability to access abortion pills was not unusual—many people who consider self-managing have little idea how to track down the medications, which can still work but are less effective by the second trimester.

"I'm pretty desperate and will do any cheap, at-home methods at this point," she wrote online. "I know how unsafe some can be but no way I can carry a baby due to mental health issues."

One person connected her to Jane's Due Process, an organization in Texas that helped minors navigate the state's parental notification requirements, offering them legal support to help appeal to a judge who would grant them a judicial bypass. Tiff texted the number, and she was able to get in touch with one of the organization's lawyers and tried to figure out what options she had. But it was the same story as always: for someone like her, there just wasn't much they could do through legal means. They didn't offer to send her abortion pills, which technically would have been against the law, and short of finding medication to take herself, the only way to get an abortion was to leave Texas, to get to New Mexico or California—the few states that were relatively close by and that didn't require at least one of her parents to sign off on her procedure. But for Tiff it just wasn't realistic. How was she supposed to leave Texas? And she was still scared of the implications: If she got an abortion elsewhere and then returned to Texas, would she have technically broken the law? Could she still get in trouble? Legally, the answer was no, but the fear was paralyzing.

Tiff still hadn't given up, but by mid-April she was in rough shape. Serious depression like hers, she knew, wasn't something that ever fully went away. You learned to live with it, and you hoped

that, with time, you'd recognize the warning signs and know when
you needed professional help, before anything too dangerous happened. But pregnancy exacerbated everything for Tiff. This wasn't
surprising: the perinatal period—that is, pregnancy and the first
year postpartum—is the most common time in a woman's life for
her to need hospital-based psychiatric care. Tiff had been on and
off antidepressants and mood stabilizers and in and out of psychiatric hospitals for years, meaning she was already at higher risk.
Immediately before getting pregnant, she hadn't been taking any
medications for her mental health. But the pregnancy felt so isolating. Tiff loved to spend time with her friends, but she felt like
she'd barely seen any of them in weeks. When she wasn't surreptitiously trying to find an abortion, she'd swing in the opposite direction, doing her best to ignore the fact that she was pregnant. But
it was hard to completely banish it from her mind. Every time she
remembered, she only felt more alone. She didn't know anyone else
in a similar situation, and it felt like nobody else really understood
what she was going through.

Manuel had stopped answering her messages for a while, but
now every time he did bother to reply, his responses were hurtful;
he told her how little he wanted to do with her, how hearing her
talk about the pregnancy made him want to run away. *If he's going to
be like that,* she thought one day, *he might as well just not text me back.*

In hindsight, she couldn't say for sure what the trigger was. Even
weeks later, it was difficult to put herself in that mental space. But,
approaching twenty weeks pregnant, Tiff snapped. She cut herself
again. It was something she hadn't done in years.

In a way, she said, it wasn't that scary. The blood was the sign she
was waiting for—the indication that this was one of the bad times
when she needed real help, the kind that only professionals could
give. She needed her mom to take her to the hospital right away.

———•———

Getting abortions in Texas had already been difficult; the years
of restrictions had chipped away at the number of clinics that
were able to operate at all. Upon enforcement of the state's 2013
ban—the law that prohibited abortions after twenty weeks and

included new regulations on how clinics and physicians could provide abortions—the number of clinics offering the service fell by half. People who lost their local health center after the 2013 law's passage had to travel fifty miles or more for an abortion. Limited access had meant Texans faced longer waiting lists for abortions, and it pushed more patients later into their pregnancies, often into the second trimester.

With Senate Bill 8 in effect, the impact was even more dramatic. More patients struggled to access care, and few of the state's clinics survived. Patients even had a hard time getting treatment when experiencing an ectopic pregnancy—a life-threatening condition in which the embryo implants outside the fallopian tube, which must be addressed by terminating the pregnancy. Doctors were concerned that, if patients were close to six weeks of pregnancy, providing the needed care would put the physician at risk of breaking the state's punitive law.

The number of patients able to get an abortion in Texas fell dramatically once the new ban was enforced, going from about 5,000 per month to near 2,500, per state data. The same data also indicated stark disparities in who would be most affected—barriers to abortion became in many cases a life-and-death issue that heightened racial inequality in the state. Prior to the six-week ban taking effect, Black and Hispanic Texans were substantially more likely than White Texans to get an abortion. They were also less likely to have access to affordable health insurance or to have the money to travel out of state for an abortion. And the health risks of pregnancy were greater for Black Texans in particular. Already, Texas has a pregnancy-related mortality rate significantly higher than the national average. Between 2018 and 2021, the Centers for Disease Control and Prevention reported 421 pregnancy-related deaths in Texas: 28.1 deaths per every 100,000 live births. And in Texas, as is true nationally, Black people are more than twice as likely to die from pregnancy compared with White people—a pattern of racial inequity that dates back at least ten years, and one that increased the significance of not being able to access abortion.

The desperation patients felt was easy to see: by the end of September, staff in clinics across the state were reporting patients coming in earlier and earlier in their pregnancies. One provider in

San Antonio said she spoke with patients who were testing themselves daily, as soon as they missed a period, just to make sure nothing was amiss. This six-week restriction had created an incredibly
narrow period in which people could terminate their pregnancies.
If someone showed up right after testing positive, they might be
too early for an abortion: the pregnancy would be so underdevel-
oped that nothing showed up on the ultrasound. Patients would
have to wait a day and come back, maybe making the same journey
several days in a row before they were able to get an abortion. Each
day that they waited increased the risk that they would miss the
window in which they qualified for the procedure—and it required
them to repeatedly pull together time off work, childcare if needed,
and the gas money for a drive that, depending on where in the state
you lived, could span hours. In southernmost Texas, one clinic—
a Whole Woman's Health affiliate in the town of McAllen—served
the entire Rio Grande Valley, a region of 43,000 square miles with
a predominantly Latino population.

Karla, an eighteen-year-old from just one town over, came to
the McAllen clinic in late September 2021, only weeks after the
new law had taken effect. She'd caught her pregnancy early, around
five weeks, and had already come once before to get an abortion.
The physician on staff, who had flown into the tiny McAllen airport from out of state, had given her the two medications that
could terminate a first-trimester pregnancy. But Karla, who worked
full-time as a cashier, was panicking. She had taken the pills, just as
the doctor said, but nothing seemed to happen. Symptoms typical with a medication abortion include cramps, heavy bleeding,
and then eventually the passing of a tiny embryo, no bigger than
a large blood clot. But Karla hadn't bled, and she didn't know what
to make of it. What if the abortion hadn't worked, she worried, and
she was still pregnant? She could try again, but what if by now she
had run out of time?

Already, Karla had paid the $650 for a medication abortion, the
standard price to end a pregnancy that early, and an expense that
in Texas—and so many states with anti-abortion leadership—was
almost never covered by insurance. But when she came back that
Tuesday, she was ready to pay it all over again if she had to. Having a child simply wasn't in the cards for her. She and her boyfriend

could barely support themselves, let alone another person. And if she became a mother now, at eighteen, how could she go to college? What was the rest of her life supposed to look like? "I can be broke now," she said as she waited to be seen. "Or I can be broke the rest of my life."

When it was finally her turn, she walked into the clinic's back area, praying she wasn't too late. For Karla, the news was good. The abortion was so early in her pregnancy that somehow she'd expelled the embryo without any bleeding. The medication had worked.

Karla had been absolutely certain of what she wanted. She had to be, because increasingly time was no longer an option for people in Texas debating what to do about their pregnancies. By January 2022, Sadler said, still months before *Roe* was formally overturned, the tenor of how patients discussed their plans had changed. In the past, clinicians had encouraged patients to take their time deciding whether to have an abortion—it was an incredibly personal choice, and one that couldn't be undone. This wasn't something to take lightly. But that was a relic of the old world. Now patients were coming in so early that many didn't know for sure whether they wanted an abortion. But what they did know was that if they didn't get one now, they'd soon be out of options.

"We pride ourselves on not rushing patients into making decisions. We give the options and allow them to make their own choices. And so it's absolutely maddening when that part is taken away," Sadler said. "Now I'd have to do the opposite and say, You may not be comfortable, but you better make a decision soon, because if not, this four-hundred-dollar [abortion] maybe could turn into three days and three thousand dollars for you to get to another state."

Of course, people continued to seek abortions, even those beyond six weeks, but the toll their journeys took was profound. Clinics in neighboring states saw a surge in patient volume: about fourteen hundred Texans left the state each month for an abortion. The largest share traveled north to Oklahoma, but clinics in Mississippi, Florida, and even Maine were affected. The journey could cost thousands of dollars; people took on credit card debt, fell behind on their electricity bills, or cut back on groceries to scrounge up the money. To cover the cost of an out-of-state abortion, one family reported eating only scraps from the fridge for a week—and because they couldn't buy dog food, they gave their dog whatever they couldn't bring themselves to eat. There were mothers seeking abortions who could not find childcare. Many would bring their kids along on the hours-long car ride, which could span hundreds of miles. Even while battling morning sickness, people boarded the first flights of their lives to make it to clinics in Albuquerque or Denver. Still others stayed in Texas, and instead found abortion medications on their own, purchased in Mexico, discreetly ordered from a medical service based in Europe, or passed along by a generous, trustworthy friend. But even that required knowing someone who could help, who knew where to look. Self-managing, as it's called, is safe and effective when done with these pills—the practice is recommended by the World Health Organization, and Doctors Without Borders has video tutorials on how to safely self-manage. Still, Texans had lost a key avenue of support: patients self-managing are supposed to have the option of calling a doctor if they need help or are concerned about the side effects.

In Texas, legal threats made this kind of self-managed abortion a medically safe but lonely process, with patients cut off from emotional or medical support systems. A medication abortion is indistinguishable from a miscarriage; the bleeding can last hours, and the pain varies. For some, it's reminiscent of a heavy period, but for others it feels akin to going into labor, all alone on one's couch or bathroom floor. And while there are medical hotlines one can call for advice, the threat of Senate Bill 8 made asking a physician in Texas, or even going to a hospital, an often horrific prospect. Sure, you could say it was a miscarriage, and no doctor should be able to tell the difference. All the same, many worried that someone in the hospital might figure out what had happened and report them anyway. And though Senate Bill 8 didn't technically outlaw miscarriage management—doctors could help end a pregnancy, legal scholars believed, if they tested for and did not detect fetal cardiac activity—the risk of a lawsuit felt perilous all the same.

The fear of criminal punishment was overwhelming for Emma, a young woman in San Antonio who found herself pregnant in February 2022. Emma's pregnancy took time to become obvious. She had felt nauseated and run-down for weeks, but attributed it to general winter malaise, or perhaps the new birth control she'd started taking. She tested herself for COVID-19 before trying a pregnancy test, counting backward as soon as she realized that her last period had been about six weeks ago. Sure enough, her pregnancy test came back positive.

Emma felt too sick to travel, but she knew people, including a friend who had recently been in Mexico and had brought back misoprostol, just to have on hand in case someone needed it. Ideally, one would take it with mifepristone for the highest chance of successful termination. But even just the one medication should work.

The night she took the pills, Emma was alone on the couch, with takeout and heavy-duty ibuprofen her boyfriend had dropped off. She thought she could sleep through the pain, nodding off to *Love Is Blind* on her couch. But not long after, she had to call him back: she was in agony, and even walking across the room was too much to bear. After returning, her boyfriend stayed with her for the next two hours, while she waited for the bleeding and cramps to stop.

It would have been worth it if the medication had worked. But when Emma's fatigue and nausea persisted—along with her revulsion at even the idea of eating sunny-side-up eggs, a food she ordinarily loved to make for herself—she made an appointment at a local Planned Parenthood. She was still pregnant, and now approaching her second trimester. Emma's friend dropped off more pills, this time managing to snag mifepristone as well. Her boyfriend stayed with her this time, too; he knew better than to leave her alone.

The pain was excruciating. Leaning on her boyfriend for support, she staggered to the bathroom, hoping to pass the blood and fetus while on the toilet. As the pain progressed, she turned to him, her face contorted in anguish. "I want to die," she screamed.

Neither the bleeding nor the pain would stop, and by hour four the young couple was starting to worry. What if something was going wrong and they didn't know what to do? If things didn't get better, her boyfriend said, he was taking her to the ER. She could always tell them she was experiencing a miscarriage—which is indistinguishable from a medication abortion—but if someone suspected she had tried to terminate her pregnancy, she feared she could get into legal trouble. Sometimes, she knew, they tried to prosecute people who self-managed their abortions for murder. Her boyfriend, who had supported her, could be seen as "aiding and abetting" her abortion, which meant that someone, even just a nurse or tech, could sue him under the law. Just before hour five, she passed the fetus, and the pain finally stopped. Emma's period wouldn't return for weeks, and neither would her taste for eggs. But her abortion had succeeded.

The strategy Emma used would, in the impending post-*Roe* world, become a model for people seeking safe, illegal abortions. Activists would talk about how easy and safe the pills were to take. Emma, too, would help more people find medication abortion pills; not all, she knew, would be as painful as hers had been. But she remained clear-eyed about the legal risks, as well as the physical and emotional toll she had experienced.

"It's going to become more and more so the only option that's acceptable, and we want people to not be afraid of that," she said in May 2022, two months after her own abortion but just six weeks before *Roe* would officially be overturned. "But we also need to be real about what they're going to experience."

"It is a thing you can do, but it's also going to be a painful thing you can do," she added. "Like, can you pull your own tooth from the comfort of your home? Yes. Is it going to be a pleasant experience? No."

———————

Texas's six-week ban had decimated access in a state where abortion had already been difficult to come by. Now, no matter where in the state one lived, getting an abortion in Texas remained nearly impossible. But for some—especially those with some level of disposable income and the independence that afforded—navigating those barriers was easier.

In April 2023, a woman named Kaleigh noticed something was off. Her period was weeks late now, and she had recently developed persistent nausea. When her pregnancy test came back positive, it felt like a gut punch. It wasn't her first time going through this. A decade earlier, when she was nineteen, Kaleigh's period was also late. Then, like now, she was pregnant. At that time, she had known she was too young to be a parent. And her relationship, she knew, wasn't right. She couldn't commit to the man who had gotten her pregnant and she certainly couldn't raise a kid with him.

In 2011, Kaleigh had little trouble getting an abortion in Dallas. She found a clinic on Google, and at eight weeks pregnant she had a minor surgical procedure to end her pregnancy. She had to wait twenty-four hours between two appointments, but there were no other barriers. More or less, she said, it was smooth sailing. But this time, ten years later, everything was different. Kaleigh and her boyfriend spent the next two days talking things over, and by the end they realized they were on the same page. Neither of them wanted a child.

Kaleigh followed abortion news in her state closely. In her conservative family, she considered herself a bit of a misfit—she and her grandmother were the only liberals, though her conservative mother did support abortion rights. When Kaleigh found herself pregnant, she knew about the state's six-week ban. She knew people were fleeing the state to get abortions. But maybe, she hoped, things would be different for her. Maybe she'd make it in time.

Unlike with her previous abortion, when she searched on Google, the first result wasn't a clinic. Instead, she was directed to a pregnancy center just outside Dallas, where she made an appointment for the next day.

The women at the center gave her a pregnancy test and an ultrasound. Even if she were at less than six weeks, they said, their facility didn't provide abortions. The whole time, they did everything they could to dissuade her from an abortion. They showed her pictures of her ultrasound and talked repeatedly about "the baby," describing an embryo that, at that point, was roughly the size of a bean. And they kept on asking her why she would want an abortion, if she was *really* sure of her decision. But the most important thing they told her was this: per their estimate, Kaleigh was already eight weeks pregnant. She couldn't get an abortion in Texas.

Kaleigh had gone to what's known as a "crisis pregnancy center," also called an "anti-abortion center": outfits where the primary goal is to dissuade people from getting abortions, and that often lure people in with the promise of a free ultrasound, which is not-so-subtly advertised on their websites and on signs outside the building. Such centers sometimes employ medical staff but often do not—and the free ultrasounds they offer are often inaccurately interpreted, providing people with wrong information about how far along they are in a pregnancy, as well as what options are in fact available to them. They are not regulated under the same laws as medical clinics, and in Texas, as is true in many other parts of the country, these centers are directly supported by taxpayer money, a product of state laws advocated for and passed by anti-abortion lawmakers.

Kaleigh drove home in a panic. She called a few abortion clinics in Texas in case they somehow might make an exception. Each time, the answer was the same: if she was already at eight weeks, they said, there was nothing they could do for her. But she should look at clinics in neighboring states and see if one of them might be able to help. Kaleigh still had some advantages that Texans like Tiff lacked. She didn't live with her parents, her boyfriend supported her decision, and between the two of them they had enough money to leave the state. She tried Louisiana first, calling a clinic in Shreveport, not even a three-hour drive from Dallas. But when she called, the person on the phone told her she'd have to wait three weeks for an appointment, a result of the barrage of displaced Texans who had been traveling to Shreveport for care. Next she tried Louisiana's other two abortion clinics. No one could see her sooner.

Three weeks would push her into week eleven, bumping up against the end of her first trimester. That wait time would limit what kind of abortion was available to her—medication abortions are effective throughout the first trimester, but they are technically only approved in the United States for the first ten weeks. Many health care providers stop giving the pills to people any later in pregnancy; the only option at that point is a minor surgery.

The idea of being pregnant that long was more than she could bear. There was the physical discomfort: by now she was throwing up each morning. But perhaps even more significant was the emotional burden. She was pregnant and she didn't want to be, and every hour of processing that reality felt more and more horrifying.

After giving up on Louisiana, Kaleigh researched abortion clinics in New Mexico. The journey would be farther: she'd have to drive west across the state of Texas, more than five hundred miles. But it was worth it if it meant she could get an abortion sooner.

Kaleigh got lucky. A clinic in New Mexico could see her Friday. She and her boyfriend could drive the nine hours on Thursday, bringing barf bags in the car just in case her morning sickness got the best of her. They'd even try to have some fun on the trip, going to a casino right by the clinic and spending the night in a hotel. On Friday morning, she'd get two pills: mifepristone to take in the clinic and misoprostol to take at home. The abortion would cost her seven hundred dollars. It was a bigger expense than they would have liked, but one that was manageable. And, more importantly, she'd no longer be pregnant. For Kaleigh, everything worked out. The clinic confirmed that she was in fact eight weeks along and provided her with the pills for a medication abortion. After the abortion was done, she called her grandmother as well as her mother. She cried on the phone from relief, happy with her decision to end her pregnancy. She would recommend the clinic to anyone she knew.

Months later, she would feel the same. But now her memories were also tinged with anger. Her previous abortion had been so easy to obtain. This one had been far from simple, and she knew that she was one of the lucky ones. She had been able to terminate her pregnancy, but countless others in the state would not have the same resources she'd had.

Two months after Kaleigh's abortion, on June 24, 2022, she would watch in horror as the Supreme Court finally overturned *Roe* entirely. Texas would enter an even harsher reality, becoming the largest state in the country to outlaw abortions almost completely. Its leadership would embrace the post-*Roe* world, proposing to direct more money into anti-abortion centers like the one she had visited in Dallas. Republican lawmakers were openly discussing legislation to limit people's ability to leave the state for abortions and to find ways to prevent them from ordering medication abortion pills by mail. "I feel like the world hates women," she said. "How can we not take it that way?"

Kaleigh felt increasingly helpless. She had tried telling her father—a lifelong conservative from Houston—about her abortion. His reaction, she recalled, was one of horror. Even her mother, a Republican who supported abortion rights, and who had validated Kaleigh in getting her own abortion, refused to discuss the onslaught of proposed new restrictions. The politics, she implied to Kaleigh, were just too unpleasant.

Kaleigh wanted to tell people what was happening, to try to help stop it. But nobody would listen.

By the end of August 2022, two states would be enforcing six-week abortion bans—laws just as profoundly limiting as the one she had been forced to navigate. Another eleven states, including Texas, would be enforcing total abortion bans. A fifteen-week ban would be in effect in Florida, and in Wisconsin, clinics would stop providing abortion services because they weren't sure what was still allowed. And even in states where abortion remained legal, the post-*Dobbs* reality had made it exceptionally difficult to access, as clinics found themselves barraged by people traveling hundreds of miles from their home states that had banned the procedure.

In a way, Texas had offered a trial run, a blurry crystal ball to see what would happen if *Roe* was overturned. But no one state could fully capture the colossal impact of erasing national abortion rights protection. When *Roe* finally fell, the effects would be massive—unlike anything anyone had ever seen.

———•———

CHAPTER 2

"It Shouldn't Be This Hard"

Oklahoma

The effects of abortion restrictions are never contained within a single state. And after Texas's six-week ban took effect—a law more punitive than any that had been enforced in almost fifty years—the consequences were immediately visible across the region. In the months to come, providers would describe it as a chance to test-drive what it would look like when *Roe v. Wade* was overturned.

The chaos began overnight. People who could no longer access abortions in Texas started calling clinics in any state they could drive to: Louisiana, Arkansas, New Mexico, Colorado, Kansas. By far, the impact was most pronounced in neighboring Oklahoma. It was an odd circumstance. Oklahoma was fully governed by Republicans who strongly opposed abortion rights, including a governor who had repeatedly vowed to sign any anti-abortion bill that reached his desk. Already, access in the state was severely limited: Anyone who sought an abortion had to wait three days—or seventy-two hours—after scheduling their appointment to actually get the procedure. When they made the appointment, which could be done over the phone, they were also required to undergo medically inaccurate, state-crafted counseling, which included telling patients that abortions might cause breast cancer or severe depression. Only four clinics operated in the entire state, with two based in Tulsa and the other two in the capital, Oklahoma City. Providers there were used to working around and within extreme restrictions. Still, under ordinary circumstances, it was hard to imagine that this state could become a haven for people seeking abortions.

But even with its constraints, Oklahoma had something going for it that few other states did: you could drive two hours from the Texas border and be at an abortion clinic. Dallas was only two hundred miles away. Austin was less than four hundred. A six-hour drive each way for an abortion—a traveling distance still unimaginable for any other medical service—was the kind of journey that patients could conceivably squeeze into a single, if exhausting, day. And so they would.

When the abortion ban's effects first became clear, Ginger Tiger was still working in an Oklahoma City hospital. An interventional radiology nurse, her primary duty involved assisting physicians with MRIs, X-rays, and ultrasounds. But she worked closely with the hospital's emergency room staff, and it was only two weeks into September when she saw the first Texas-based patient come in. One by one, Tiger noted her symptoms. The woman had uncontrollable chills, an escalating white blood cell count, a climbing pulse, and blood pressure creeping downward. The diagnosis was easy: sepsis, which is the body's natural reaction to an infection. If treated quickly with antibiotics, sepsis need not be life-threatening—people who experience it do generally recover, though they may continue to experience symptoms for months. But it is by all accounts a medical emergency, and it brings a not-insubstantial risk of death, especially if patients cannot access timely care.

Tiger had seen septic patients countless times before. This, however, was the first time someone came into her hospital, into her emergency room, septic because they had tried and failed to induce their own abortion. It was a trend with historic precedent: in 1968 alone, a public hospital in Los Angeles County reported admitting 701 women with sepsis induced by illegal abortions, or one such case for every fourteen deliveries it saw. When *Roe* became law, hospitals eventually shut down the whole wards they had devoted to caring for patients with so-called septic abortions. This was supposed to be a relic of the past, not a health phenomenon reappearing in 2021.

The woman was frank with Tiger. She lived in Texas, she was pregnant, past six weeks, and she needed an abortion. Since she couldn't find one in her home state, she had tried to terminate her own pregnancy, through mechanisms she never specified to Tiger. She had no idea if it had worked, but when she felt the fever come on, she knew she needed help. Given the state's ban, though, she was too afraid to go to any hospital near her. The doctors might figure out she had attempted an at-home abortion, and she didn't know if that would put her in legal jeopardy. So instead, with her condition deteriorating and fever worsening, she drove herself the hours-long trip from Texas to Oklahoma City, where she could find a hospital that would take care of her, where abortion was legal, and where she didn't have to fear the potential legal consequences for her or for someone she loved.

It was a moment that changed Tiger's life. She had worked in nursing for years, but she had never taken a particular interest in reproductive health before. Now, however, it seemed like there was no cause more vital.

"That's definitely when it hit," Tiger said. "These women are going to find a way. And the fact that they're putting their own lives at risk? It's devastating."

She spent two more weeks working at the hospital, watching as more patients from Texas continued to trickle in, each reporting medical complications after their efforts to terminate their own pregnancies had gone awry. By October, Tiger had found her calling. People were risking their health and their lives because they couldn't access a safe, legal abortion. As a medical professional, it was her duty to help. And where would she be more effective than at an abortion clinic?

When Tiger joined the staff at Planned Parenthood, they, like every abortion clinic in Oklahoma, were already underwater from the surge in patients. In the past, you could call for an abortion and get an appointment within the week. Now, though, wait times were stretching to three weeks. Research would ultimately show that, in the first six months of Texas's six-week abortion ban, 45 percent of people from the state—almost one in two—who went somewhere else for an abortion would go to one of Oklahoma's four clinics. In both 2020 and 2021, about 10 percent of all Oklahoma-based abortions would be performed on people who had traveled from Texas;

in 2022, more than half would be. In 2019, in comparison, Texans made up only 2 percent of Oklahoma's abortion patients.

Clinic staffers like Tiger didn't need the data, though; they could see it with their own eyes. In Oklahoma City, the Planned Parenthood clinic opened at nine a.m. When Tiger arrived, she would see patients already lined up outside the small medical building—uptown, on the rapidly gentrifying side of the city—waiting for their appointments. They had woken up before dawn, sometimes at three or four in the morning, and made the hours-long drive to come here. Some were using their rent money to pay. One woman said she had sold her car to cover the price of her abortion, and then hitched a ride with a friend to Oklahoma City. Patients waited hours in the clinic before it was their turn to get a sonogram, to figure out how far along they were in their pregnancy—and, depending on the answer, to figure out if there was a doctor on-site that day who could perform the type of abortion they needed. Those in their second trimesters required a medical provider who was able to perform a minor surgical procedure, and those physicians weren't available every day. Abortion doctors at most of the state's clinics typically flew in from out of town, a common arrangement in states with harsher abortion restrictions, where abortion providers are even more likely to face the threat of harassment, stigma, and violence. Sometimes, one staff member recalled, patients who had spent hours waiting for an appointment would give up and drive home to Texas. Some were tired of waiting, and they hoped they might have better luck on a different day. Others were already parents, and they didn't have the childcare lined up to stay away much longer.

In this post–Senate Bill 8 but pre-*Dobbs* world, the Planned Parenthood in Oklahoma City typically saw three dozen abortion patients a day, though there were days when the number crept up to fifty. Eight-hour workdays stretched to twelve-hour ones, with nurses and health assistants running around to make sure as many patients were seen and treated as possible. The strain was visible even in the shoes that clinic staffers wore to work each day: Crocs with rainbow socks or running shoes that might allow them to withstand hours on their feet. Tiger, a veteran of emergency rooms, lived in her beloved New Balances. They had to be deliberate in carving out time to eat and drink water, Tiger recalled; if they didn't, they'd crash before the day was done, when there were still patients in need of their help.

The toll was more than just physical. Months later, Tiger would still recount the desperation she heard in patients' voices on the phone, the fear and need she saw in their eyes. One woman, who called the clinic from Texas, told Tiger that she had read online that taking chemotherapy medication might terminate her pregnancy. She had given it a try, but she was still pregnant and carrying a fetus that likely now would not survive outside the womb. What did Tiger suggest she do?

Abortion clinics typically operate on shoestring budgets, with just enough staff to get by. Often, clinics perform abortions only a few days a week, offering other family planning and reproductive health care the rest of the time. But after Texas's ban took effect that wasn't an option. The Oklahoma clinics expanded their hours and offered abortions on more days. There were so many more patients calling—and so many from Texas specifically—that Oklahomans could no longer find timely abortions in their home state. Instead, they started driving across their own northern border, finding appointments in Kansas. Trust Women, which operated health centers in both Oklahoma City and Wichita, reported that both of its clinics were now treating mostly out-of-state patients. In Oklahoma City, they saw mostly Texans, and in Wichita, it was mostly Oklahomans.

For Andrea Gallegos, the transition was abrupt and difficult to swallow. Gallegos, a Texas native, had been running two abortion clinics since 2019: one in San Antonio, and the other farther north, in Tulsa. It felt like she'd been in this business her whole life. Her father, Dr. Alan Braid, had been providing abortions to Texas-based patients since 1973, when the *Roe* decision came down. Gallegos, with curly brown hair and a voice that sounds like an elementary school teacher's—soft, yet tinged with a no-nonsense firmness—had grown up going to abortion rights marches and talking to her parents about abortion restrictions at the dinner table. A social worker by trade, she'd previously managed a senior living facility. She'd liked the job, but her heart had never been in it. Abortion access—helping people find reproductive autonomy—was her real passion. When her father, now in his seventies, asked her to start running his clinics, she knew that this was what she was meant to be doing.

After September 1, 2021, Gallegos saw the traffic at her San Antonio clinic slow to a trickle, with most patients too late in their pregnancies to get an abortion in the state. In Tulsa, meanwhile, the number of patients they saw doubled. Before the six-week ban took effect, the Oklahoma clinic saw maybe 230 or 250 abortion patients per month. Now it was more like 500 patients per month, sometimes 550. Out of every five patients, three were coming from Texas, with some driving as far as twelve hours each way. It was surreal, Gallegos said. She was living in two worlds, one where her staff couldn't care for most patients, and another where they couldn't see enough people. Underlying that contrast was a more complex truth: the loss of most abortion care in one state made abortion increasingly hard to access in both Texas and Oklahoma. In the former, clinics weren't allowed to provide abortions; in the latter, caring for people from two whole states was simply too big a burden for the already fragile ecosystem of reproductive health care.

Gallegos kept hoping things would get better. Soon, she told herself, the six-week ban would be overturned. Someone would intervene. Until then, she didn't know how they were supposed to sustain this. It would take maybe six months for the reality to sink in, for her to realize that things were never going to improve. In fact, the only change she could count on would be the situation worsening.

She started splitting her time between San Antonio and Tulsa, staying in hotel rooms or Airbnb rentals for the two weeks each month she spent working at the Oklahoma clinic. Sometimes her mom would drive up with her for company. Once, she brought her two daughters on the journey, though normally the kids stayed back with her partner, who took over childcare responsibilities at home. Only her older daughter, who was sixteen at the time, understood what Gallegos was doing. The other kids, ages three and five, just knew that sometimes Mom wasn't going to be home.

Running the clinics became part art and part science. The staff knew that not everyone would be able to come for their appointments in Tulsa—money, time, or life would get in the way—so they

tried to book more patients than they had room to see. The idea
was to overschedule just enough so that they never wasted an
appointment slot, but not so much that they wouldn't be able to see
everyone. They would stay through the evenings, past seven p.m.
if that was what it took to care for all the patients on the books.
Occasionally, if they really needed to, they'd schedule a Saturday
clinic. But for the most part they tried to work five days a week.
Otherwise, the workload just wasn't sustainable.

By now, Gallegos was growing increasingly well-versed in the
delicate, painful practice of telling people that she was sorry, but
they were too late in their pregnancies, there was nothing the staff
here could do. She knew how to sit on the phone as patients sobbed,
begging her to help them find somewhere else to go or another
way to get an abortion. It was the kind of conversation she would
have again and again in the months to come.

Still, she tried to develop contingency plans. If a patient at
the Texas clinic could not get an in-state abortion, her staff would
offer to reschedule them for the Tulsa sister facility, hoping for
an appointment as soon as the next week. But that wasn't always
feasible. They couldn't find any doctors in state who would perform surgical abortions at the clinic; the lone on-staff physician
from Oklahoma had been trained in performing only medication
abortions. (The surgical procedure for an abortion, while simple
to perform, requires basic training, and most state laws allow only
physicians to learn to provide this care.) If someone needed a surgery, they would have to wait a week for another doctor to fly in—
maybe from Idaho, maybe from Montana. Sometimes, the wait time
for an appointment could be a month, pushing a patient later into
their pregnancy, which grew only more physically and emotionally demanding as it progressed. And no matter what resources the
clinic offered, there were always patients who were unable to make
the journey. Even one state away was sometimes too far to travel.

The worst part was what Gallegos knew in the back of her
mind: the hundreds of patients she was seeing in Tulsa represented
only a fraction of the people in need. There were so many more
who couldn't find their way to a clinic, who didn't have the money
to pay for gas, who couldn't get the time off work to travel hundreds
of miles, or who couldn't line up someone to take care of their other

kids. For them, abortion was so inaccessible it might as well be illegal. She didn't know what would happen to those patients, and even as she desperately wanted to help, she didn't know how she could.

———————

When Kelly's pregnancy test came back positive, she felt her heart sink. The timing was all wrong. At twenty-six, Kelly had been with her boyfriend for less than a year, even though she'd known him since high school. She worked a part-time job with no benefits, had no health insurance, and had barely two hundred dollars in her savings account. In Texas, one of the few states that had declined the health insurance expansions created in 2010 by the Affordable Care Act, she was still somehow too rich to qualify for Medicaid, the health insurance program specifically created for low-income people.

She'd had an abortion only seven months ago in Houston. At the time, she'd heard rumblings that a new law was coming, something that would make it harder to access the procedure in Texas. Still, she didn't really know what that meant. It turned out that the only way to understand was to experience that shift firsthand.

On the same day that she took her test, her boyfriend came to her with good news. His mom was looking for an office assistant. The pay would be better, and she'd get benefits, too. Objectively, it was an exciting development, but it was hard for her to feel any real joy.

"That's great," she said. "But I'm pregnant."

Kelly took the job and, in her free time, started calling abortion clinics near her. Even if they couldn't help, she reasoned, maybe they could tell her where to go. Instead, the voices on the other end of the phone spoke quickly, almost as if they were afraid to even mention the word "abortion." They told her there was nothing they could do to help her.

Kelly turned to the internet, where she plugged in the words "cheap," "affordable," and "ultrasound." She didn't realize that this would lead her to an anti-abortion center, and how significantly those facilities differed from proper abortion clinics. All she hoped was that they would tell her how far along she was and where she might be able to get an abortion. When she showed up at the center a week after her positive test, her internal alarm bells started to go off. Someone took her to the back room for a pregnancy test, but it wasn't the kind she'd ever seen in doctors' offices. It looked like they'd picked up the same brand she'd bought at Family Dollar. After the test, a woman took her to another room, where she peppered Kelly with questions. Why did she want an abortion? How did she feel about being pregnant? Had she considered carrying the pregnancy to term, and then having the child placed in foster care? Increasingly uncomfortable, Kelly refused to answer. None of these questions, she reasoned, were any of this woman's business.

Done with the interrogation, Kelly went for her ultrasound, where again something felt wrong. There were no framed medical diplomas on the walls—only pictures of newborn babies. On the table nearby, she saw a model of a fetus inside a womb. The woman managing the ultrasound told Kelly she was eight weeks pregnant and played the sound of early cardiac activity, describing it to Kelly as a heartbeat. And then she asked: Did Kelly want to record the sound and bring it home with her? Then she could play it for her boyfriend, too. Furious, Kelly declined, and then went home, still stunned. The women at the center had already scheduled her to come back the next week. Unsure what to do, she kept the appointment, and a week later she returned to ask the only question that she truly needed answered: Where could she get pills for an abortion?

Nobody was willing to help her, though they sent her home with Scripture-filled pamphlets, a loofa, and travel soap. Kelly had lost two precious weeks since that first positive test. Back home and now nine weeks pregnant, she tried to imagine where she could go. A plane ticket was out of the question; neither she nor her boyfriend had the money. Instead, Kelly searched for clinics in Oklahoma, where she came across Trust Women, in Oklahoma City, and Gallegos's Tulsa-based clinic. She called the phone numbers for both, hoping one might be able to see her. She and her boyfriend would find a way to make the drive, somewhere between six and eight hours each way, if it meant she could get an abortion.

At both clinics, the staff on the phone were so kind. They told Kelly what she was starting to suspect: her experiences at the crisis pregnancy center were not appropriate medical care. And, they told her, they could book her an appointment later in the month for an abortion. But there was one catch: the only slots available to her were on weekdays. Kelly was stuck; she had just barely started working at her new job and hadn't earned any vacation days yet. There was no way she could take a day off midweek to leave the state for an abortion. It was only one barrier, but it was enough to put Oklahoma out of reach. Abortion clinics were legally providing care less than five hundred miles away, but as far as Kelly was concerned they might as well not exist at all.

Those were a bad couple of weeks, and the emotional burdens of pregnancy made everything feel worse. Kelly's boyfriend tried his best to be there for her, to help brainstorm solutions, and to offer whatever support he could. Despite his best efforts, though, he couldn't fully understand how she felt. She was still alone.

"It's your body going through this—no one else's," she said months later.

Kelly couldn't travel for an abortion, but she kept searching for an alternative. Unlike Tiff, who had struggled to find helpful advice online, she found a post in a forum for abortion seekers, referencing a website called Plan C. She'd never heard of it, but when she went to the page she found a repository of online health services that could directly mail her the pills for a medication abortion—she could take them at home, on her own. One health service would even connect her with a physician, someone who could talk through the process with her before and after, who could help guide her through any questions she might have about what the abortion would feel like.

Technically, the service Kelly used didn't ship abortion pills to Texas. But through sheer determination, she was able to finagle a workaround. One website she read suggested that, if she got officially notarized, she could sign herself up for a virtual mailbox in Colorado, at a postal address that she technically didn't occupy. After her online medical consult, the pills would be sent to that Colorado address. From there, she could have them emergency shipped to her home in Houston.

Kelly followed this improvised plan, but still, the waiting was brutal. She felt herself counting the weeks of her pregnancy, watching all the ways her body seemed to change. Every day, she would come home from work and just sit in the car, breathing heavily and trying to process what was happening to her. If the pills didn't work, she didn't know what other options she had. When Kelly finally got her abortion pills, she was approaching week twelve, the end of her first trimester, and the phase in pregnancy when abortion pills become less effective. She didn't have any time to waste. Kelly took the medications twenty-four hours apart, taking the second set on a Thursday. On Friday she called in to work sick, saying she had food poisoning. She sat on the toilet for hours, nursing her cramps—uncomfortable, but not worse than her worst periods—and watching the blood. Later, standing in the shower and sensing she might soon vomit, she saw what she had been waiting for: a blood clot passing out of her body.

It would take weeks for Kelly to recover from the emotional roller coaster of her abortion. Her twenty-seventh birthday, just a month later, was one of the lonelier ones she could remember. Kelly didn't feel the regret that the women at the crisis pregnancy center had foretold. She was grateful for her abortion, but she felt drained and exhausted after navigating so many obstacles just to stop being pregnant.

"No one really understood what I just had to go through—all by myself," she said.

— · —

By mid-February 2022, it was becoming clear that Oklahoma had emerged as an unlikely abortion sanctuary for people traveling from Texas. But that wouldn't remain the case for long.

Tiger, the Planned Parenthood nurse, was still holding on to hope. Her home state was more progressive than Texas, she told herself, and most people here didn't support a ban on abortions. Yes, abortions were largely outlawed just one state to the south, but it couldn't happen here. It wouldn't.

This was wishful thinking. Oklahoma's Republican caucus was pushing two competing abortion bills. In the senate, they had legislation that would directly replicate Texas's abortion ban. In the house, there was an even more extreme proposal—a bill that would also use Texas's private lawsuit scheme, letting private citizens sue anyone who performed an abortion or aided and abetted someone in seeking out the procedure. Instead of stopping at six weeks, though, that bill would ban all abortions. If signed and enacted, both bills would take effect immediately. Among their motivations, state lawmakers cited a disappointment that Texas had beaten them in ending abortion access. And, they added, they were dismayed that their state had become a resource people could turn to for safe and legal abortions.

Either proposal would be catastrophic for abortion-seeking patients. A six-week ban in Oklahoma would put an end to the state's status as a refuge for unmoored Texans, and it would deprive Oklahomans of most abortions. A total ban would be even more consequential. In the clinics, staff did their best to stay focused on their work, at least for as long as they were able to. After all, they barely had the time to see their patients, let alone keep track of all the bills moving through the capitol.

On the morning of March 10—the day Oklahoma's state senate would vote on its proposed six-week ban—Tiger was working at Planned Parenthood, caring largely for medication abortion patients. The staff had put a livestream of the legislature's debate on the computer so that they could monitor the situation while they worked. In their building, barely two miles from the capitol, Tiger listened to lawmakers spar over nuances of their bill, including whether the state should add new provisions that would punish pregnant people seeking abortions.

"I don't see much nuance in performing abortions," Tiger heard one woman, the bill's sponsor, say. Later, she added, "I'm bringing this bill in an effort to stop abortions in Oklahoma."

Said another lawmaker, a man who worried the bill didn't go far enough: "While I wholeheartedly agree with the sentiment of saving innocent life, shouldn't we also be providing justice for those who are murdered?"

Tiger couldn't understand these people. The "murder" they were describing was nothing like what she saw in the clinic. This was health care sought out by pregnant patients who were desperate for help. What they were saying felt ignorant and cruel; it showed that the lawmakers regulating abortion had never actually spoken to any patients who needed this kind of care.

As the debate progressed, abortion patients started one by one to poke their heads out from their curtain-covered chairs. What was happening? Could they come out and see? Tiger watched as the patients climbed from their chairs and stood next to one another, watching the computer screen as state legislators—mostly but not exclusively men—debated whether abortion was, in fact, necessary. Over the course of the debate, Tiger stole a few glances at her patients. She saw tears streaming down each of their faces.

That day was only the beginning. Over the next six weeks, clinicians would watch the statehouse anxiously, wondering each day if tomorrow they would wake up and find out their government was about to pass a bill that would immediately outlaw all abortions. Kailey Voellinger, the clinic director at Trust Women, fell into a routine of checking the clunky state government website each night, just to make sure a vote hadn't been scheduled for the next morning, and that there wasn't a chance the legislature would give the governor an abortion ban to sign into effect. If that happened while her clinic was caring for patients, she didn't know how they'd handle it—if they would have to immediately halt everything, if they'd have to turn away patients who had waited for hours that day to be seen. If someone was mid-procedure when an abortion ban took effect, no one could say for sure whether they'd have to stop providing care halfway through.

The uncertainty created an ethical quandary, too. Knowing how much patients relied on Oklahoma clinics, did you keep scheduling abortion appointments, even if there was a chance that the procedure would be outlawed that same day? Was it in patients' best interest to send them somewhere else? And how did you keep paying for doctors to fly in from states like California and Florida, when there was a good chance that they'd land here without the ability to see patients? Barraged by the looming abortion bans, both of Oklahoma City's clinics made the decision in April to suspend abortion services, even though no new law had even been passed. Simply the fear of a ban was enough to cut off access.

———

Monica Martinez, thirty-seven, had known she never wanted children. She and her boyfriend had talked about it repeatedly. So in early April, after a few weeks of anxiously waiting for her period to start, she grabbed a handful of home pregnancy tests during her Sunday Walmart run. There was no harm in checking, she figured.

As soon as she saw the positive result, she knew she needed an abortion. In the back of her mind, she recalled a news report she had read saying that Texas, her home state, had passed an abortion ban. But she wasn't sure if it had taken effect or what it would mean for her. Still in denial, she scheduled an appointment for the next day at the nearby Planned Parenthood, just a short drive from her home in Fort Worth. She'd get tested there, have an ultrasound to see how far along she was, and find out what her options were.

That Monday, Monica learned she was just at six weeks—she had caught her pregnancy early, but there was still nothing she could do in Texas. Her health added another complication: Monica took blood pressure medication that wasn't recommended for use while pregnant. But even if she didn't have any medical risks, she wouldn't have changed her mind. She knew she did not want to be a parent. The staff handed her some pamphlets and a list of clinics out of state that she could try. Shaken, she walked out of the clinic and drove straight to her boyfriend's house. She hadn't yet let him know about any of the tests she'd taken, about the visit to Planned Parenthood. Now, face-to-face, she told him the news: she was pregnant. Saying the words out loud, the reality of the situation started to sink in. Then she got to the worst part—that the abortion she knew she needed was impossible to find in Texas. As she finished the thought, she began to sob.

She didn't want to keep the pregnancy, and he would support whatever she wanted. No matter what she wanted to do, where she wanted to go, he promised he would help. He could drive the car or help cover the cost of any procedure. But having to leave the state, driving for hours each way, just seemed so daunting. Monica waited a day before she started her research. Already, she was feeling anxious about what the process would look like, how difficult and exhausting it would be. She lived five minutes from a Planned Parenthood that, only a few months ago, would have been able to perform her abortion. The fact that she couldn't just go there now felt ludicrous.

Before calling the list of clinics, she looked online too, just the way Kelly and Tiff had. If she could get abortion pills sent to her house, that would be much easier than traveling hundreds of miles. But when she tried searching, she was quickly lost. Monica couldn't figure out how to get the medications mailed to her Texas address. It never occurred to her that she could or should go through the process of setting up a second mailing address, and then get pills forwarded to her. After all, what other medical services required that kind of subterfuge?

Running out of options, Monica started going through the list she'd gotten from Planned Parenthood, calling abortion clinics in other states one by one. The closest to her, in Shreveport, Louisiana, was booked for weeks, but they could put her on the waitlist. Next, she called the Planned Parenthood in Oklahoma City, where she struck out again. Spooked by the pending abortion bans, the clinic wasn't scheduling patients who wanted to terminate a pregnancy. Finally, she called Trust Women, Oklahoma City's other abortion provider.

Her timing couldn't have been better. For most of the month, that clinic had also stopped providing abortions. But the day before Monica called, Trust Women's leadership decided to change course and to resume abortion services for as long as they could. They knew that they ran a risk and that every patient they booked might show up in the morning to learn that abortions were no longer legal in Oklahoma. But the alternative—sitting on the sidelines, watching and waiting and telling patients they couldn't help—was more than they could bear.

Their first batch of appointments was slated for Friday morning, and the schedule was already full. But the woman on the phone gave Monica an appointment for Monday. Oklahoma City was only a two-hundred-mile drive each way, and she and her boyfriend could make the trip in a day. But the employee on the phone warned her that there was a chance her appointment could be canceled. They were sorry, but they just didn't know if abortion would still be legal in a week. If they were unable to help her, though, they could put her in touch with their affiliated clinic in Kansas, which was another two-hour drive each way.

Even with her abortion scheduled, Monica felt the anxiety eating away at her. She stopped sleeping properly. Between the stress and her newfound morning sickness, she could barely eat. Her boyfriend kept pointing out how different she seemed, how unlike herself.

I shouldn't have to be in this position, she kept thinking. *It shouldn't be this much work. It shouldn't be this much money.*

In her head, Monica kept going over everything that could go wrong. If she couldn't get an abortion in Oklahoma, would she have to go to Kansas that same day? Would she have to make another appointment on a different day, taking more time off work? Would she have to stay overnight in another state, finding the extra few hundred dollars for a hotel room? And if Kansas didn't work out either, where would she go instead? Briefly, she and her boyfriend floated the idea of going to Arizona or Colorado, or heading south to the Texas-Mexico border, maybe trying to find someone who could sell them abortion pills there. They tried to focus on places where they could drive. Already, they had little in savings and were living just about paycheck to paycheck. She had no idea how they'd afford to fly somewhere for an abortion, especially if she needed a last-minute plane ticket. If they had to travel farther, maybe they would just put the expenses on a credit card and hope that some-day they could pay it off. Her parents, she knew, wouldn't be willing to help. Her boyfriend's parents had been understanding about the abortion, but Monica had kept it a secret from her own family. Avowed Catholics, they deeply opposed abortion; Mexico, where the Martinez family was from, had only recently decriminalized the procedure, and stigma was still widespread. She feared that if she told them she was terminating a pregnancy, they'd never look at her the same way again—she would be a sinner, even a murderer.

The uncertainty and secrecy even made her question herself. She knew she didn't want to be a parent, but finding an abortion was so much harder than she ever thought it would be. Would it be easier to just have a baby?

Finally, Monday came. Monica and her boyfriend left Fort Worth at four in the morning. By eight a.m., they reached Trust Women—a small, unassuming medical clinic on the city's south-western side, surrounded by churches, fast-food joints, and taque-rias. The clinic staff had recommended coming right when they opened. They had a full roster of patients that day, but if Monica came earlier, that increased the odds she would be seen quickly. And getting in right away meant she would miss the bulk of the protesters: anti-abortion advocates who set up shop each day outside the clinic's walled-in parking lot, brandishing posters and shouting into their megaphones about the murderous sins of abortion. Like virtually all clinic protesters, they based their arguments on their religious views: This was against God's will, they shouted. If you got an abortion, you were going to Hell. The religious framing is a common strategy, an effort to dissuade people from seeking abortions, which are already incredibly stigmatized. Abortion clinic staff at Trust Women were largely used to this kind of interference, though many tried to keep their professions a secret from other people in their lives, to avoid judgment and harassment. But for a patient like Monica, it was the first time coming face-to-face with the vitriol these protesters spew at people who choose to terminate their pregnancies.

Monica was allowed to go inside the building; because of the clinic's precautions surrounding COVID-19, her boyfriend would have to wait in the car. He would sit outside all day, doing his best to block out the screams of protesters. Once inside, she waited in her sticky chair, where she sat for eight hours before the three p.m. surgical abortion she had scheduled. She had wanted something quick and easy, and the idea of coming back to Oklahoma for yet another visit was more than she could handle. From that perspective, a surgical abortion made the most sense. It rarely requires a follow-up visit of any kind, and it can be taken care of within a day.

Apart from the phones ringing and staff chatting, the waiting room was quiet. None of the patients spoke to one another. Normally, she might have passed the time by scrolling through social media or reading the news. But today Monica was so anxious she couldn't even look at her phone. Occasionally, she could hear the voices of the protesters trickling in from outside.

When it happened, the abortion itself was quick. The fetus was tiny, a nurse told Monica. The doctor reminded her too that, if Monica ever did want to become pregnant, it would be a medically tricky undertaking—not because of the abortion itself, which has no impact on fertility, but because of her blood pressure condition. Monica remembered some pain from the surgery. But then, when the process was over, all she felt was relief. The journey had been so difficult, but, after everything, they had done it. It was like a load she had been carrying all week had suddenly evaporated.

She fell asleep in the clinic's recovery room; when the staff woke her sometime later, they checked her vitals and cleared her to leave. Her boyfriend took her to a restaurant maybe a mile away. As they ate, he looked at her. At the risk of stating the obvious, something was different. It had barely been a few hours, but the cloud that had hung over her was already disappearing. She was starting to seem like her old self again.

After dinner, they began the three-hour drive back to Texas, watching the long day slowly fade into night. When, at nine p.m., they finally made it home, both were exhausted. They would later add up the time they had spent traveling, waiting, getting the abortion. Altogether, it had taken them almost eighteen hours.

Eight days after Monica's abortion, on the evening of May 3, the Oklahoma governor signed a bill banning abortions for anyone beyond six weeks of pregnancy. The bill was a near carbon copy of Texas's ban. In some ways, passing it didn't make much sense. Just the day before, news had broken from Washington, D.C., in the form of a leaked draft of the court's opinion, that the Supreme Court was set to overturn *Roe v. Wade.* A decision could come anytime this summer, and, if and when it did, Oklahoma already had laws on the books that would outlaw all abortions. But lawmakers in Oklahoma had a chance to cut off abortion access now—a goal they had been chasing for years. How could they not take it?

The timing highlighted just how lucky Monica had been. Had she come for an appointment even a week later, Oklahoma would no longer have been a viable option—and what would she have done then? More than anything, she felt angry. She'd spent years worrying that someday Republicans would make good on their promise to end abortion access. It had been a litmus-test party issue in Texas politics for as long as she could remember. Still, people had always told her to calm down, that she was being hysterical. A few years ago, she recalled, one of her coworkers had insisted to her that no one would ever outlaw abortion. Now Monica was proven right. "There was truth to it," she said. "We could see this coming."

Oklahoma was the second state to pass a law that would ban abortion, and it seemed as if no one outside the state really cared, not in the same way they had about Texas's law just eight months before. Time had already inured them. The White House, which had been quick to condemn Texas's six-week ban, put out no statement when Oklahoma's took effect. The Department of Justice, which had already failed in its efforts to block the Texas law, never stepped in or even attempted to challenge Oklahoma's six-week abortion ban. The media frenzy that had descended upon the Lone Star State never came to any of Oklahoma's abortion clinics. For some abortion providers in the state, it was a familiar feeling of neglect, and one they weren't surprised to see. They knew that those who didn't live there assumed that in Oklahoma everyone wanted abortion outlawed—even though polling data showed that about half of all state residents supported keeping abortion legal in most or all cases. For people who didn't see firsthand what it meant to lose abortion rights, the consequences were easy to ignore from afar.

"There's kind of this view of these states as disposable—that there aren't valuable people that live here," Voellinger of Trust Women said soon after the Oklahoma ban passed. "It feels like we're afterthoughts."

The era of legal abortion was coming to an end—and even this early there were clues as to what it would mean across the country for bodily autonomy.

In Oklahoma, as in Texas, abortion access and gender-affirming care for trans people had long been grouped. They were frequently provided at the same medical centers and were targets of kindred vitriol from socially conservative state lawmakers. Many of the states that had passed laws meant to ban abortion—Arkansas, Alabama, Texas, and Arizona—had already imposed restrictions on health care for trans people, though all but Arkansas's had been blocked by state courts. But efforts to restrict care would intensify in the future, in what health care providers in a state like Oklahoma would see as part and parcel of a larger effort to curb people's access to reproductive health care.

In the beginning of 2023, with abortion successfully banned, Oklahoma's legislators followed the lead of other conservative states, turning to prioritize legislation curbing access to gender-affirming care, such as hormone therapy or medications that delay puberty. One proposed bill would ban treatment until patients turned twenty-six. Such policies would be devastating; research shows that denying access to this particular health care increases the risk of suicidal ideation, while receiving care improves mental health outcomes. Trust Women, which would soon work to start providing gender-affirming care to Oklahoma patients, emerged as a sharp critic of those restrictions. As far as Voellinger was concerned, the progression from abortion bans to limitations on gender-affirming care was hardly a coincidence. It was part of the same playbook; all, she worried, would police people's abilities to access the health care that they needed. An argument to block one such procedure opened the door for lawmakers to justify blocking another.

"If you can understand why someone might need an abortion, I think it's a fairly easy extension to understand why someone might need to be on testosterone or why somebody might need top surgery," she said. "We know that these are life-affirming and lifesaving medical practices."

Soon enough, she knew, none of them would be available for the people her clinic served. The loss of that care, she feared, would kill people.

———

On May 3, 2022, Andrea Gallegos had to start making the calls she'd been dreading. With an abortion ban looming, Gallegos had been slow to schedule patients too far out. But that morning she'd checked the news first thing, and the governor hadn't signed an abortion ban yet. She was working in Texas that day, but she knew that the Tulsa clinic was booked solid. While seeing patients, she contacted a few more people to tell them that they could in fact come to Tulsa for an appointment tomorrow; it looked like abortion would still be legal in the state, even if just for another twenty-four hours.

But when news reports emerged just after five p.m. that day that the governor had signed a six-week ban—effective immediately—

Gallegos didn't have time to be shocked, to sit and digest the news. She had an urgent job to do: letting her patients know that, unless there was any chance they were earlier than six weeks pregnant, there was little point in coming into the clinic tomorrow morning. They'd be better off saving their time and gas money, repurposing it for a trip to another, safer state. Gallegos's grief was something she'd have to process later.

By now, Gallegos was used to being the constant bearer of bad news. But still, it was a miserable prospect. Sitting at home that evening, she went through the list of patients, calling those who were past six weeks: some Oklahomans, as well as every Texan scheduled to drive up to Tulsa the next day. The calls were brutal. On the other end of the line, every person she spoke to responded with a mixture of anger, shock, and confusion. Often, she noticed, she was the first one telling patients about Oklahoma's six-week ban. When she told them about their other options—traveling to Kansas, Colorado, New Mexico, Illinois—patients responded with disbelief. And because Oklahoma was at the time one of the few states to explicitly criminalize self-managed abortions, that wasn't a route she felt comfortable advising her patients to follow. (After *Dobbs,* the state's self-managed abortion ban ceased to be in effect, superseded instead by the state's new abortion "trigger ban," which had been written to take effect if *Roe* was ever overturned.)

Amid patients' incredulous replies, there were phrases she kept hearing over and over again, every time she told them that they'd now have to travel one state farther for an abortion. *"What do you mean I've got to go out of state?" "That's crazy." "I can't afford to take off work." "I can't leave my kids that long."* Then there was the kicker, the one that summed it all up: *"How am I supposed to do that?"*

She didn't have an answer. Gallegos would spend the next years of her life helping patients travel out of state for an abortion, being reminded over and over again just how difficult it was for patients to drop everything and leave. And never would she come up with a good answer for how people were supposed to pull together the time and resources, under legal threat, just to seek medical care.

In the days to come, Gallegos would experience a strange déjà vu. Just like it had in Texas, traffic in the Oklahoma clinic would slow to almost nothing. Frankly, she wasn't sure how long they could sustain something like this; while some clinics offer other reproductive health services as well, hers focused only on abortions. (And even when health centers do provide other forms of care, abortion is, from a financial standpoint, often the most important one.) From caring for between two and three dozen patients daily, they were down to providing abortions for maybe eight patients one day and ten another. Those numbers represented only half the people who showed up to the clinic. The rest were too far along in their pregnancies and had to be told that, if they wanted an abortion, they'd have to go elsewhere.

Gallegos would keep thinking about those patients. She had no way of knowing what would happen to them—if they could make it to a clinic out of state, if they found a way to safely induce an abortion on their own, or if they'd be forced to carry their unwanted pregnancy to term. She worried most about people who might try to terminate their own pregnancies but who didn't know how to do so safely, and who didn't know where to find reliable information about how to get medication abortion pills. In the pre-*Roe* world, she kept thinking, people died from unsafe attempts to do their own abortions. This, she was convinced, was where the country was heading once more.

And even this nightmarish reality wouldn't last long. Oklahoma passed another ban only three weeks later. This time, it would outlaw abortion entirely. Soon after, Gallegos's clinic would shut down. If someone called at any stage in their pregnancy, the most her staff could do was redirect them to a clinic in another state. No more were people like Monica able to rely on Oklahoma's abortion clinics. No more were Planned Parenthood nurses like Tiger able to provide care to the people who had driven day and night to reach them, instead pivoting to provide other forms of reproductive health care, as long as they remained legal. By June 24, 2022, when the Supreme Court overturned *Roe v. Wade,* it was—in Oklahoma, at least—a formality. Abortion had already been gone for weeks.

Gallegos tried to figure out how she could help the people who needed her at home. But in Texas and in Oklahoma, she would quickly realize there was nothing she could do. Soon, Gallegos would start planning for a future she could never have imagined: one that would take her out of Texas, and out of Oklahoma, to cities and states she had never visited before, but that would soon become the only realistic access points for people in her home states who wanted or needed an abortion.

Pregnancy is a medical condition, and one that brings with it its own host of complications and comorbidities. And yet it's a condition that the American health care system is often ill-equipped to handle. Even prior to 2022, pregnancy-related deaths had been on the rise in the United States, a stark contrast to other wealthy nations. Medications are often not tested before approval to ensure they can be safely provided to pregnant people. In large swaths of the country, it's impossible to find an ob-gyn within fifty miles, let alone one who accepts health insurance or who is comfortable caring for a patient with other health conditions in addition to being pregnant.

Tiff assumed that treatment for her latest bout of serious depression would be similar to what she'd experienced during previous episodes. But she had never sought inpatient mental health care while also pregnant, and the hospital, which specialized in pediatric psychiatry, wasn't quite sure what to do with her. Only one of its physicians had expertise working with pregnant patients specifically, and he wasn't in at the moment. Could she wait until he was on duty?

There was no way they were waiting—both Tiff and her mom knew that this was an emergency. Together, they drove to the emergency room, where she spent close to twenty-four hours before being checked into the proper psychiatric unit. She would stay for just under a week.

In a way, it was a transitional moment. Because her friends had known her for so long, few saw her as the pregnant girl—pregnant just happened to be her current state. They generally didn't treat her any differently so, when she wasn't secretly looking for an abortion, Tiff, too, had for the most part spent as much time as possible trying to forget that she was pregnant.

At the hospital, though, she couldn't escape it. Her pregnancy dictated how people treated her. Before group therapy, all the kids always got snacks—fruit gummies, Rice Krispies Treats, and short-bread cookies—but because she was pregnant the hospital staff made sure she got extra food. For three days in a row, someone would come by at five in the morning to check her blood sugar. She saw a different doctor from everyone else, the one who specialized in pregnant patients specifically. People kept asking her how she felt. Because the facility had extra-heavy chairs, weighted so that patients couldn't easily pick up or throw them, people kept offering to move the seats for her.

Even her treatment options were different. Tiff had taken anti-depressants before, but she wasn't taking any meds at the time. Data has historically been limited regarding what medications are safe for pregnant people to take, including psychiatric drugs. There is some research suggesting that, especially when taken earlier in pregnancy, particular medications may increase the risk of birth defects. But it's not always fully clear which ones, how much greater the risk becomes, and how to balance that risk against the benefits of treating people's mental health conditions. In particular, physicians don't always agree on whether to prescribe pregnant people many commonly used antidepressants, even though they are in agreement that untreated depression increases risks for both the pregnant person and the fetus. (Newer research, published well after Tiff's hospital stay, would underscore the fact that most antidepressants are generally safe to take during pregnancy.) In her case, the only prescription the hospital gave her was one that she had taken before, a mood stabilizer generally known to be safe for pregnant patients. Previously, she had found it to be most helpful when paired with other medications; this time, however, she could take only the one.

As she watched the way people treated her, Tiff's perception of her pregnancy started to shift. "It just made it real," she said. "In the hospital, they meet you as pregnant. So that's what they're thinking about."

Tiff was feeling better when she left. Just like always, she'd made new friends at the hospital, people she'd stay in touch with for months after. She was taking medication again. In the coming Texas summer—one of the hottest on record, and her last one as a mostly unencumbered kid—she'd start spending more time with her friends, ones she knew from school, and her cousin who lived down the street. In July, seven months into her pregnancy, she went to Houston's Pride Celebration Festival with her best friend, though the heat and crowds almost made her pass out, forcing her to end the day early. When the hot weather got to be too much, she stayed indoors playing her favorite game, *Roblox*.

At one point, her mom even tried to plan a baby shower. But the logistics were too complicated and a party too expensive to pull off. Her friends, seeing her belly grow, brought her gifts anyway. Manuel kept his distance, but his family showed up with a baby swing, a car seat, and a crib. He still wasn't speaking to her, but his family loved her all the same.

By now, she was starting to envision this alternative life for herself—the one where she had a baby and became a mom. But she couldn't fully grasp just how much having a baby would take over her life. She started making plans. Sometime after giving birth—before the end of 2022 if she could—she'd find time to take her final GED test. Then, when she turned eighteen, she could work to get certified as an EMT. The course was only fifteen weeks. And, if she liked the work, then eventually she could enroll in community college and study to be a paramedic. Her parents were older, sure, but she had no doubt they'd be able to help take care of the baby while she studied.

By Tuesday, August 9, 2022, Tiff's stomach felt huge. And that day she was in more pain than usual. She was still another three weeks away from her due date, but far along enough by now that, whenever she gave birth, the baby probably wouldn't need extra medical care or face any major health problems. She'd picked out a name already: Mateo.

Tiff and her mother were already in Houston for a checkup with her ob-gyn that would turn out to be her last doctor's visit before she gave birth. When Tiff mentioned the pain in her stomach, how it felt sharper than she was used to, the physician frowned.

Tiff had to get to a hospital quickly, she said. This late in pregnancy, upper abdominal pains could mean preeclampsia, a high-blood-pressure condition that can endanger the pregnant person and is only treatable by quickly delivering the baby. Common consequences can include having a baby with low birth weight or the pregnant person experiencing placental abruption—a rare and dangerous condition in which the placenta detaches from the uterus, causing heavy bleeding and making it harder for the fetus to breathe. What the doctor didn't say aloud was that, if it was in fact preeclampsia, and if Tiff didn't get treated soon, she could die.

They drove straight to the hospital. For hours, she waited as staff ran a series of tests, including what's called a "biophysical profile"—a way to assess high-risk pregnancies, measuring how much amniotic fluid surrounded the fetus, the fetus's movement, its muscles, and its breathing. For Tiff, that last part was critical. A fetus finishes developing lungs around thirty-six weeks of pregnancy, and after that it's supposed to spend the next four "practicing" breathing: contracting and expanding its diaphragm so that, when it's born, the baby has strong, healthy lungs that can process oxygen. But when the doctors looked at Tiff's tests, they saw no sign of that fetal breathing movement.

Tiff was terrified. So much was happening, and she could barely process what it all meant. There were other concerns, about Tiff's own health. Her blood pressure was high, and the protein levels in her kidneys seemed off. The longer Tiff stayed pregnant, the doctor told her, the greater the risks to her health. They were admitting her today and would induce labor promptly. Tiff remembered being taken by surprise when she found out that she'd be giving birth soon. And then she started to cry.

By the time Tiff was transferred to the labor and delivery ward, it was nighttime, and the hospital was closed to visitors. The next two and a half days were a miserable blur. It took hours before the fetus dropped near her pelvis, a sign that she would soon begin labor. A nurse gave her an epidural in the afternoon, but the physician delivering her baby didn't reach her room until after it felt like the medication had worn off. When she finally did give birth, Tiff felt each contraction. It was a pain unlike any she'd ever experienced.

On August 11, it finally ended. Mateo was healthy, and so was Tiff. Her pregnancy had been awful, and her delivery a nightmare all the way through. But it was over. As she looked at her son, it sank in once more. Tiff was now seventeen years old, but she was somehow a parent. From this day forward, her life would be completely different from what she'd experienced until now, or what she had envisioned for herself.

Six days later, after settling back in at home with her parents, Tiff wasn't as tired as she thought she would be. Her life revolved around the baby now; she snuck in half-hour breaks for herself whenever Mateo took a nap, but it was hard to predict when he might fall asleep. And when the baby was awake, he kept wanting to eat. Her breasts were leaking milk nonstop. When she wasn't feeding Mateo, she was pumping. Tiff's mother kept telling her to sleep when she could, but all the feeding just left her hungry. It was hard to process how quickly she had learned to love Mateo, this baby she had never wanted. But still, she couldn't shake the feeling that this wasn't how things were supposed to be. The next few months would be some of the hardest she'd ever live through, and she still couldn't imagine what the rest of her life would look like. She was grateful her child was a boy, she confessed. He would never have to worry about pregnancy or about needing an abortion while living in a state like Texas; he would never have to endure what she had.

"As much as I love this baby, I would wish this on absolutely no one," she said a few days after she gave birth, while Mateo finally slept for a bit. It was a sentiment she'd reiterate over and over in the months to come, as she continued to process just how irrevocably her life had changed.

"I still ideally would have had that abortion."

PART II

Angela

ACROSS STATE LINES

CHAPTER 3

Not Strong Enough

New Mexico and Illinois

On a normal day, Hope Clinic might have gotten 150 calls from people in and outside of Illinois seeking an abortion. But Friday, June 24, 2022, was anything but a normal day.

That morning, the first hundred phone calls to the clinic came within an hour—specifically, the hour right after the news broke that the Supreme Court had finally ruled in the *Dobbs* case, issuing a decision that completely overturned *Roe v. Wade*. The decision had opened the door for states to ban abortion entirely, and many would start doing so almost immediately. But Illinois, where Hope was based, was taking the opposite tack: the state government had already passed laws explicitly protecting the right to an abortion. Still, abortion providers in the state were about to find themselves at the center of the post-*Roe* world: overwhelmed by people calling from out of state and in dire need of help.

By the end of that Friday, the staff had recorded 650 callers. Some were people who lived in Illinois, who were confused and wanted to know if abortion was still legal. Others asked if their appointments, which they had already scheduled days ago, were about to be canceled. And then in the last group were perhaps the most desperate people: the ones calling from states like Missouri, Kentucky, Tennessee, and Alabama. They needed abortions, maybe had already scheduled something at another clinic closer to home, and their states had now begun enforcing laws to ban the practice. Hope Clinic, in Granite City, Illinois, near the Missouri border, was their only realistic option. Could someone see them? And how quickly could they get an appointment?

In states like Illinois and New Mexico—places where the government had vowed to protect access to abortion, and that were surrounded on virtually all sides by those that had banned access to the procedure—June 24 was only the beginning. In the months and years to come, health care providers in these states would be tested over and over again, watching as the post-*Dobbs* world cemented their status as some of the nation's most critical access points for abortion. It was a heavy burden, and one that arguably neither state was strong enough to bear.

Chelsea Souder had known for months in advance that her clinic would become a destination. Even before *Dobbs,* its staff largely saw patients from out of state: mostly pregnant people who traveled from Missouri, where abortion restrictions were so onerous that, even prior to *Roe* being overturned, all but one clinic had already shut down. So far in 2022, they'd already been seeing 20 percent more patients than usual, a change Souder attributed to more people traveling to Illinois after Texas's six-week abortion ban took effect. It was only reasonable to expect that, without federal abortion protections, the demand for their services would skyrocket. This was just plain geography: Illinois's government had vowed to protect abortion, and the clinic was close enough to other states likely to ban or heavily restrict the procedure.

For months leading up to the Supreme Court's decision, Souder, who co-owned Hope Clinic, had tried to work with her staff to better understand what it would look like when states on all sides of them began enforcing abortion bans. She had even planned a physical expansion of their building and started trying to hire more people. Still, she would say later, nothing ever could have prepared her for the onslaught of patients who would soon come calling.

Those first days were a blur. In the past, Hope Clinic had been able to book patients for appointments within a week of them calling. By Tuesday, just four days after the court decision, they were scheduling people three weeks out. By Wednesday, Souder had lost count of how many people had called her clinic—it easily surpassed a thousand, well beyond what they had previously imagined was even possible. There literally weren't enough people working to answer every phone call. In the days that followed, Hope Clinic would start booking sixty patients per day, hoping as many as forty would show up. The staff would work ten- to twelve-hour days, even as everyone acknowledged that, eventually, they'd have to slow down if they wanted to keep this going. They would start offering abortions six days a week, instead of five. She hoped that if they hired more medical providers, the clinic might bring down its wait times; two to three weeks was too long to ask someone to wait as their unwanted pregnancy progressed. It was a tall order, and one they would struggle with—even months later, patients calling Hope were still told they'd have to wait two weeks before they could get an abortion.

Souder knew that no matter what they did, it was never going to be enough. They were just one clinic, too small, too fragile. And the responsibility they were asked to take up now was just so gigantic. It was a painful reality to accept, one she had to keep reminding both her staff and herself about.

"We're not going to be able to help every person who calls us," she said a week later. "That's a hard pill to swallow."

———————

In the weeks, months, and even years after *Roe*'s overturn, the responsibility of abortion care for whole regions of the country would fall overwhelmingly on clinicians in Illinois and New Mexico, which were close to states that banned the procedure but which were unlikely to do so themselves. Surrounded by hundreds of miles of mostly flat land, these states were easy to drive to, and a far easier option than, say, hopping on a plane to Colorado or California—at least in the warmer months. When the seasons changed, Illinois's notoriously treacherous winter would derail countless patients from making it up north for an abortion.

In both states, providers had had some practice caring for

people who had fled abortion restrictions in their states. Illinois had been a refuge for Missourians as well as for countless abortion-seeking patients displaced after Texas's ban took effect. New Mexico, meanwhile, neighbored both Texas and Oklahoma, and providers there would darkly joke that, as far as they were concerned, *Roe v. Wade* had been undone the moment Texas's Senate Bill 8 took effect. Wait times kept growing due to the volume of out-of-state patients. By September, only months after *Dobbs,* one clinic in Albuquerque—where physicians provided abortions every day of the week—still had an average wait time of four to six weeks for an appointment. In that much time, worried Dr. Eve Espey, a physician there, someone's pregnancy could progress from first to second trimester, or even from second to third. Medically, it was a real problem. Abortions are very safe—safer than childbirth in many cases—but when performed later in pregnancy they do become more involved and invasive, a development that naturally makes the procedure riskier. In New Mexico, there was no legal limit on when in a pregnancy someone could get an abortion. But in Illinois, the procedure was banned after around twenty-four to twenty-six weeks—typically enough time, but a far trickier deadline to meet if six of those weeks were spent waiting for an appointment. The problem, Espey kept reiterating, was the pattern that had begun to emerge the day *Roe* fell: there simply weren't enough clinics or appointments to provide appropriate, timely abortions for all the patients who kept calling.

In theory, abortion providers in these states would work with support from their state governments. The governors of both Illinois and New Mexico had promised to use all their powers to protect anyone who provided abortion. But little aid appeared immediately, and what did emerge simply didn't suffice.

Illinois's governor, J. B. Pritzker—who in the summer of 2022 was running for reelection and eager to tout his support for abortion rights—promised the very day *Roe* was overturned that he would call the state legislature back into a special governing session, so that they could swiftly pass even more state laws protecting abortion clinics. That could mean special laws protecting abortion providers if they cared for people who traveled from somewhere that had banned abortion. It could mean allocating more money to support the state's overwhelmed abortion clinics as well as the independent abortion funds that were now fielding phone calls from people across the region, all asking for help with paying for the procedure and the exponentially more burdensome travel now associated with getting to a clinic. The governor's promise never materialized. Only a few weeks after the *Dobbs* decision, abortion rights organizations in Illinois learned that the state government wouldn't be coming back into session anytime soon—at least, not before Election Day in November. There were no new laws that might protect them, no immediate state support they could count on. In Chicago, the biggest city in the state, the mayor's office took some action on its own, directing the city government not to cooperate with out-of-state investigations into abortion provision and issuing $500,000 in grants to the Chicago Abortion Fund and Planned Parenthood of Illinois. But in the immediate term, it still wasn't enough to address the enormous strain on many of the state's clinics.

In New Mexico, by contrast, the state government had made significantly more direct investments in expanding access. By the end of that August, the governor, Michelle Lujan Grisham, had directed her administration to take concrete action to expand access to abortion as much as possible. That meant investigating whether the state's health department could start providing medication abortions and putting $10 million in state money toward opening a new abortion clinic. That clinic, located in southwestern Dona Ana County, would be specifically intended to serve patients traveling to New Mexico from the West Texas border. It was a tremendous investment, and an unprecedented one, too. Congress has long prohibited the use of federal funds to pay for abortion. With that constraint, a state project like New Mexico's required using money it generated on its own, from state-specific taxes, and convincing state residents that this was a worthy use of their locally generated funds. Never before had a state used that money to directly fund the creation of a new abortion clinic. Providers in the state hailed the governor's efforts, emphasizing just how much they needed the support. But, they acknowledged, it would take months—at a minimum—for her work to have an impact. Building new clinics takes time, and the state government wouldn't even start planning the project until 2023, more than six months after

Roe's overturn. Espey, an adviser on the project, worried it could be years after the decision before the new state clinic opened. Just saying that out loud made her nervous. Patients desperately needed help, and it felt like there was little providers could do.

Post-*Dobbs,* anyone paying the slightest bit of attention could see just how seismic the change had been and how dramatic the implications would be for access to health care. But taking the next step—treating the crisis as an actual emergency, and one that merited sweeping and immediate interventions—seemed impossible. Even the most aggressive state response would inevitably fall short.

The story of abortion is one of health care, but also of so much more. For decades, restricting access to abortion has also exacerbated deep-seated inequalities in America. The best evidence available, a landmark body of research called the Turnaway Study, demonstrated indubitably that when people are denied access to abortion they are more likely to fall into poverty and then stay there. There is a vicious cycle to it, and one that abortion bans have reinforced. People who want to end a pregnancy are usually already parents, and often they are concerned that they cannot afford to raise another child. At the same time, because they have less money, the cost of leaving the state for care poses a more immediate hardship. The racial implications, too, are obvious and undeniable. Because of decades of discrimination, and a wage gap that penalizes all women but most deeply affects women who aren't White, the people who cannot afford another child—who are therefore most likely to need an abortion and least likely to be able to pay for one—are more often Black women and Latinas. Although abortion bans would affect virtually everyone, women of color would shoulder perhaps the heaviest burden in the post-*Dobbs* world.

This wasn't a story that Angela, a twenty-one-year-old woman in Texas, ever thought she would be a part of. Her grandmother had immigrated to Texas from Guatemala, and in their home of San Antonio, that shared heritage felt distinctly meaningful, offering the family strength and solidarity in a city, state, and country that felt foreign. Angela loved her family deeply and treasured her connection with them, even when her grandmother sometimes chastised her for being "too American"—and, by implication, not Guatemalan enough. Her family also had warned her about the evils of abortion. The argument was both cultural and religious: the Catholic beliefs her relatives had carried with them long before coming to America and that felt even more important to retain in the new country. The Church was like a piece of home; keeping alive the tenets and traditions they'd known before immigrating felt essential to holding on to their identities. She understood why she'd heard the same words over and over, since she was a girl: Abortion was a crime against God. Pregnancy, no matter whether you wanted it, was a gift.

Angela had already been forced to grow up more quickly than she would have liked. She'd become pregnant with her son at nineteen, when she still barely felt like an adult. Years later, she was quick to note just how deeply motherhood had changed her, fundamentally shifting her sense of purpose. Her boy was now the reason she woke up each day. But at her core Angela was still the same person she had always been. Irreverent and sarcastic, incredibly self-aware and intensely curious about the world around her, she loved to imagine a life that took her beyond her home in South Texas. Maybe, she dreamed, she'd live in Europe someday, where together she and her boyfriend could raise their young son.

Early in the fall of 2022, with her son not even a year old, she hadn't considered she might be pregnant again. The signs were subtle at first: days of unabating back pain, headaches, and a late period she initially attributed to stress. Finally, when none of her symptoms got better, she forced herself to take a pregnancy test.

Those three minutes of waiting were agonizing. And when she saw the result—"pregnant"—her jaw dropped. A sonogram at a doctor's office confirmed that she was already eight weeks along; where she lived, her only option was to carry the pregnancy to term, giving birth to a baby that she could either keep or give up for adoption. *Dobbs* had come down only two months earlier; abortion was illegal in Texas.

Angela couldn't imagine a worse time for her to have another baby. She still owed almost a thousand dollars in medical bills from the last time she had given birth. Her boyfriend, Nigel, was supposed to go back to school in January. Eventually, she hoped to do the same, but their little family was still mired in debt—even beyond her outstanding medical bills—which she knew she had to pay off before she could become a student again. Her contract job, which paid decently, was set to expire in the new year, and she didn't have anything lined up for after.

Angela knew firsthand what an intense responsibility parenthood was. Her son was a surprise baby, but she still loved him desperately, understanding on an innate level how completely he depended on her to live. Her own childhood had been difficult; she was raised by extended family while her mom floated in and out of Texas. Before getting pregnant, Angela said, she'd never really known how to take care of herself, especially when it came to alcohol. Back then, she drank heavily—in retrospect, she suspected it had been an effort to forget, however briefly, just how miserable her adolescence had been. It felt like everything had changed when she became a mom, though. She cut out alcohol completely, and she was pretty sure doing so had saved her life. Watching her son grow even just these past few months, with a face that looked like hers on some days and Nigel's on others, she'd begun to imagine a new life for herself, too. Eventually, she would go back to school, finish her degree—she was thinking nursing or accounting—and someday earn a good living to help support her son. The three of them would be a family, and her boy would grow up with so much more than she had.

But the new pregnancy had thrown a wrench into all those plans. How was she supposed to finish school now, with not one small kid but two? Already, they were struggling. Another baby would put her even further behind on getting back to school, on getting the right job to help take care of everyone. Angela needed an abortion for a million reasons, but, most importantly, getting an abortion would help her be the parent she wanted to be. She needed to do this so she could take care of the baby she already had.

In that regard, Angela really was just like the bulk of Americans who seek abortions. Years of data have shown that around six in ten people who terminate a pregnancy in the United States are already parents—people who know intimately what it means to take on the responsibility of having a child. One in ten has three kids already;

a quarter of all abortions are done for people like Angela, with just one child at home. Around six in ten are in their twenties, the same age range as Angela. And government data also show that Hispanic women, like Angela, have significantly higher abortion rates than White women, a product of the systemic racism that means they often earn less money.

It was still hard to believe that this was happening to her. Angela and Nigel used condoms whenever they had sex, in an effort to ensure she wouldn't get pregnant again. And ever since she was young, her family had taught her that a fetus was alive from the moment of conception—for much of Angela's childhood, she too had believed that getting an abortion was tantamount to murder. Her mother had always been loudly judgmental of people who got abortions; one time, she recalled, her mom had even suggested that anyone who got an abortion should go to prison.

It wasn't until Angela was a teenager that she changed her own mind, after meeting people who'd become pregnant as a result of rape or who knew they couldn't afford another kid. And, from everything she knew, the state's foster care system was already over-run; it seemed wrong to have a child if you couldn't take care of it yourself. In that regard, too, the evidence suggested she was right. National data show that children placed in the foster care system suffer substantially higher rates of mental health problems, including post-traumatic stress disorder. And Texas's foster care system specifically has come under fire for a stunning lack of resources, including insufficient placements for children, funding shortfalls, and an inability to account for hundreds of children who go missing each year.

Maybe, Angela had begun to tell herself, abortion wasn't the horror she'd been told. It was a lonely realization to come to, and she hated the feeling of knowing how differently she viewed the world compared with so many people she loved, and knowing too that they thought less of her for it. So she learned not to talk too much about the issue. It just wasn't worth fighting with her family about it.

This meant that if Angela wanted an abortion—and the more she thought about it, the more she knew in her gut that she did—she wouldn't be able to tell her family the truth. They would look at her differently, like a murderer, someone who had violated a tenet of their faith and rejected God's own blessing. Already, they judged her for supporting the right in theory, telling her on the rare occasion their disagreement came up that she supported the murder of babies. If she shared that she too was one of those murderers? She would lose their respect for the rest of her life.

It was a conundrum that countless people across the country just like her would face and have faced for decades. The Catholic Church has long staunchly opposed abortion, a viewpoint that has shaped not only its legality but also how people perceive it. In Guatemala, Angela's family's home country, abortion is still illegal and birth control remains difficult to come by, a result in part of the Church's still-pervasive influence. And in her home state, Texas, major anti-abortion groups—for instance, the influential Texas Alliance for Life, which supported laws such as Texas's six-week abortion ban—boasted strong ties to the Church, including organizing anti-abortion marches with the Diocese of Austin, situated right by the state capitol building. It's a view out of step with most American Catholics: data show that most people, including people who are Catholic, and including people who identify as Hispanic and Catholic, agree that abortion should be legal in most cases.

But there is a difference between believing that the procedure should be allowed in theory and in accepting it for the people one knows and loves. Across the country, the judgment reserved for people who get abortions remains incredibly potent, and people with Catholic families are far more likely to report facing stigma if they terminate a pregnancy. The threat of abortion stigma in turn can result in long-term psychological distress, especially for people like Angela, who had a history of depression or anxiety. When *Roe* was overturned, she recalled, her family had seemed genuinely happy; she didn't want to risk another fight by arguing for what she believed in.

For Angela, the fear of judgment meant that, with the exception of Nigel, there was no one she could talk to about her decision-making process and no one she'd be able to lean on for support in the lead-up to her procedure, or in the weeks and months after. And telling people what she had done or even considered doing could lose her virtually every relationship she held dear. If she wanted to make this choice, she'd have to commit to doing it on her own. It was perhaps the loneliest decision she'd ever made.

"It's such a hard thing to do as it is, to make a choice like that. I've never had an abortion, and I made that choice," she said. "Having this right taken away and just being looked down upon for doing something like that? It does make it hard."

Before abortion became illegal in Texas, Angela hadn't worried too much about it. She thought that she wasn't going to get pregnant, so the state laws weren't going to affect her. Someday, once they'd saved up enough money and found the right jobs, she and Nigel planned to move out of Texas, to somewhere with more progressive leadership that better aligned with their values. She wanted to raise her son somewhere they could count on the state to protect access to abortion, to help people afford things she deemed essential, like health insurance.

But now here she was, at eight weeks already in a state that had opted to ban virtually all abortions, with strict penalties for anyone who aided or abetted someone in getting one. The only exception to the state's ban was for medical emergencies, and that provision was, in practice, typically invoked only if a patient was quite literally about to die. If this had all happened a year or so earlier, Angela could have gotten an abortion at a clinic in San Antonio. It would have been a short drive, and she could have recovered at home. She wouldn't have had to make any excuses—take off work or explain her absence to anyone who asked too many questions. It would be a private decision she made with her partner, and there would be no need to make up stories or lie about where she was.

Instead, she'd have to find a way to get to another state, a place where she could safely, legally get her abortion. Just looking at a map, she considered her options: a fourteen-hour drive to Denver, perhaps, or an eleven-hour journey to Albuquerque. It was hard to conceive of how she could afford to pay for either. But what other choice did she have?

———————

In both Illinois and New Mexico, the need for abortion services had only grown more acute, and the impact was spreading quickly.

Some clinics in the state had to temporarily suspend scheduling appointments altogether. Eve Espey, in Albuquerque, said that the demand was so overwhelming that the clinic she worked at struggled to schedule in-person visits for other family planning services, such as birth control consultations. She knew that over the long term there would be consequences. Fewer people able to access comprehensive contraception could mean only higher unintended pregnancy rates down the line; reproductive health clinics that were unable to schedule as many cervical cancer screenings could yield higher complication rates for a disease that is far more treatable if caught early. Although new clinics would come to New Mexico, ostensibly to help undercut the surge, most focused on abortion, leaving other reproductive health services more underaddressed than they ever had been. At Espey's clinic, they tried to develop a sort of triage system: hiring a new nurse practitioner who could focus specifically on birth control, while anybody able to provide abortion care was told to focus on that. Still, she worried about how they could provide care for everyone in need and continue offering all the services for which patients depended on them. She didn't think it was possible.

As clinics were increasingly stretched thin, the cases doctors like Espey saw were becoming more time-consuming and medically complex to address. It was entirely predictable. Patients were having to travel farther for abortions, making journeys that were more logistically and financially difficult to plan—meaning it took them longer to come in for care. One patient, she recalled, drove seventeen hours each way for an appointment. Increasingly, they saw patients who had a history of multiple cesarean section births, which increased their risk of complex pregnancies and, in turn, complex abortion needs. And at the same time, the wait times for appointments continued growing.

In the past, most people who got abortions had been solidly in their first trimester. Per federal health data from 2020, about four out of five abortion patients in New Mexico that year were less than thirteen weeks pregnant. After *Dobbs*, though, more and more, patients calling for appointments were well within their second trimester. The delays in care inflicted emotional burdens on patients, forced to feel their unwanted pregnancies progress. Critically, abortions later in pregnancy are also typically more expensive, sometimes costing thousands of dollars instead of hundreds. And later abortions can necessitate more complex procedures, often requiring two days of in-person medical care as opposed to one, or rescheduling someone's visit from an outpatient clinic to a hospital. Medically, it was far from ideal. The laws and obstacles that had forced people to delay their abortions had as a result put them at greater medical risk.

At the same time, the delay in when people could get abortions created new financial hurdles for patients, who now needed to scrounge up even more money to pay for their procedures than they would have in the past. And it added to the challenges providers faced. Already, they didn't have enough doctors to care for everyone in need. Now those same doctors had to do more two-day abortions—which meant fewer appointment slots available to care for everyone in need.

It wasn't an entirely new pattern. After Texas's six-week abortion ban took effect, something that now felt like a vestige of a previous lifetime, doctors in neighboring states had witnessed a similar phenomenon, reporting to one another that they had started seeing more and more patients who were later in pregnancy, whose abortions had been delayed for weeks because finding an appointment was far more difficult now. But the increase in states banning abortion had amplified the problem exponentially, affecting more patients and straining an under-resourced medical system that already had almost no slack left.

In New Mexico, abortions were legal throughout pregnancy, but there were still limitations when it came to what kinds of procedures a clinic's staff felt comfortable and equipped to actually do, and what practically they had time for. Part of the challenge was sheer math. Because abortions later in pregnancy take longer to perform, doing them limits how many patients the clinic can see in a day. With more patients coming to New Mexico clinics, providers had to make a choice—whether it was worth seeing the rare patient who needed an abortion past twenty-four weeks, or whether they should conserve their resources to care for as many people as possible.

By 2023, only about six months after *Dobbs,* the effect was clear:

despite the state's permissive laws, there was no longer a single abortion clinic in New Mexico that performed abortions for anyone later than twenty-four weeks. Espey's went up until twenty-three weeks and six days, and she had patients calling who were two weeks shy of that deadline. When people called who were that late in pregnancy, providers had little choice but to push them to the front of the line—in turn postponing abortions for people who were earlier in pregnancy, making them wait longer and watch their pregnancies progress further before they could get care. By the time she saw patients for their abortions, she said, many had experienced an intense range of emotions: first desperation, anger, fear, and, finally, relief.

"It's so awful. A lot of them internalize it and feel like it's their fault, which is really painful," she worried. "And for us, to see patients who can't access this basic health care . . ."

She couldn't see when, if ever, things would get better. No one could.

———◆———

Back in San Antonio, and still desperate for an abortion, Angela was surveying her options. After searching online for nearby states where the procedure was legal, she'd started calling clinics in Colorado and New Mexico, seeing which ones might be able to take her, how quickly she could get an appointment, and how much it would cost. Surgery made her nervous. She wanted a medication abortion, which meant she needed to be seen within her first twelve weeks of pregnancy. Now that she was already halfway through her first trimester, and with clinic wait times expanding daily, she knew she didn't have much time.

None of the Colorado clinics she called could offer her an appointment anytime soon. But in Albuquerque, the voice on the phone told her she could be seen in two weeks, on a Friday morning. It felt like an eternity to keep her pregnancy even that much longer, despite knowing she'd eventually be able to get the abortion she needed. But, she'd come to realize, this was as good as things were going to get.

She needed to get to New Mexico without anyone knowing why. So Angela and Nigel made their plan. They could leave Wednesday and drive through the night, reaching their Albuquerque Airbnb on Thursday. On Friday, she'd go to her appointment and receive mifepristone. The next day, Saturday, she'd take the misoprostol, and on Sunday they would drive home. Her family would watch their son while the two of them were gone. And they would tell their relatives that the trip was in honor of Nigel's birthday, a date that, coincidentally, happened to fall on the same weekend.

People admittedly seemed a bit confused when she told them that they were leaving town for the weekend. Everyone knew she and Nigel were struggling. Why would they drop all this money on a last-minute weekend getaway? She was grateful they didn't ask too many questions, though; Angela wasn't sure how much scrutiny her story could withstand.

She hated lying, especially to her mother. They'd only recently begun working to rebuild their relationship. And it hadn't been easy: Her mom had left Texas for the first decade of Angela's life, relocating to Canada with a new boyfriend and leaving Angela's grandmother to raise her. Even when her mother came back, she'd exhibited what Angela considered a less-than-perfect approach to parenthood: needling her daughter about her body, tracking Angela's calories on a calculator whenever she ate. Now, as an adult, Angela drew a direct link between the way her mother had treated her as a child and the eating disorder she still struggled with.

Developing a real relationship—one where spending time together felt supportive and good, where she actually looked forward to their weekly dates—had been one of the hardest things Angela had ever attempted. In retrospect, it was worth it: she relished the trust and comfort they had finally developed with each other. At long last, their relationship felt somewhat close to that of a normal mother and daughter. But she knew her mother didn't believe in abortion and that telling her could ruin the relationship they had just rebuilt—this time, she feared, maybe beyond repair.

In theory, Angela and Nigel could have cut their New Mexico trip in half, eliminating at least some of the financial costs. Mifepristone, the first medication Angela would take, can be administered either at a doctor's office or at home. But misoprostol, the second medication, is almost always taken in one's home, and the cramps and bleeding associated with this kind of abortion don't begin until after taking the misoprostol. There was no medical reason to stay in New Mexico after taking Angela's first set of medications; from a purely scientific standpoint, the two of them could have driven home Friday night. She could have taken the second drug in their apartment on Saturday, saving them two whole nights' worth of lodging, money they badly needed.

But the laws around medication abortion were and still are intensely confusing. Medically, an abortion starts once you take the first medication, but abortion providers and lawyers couldn't answer for sure if someone like Angela taking the second pill in San Antonio would technically count as her having an abortion in Texas—and if that would break the state's law. Without some level of certainty, Angela couldn't take that chance.

When they crossed state lines, she felt the relief course through her like adrenaline. The shift was visible right away: on the side of the road, she could see signs specifically advertising that here abortion was legal. Even if you came from somewhere else, the doctors in New Mexico would help you safely terminate your pregnancy. That reassurance provided a sense of security she hadn't experienced in weeks—she'd almost forgotten what it felt like to know that she had the right to make her own medical choices.

Still, the weekend was grueling. That Friday morning, volunteers from a neighboring crisis pregnancy center waved posters outside the abortion clinic, offering her brochures. If she just followed them, they said, they'd do a three-dimensional ultrasound for free and then show her a picture of her "baby." They kept using that word, the same kind of language she'd heard so often growing up, that she knew her mother or grandmother would use if they knew what she was doing. It was enough to make her wonder about whether this was right, to once again fill her with anxiety. *Maybe I should rethink this,* she thought.

The hesitation lingered in her mind for only a split second, before Angela reminded herself that right now this eight-week-old embryo—not even two centimeters long yet—wasn't something she could afford to let uproot her life.

Angela brushed past, going inside the clinic for her appointment, into a waiting room full of people. She chatted with the other patients as they waited: some said they were as young as fifteen, and most, like her, had come to Albuquerque from another state. One woman told her she'd also driven there from San Antonio—if they'd known, they could have traveled together, splitting the cost. Before seeing her doctor, Angela filled out a piece of paper, certifying that the clinic wouldn't disclose any information about her abortion to anyone. She understood why the form was there, but it instilled in her a fear that something illicit was happening and the sense that what she was doing could put her in legal danger.

She could tell that the other patients were on edge that day, a by-product of the circumstances that had forced them to flee their homes, driving hours across state lines for this care. Having to travel so far, having to get your abortion in secret—it made you question what you were doing, letting in doubt that otherwise wouldn't be there. Angela kept thinking about her family. Was it wrong she hadn't told them what she was really doing? Would she someday tell them the truth?

When it was her turn, she went to the clinic's exam room, where she met with a physician who would give her the medications she needed. She told him what she had been through, how far they'd had to drive to come here. The doctor, she recalled later, was sympathetic to her plight and angry at what she and her fellow patients had endured to get to the clinic that morning.

It wasn't fair, he said, to force people onto a plane or to make an eleven-hour drive like she had. This was a routine medical service they should be able to get at home.

After giving her the medications, he told her she'd have to come back in four weeks, when they'd do a follow-up appointment to see how her body had recovered after the abortion. It was a reasonable request: medication abortions are safe and straightforward, but, when possible, a subsequent check-in visit is often recommended, just to make sure the abortion medications worked and that there are no fetal remains lingering inside the patient. But Angela wasn't ready to prepare for yet another days-long journey back across state lines, and, more importantly, she didn't know how she would be able to afford it.

Abortion bans in the years before *Dobbs* had been part of a larger political project: laws were written largely to please a segment of anti-abortion activists, often crafted almost entirely by a select few national anti-abortion advocacy groups, in some cases in an effort to prompt court cases that might challenge *Roe* or push a more conservative court to weaken its protections. But many of the Republican legislators who pushed abortion restrictions hadn't prepared themselves for *Roe* to actually fall, had never considered it worth their time to seriously consult actual physicians or medical experts, or to educate themselves as to how abortion actually worked. What was the point of doing so, when these bans weren't going to take effect—and when an abortion, as far as they understood, was something they would never get themselves?

With *Roe* gone, the bans being enforced were incredibly vague, written without the nuance or attention to detail that might have been applied to an issue like road maintenance or energy policy. There was little specificity about what actually constituted an abortion—and the uncertainty over how exactly the laws worked meant that, even if a medical provider practiced and offered care in a state with enshrined abortion protections, they could still possibly face criminal charges if they ended up treating anyone who had traveled from a state that had banned the procedure.

A core issue was the two-drug mechanism recommended for medication abortions: the mifepristone, the twenty-four- to forty-eight-hour wait, and then the misoprostol. It was the same question Angela had struggled with. If someone traveled to a state with abortion protections, and if they took the first medication there—the one that effectively started the abortion, but did not complete it—would they have to stay in the state another twenty-four hours and take the second drug there? Would they have to spend another two nights away from home, paying for a hotel there and a babysitter at home, waiting until they had passed both blood and an embryo before they could finally go home? Did taking the second medication at home count as getting an abortion in a state that had outlawed the practice? And if so, would doing so open up a patient's loved one or their doctor to criminal punishment? (At that point, abortion bans generally didn't punish the patients themselves, a political concession made so that abortion opponents could attempt to position themselves as protecting pregnant people.)

This was uncharted legal territory, and a question few had spent time interrogating before *Roe* was overturned. When patients asked what, legally, they could do, doctors and clinic staffers couldn't answer with certainty. Without ironclad legal protection, few abortion providers wanted to risk becoming the sacrificial test case—and possibly face charges levied by an overzealous county prosecutor or politically ambitious attorney general from another state. They certainly could not tell patients in good faith that taking the second medication in their home states would not expose them to any legal risk.

Both forms of abortion are safe and effective, but there are all sorts of reasons a patient might prefer a medication abortion over a surgical procedure. In 2020, just two years before *Roe*'s overturn, medication had actually become the most common form of abortion, a shift that was long in the making, but that reproductive health researchers believe was accelerated by the COVID-19 pandemic and the option of taking the pills entirely at home. Unlike a medication regimen, an in-clinic abortion procedure can require minor sedation, meaning the patient needs someone to drive them home. Some patients also said the medication process felt more "natural" to them, and they preferred the idea of taking the medication in a private setting. And medication abortions are easier to administer, requiring fewer staff resources and appointment times. Depending on the clinic, these kinds of abortions can also be cheaper for patients.

Yet when faced with the legal risks and uncertainties, abortion clinicians said, more and more patients found themselves switching to surgeries. It was the only way they knew they'd be legally safe.

Days after *Roe* fell, staff at Hope Clinic were still struggling over how to handle the issue. They were working nonstop to care for all the patients now booking appointments in Granite City. They had given up on answering every phone call they got; frankly, there were just too many. At this point, the clinic was transitioning. In a few months, it would serve mostly people who had traveled from out of state, estimated Julie Burkhart, who co-owned Hope along with Chelsea Souder. The number of Tennesseans in particular was creeping up—four days after *Dobbs*, that state had begun enforcing a six-week abortion ban. (In August 2022, that state's total ban would take effect, forcing even more Tennesseans to get care outside the state.) People from Oklahoma and Missouri, who could no longer access any abortion care whatsoever, were also flooding Granite City. Meanwhile, Burkhart feared, the neighboring states' abortion bans were making it harder for people who actually lived in Illinois to access abortions. When she looked at the clinic's patient data, Illinois residents seemed to have "gotten lost in the mix," making up an increasingly small percentage of the people Hope served. She had no idea where the state's residents were going for abortions; she just hoped that some other clinic was able to help them.

At a clinic like Hope, where most patients were coming from elsewhere, the risk of out-of-state prosecution was naturally greater. They were treating more people who came under legally risky circumstances. Illinois still hadn't enacted protections that might at least attempt to shield state clinicians from out-of-state prosecutions; it wouldn't do so until January 2023, months after the state's abortion clinics had already seen hundreds of people from elsewhere. Unlike employees at the clinics in Chicago, the staff at Hope couldn't expect any open support or protection from their local government. Granite City, a former steel town, had swung for Donald Trump in the last presidential election, and securing the right to an abortion wasn't the kind of issue you used to win votes. For the first six months after *Dobbs,* the absence of state or local protections meant that if providers here did face criminal charges—levied perhaps by an ambitious public attorney in Tennessee or Missouri, someone who wanted to make headlines with an envelope-pushing anti-abortion prosecution—they couldn't even count on their own state for help.

With so much up in the air, and little guarantee of safety, Burkhart and Souder made the call. They would start giving patients both abortion medications at the same time, abandoning the twenty-four- to forty-eight-hour waiting period that is typically recommended. It was a compromise. If patients took both medications at once, they wouldn't have to spend another day away from home, incurring the costs of lodging, food, childcare, and lost wages. Hope Clinic, meanwhile, wouldn't have to worry about facing legal charges from another state.

Still, the choice wasn't without consequences. When taken twenty-four to forty-eight hours apart, the mifepristone-misoprostol combination is around 97 percent effective at ending a pregnancy. Little research existed assessing the regimen without the time lapse. And what did was not entirely comforting, with one study finding a drop in effectiveness of 2.5 percentage points if patients took the medication simultaneously—a failure rate of about one for every twenty patients. To insulate themselves from legal risk, medical providers had to recommend care they knew was in all likelihood less effective.

For Burkhart, it wasn't an easy decision. She was a veteran of abortion care and no stranger to the risks providers faced. In the past, she had stared them down without blinking. One of her former mentors, Wichita physician and abortion provider Dr. George Tiller, had been murdered by an anti-abortion extremist. After Tiller's death, Burkhart bought his Kansas clinic, running it in addition to an Oklahoma outpost until 2021. Walking in to work each day, she regularly faced threats from the anti-abortion protesters who camped outside her facilities. It was so familiar that she and her staff could recognize individual protesters by face and name. Even more recently, Burkhart had come face-to-face with the dangers people in her line of work faced. In the spring of 2022, Burkhart had taken steps to open an abortion clinic in Wyoming, only to see the facility torched in late May. Authorities suspected arson. Still, abortion was legal in Wyoming—for the moment—and she had pressed on in opening a clinic, even though that meant rebuilding their facility.

But this time the dangers felt different. In a post-*Dobbs* world, the risks to providers—physical and legal—felt heightened in a way they hadn't before. States really were banning abortion, and anti-abortion lawmakers said they were looking for ways to crack down on out-of-state travel. Who knew what they would do next? Burkhart frequently woke up with a pit in her stomach, a sense of deflation and defeat that, after all these years, the reproductive rights movement had lost, at least for now.

"It comes down to what's your tolerance for risk. And that's a hard call," she said. "In this culture we're living in now, we have to think not only about patients and the care we're giving to patients.

But it's—you know, is a rabid AG going to come after the clinic? Come after our physicians?" If one did, she didn't know how she could protect them.

———◆———

If the gravity of the situation wasn't already obvious in the weeks after *Roe* fell, it would be unmissable by the fall of 2022, with patients from both in and out of state falling by the wayside. Anti-abortion activists, including those in abortion-friendly states, did all they could to undercut access to care, yet another challenge for providers already fighting to meet patient need. Anti-abortion centers had already existed in New Mexico, but after *Dobbs* even more began to set up shop, picking locations near newly opened abortion clinics. Their goal was to deter patients from getting abortions, or even in some cases delay or distract them just long enough that they might miss their appointments. Some municipalities even tried to ban abortion within their borders, with one—Hobbs, New Mexico—passing a local ordinance to declare itself a "sanctuary" for the unborn. The move was in some ways symbolic, since no abortion clinics existed in the town, but bans such as that, if enforced, could deter clinicians from opening a new facility and spark fear in patients there who had hoped to travel to another town for an abortion. In time, support from state governments would come. In March 2023, New Mexico would pass a law prohibiting cities from attempting to ban either abortion or gender-affirming care. Still, the fact that the law didn't pass until more than half a year after the fall of *Roe* indicated another challenge. The pace of legislative work still felt stunningly slow, especially in the face of a dynamic and escalating public health crisis.

And yet nothing the state had done could address the desperation clinicians faced every day. By the time more meaningful government aid might come, abortion providers kept asking, who knew how many patients would have been forced to carry unwanted pregnancies to term?

In the meantime, the only help they could count on was from the only people who truly understood: other abortion providers.

During the summer of 2022, some clinic leaders had started to announce their next steps. Mississippi's last abortion provider—Jackson Women's Health Organization, the defendant in the Supreme Court case that overturned *Roe*—was moving to Las Cruces, New Mexico, a desert town near the Texas border. Planned Parenthood began preparing for an expansion in New Mexico. Whole Woman's Health, which had previously operated abortion clinics in Texas, would open in Albuquerque in the spring of 2023. A medical group called Choices, which operated an abortion clinic in Memphis, Tennessee, was opening a new outpost in Carbondale, a college town on the southwestern tip of Illinois. Choices' Memphis clinic would stay open and continue to provide Tennesseans with other reproductive health care.

Andrea Gallegos, with her Oklahoma and Texas clinics no longer able to operate, planned to relocate to Illinois and New Mexico. There would be a Carbondale clinic and another in Albuquerque. Carbondale especially intrigued her. Before *Roe* had fallen, the town didn't have any abortion clinics—under pressure from local conservatives, the city's hospital board had voted decades ago to stop their facility from performing abortions, and the people who lived there typically drove two hours to get to Hope Clinic. But the city was a manageable enough distance not only from Missouri but also from Kentucky, Mississippi, Tennessee, and Arkansas. There was an old LASIK center for sale just off the main highway; with a bit of remodeling, she could easily turn it into an abortion clinic. And when she spoke to the owners at Hope Clinic, they assured her they could use all the help they could get. Gallegos's clinic, along with the new Choices outpost, could play a critical role in alleviating the pressure they faced.

Between the numbers and the geography, Gallegos knew there was no more important place she could be. Abortion was her calling, and these were the states where her patients were going. This was where she could have the most impact. But it still felt so surreal. Gallegos was a Texan born and raised, an identity that felt impossible to shake. Her father still lived there. Commuting part-time to Oklahoma was one thing. But were she and her three school-aged children really all supposed to pack up their lives and move west to New Mexico or up north to Illinois? She didn't even own snow boots or a coat thick enough to insulate herself against the midwestern winter, which she knew about only secondhand. Was she really ready for this to be her new home?

Right away, she decided she wouldn't move full-time. Gallegos's oldest child, a daughter, had one more year of high school left. Instead, she'd find a way to juggle parenting while managing two out-of-state clinics. She'd commute part-time to Carbondale and part-time to Albuquerque. In between, she'd make sure to be home for her kids' honor society ceremonies and karate demonstrations. Somehow, she'd make it all work.

Opening a new abortion clinic was difficult, though—maybe harder than anything Gallegos had ever done. The Albuquerque clinic opened on schedule, in mid-August 2022. By the fall, they were seeing dozens of patients from Texas each week. But in Carbondale, the construction took weeks longer than she anticipated; the clinic couldn't start seeing patients until November 2022, much later than she had hoped. Then there was getting to Carbondale, which required Gallegos to take a two-hour flight from San Antonio to St. Louis, pick up a rental car, drive another two hours to the clinic, and then get straight to work. In just a few weeks, she became adept at finding the cheapest flights, booking one-ways out of pocket and using the points she earned on those flights to pay for her returns. Every dollar she spent on travel was another she couldn't use directly on the clinic. And there were other, more granular details: she had to find a new bank—the one she worked with in Texas and Oklahoma didn't have a branch in Carbondale—and hire new staff, most of whom had no experience in abortion care specifically, even if they'd worked in other health care settings. To ensure they knew what to do, Gallegos paid for her new employees to fly from St. Louis to Albuquerque, where they could learn how to perform an ultrasound, how to counsel a patient, and how to help people recover after an abortion. She'd found a collection of doctors who would take turns staffing the clinic and providing abortions. The closest one traveled from Memphis, three hours each way.

In the first few weeks of business, it felt like there was always something they needed to fix. One brisk November morning, staff had to wear their hats and coats inside the building because the heat wasn't working. Another employee was stuck on the phone, trying to figure out how to make their credit card reader work. They were still waiting on medical equipment to be delivered. At home in Texas, Gallegos would have known which contractors might refuse to work with her because she provided abortions. In Illinois, she was starting from scratch, something she was reminded of when one company she'd hired to build a front sign eventually stopped returning her calls. And then there was the issue of finding patients. Her clinic wasn't appearing in Google searches, a source of constant frustration. Despite her efforts to raise awareness—buying online ad space and keeping the phone lines open in San Antonio and Tulsa, in case anyone called there—patients kept telling her that they'd struggled to find the clinic. And already, hazardous weather, including early-season snow, had delayed or even thwarted some patients' efforts to travel for an abortion. The only benefit of their relative anonymity was that, at least when they first opened, anti-abortion protesters hadn't yet set up shop outside the facility. Only twice had she seen people attempt to dissuade patients from coming inside for their procedures. Soon enough, protesters would start showing up with regularity, but even the brief respite offered some relief for Gallegos, her staff, and her patients in the early days of providing care.

The trickiest part still was figuring out how many patients would actually show for their appointments, and for how many the journey to Carbondale simply wasn't feasible. On Saturdays, they'd started seeing a dozen patients, sometimes more. But weekdays were still slow; one Wednesday morning in their first month of business, only four out of the ten patients she'd scheduled made it in for their appointments. For all of them, Carbondale had been a lifeline, providing abortions they couldn't get in their home states: Arkansas, Tennessee, and Oklahoma. Still, Gallegos knew that the low numbers—such a stark contrast with what she'd gotten used to in Tulsa—were a poor reflection of how many people needed care.

All the same, she kept reminding herself, every patient they saw was still someone who mattered. One day, a woman from Arkansas was so grateful for the care she had gotten that she hugged the staff after receiving her abortion. Just the week before, three minors had come from other states where abortion was illegal. One, who had come from Mississippi, was only twelve years old. Every time Gallegos processed just how far people had traveled to get to her clinic, she felt that familiar sense of anger and despair, but looking at the youngest patients was still the most painful. When Gallegos looked at one of those girls, she saw her own children.

She'd never doubted that this was the right thing to be doing, that this was where she belonged. And in time, she told herself, running the clinic would get easier. Eventually, more patients would find their way to southern Illinois. Every time she came back to Carbondale, Gallegos met someone new who told her how much they appreciated the work her clinic did and promised to help in whatever way possible. On her desk, she kept an unsigned thank-you card they'd received in the mail. It was decorated with red, pink, and lavender hearts, mailed from someone with an Illinois return address.

Sometimes, she still couldn't believe they'd made it to this point, and that after all this time abortion was fully illegal in so many states, including her own, and that this was maybe the only way she could keep providing care. But on other days it didn't surprise her at all. The loss of abortion rights, she said, was part of something bigger. It was something she'd talked about with her father for years at the dinner table—something that they'd all seen coming. It was a direct attack on bodily autonomy, and specifically on the rights of people who wanted to control their own reproductive health.

"*Dobbs* made me and others like me second-class citizens," she said. "The attack on reproductive rights—which isn't always but is typically spearheaded by White men—it's definitely a result of misogyny."

———

In New Mexico, Angela had just returned from the abortion clinic to her Airbnb. The past three and a half days had been nonstop, and by now she was bone-tired. She couldn't believe she was supposed to make this trip again in just a few weeks. She didn't know what she would tell her mother, how she would explain her second absence from San Antonio in barely a month. And she couldn't begin to imagine how she would pay for the journey all over again.

It was Saturday afternoon in September, and finally she'd taken her misoprostol. Right now, she was waiting for it to kick in. It was hard to know what to expect: Some people, she knew, compared it to little more than a bad period. But she'd also heard about the others who had intense reactions to medication abortions, with heavy bleeding and agonizing pain. Still, whatever happened, she had only one day left in Albuquerque to process it all. Tomorrow, they were driving back home.

Right now, Angela was exhausted in every sense of the word. All she wanted was to be recovering in her own apartment, in her own city. Instead, she was in a stranger's house, and she and Nigel were counting out how much money they had left to get through the weekend. They'd set aside two thousand dollars, or the sum of one paycheck from each of them, to cover gas, food, medical expenses, and lodging. They had about two hundred dollars left to pay for the drive home; with gas prices around $3.68 a gallon, she estimated they'd use most of that money. The trip had been so draining—financially, physically, and emotionally—that they decided to scrap their plans of doing something small in honor of Nigel's birthday.

She didn't regret her abortion at all, but she hated how this felt. She couldn't stop thinking about the circumstances that had brought her to New Mexico, about the fact that she didn't know how they'd pay their bills for the next month, or that she'd lied to her family, and Nigel to his. None of it had to be this way.

"I can't just be okay in my home," she said, her voice trembling. "I'm staying at someone else's Airbnb, in pain, feeling guilty that I had to lie to my family, and feeling stressed about the financial hit that I took from this."

The money was maybe the part that worried her most. When would she pay back her other debts? She didn't want Nigel to be responsible for paying all the rent and bills himself, especially when he'd be a student in just a few months, losing his own source of income. Back in San Antonio, their one-bedroom apartment was falling apart, with doors literally coming off the hinges, and ants so pervasive that they would crawl into her son's crib and bite him throughout the night. It was no place to raise a child. They'd been saving for months, hoping to move somewhere even just a bit better. But now she couldn't see how they would do that anytime soon.

In just a few weeks, she'd be making this trip all over again. Adding insult to injury was the knowledge that, if she lived in another city, in another state, she could have probably gotten this same care by driving just a few miles. The money she'd spent to come to New Mexico for a few days would still be in her bank account.

It was difficult to fathom that, despite how difficult the journey had been, and despite how much it would set them back, she was still lucky to get an abortion at all. She could see how crowded the clinics were, how many people were traveling even farther than she had. If she hadn't made it to her appointment in Albuquerque, she wasn't quite sure what she would have done. Already, pregnant people in San Antonio were starting to get abortion pills from aid networks in Mexico. She'd heard that you could buy abortion pills on the internet and get them mailed from another country. But she hadn't looked into it for herself. The prospect frightened her—she worried about somehow getting in trouble with the law for procuring pills she wasn't supposed to have or for taking them in a state where using them for an abortion was illegal.

In retrospect, she said, if she hadn't been able to get an appointment, she'd have tried to terminate her pregnancy on her own. She didn't know how exactly to do so, and the prospect of hurting herself in the process was terrifying. What if she made herself sick or even died? That her choices were so limited made her feel like less of a person—like someone who didn't matter.

"I just felt like my human right was taken away," she said, as she waited for the misoprostol to take effect. "It's very hard to be put in that situation where you have to go behind everyone's back and you have to do it so secretly and there's obviously that fear of getting caught and someone finding out, or me getting in trouble. Just because I want to make that choice for my body. Because I know I'm not ready to have another kid."

—◆—

CHAPTER 4

A Haven, for Now

Kansas

Melissa really hadn't been paying any attention to the whole abortion issue. After all, she'd never been pregnant herself, and, as far as she was aware, nobody she knew had gotten an abortion. She'd gathered that people were upset *Roe v. Wade* had been overturned, just from the snippets of news she saw on TV or online. Her life hadn't been changed by the decision, though; it was easy enough to ignore.

But by the evening of August 2, 2022, everything had changed. In just a couple of weeks, the issue of abortion rights, particularly in her home state of Kansas, had developed a new sense of urgency. That night, Kansas would be the site of a sort of referendum on the *Dobbs* decision. The state's election had drawn national interest: it was the first time since June 24 that people could vote directly on whether the state should protect abortion rights.

That August evening, Melissa could think only about the election. She'd voted that morning. Less than a week ago, she had fought with her mom about abortion, trying to convince her of the need to protect access. Now, alone in her apartment, she searched for the election results and kept pressing refresh—waiting to see whether Kansas, by all accounts a conservative state, would protect the right that she had once barely considered.

Like so many Americans, Melissa had for most of her life taken abortion protections for granted. But this year, the summer of her twenty-eighth birthday, the right to terminate a pregnancy had become paramount.

Earlier that summer, she'd met a guy online. He seemed sweet and attentive, and they'd dated for about a month. But by mid-July, something began to seem off. He'd started talking to her in a more aggressive tone, she said, and she felt unsafe when she was with him. Finally, she cut ties with him, and she hoped that would be the end of it.

But just a day later, she started noticing the changes in her body: mainly the cramps that felt stronger and more uncomfortable than her typical menstrual cycle. Still, she didn't think it was pregnancy. Before she'd ended things, they'd had sex without a condom, but she'd taken Plan B soon afterward. Maybe, she told herself, the pain she was feeling was just the side effects of the birth control. Still, on July 25, she drove to a nearby store and bought a pregnancy test. It couldn't hurt to double-check.

Melissa had read online that pregnancy tests worked best in the morning. So the next day, when her alarm rang at five a.m., she climbed out of bed. She liked to start her days by lifting weights at the gym, but before heading out she took the test, just to be sure.

When she saw the positive result, Melissa felt her heart jump into her throat. She couldn't follow one train of thought for longer than what felt like a millisecond. Breathing heavily, she tried to focus. *I need to tell someone about this. I need to talk to someone.*

The sun hadn't yet risen, and nobody she knew was awake. She certainly wasn't going to discuss this with her parents. Instead, Melissa tried to text the guy she'd been seeing, since he was the one who'd gotten her pregnant. She kept waiting for the message to show up as delivered, but it never sent, which somehow made things even worse. He must have blocked her number, she realized. Out of options, she swiped to the app she used to talk online with her therapist. Yes, it was before six a.m., but the therapist had told Melissa that if she ever had an emergency, go ahead and message her right away. And this was definitely an emergency.

All Melissa could think about was what she was going to do. At her desk job that morning, she waited anxiously, half glancing at her phone for a response from her therapist. It was hours before she heard back. Her therapist had no slots today, but Melissa could set up a virtual appointment in a couple of days. They'd talk through how she was feeling and what she was going to do. On that point, Melissa was certain: She was calling Planned Parenthood. She needed an abortion.

For Melissa, the timing couldn't have been worse. Yes, *Roe* had been overturned a month ago now, but abortion was still legal in Kansas. In a little over a week, though, voters would weigh in directly on whether the state should continue to protect abortion rights, a question with massive ramifications for access in the Midwest. But the framing was complicated, to say the least. A few years earlier, Kansas's state supreme court had said that its state constitution—which enshrined a right to "bodily autonomy"— implicitly protected abortion access. That decision had been used to keep the state's Republican lawmakers from passing stricter abortion laws. Now the state was putting the question to voters, asking them to amend their constitution so that it specifically did not protect abortion rights. The wording was particularly confusing. A "yes" vote on the amendment was a vote against abortion rights; it would eliminate the state's abortion rights protections. A "no" vote would leave the state's abortion protections unchanged. The vote, scheduled for an early August primary without many competitive races, seemed engineered to attract few voters. But in the freshly post-*Dobbs* world, the Kansas initiative had become a national flashpoint. Throughout the country, pundits, organizers, and activists across the political spectrum were treating the election as a lens through which they could better understand whether Americans really cared about abortion rights—and if so whether it was enough to drive them to vote.

To Melissa, though, none of that context really mattered. She cared only about whether her state was about to ban access to something she desperately needed. When she called the Planned Parenthood clinic in Overland Park, right outside Kansas City, the first day they could schedule her was a week and a half from then, on August 4. It was one day before her birthday and two days after the Kansas vote.

Melissa tried to be rational. If the yes vote won, nothing would change immediately. Passing the amendment would just open the door for the state government to pass laws later that could ban or otherwise restrict abortion—something that probably wouldn't happen for months, well after her abortion. That was what the woman at Planned Parenthood told her over the phone. No matter what happened on Election Day, she'd be able to get her abortion.

Still, it was difficult for her to accept. In Kansas City, the lawn signs were everywhere, telling people how to vote on the abortion measure. It felt like no matter where she looked she saw another reminder that in just a few days her neighbors and peers would get the chance to decide how much decision-making power she deserved to have over her own body. Worried and still unsure what the results might be and what they could mean, she booked an extra appointment at an abortion clinic in a neighboring state, just in case she might need it. In states where abortion rights were tenuous, it was an increasingly common practice, with patients frequently booking multiple appointments in several clinics, just in case one place fell through or another one could see them sooner. For patients, that level of caution was just common sense, and a way to make sure they'd be seen, no matter what. For abortion providers, it meant never truly knowing just how many patients they'd see in a day and how many wouldn't show up for their appointments.

Election Day came. Whenever Melissa opened her phone for a quick social media scroll, all she saw were abortion rights posts from her friends. Almost all of Melissa's coworkers were women— and all day, the only things they could talk about were if they'd voted yet, how they'd voted, and their worries about what came next. Not a single person she spoke to had cast a ballot in favor of eliminating abortion rights. It gave her some comfort. Still, she knew that her office, which was located in the state's most liberal county, was a small and, she told herself, probably inaccurate sample.

That night, the results came in far earlier than anyone had expected. Melissa was home alone, refreshing her Google search page every few minutes, almost on autopilot, and texting the one friend in whom she had finally confided the details of her scheduled abortion. At some point, she kept hoping, there would be good news.

Just before nine p.m., enough votes had been tallied to forecast the results. In a lopsided vote, Kansans had resoundingly rejected efforts to eliminate their state's abortion rights protection. Republicans, Democrats, and independents alike had turned out in massive numbers to vote the amendment down. When Melissa saw the results, she couldn't quite believe it, but she sat there, letting the news sink in. She could get her abortion. She wouldn't have to leave the state, and she wouldn't be forced to stay pregnant. Her relief was more palpable than anything she had ever felt before—maybe anything she would ever feel again.

Two days later, Melissa got her abortion, which she paid for using the birthday money her parents had given her and the remaining chunk of her paycheck that hadn't already gone toward rent. Certainly, she was thankful to terminate her pregnancy, but she'd already gone through all the emotional turmoil she could stomach. For her, election night was the climax. The abortion itself felt like an afterword.

———

In their decision to overturn *Roe,* the Supreme Court's conservative justices had made the argument both implicitly and overtly: eliminating a federal right to an abortion would, they claimed, allow for a purer, more direct democracy. The abortion question would be decided by states and the officials chosen by their residents, as opposed to unelected judges in Washington. This would simply allow the nation to return to its natural order.

It was a framing that disguised the radicalism of the *Dobbs* decision—and, just as importantly, one that would prove false time and time again in the months and years after. Reproductive rights organizers have long made the argument that efforts to restrict abortion rely on undercutting voting rights as well, on building systems of governance that can be insulated from what the majority of Americans actually want. It was a truth that the post-*Roe* reality had only accentuated. After *Dobbs,* it became clear that few Americans supported laws banning abortion and that, given the chance, they would come out in droves to vote down laws that might prohibit people from accessing it. But those victories were usually incredibly hard-won, and, just as importantly, they wouldn't always translate into actual health care access. The chasm between what Americans supported and what their lawmakers would do—in some cases, without having to worry about electoral accountability—remained a gap too large to bridge.

The Kansas vote had seemed like a turning point, a feeling that only grew a few months later, when in November 2022 abortion rights groups won similar ballot races across the country, in Kentucky, Michigan, Vermont, and California. But the repeated success belied just how much time and money it took to secure abortion rights at the ballot box. In Kansas, abortion rights organizers had planned for their state's campaign for more than a year, spending millions of dollars and building virtual armies of people to canvass the state. Despite all that work, the results didn't actually expand access to abortion. They simply maintained the status quo, and they certainly wouldn't stop anti-abortion lawmakers from trying to restrict access to the procedure there or in other conservative-led states. In some states, it remained impossible to translate the electoral victories for abortion to real-life access. Kentucky offered one such example. Clinics there had challenged the state's abortion ban in court, arguing that the Kentucky constitution protected the right to terminate a pregnancy. When voters there rejected a proposal that would have amended Kentucky's constitution to allow the state government to enact an abortion ban if it so chose, it seemed like the question was settled. People who lived in Kentucky understood that their state implicitly guaranteed the right to an abortion, and they wanted it to stay that way. But in February 2023, only four months after the vote, the state's supreme court ruled the opposite way, holding that the state's abortion ban could stay in effect, ensuring that anyone who lived in the state would be forced to travel to Illinois or Virginia for care.

Still, maintaining abortion rights in Kansas—which had been an unlikely abortion haven for years—had incalculable significance. In a way, it was fitting: this was a state whose residents prided themselves on their progressive history, down to their pre–Civil War founding as the free-state alternative to slaveholding Missouri. Even before *Roe* was overturned, close to half of all abortions in Kansas were performed for people from another state, mostly Missouri. George Tiller, the doctor who mentored a young Julie Burkhart, had become a national target because of his work providing abortions to the people of Kansas, as well as those who traveled there. It was a service he had provided up until the day he was shot.

Without *Roe,* the state's abortion network was more important than it had ever been. With Arkansas, Tennessee, Missouri, Texas, and Oklahoma all outlawing abortions, thousands more pregnant people turned to Kansas's abortion clinics, which were the closest to which they could reasonably drive. Five clinics in the entire state—two independent clinics and three Planned Parenthoods, including one that had just opened the summer of *Dobbs*—were the first, best, and only option for an entire region of the country. Per one study, Kansas saw one of the largest percentage-based increases in abortions in the first two months after *Roe* fell, with the number performed increasing by 36 percent. (In Illinois, with far more clinics available, abortions had gone up by 28 percent.) State data made the jump even more stark. In 2022, Kansas recorded 12,318 abortions—a 57 percent increase from the year before, fueled entirely by out-of-state patients, who that year made up close to 70 percent of the people getting abortions in the Sunflower State.

And, unlike those in Illinois or New Mexico, Kansas clinics couldn't count on anything more than quiet, understated public support. When the state's most powerful Democrat, Governor Laura Kelly, was up for reelection four months after *Dobbs,* she barely talked about the issue, avoiding even mentioning the word "abortion." Few expected her to go out of her way to make care more accessible, whether through devoting state money to support clinics or expanding legal protections for physicians and clinic staff. Clinic leaders knew she was the most they could hope for: someone who would reliably oppose any anti-abortion proposals. But they also knew that, if Republican lawmakers voted as a group, they had the power to override her efforts to veto restrictions.

All the same, in the weeks after the August 2022 vote, abortion providers allowed themselves something they hadn't felt in a long time: hope. Emily Wales, who ran Planned Parenthood Great Plains, started talking about expanding the organization's presence in Kansas. Maybe they could open another abortion clinic. Planned Parenthood already had a strong presence near the Missouri border, but they could open another outpost on the state's southern end, closer to Oklahoma. By 2023, another independent clinic had opened in Wichita, this one offering only medication abortions for people in their first trimester and focusing on out-of-state patients.

It marked a small but meaningful increase in the number of abortion providers in the state; now there were six clinics in Kansas.

But the need for abortions was far greater than what these providers could handle. So many people were calling for abortions that, as one employee at the Wichita-based Trust Women put it, they could probably schedule people out for the next nine months and still not get to everyone in need. It was a refrain that staffers across the clinic repeated: they could stay open every hour of the day, see patients 365 days a year, and never reach every patient who sought their help. Doctors from other states started working to get certified in Kansas, so that they could travel there and offer abortions. Some, like Selina Sandoval, shaped their careers around Kansas. An ob-gyn born and raised in California, Sandoval relocated to Kansas City as soon as she finished her medical fellowship, taking a job as an abortion provider at Planned Parenthood. It was some of the hardest work she'd ever done—she regularly saw patients who had driven nine or ten hours to get to her clinic, and the majority had come from Texas. She knew there were few places she'd be more valuable. And she also knew that, as things stood, the clinics she worked at simply couldn't do enough.

Clinic employees from Oklahoma City's Trust Women started working in Wichita, commuting between states to come in to work or in some cases moving across state lines. One nurse, who had originally planned to leave the state, recommitted to Kansas after the August election results, buying a house with her husband so she could keep providing abortion care to all the patients who would travel to Wichita. The picture looked drastically different compared with what things had looked like even a few months earlier in Oklahoma, noted Jody Steinauer, a California-based ob-gyn who, when the Oklahoma ban took effect, promptly started working at the Kansas clinic. In Oklahoma City, the vast majority of patients she saw had come from Texas. In her new Wichita-based role, Texas was still the biggest individual source of patients. But now she also cared for patients from across the region—Arkansas, Missouri, and Oklahoma, to say nothing of the people who actually lived in Kansas. The switch underscored a truth many knew, even if it was often difficult to say out loud: people from the neighboring abortion deserts were relying on the Kansas abortion providers far more than they ever had before. And without Kansas, few knew where they'd be able to go next.

For many patients, though, even getting to a clinic in Kansas was a struggle. When Anna, a seventeen-year-old from just south of Oklahoma City, learned she was pregnant, she had had sex only three times in her life, all with her boyfriend, and all while using condoms. She discovered the pregnancy only when she went to the doctor to get started on hormonal birth control. It had been more than a month since they'd had sex, so by the time Anna found out, she was already six weeks along.

Anna had no intention of staying pregnant, let alone becoming a parent. But until now she had never given abortion much thought. As a child, she'd been raised by her deeply Christian mother to believe abortion was a sin; the first conversation they'd had about it was at the dinner table, when she was maybe ten years old. It wasn't until *Roe* was overturned that Anna had begun to interrogate her mother's view, reading news articles and browsing on social media to see the stories people shared about why they had chosen to end a pregnancy. She was still religious, and she still believed in God, even if she went to church far less than she used to. But now, unlike her elders, she believed abortion was a good thing, even empowering, and something she could support even while holding on to her faith. Abortion, she thought, was something that helped people who weren't ready to be parents. But it still wasn't something she expected ever to need herself. She'd always assumed she would delay sex until she was older—the first time she and her boyfriend had intercourse was completely unplanned. And if she didn't have sex, she wouldn't get pregnant; she'd never need to worry about terminating a pregnancy. Now that everything had gone awry, she was stunned to learn that her state had banned abortions entirely. If she wanted a doctor to end her pregnancy, she'd have to travel to Kansas.

As road trips go, it could have been worse. Wichita, home to Kansas's southernmost clinics, was less than three hours away. But Anna was in a distinctly vulnerable position; she didn't have a car or a full-time job. As an incoming high school senior, she worked part-time after school and on weekends at a local medical practice, which she hoped would help her someday become a physician's assistant. She didn't earn enough money to cover the cost of the abortion, let alone to pay for a car to help her get across state lines. To leave Oklahoma, she needed someone to help her. She'd have to ask her mother, who, like Angela's, strictly opposed abortion and viewed it as a sin incompatible with her religious beliefs. But, unlike Angela, Anna had no choice but to rely on her mother. Without her, it would be impossible to leave the state and get to a clinic.

Anna's mother spent days trying to convince her not to get an abortion; she referred to the pregnancy as the grandchild she'd wanted for years and dragged her daughter to a Christian-affiliated anti-abortion center. There, the staff encouraged her to keep the pregnancy, or maybe have the baby and then consider adoption. They told Anna that if she got an abortion she would be condemning her soul. She had to find God, they told her—though Anna replied that she already had and that her belief didn't stop her from knowing that right now an abortion was what she needed. Though the pressure and shame didn't change what Anna knew intellectually, they still took their toll. Coming home from the anti-abortion center, Anna cried to herself, turning over in her mind the harsh language the staff there had used, words that would stay with her. Maybe they were right and getting an abortion meant she was a bad person—maybe she should hate herself for doing this.

Even with the pressure building, Anna made herself stand her ground. She kept talking to her boyfriend, who seemed to be the only person who supported her decision. He kept reminding her what she knew: they weren't ready to become parents, and she didn't have it in her to carry a pregnancy to term, only to then give up a child for adoption. Finally, she convinced her mother to call Trust Women, the Wichita clinic, and to schedule her an abortion.

As a policy, the clinic was scheduling patients only up to two weeks out; by Anna's appointment, she expected to be just over nine weeks pregnant. But even those two weeks of waiting were agony. Her morning sickness was getting worse, and she could barely keep down anything she ate. Meanwhile, she said, her mother kept threatening to cancel the appointment if Anna did something that upset her. And, though she was a teenager on a part-time salary, Anna would have to promptly pay back every cent her mother spent—on the abortion, on a hotel in Kansas, and even on gas for the trip. She'd have to take on extra shifts at work to cover the costs: eight hundred dollars in total. Each conversation got worse, and with each one Anna felt another swell of terror. Was this the time her mother would snap and cancel the appointment?

"I stopped talking to her because it was just scary," she said. "I didn't want to be stuck with the kid because that's what she wanted."

They drove up north the day before the abortion, spending the night in a hotel and reaching the clinic around ten the next morning. Just being outside was surreal, Anna said; by the clinic's gated parking lot, she saw a truck adorned with an image of a fully developed fetus. Despite the childhood lessons she'd received from her mother on the evils of abortion, she'd never seen anything like these images before.

She felt safer once she got inside, passing through the clinic's metal detectors. A security guard checked to make sure she had an appointment, inspecting her bag for weapons before instructing her to wait with all the other patients. She did schoolwork while she waited her turn—or tried to. The stress of the day weighed too much on her, and she spent most of the morning struggling to maintain her composure. She was so close now, but what if something happened and they couldn't give her an abortion?

When eventually they called her name, Anna went into the clinic's back room. She spoke to a nurse and a doctor, who assessed how far along she was and performed a general health check to make sure there would be no complications if she got an abortion. Finally, around two p.m., they gave her what she had come for: the pills to terminate her pregnancy. She took the first set in the clinic and packed the second to take the next day at home.

Anna couldn't describe the magnitude of her relief. Finally, *finally*, the thing she had spent weeks worrying about had happened. By the end of the next day, she'd no longer be pregnant. She could try to go back to her normal life, working, finishing school, planning for college someday. But the drive back to Oklahoma was miserable. Her mom yelled at her in the car the whole way home. She was furious at her daughter, who she kept saying had killed *her* baby. To Anna, the emphasis was shocking. There was no baby at this point. And, even if there were, it certainly didn't belong to her mother—someone who wouldn't have to carry the pregnancy, with all its physical demands, or have to commit to a lifetime of parenthood. This was Anna's choice, something she deserved to opt in to (and out of) willingly. And though pregnancy and parenthood were things that she might be ready to do someday, she certainly wasn't right now.

When they got back to the house, her mother was still livid. For a while, she wouldn't speak to Anna or would respond only in terse, one-word replies. When she did speak, she'd berate Anna about the abortion, even characterizing it as murder. Anna's stepfather also gave her the silent treatment for days.

The next day, Anna took her second set of pills; about thirty minutes later, the excruciating cramps set in. They were far worse than anything she'd felt before; she even vomited from the pain. When she felt able to move from the toilet, Anna drew herself a bath, hoping the warm water would provide her some physical comfort. From the tub, she waited, watching the blood leak out and then, at long last, the fetus. She put the remains inside a cup, and she figured they'd find a way to dispose of it.

If she'd had anyone else to ask for help, she would have. But physically she was too exhausted to clean up by herself, and her mother, angry as she seemed, was still the person who was supposed to take care of her. And maybe, Anna told herself, her mother would be less upset now. The abortion was over, and there was nothing she could do to reverse it. But when her mom walked in, she took one look at the remnants of the abortion before starting to cry. She took the fetus out of the room; later, she would bury it in their backyard. It was a painful thing to see—for Anna, it felt in a way as if her mother had dismissed the choice she had made, and that she saw her differently now.

When her mother started speaking to her again, they simply never discussed the abortion. Anna never told her older brother or much of her extended family or friends what had happened. She didn't know what they would think of her or how they might judge her now. She didn't want them to think less of her because she'd had an abortion.

Anna didn't doubt herself or her decision. It was clearly the right thing to do. But, she kept thinking, it shouldn't have been so hard. If this was how her state worked—if this was how her country worked—something must be wrong.

"It's just, like, crazy to me that something that was legal before is just completely gone," she said. "Just because a couple of people that were voted into power—not by the whole entire United States—just got to have a say over everyone else's voices."

The August 2022 vote that maintained Kansas's abortion rights protections had certainly been a victory for the state's abortion providers and for anyone seeking access to care. But clinicians in the state still worried that lawmakers would continue to pursue new restrictions on how they operated—limitations that they could ill afford, especially given how many people were relying on them. For one thing, the constitution's abortion rights guarantee was something issued by a collection of judges, ruling in a 2019 case. There was no guarantee that someday, years down the line, a different group of judges wouldn't feel differently and overturn that decision—just like the national courts had just done with *Roe*. But there was still a more immediate threat: the Republican Party's stranglehold on the state legislature. Lawmakers may not have had the power to pass a total abortion ban, but few doubted that they would keep trying to restrict access, passing other laws that might make it harder for clinics to operate.

———◆———

Politicians who support restricting abortion rights often describe their views as a natural extension of their religious beliefs. And in Kansas, the Catholic Church remains the biggest, most powerful entity opposing abortion rights; the Archdiocese of Kansas City spent well over a million dollars in 2022 campaigning to eliminate the state's abortion protection, far beyond the amount usually spent on state-level ballot initiatives. Outside the state's abortion clinics, the protesters who screamed at abortion-seeking patients, brandishing images of mutilated fetuses in their efforts to dissuade them, often framed their arguments in religious terms. Still, religion alone remained a poor indicator of the public's views on abortion access. Almost as soon as *Roe* fell, polling showed widespread disapproval of laws that would ban abortion entirely. Only days after the court decision, data collected by the Public Religion Research Institute indicated that the majority of American Catholics—64 percent of White Catholics and 75 percent of Hispanic Catholics—said they supported access to abortion in most or all cases. Most Americans of faith support abortion rights, and in the months to come numerous Jewish-led organizations would even file lawsuits arguing that bans on the procedure violated their religious beliefs, saying that the laws should be struck down as a result. In fact, research has consistently shown that White evangelicals are the only religious group where a minority believe abortion should generally be legal. (Of course, as people like Angela would repeatedly be reminded, favoring access in the abstract didn't necessarily translate to supporting individuals who sought abortions.)

The Kansas election had made that tension even clearer. Even as the Church's leadership campaigned to eliminate the state's abortion rights protections, two local nuns—both residents of Kansas's most liberal county—came out on the opposite side, writing in a letter to *The Kansas City Star* that they would be voting to keep abortion protected in Kansas.

It was a pattern that would play out over and over again. When, in the November 2022 elections, voters in Kentucky—a state with an even larger evangelical population—similarly rejected an effort to eliminate abortion rights from their state constitution, polling from the Associated Press suggested that 60 percent of Catholic voters in Kentucky opposed their state's proposed amendment, along with a third of the state's evangelical voters. Among Kentucky's evangelicals, even those who opposed abortion in general came out against laws that would ban the procedure entirely. Such prohibitions were simply too extreme.

In retrospect, it made a surprising amount of sense. Morally opposing abortions, or judging people who have them, is different from believing the procedure should be outlawed completely, noted Melissa Deckman, CEO of the Public Religion Research Institute, the foremost authority on how religious views inform political ones. "Many Americans would recognize there might be some times where abortion should be legal—even if you're generally opposed to abortion, even for religious reasons," she said. And in the months after *Roe*'s overturn, she argued, that view would grow more prevalent, as people were confronted with some of the impact of abortion bans, hearing stories of people with life-threatening medical conditions who were denied medical care, of survivors of rape and incest being unable to access abortions, and

of children like Anna who were forced to cross state lines to terminate their pregnancies. On a widespread policy level, people of
all faiths would agree that the harsh abortion bans being inflicted
across the country were a bridge too far, and they voted in droves
to oppose them.

In Kansas, November 2022 brought clinicians a tiny bit of
relief. When Kelly, the Democratic governor, won a second term,
the state's clinicians knew that they had retained at least one ally in
Topeka. And they needed all the support they could get. Kansas's
legislature, dominated by Republicans, had become conservative
only in recent years, particularly on the issue of abortion. Based on
existing state precedent, the courts would likely strike down any
effort to ban abortion outright. But many worried that protection
ultimately wouldn't stop lawmakers from trying to pass a ban anyway, or even a law prohibiting abortions after fifteen weeks. They
might also try other kinds of limitations: making people wait longer before they could get an abortion or pushing for new regulations on the operation of the state's clinics, overwhelmed as they
were.

Staff at Trust Women could easily delineate the shift between
the time before *Dobbs* and after. The Wichita clinic was no stranger
to out-of-state patients. After Texas's six-week ban took effect,
they'd become the spillover site people went to if they couldn't
get to a clinic in Oklahoma. When Oklahoma banned abortion,
Kansas, and Wichita specifically, truly became a nexus, a status it
would retain in the post-*Dobbs* world. Trust Women was only a five-
hour drive from Dallas and an eight-hour drive from Austin. They
increased their staff, going from six full-time employees to about
twenty—though it all happened so fast it wasn't easy to keep track—
and worked with additional out-of-state doctors, paying for their
flights and lodging when they came to Kansas. As is true in many
areas with a strong culture of anti-abortion activism, few doctors
in the Wichita area provided abortions, a product of the years of
stigma and violence directed toward abortion providers, including
Dr. Tiller's assassination. The clinic—which used to provide other
forms of reproductive health care, including gender-affirming
care—pivoted to providing abortion full-time, along with the offer
of contraception for people who came in to terminate pregnancies.

It was a switch they regretted having to make, and emblematic of how the pressure on abortion care networks in turn limited access to other forms of health care as well. Already, gender-affirming care in Kansas was difficult to come by, with few health care providers equipped to offer the service and looming new restrictions being passed by the state government. But the staff at the Wichita clinic, like others across the country, felt like they had little choice. There were only so many of them, and the demand for abortion so great.

One Monday morning, the physician providing care for the day, Dr. Jennifer Kerns from California, had barely made it in. Her flight the day before had been delayed over and over again. She got to Wichita at one forty-five in the morning. A little over six hours later, she was at the clinic, clad in black scrubs with her brown-blond hair tucked to one side, drinking coffee she'd grabbed on the way to work and preparing to care for patients. Today and tomorrow, she'd see close to forty patients each day, a good chunk of whom were in their second trimester. Two on the books were minors, a seventeen-year-old from Oklahoma and a teenager from Wichita who estimated she was sixteen weeks pregnant. On Tuesday night, Kerns would fly from the tiny Wichita airport back to California. She'd work a night shift in San Francisco the next day. And in a month she'd fly right back to Kansas.

Everything operated on a far larger scale post-*Dobbs*. The clinic partnered with nonprofits and abortion funds, allowing them to offer exponentially more financial aid for patients. In the spring of 2022, a clinic employee who handled its abortion fund programs estimated that Trust Women distributed between $30,000 and $40,000 in aid per month. By the end of the year, she was allocating more than six times that—approximately $250,000—each month. It meant that, as of October 2022, patients who traveled to Wichita from states with abortion bans could, if they were within their first trimester and earned less than a certain amount, get an abortion at no cost. Virtually every patient who got an appointment at Trust Women qualified for some kind of financial support, said Ashley Brink, the clinic's director. It could make a trip to the clinic attainable when it otherwise might not have been, even if it wasn't enough to cover both the cost of the procedure and travel expenses. One patient, a thirty-seven-year-old woman named Natalie, had qualified for aid in getting her abortion, but still had to find the money to pay for her trip to Wichita. Sitting on a medical recliner in the clinic, she quickly ran the numbers to calculate how much it had taken to travel from Dallas, including gas, snacks, and a hotel room for herself and her twin sister, who drove while she battled morning sickness. Ballpark, she said, the trip cost her just shy of a thousand dollars—money she hated spending just before the upcoming Christmas holiday, especially when she already had two daughters at home. Still, she was grateful the abortion hadn't cost even more. And she would have gone wherever she needed to terminate her pregnancy, she said, even if that meant traveling as far as New York or Washington.

Telling patients that they would be able to get help felt good. "I'm like the abortion fairy," said one clinic employee, a blue-haired woman named Stormi. She had just spoken to a woman calling from Atlanta, Texas—a seven-hour drive away. She'd heard the trepidation, even the sound of defeat on the phone after telling the caller what a medication abortion would cost at that point in her pregnancy: $750. When the woman found out about the grant program, and that she wouldn't have to pay anything herself for the abortion, Stormi could hear the relief in her voice. "She went, 'Oh my god, really?'"

But there was still an unspoken truth, a subtext that grew harder and harder to ignore. Tens of thousands of patients had been displaced by the newly enforced state abortion bans, and the Kansas network of clinics—which included fewer abortion providers than used to operate in the city of Houston alone—wasn't big enough to fill the gap. In Wichita, they realized it was futile to try. In November 2022, a month that would typically have been slower, Trust Women cared for almost 500 patients. Of those, 257 came from Texas. Another 100 came from Oklahoma, and 20 more came from Missouri and Arkansas. It was a heavy load, with between 30 and 40 patients getting an abortion most days, and closer to 50 patients on Fridays. Before, they'd seen maybe half that many people in a day and done abortions only twice a week. There had once been days when the phones didn't ring at all, an almost laughable concept now. With *Roe* gone, there was no such thing as a slow day. The growth had happened so quickly that the clinic didn't have enough chairs for everyone to sit in or enough employees to see everyone. They didn't even have enough parking spaces for all their patients.

Even this situation was tenuous, with the delicate balance at risk of being upended the moment lawmakers found a way to circumvent or undercut the state's abortion protections. In the spring of 2023, the legislature overrode the governor's veto to pass a bill that would force abortion providers to inaccurately tell patients that medication abortions could be reversed—they cannot be—and blocked her effort to veto a budget item expanding funding for anti-abortion centers. A few Democratic legislators joined them in passing a bill that would ostensibly protect infants born "alive" after a failed abortion, a scenario that does not actually exist. And though they failed to garner enough votes for other restrictions, Republican legislators still pushed other anti-abortion bills, including one that would have banned the use of telemedicine for medication abortion. The fights at the statehouse underscored just how fragile abortion rights remained: maintaining the status quo felt untenable and unsustainable, but it was still the most that clinicians could hope for.

Providers' sense of defeat and fatigue echoed what providers in Illinois and New Mexico too had experienced. One day, Trust Women recorded sixteen thousand phone calls to the clinic, with at least one person calling more than two hundred times to try to get an answer. Brink only half joked that it was impossible to reach a colleague by dialing their extension—every time you picked up the phone, you'd be inadvertently answering a phone call from someone asking about an abortion. The circumstances changed the kind of care they gave, too. When giving patients the pills for a medication abortion, Kerns always made sure to provide extra doses of misoprostol, encouraging patients to take more if they were concerned the abortion wasn't progressing as it should. She didn't want them to worry about making the trip back to Kansas if the abortion, for whatever reason, didn't work. And because getting an appointment had become so much harder, more patients were now further along in their pregnancies when they finally made it to Trust Women, requiring more involved procedures and taking more time and resources to complete. The staff did their best to book second-trimester procedures earlier in the day, so that abortions that might previously have been done overnight—dilating the cervix alone required four hours—could be finished within a day, so that patients could quickly get back home. And it seemed that more of them required increasingly medically complex care. Kerns saw patients in Kansas who had traveled from other states because they had ectopic pregnancies; they needed an abortion—in this case, an emergency surgery—and delays in getting one could kill them. But nobody in their home state had been able to give them care.

Similar stories had emerged in Texas in the months after Senate Bill 8 took effect, but in states with abortion bans, legislators had promised that their laws allowed exceptions for people with ectopic pregnancies to get an abortion. In practice, it wasn't true. Doctors largely did not feel safe providing care until the ectopic pregnancy had progressed to the point that the patient was at death's door. The only option patients had was to travel to a state where abortion was legal.

A few staffers at Trust Women were devoted to booking every slot they had available and answering as many calls as they could. But they knew that the patients who made it to the clinic were the ones who had been lucky enough to have someone pick up their first call, or who had the time and flexibility to keep calling until finally someone answered. In other parts of the clinic, staff lowered their phones' volume, doing their best to ignore the persistent buzz. The ceaseless ringing was too painful a reminder of everyone they'd never be able to help.

———◆———

After Angela and Nigel returned from New Mexico, she was still struggling to maintain the lie she'd told her family about getting an abortion. She hadn't told her mom about the pregnancy, let alone her choice to terminate it. But for two weeks after, she still felt residual pain, and the bleeding hadn't fully stopped. She'd even bled in the car while Nigel drove them home from New Mexico, clutching her midsection in pain. Now, back in Texas, she'd followed the standard post-abortion advice, holding off on physical activity—which meant skipping out on the workouts she typically did each week with her mom. Every time she bailed, Angela offered her mom a vague excuse: she had to work extra those days, and she wouldn't have the time. She knew she sounded evasive. There was no way her mom couldn't figure out that, at the very least, Angela was hiding something. In all honesty, it wouldn't have surprised her if her mom had guessed what had happened. But she couldn't tell her mom about the abortion. With anyone else, the deception wouldn't have been this difficult. But her mom shared everything with her, including things she'd never told anyone else. Nigel did his best, asking how she was doing, reminding her that she hadn't done anything wrong, but it wasn't the same. She was hungry for someone—anyone, even a friend or sympathetic stranger—to talk to about how she felt. She would pour her heart out, if only given the chance.

Angela didn't regret her abortion at all, but she hated how alone she felt and how the stigma and judgment that accompanied abortion in a family like hers had cut her off from that support network. Instead, she had to carry this memory on her own, much as she would welcome the chance to process her feelings and experience out loud. "I feel like I have to walk on eggshells with them," she said one day. "I'm afraid of my family ever cutting me off for this."

Two weeks after she came back from the clinic, Angela was starting to worry. She was due back in New Mexico in a week for her follow-up visit, and it seemed like an important appointment to keep. Her pregnancy tests were negative by now, but she wanted to be sure there were no fetal remnants still in her uterus. And she wasn't quite sure if the abortion might affect her health in other ways; already, she suffered from anemia, and she had bled a fair amount as a result of the medication. When she'd given birth to her son, still less than a year ago, the doctors had warned her that substantial blood loss could be even more dangerous for her than for other people. She'd feel more reassured if she could return to the clinic, just to make sure everything was okay. She certainly couldn't go to any doctor in Texas to ask them. She wasn't about to tell them she'd left the state for an abortion.

But she and Nigel were still recovering financially from how much they'd spent going out of state the first time. They were cutting back everywhere they could, and Angela had even been buying less formula for her baby. Their budget was so tight that she tried to minimize how many times she left the apartment, to save on gas money so that each tank lasted as long as possible. They'd given up on getting a bigger apartment, instead signing another year-long lease and hoping that things would someday improve. Maybe eventually, if she kept calling, the building management would take care of the ants. It wouldn't fix the place, but it would be something.

Still, Angela worried, they were barely making ends meet. Feeling like she had no other option, Angela called the clinic and canceled her follow-up visit; they couldn't afford it. The employee on the phone was understanding. She told Angela to just pay attention to how she felt and that in all likelihood she was probably fine. She was hardly the first person to cancel a follow-up visit because she couldn't find the money to travel out of state again. If anything, it was something staff had become used to.

A week later, Angela couldn't stop thinking about how lucky she was to have gotten in when she had. Most of her post-abortion symptoms had disappeared, and she was close to feeling like herself again.

That Wednesday, she found out she was losing her job—a contract position she'd expected to hold for a few more months that instead would be ending earlier than she'd been told. She had two days' notice. Angela had already started applying for new positions, but she'd thought she had more time. All she could do was keep applying, hoping that eventually she'd find something that could help them stay afloat, rather than the minimum-wage jobs she kept seeing.

At the very least, she told herself, she'd gotten her abortion. She couldn't imagine dealing with all this along with the physical and emotional burdens of pregnancy. Her previous experience had been so difficult; during and after pregnancy, she'd faced debilitating depressive episodes. The weight gain associated with pregnancy had functioned as a psychological trigger, especially given her history of disordered eating. And then there was the sense of shame. There is already a strong cultural stigma against single mothers, with almost half of all American adults saying single motherhood is "bad for society." For Angela, that judgment was overlaid with overt racism. Back when she was pregnant with her son, Nigel's mother had accused her of getting pregnant on purpose, as a ploy to "trap" her White boyfriend into staying with her. It wasn't the first time someone had said something like that to her—she'd once had a boyfriend whose father warned him that she might "pull a knife on him," employing an offensive stereotype insinuating that Latina women were more violent. Angela still remembered how much effort it had taken to get Nigel to defend her from his mother's accusation and how he didn't seem to understand intuitively how painful it had been. And she knew for a fact that his family had never treated Nigel's other girlfriends that way. After Angela gave birth to their son, the stress of new parenthood, combined with her postpartum depression and his mom's treatment of her, stretched their relationship to the breaking point, almost driving them to end things. The situation had finally improved with his mother, who genuinely seemed to love her new grandchild and who had in the past few months tried her best to make amends with Angela. Things were better too with Nigel, with whom Angela had begun to discuss marriage. But she couldn't imagine going through the hell of pregnancy again.

In the days and weeks following the abortion, Angela would try to focus on everything that was going well in her life. Her son was healthy, and her boyfriend loved and supported her. But sometimes it felt like that was where the list ended. On her darkest days, she felt almost guilty about terminating her pregnancy. It didn't override the relief she felt, the knowledge that she had made the right choice. But still, she kept telling herself, if she didn't have a job and she wasn't in school, maybe she didn't deserve to have an abortion. If she wasn't contributing anything else to society, if she wasn't good for anything else, she might as well have had another kid. And then, at least, she wouldn't have had to lie to virtually everyone about what she'd done.

Only when she finally got a new job—one that paid enough to start saving up to move out of the apartment and to eventually return to school, even if she wouldn't do so anytime soon—did Angela's guilt finally go away. But the anger she felt never dissipated.

"This feels like a personal attack on me, on women. It really does," she said. "It takes away our right to choose, our right to decide what we want for our future. They took away that choice."

PART III

Darlene

THE SAFE HAVEN MYTH

———

CHAPTER 5

The Promised Oasis

California

Darlene Schneider recognized this feeling. The unending fatigue, the daily nausea. She'd felt like this only once before: three years ago, when she was expecting her daughter. But this time, she told herself, it couldn't be that. There was no way.

Only two weeks ago, in mid-January, she'd undergone surgery that removed fibroids, noncancerous tumors that had formed inside her uterus and caused nightmarish periods and overwhelming pain. Fibroids of that size meant she couldn't become pregnant again, she'd learned; the growths blocked any fertilized eggs from properly implanting in the womb. And she desperately wanted a second child, a chance to see her young daughter become a big sister.

The doctor had initially suggested a hysterectomy—a surgery that involved completely removing her uterus, fibroids included—to ensure the procedure would work, but that would have involved an overnight surgery, and Darlene had never been away from her daughter that long. And she was worried about spending that much time in the hospital. COVID-19 cases were especially high in Texas, and she didn't want to bring a virus home with her, potentially infecting her whole family. So instead she'd had what's called a myomectomy: her uterus was opened up, the growths removed, and then her womb stitched up again. A key difference between the two types of surgeries is that, after recovering, people who have myomectomies can safely get pregnant.

Her body was still healing from the procedure; typically, doctors recommend that people who have fibroids removed wait three to six months before trying to conceive. Otherwise, their uterus might be too fragile to hold a growing fetus. The worst-case scenario is that the uterus could break during the pregnancy, potentially killing both the fetus and the person carrying it. To ensure she wasn't pregnant, Darlene had been given a pregnancy test right before her surgery, so the doctors could ensure that it was safe for the operation to proceed.

When she called the doctor's office about her symptoms, they told her it was probably nothing. She must be feeling the side effects from the surgery. The physician prescribed her some medicine to improve her nausea and told her to follow up if things didn't get better. But later that week, on her forty-second birthday, Darlene was feeling even worse. Her husband was equally baffled. All signs pointed to her being pregnant, but they couldn't believe that was it. The doctors had told her she probably wouldn't be able to conceive before having the surgery. Separate from the pregnancy test she'd had in the hospital, she'd even taken a home test the night before surgery, and it had come up negative. Darlene and her husband told each other they wouldn't worry. It must be something else, but she'd ask her doctor as soon as she could.

The symptoms continued for almost two weeks. Just five days shy of Darlene's six-week follow-up appointment, wandering through the meat section of the grocery store, she almost vomited, with her daughter sitting in the cart. That evening, she took three pregnancy tests. Each one was positive. By her calculations, she must've been pregnant when she'd had the surgery. It had just been too early for the tests to detect it.

When she saw her doctor five days later, her physician seemed unsure. Still, he agreed that it couldn't hurt to check, just to rule things out. They gave her a sonogram, and when he saw the image, Darlene recalled, his entire expression changed. His eyes kept darting back to the screen, and as he spoke it seemed like he was talking less to her and more to himself. He wasn't a sonographer—he told her they'd have to get someone else in to confirm the images, to make sure that he was correctly interpreting what he was seeing. But as far as he could tell, this looked like a nine-week-old fetus, at least. In all his years of providing ob-gyn care, he'd never seen something like this.

Then he muttered to himself, "I can't intervene. I can't intervene. I can't intervene."

Darlene could see what was happening. She knew that here in Texas abortions were largely illegal. And she could see what course of action her physician clearly wanted to recommend, and what the laws wouldn't allow him to say. What she didn't know—what she couldn't fully understand in that moment—was how grave the threat to her life was. Only in the coming days, as she sat with the news, would she begin to process just how much danger she was in.

———

Almost two thousand miles away, in Oakland, California, Dr. Jennifer Kerns had been planning for months for *Roe*'s overturn. She knew she had to find a way to help—there were too many people whose lives were at risk.

When Texas began enforcing its six-week abortion ban, Kerns got certified to provide abortions in Oklahoma. She wanted to be able to make a difference. Starting in March 2022, she made monthly trips to the Trust Women clinic in Oklahoma City. She'd fly in on a red-eye and sleep for a few hours at a downtown hotel before working close to a ten-hour day. At night, she'd fly back home to her family, including the two kids who still lived at home. When Oklahoma banned abortion that May, she simply moved one state north, getting licensed in Kansas as well. It was a simple formula, as far as Kerns was concerned: find the place she could help the most and go there.

Kerns, a devoted triathlete who even on a few hours of sleep sounds as calm and collected as a public radio host, had been providing abortions for more than two decades. It was a skill she'd had to deliberately seek out. Ob-gyn residency programs have long been required by accreditation boards to give trainees a chance to learn about abortion care, but adequate training wasn't always readily available. In the post-*Dobbs* world, it has become far more difficult for future physicians to actually gain this kind of training, since hospitals in states with abortion bans cannot themselves train people to provide the procedure.

More than twenty years earlier, Kerns was the type who had known from the beginning that this was what she needed to do. In med school, she'd gotten involved with Medical Students for Choice, a club that served almost as an incubator for future abortion providers. When, after graduating in 2004, she moved to New York City for residency, she saw firsthand just how difficult abortions were to obtain, even for people living in states that nominally protected access. People in Washington Heights, where she worked, would frequently go to the pharmacy to buy misoprostol, which was available if you knew where to look. They asked for the pill that would "bring down their periods." It made sense: a pharmacy was cheaper than going to a clinic, especially if you didn't have health insurance or if you couldn't use it to pay for an abortion. It was also more discreet for anyone who needed to hide their abortion from any family members and wanted to eliminate the risk of any paper trail—insurance statements or bills—that might betray to others that they had sought to terminate a pregnancy.

Even back then, this demonstrated something Kerns would be reminded of again and again: the protections granted by *Roe v. Wade* were never enough to ensure that everyone could easily, safely access legal abortions. And even in places like New York and San Francisco it was hardly an easy thing to come by.

In 2022, Kerns could see that *Roe* was on the verge of disappearing. Outside of her work as a medical provider, she studied abortion academically as a professor at the University of California, San Francisco, one of the nation's premier medical research centers. She knew better than most just how many people would be denied care when abortion rights were gone and just how devastating the implications would be. Still, when the *Dobbs* decision came, she didn't expect to see much immediate change in the Bay Area. Her home felt worlds away from the patients she saw on her sojourns to the Midwest. She knew her colleagues in Los Angeles and San Diego would face countless out-of-state patients, people traveling from Arizona or Texas. But why would someone come all the way to San Francisco, hundreds or even thousands of miles away from where they lived? They probably had better options closer to home.

It didn't take long to see how wrong she'd been.

The loss of *Roe* was simply too massive, the number of unmoored patients too gigantic, for any part of the country to remain unaffected. By September, Kerns had seen patients from all over the country travel to her Bay Area clinic for an abortion. There were people coming from Texas, Georgia, and Kentucky, just to name a few, all showing up at the Women's Options Center, the outpatient family planning unit at the city's public hospital, Zuckerberg San Francisco General. Because it was part of a hospital, the center had always seen a mix of patients: straightforward pregnancy terminations, but also patients where an underlying health risk—a history of multiple cesarean section deliveries, for instance—might make the abortion more complicated.

Post-*Dobbs,* the people flying to San Francisco were distinctly from the latter category: patients often later in pregnancy who had developed complications for which abortion might be the best, safest, or even only option. In the past, those cases could have been referred to a nearby university medical center within the same state, where doctors were used to dealing with complex pregnancies and terminations. But those physicians no longer felt comfortable caring for someone whose pregnancy might have evolved into something potentially lethal.

In some states, like Idaho, the threats to providers were so great that some hospitals were actively shutting down their labor and delivery wards, meaning that patients would be expected to drive hours from home to reach a medical center where they might be able to give birth. This too emphasized another truth that medical providers and researchers such as Kerns had long understood: pregnancy-related health care in the United States had been in trouble well before the end of *Roe.* Providing ob-gyn care outside dense metropolitan areas was already incredibly difficult—it is often reimbursed at lower rates by insurance and more financially challenging to provide, in part because the high risk of complications drives up the price of securing malpractice insurance. Prior to 2022, the distance many people had to travel for reliable ob-gyn care, let alone abortion, already made pregnancy a riskier proposition. The farther pregnant people have to travel for care, research shows, the greater the likelihood they will face medical complications in giving birth, including death. *Dobbs,* it quickly became clear, had only amplified the crisis.

With new abortion bans in place, doctors didn't have any systems or protocols to refer patients to another state—most had never before needed to transfer someone out of state to treat a high-risk pregnancy. Out of options and with no clear map of what to do, they were racking their brains, calling up old medical school colleagues, and advising patients that, if they really wanted the best care possible, they'd better hop on a plane and book an appointment at a hospital in a reliably blue state that was known for treating high-risk pregnancies. Often that meant figuring things out as they went—"giving out piecemeal information," as Kerns said. One patient from Georgia, she recalled, had had complications in her last pregnancy, when she had a bad reaction to anesthesia. She wasn't sure how this would affect her current pregnancy. In the past, that patient probably would have simply been referred to a medical facility such as Emory University Hospital; getting to Atlanta would have taken far fewer resources and less planning than boarding a plane and flying five or six hours to California. But with abortions in Georgia banned after six weeks, physicians weren't sure she'd get the best or most comprehensive treatment if she stayed in state. Her doctor told her she had only two options: go to New York or go to San Francisco. Kerns, who traveled once a month to Kansas to provide abortions, had helped transfer one of her medically complex patients from Wichita to the Bay Area, too. It was the closest place where they could guarantee abortion patients would get care while having access to anesthesia and a hospital blood bank, and where they had the resources to cover the cost of her patients' travel. The need was so frequent that she had started building a more formal transfer arrangement between her Kansas clinic and her San Francisco center.

It was a haphazard system that spoke to a larger concern: clinics in border states were so under siege that people no longer felt able to rely on them for a timely abortion. Instead, they started calling for appointments in whatever state they could get one—maybe not the closest state to them, but one where they had a friend or relative who might put them up for a night, or where the doctor knew someone whom they recommended. This, more than anything else, was the main predictor for who traveled to San Francisco, reflected Dr. Eleanor Drey, the medical director at the Women's Options Center. But that also meant nobody could really anticipate when or where the next increase in patients would materialize—let alone allocate resources or expand capacity in time.

At San Francisco General, the influx, though far smaller than what clinics in Illinois or New Mexico or Kansas were experiencing, was enough to cause concern. Unlike in states bordering those with abortion bans, clinicians in the Bay Area were new to this kind of challenge. After *Dobbs,* the volume of phone calls at the Women's Options Center was far higher than ever, and for the first time, Drey said, she knew they couldn't offer an appointment to every patient who called looking for one. Instead, she began encouraging her staff to, in her words, "slow walk" the phones. If callers were earlier in pregnancy, and if they had the means to go, really, anywhere else, the clinic should encourage them to do so.

"It just feels like this big black hole—what's happening with those people who don't even get on our lists?" Kerns worried. "Like, where are they going? It's a little bit of a tortured feeling."

The patient influx added another worry: resources were finite, and there was only so much they could do to ask staff to scale up what care they provided. This clinic was a local safety net, one known for providing affordable abortions to those who couldn't go anywhere else. A twenty-four-week abortion there, for instance, cost less than $1,500, far below the typical price for an abortion at that point in pregnancy, which is often closer to $6,000. If more people came to San Francisco, doctors wondered, what would happen to the people the hospital usually took care of—the locals who came in from Oakland, just across the Bay Bridge, because they didn't have the money to go anywhere else? Where would they go now?

"I didn't want to lose track of trying to help our standard patients," Drey said. "You only have so many slots."

In theory, California residents' abortion rights hadn't been changed whatsoever. They were still protected by the state government. But, in practice, actually accessing a timely abortion was now more difficult. "We're the county hospital in San Francisco. And we are really committed to serving people in our community," Kerns said. "That's been interesting: thinking about how to balance these, not competing groups of people, but just more people."

Meanwhile, other concerns had emerged. The staff in San Francisco were no strangers to threats of violence: in March 2022, just months before the *Dobbs* ruling, their facility had been infiltrated by anti-abortion protesters—per a lawsuit filed by the city, one protester impersonated a pregnant woman seeking medical care so that the protesters could enter the clinic, where they began filming employees and patients. The episode left employees shaken for months. Drey even remembered the protesters chanting her name as they came inside. *Dobbs* had further emboldened anti-abortion activists. They'd increased their presence and even tried to sue the hospital for records of how the health center's staff disposed of fetal tissue. Everyone was on edge, and the threat of physical violence felt more potent.

The subtext was unmissable. Bans that had passed on the other side of the country radiated hundreds of miles away. They had already begun to undercut access for people in San Francisco, a purported haven in a state that prided itself on its efforts to secure abortion rights.

———

Darlene's doctor had an update for her a few hours after her appointment: she wasn't nine weeks pregnant—she was at eleven weeks, closing in on her second trimester. When she'd gotten her surgery, six weeks ago, she'd already been about four and a half weeks along. The doctor had never seen a case like hers before, but he was making some calls. He'd learn what to do next, he said. She just needed to sit tight.

For two weeks, Darlene waited, crying frequently and doing her best to hide her tears from her toddler. She didn't want her daughter to see just how scared she was.

She kept replaying his words to herself, over and over again. *I can't intervene.* They were words he'd repeated with something approaching desperation, sounding to her like he knew that, from a medical standpoint, the best thing to do would be to end the pregnancy. But at that point in Texas, abortion after six weeks was banned; in the months to come, it would be outlawed completely. Her doctor couldn't be caught helping her terminate a pregnancy.

The worst part was that Darlene and her husband wanted another child. She loved being a mom, and ordinarily they would have been thrilled at the prospect of their daughter getting a younger sibling. But this wasn't the way it was supposed to happen, when having another baby could put her own life at risk.

No matter what happened, her husband told her, he would support the choice she made. But it was up to her to decide.

Darlene was about thirteen weeks pregnant when she finally heard back from the doctor. After calling around, the doctor had learned about a case similar to hers, from a colleague he knew in Germany. That woman had given birth at thirty weeks—an incredibly early delivery that was facilitated by cesarean section, which brings risks of hemorrhaging and infections—and her baby required immediate intensive care. It sounded like giving birth was still possible for Darlene, the doctor said, but he sounded nervous even as he described it.

Every time Darlene asked a question—and she had a lot of questions—his responses felt vague, even timid. It seemed to her like he wanted to recommend abortion but didn't feel able to do so. But he kept urging her to get a second opinion from another doctor. Maybe they might be able to help her.

She found someone in Houston, a specialist recommended to her by her primary care physician. The doctor was an expert in intrauterine procedures—if anyone would know about the risks she was facing, and what she needed to do next, it would be a doctor like this one.

By now, Darlene's pregnancy had begun to show, just a little bit—early for most pregnant people, but visible to her. Still, she told few people about what was going on. Her secrecy made sense. There were legal concerns, for one thing. If she did get an abortion, people would know she had terminated her pregnancy, going against state law. More importantly, though, she feared judgment. She didn't know what people would think of her decision—friends, but especially her parents. Since she'd been a child, her mother and father both had impressed upon her that abortion was a sin. If she or her sisters ever got pregnant, they told her, abortion wasn't on the table. They would help her raise the baby, or they would help her find a loving family to adopt it. For them, it was a black-and-white issue of right and wrong. Never did they discuss a case like hers, where an abortion very well could be the thing that kept her alive.

When the Houston doctor saw her, he was stunned. In his view, every day that she stayed pregnant put her life in more danger; he didn't see how she could safely carry her pregnancy to term. He thought he should be able to provide an abortion. But when he asked his supervisors, he was shocked to learn that the answer was no. Because she wasn't literally about to die, they didn't believe Texas's medical exceptions to its abortion ban would apply here. The threat to Darlene was looming, but not yet imminent enough.

She didn't have any other options, he said. She had to get out of the state as soon as possible, to see a doctor whose hands weren't tied the way his were. And until she made it to her abortion, he urged her never to be too far from a hospital. At any point, he feared, the fetus could grow enough to burst her uterus—and if she didn't get care quickly enough, he said, she would probably die.

At that point, abortion was still legal in most states. But with *Roe* about to fall, the number of states where it would remain a viable option—where she'd be able to get the full, comprehensive set of options to manage her pregnancy—would quickly dwindle. For now, though, there were two places where he suspected she'd be able to find the right kind of care, no matter what: New York City and San Francisco. The question now was simply getting there.

———

After the *Dobbs* decision, California was expected to become a mecca for reproductive health care, the destination state that would support half the country for whom access had disappeared. One estimate from the Guttmacher Institute, one of the most reputable reproductive health policy research groups in the country, suggested that, if every state with anti-abortion leadership banned the procedure, the number of abortion patients in California could increase by as much as 3,000 percent.

Even before the Supreme Court's decision, the state's governor, Gavin Newsom, who was widely believed to be considering a presidential bid, had vowed that his state would protect abortion rights. In September 2022, just shy of three months following the court's decision, the state launched a website and billboard campaign, encouraging people from states such as Texas, Indiana, Michigan, Oklahoma, and South Carolina to come seek abortions in the Golden State. (This was despite the fact that abortion was at that point legal and available in Michigan and South Carolina.) Later that month, Newsom approved a budget allotting $200 million to support abortion access—money expected to help cover people's travel costs if they visited the state for an abortion, to provide clinic security and other new expenses providers might face. The state also passed new laws meant to encourage more people to become abortion providers—a critical investment if thousands or even tens of thousands more Americans were in fact expected to travel to California for care—and to clarify that the state would not comply if another state tried to prosecute California abortion providers for treating patients who had traveled there. In Los Angeles County, closer to the Arizona border, the state put $20 million toward a program that would create a special "safe haven" for people seeking abortion, funding pilot initiatives meant to expand access to abortion in the region, focusing on training more abortion providers, helping people get childcare and transportation support when seeking an abortion, and steering them away from crisis pregnancy centers. But the first round of pilots didn't even launch until April 2023, rendering the program's impact unclear even a year after *Roe* had fallen. And Dr. Susie Baldwin, medical director of the county health department's Office of Women's Health, tempered expectations about how many out-of-state travelers the initiative would serve in the immediate term. "My hope is that we're going to be serving everybody," she said. "But there are a lot of crises in our communities."

Politically, it made sense that California could become a sanctuary. In the 2022 elections, voters turned out in overwhelming numbers to enshrine abortion rights in the California constitution.

There were plenty of places in the state to terminate a pregnancy: California was home to more than four hundred abortion-providing facilities, and less than 5 percent of people in the state lived in a county without one. The only statutory restriction on the procedure was a law banning most pregnancy terminations after the fetus could independently live outside the womb, something that typically occurs between twenty-three and twenty-five weeks. (This same limit exists in many other "haven" states.) The state, the largest in the country, had already been home to the most abortions done per year. And already some people traveled from out of state to get there: just in 2021, Planned Parenthood reported that seven thousand out-of-state patients visited its clinics, with most coming for abortions. That figure still constituted a tiny fraction of the number of abortions performed in California—though the state didn't collect data, estimates from Guttmacher suggested that more than 150,000 abortions took place in California each year. But the out-of-state contingent wasn't nothing. If given enough support, the thinking went, far more people would be able to travel from states with bans to at least one of California's countless providers. In this state, if nowhere else, they'd be able to find someone who could care for them in a timely manner.

But in actuality the situation was far more complicated. California's abortion infrastructure would undoubtedly face newfound strains as more patients traveled there from out of state, but the increase looked different from what clinics in other states were reporting. The explanation was simple: not enough people were able to make the journey to take advantage of the Golden State's resources.

"It's not realistic," Drey said. "People who need this service already couldn't get to us—from even across the Bay Bridge. Do you really think that undocumented women from Texas are going to be able to make it to San Francisco? Who really thinks that's a reality?"

Still, the needs were undeniable. Clinics overseen by Shannon Connolly, the associate medical director at Planned Parenthood of Orange and San Bernardino Counties, saw a 200 percent increase in patients after *Roe v. Wade* was overturned, almost entirely people coming from neighboring Arizona. It wasn't the first time that patient demand had spiked; after Texas's six-week abortion ban took effect, more than a year earlier, Planned Parenthood had experienced a 350 percent jump in the number of patients it saw. Pratima Gupta, an ob-gyn in San Diego, could also attest to the growth. A professor at the University of California, San Diego, she had taken up shifts at the nearby Planned Parenthood, eager to help however she could. The clinic's wait times grew longer—not as bad as in states like Kansas, Illinois, or New Mexico, but still by as much as ten days. It was enough to be noticeable and to cause her worry about what would happen to the patients who couldn't wait that long, for whom the delay could push them into another trimester or even past the legal limits. Each day at the clinic, Gupta met with patients who'd driven hours from Arizona and Texas to see her, overnight journeys that many spent sleeping in their cars, because they didn't have extra money for a hotel. The need was also clear to Quita Tinsley Peterson, who ran the state's largest abortion fund, called Access Reproductive Justice. They saw it when they looked at their records each night. In January 2022, months before *Roe* was overturned, their fund got 110 calls from people—predominantly but not entirely Californians—seeking help paying for their abortions. Only seven months later, in August, the number of callers had more than doubled: now 284 people had asked the fund for help paying for an abortion. The increase was largely sparked by new people coming to California from other states.

Little more than a month after the Supreme Court's decision, the fund could help only a fraction of those callers: barely more than sixty people. Peterson, a Georgia-to-Oakland transplant, knew that the need far outstripped what their organization could provide. They also knew that the people calling their fund represented a tiny share of the people coming to California's abortion providers. It would take time—months at the very least—for their fund to see any of the money allotted by the state, which was intended to support abortion funds and providers. They were grateful for the government's support, hyperaware of the stark contrast with what they had battled back in Atlanta, fighting against state leaders keen to eliminate abortion as much as possible. But they worried about how long it would take and what would happen to the people in immediate need.

Still, although the demand in California was more than the

state's vast reproductive health care system could easily and comfortably bear, it was, at least in the immediate term, far less than what abortion providers and funds in other states had seen. In the first six months after *Roe*'s overturn, some clinics in California still reported little to no changes in their wait times, despite seeing an increase in out-of-state patients. There were enough medical providers in the area that, if they added on another day of services, they could still provide care for everyone in a timely manner. It was a sharp contrast to states such as Illinois, New Mexico, or Kansas. Research conducted out of the University of California, San Francisco, emphasized this difference. Abortions in California went up by only 1 percent in the first two months after the *Dobbs* decision. A year out from the *Dobbs* decision, California had seen one of the largest surges in terms of raw number of abortions performed in the state. But because the state is so large and the site of so many abortions, the increase felt much smaller: a year after *Dobbs,* the monthly average of abortions in the state had gone up only about 2.1 percent.

Many abortion providers remained skeptical that this equilibrium would hold. In years to come, they acknowledged, the demand for their services would likely grow, especially if more states passed abortion bans and people had fewer other options for accessing the full spectrum of reproductive health care. By the beginning of 2023, abortion was virtually unavailable in fourteen states. In another half dozen states, abortion bans had been blocked by state courts, and other states—Florida and North Carolina among them—were weighing their own new restrictions.

But even if California remained the rare and reliable option, the data immediately after *Dobbs* underscored an uncomfortable truth. In reality, this "haven" state was just too far away for most people to get to. The patients in health centers like Kerns's were largely those who had enough money to purchase a last-minute plane ticket to San Francisco—which could cost anywhere from three hundred to eight hundred dollars per person—who were used to flying, whose flights weren't the ones canceled or delayed, and who'd then still have money set aside for a hotel, too. "It's a really, really far distance for people to come," Kerns said. "California is a little— It might serve some little slice, being a haven state of some sort. But I don't know that it can really do that in a huge way, just because of the geography."

———◆———

If patients couldn't come to California—a state full of abortion providers willing to care for them—was there any way doctors could bring abortions to them? Or was there any other way that the state's vast abortion care infrastructure could be of help?

Already, the threat of litigation kept patients and providers alike nervous about performing abortions for people who had traveled from out of state. In California, medication abortions are allowed to be dispensed entirely through telemedicine. As long as someone had an in-state mailing address, they could have the pills sent directly to them, bypassing any hours-long clinic visit. Still, that required having an in-state mailing address—whether it was a mail forwarding address, a post office box, a hotel, or a friend or relative's home.

The fear of criminalization was potent in Gupta's San Diego clinic. The patients she saw seemed so scared of what would happen when they returned home if someone found out where they had been. One, she recalled, asked for her help in deleting any reference to abortion from her text message history, just to be safe. It was a reasonable fear to have. In a high-profile case post-*Dobbs*, the State of Nebraska prosecuted a mother and daughter, using the daughter's Facebook messages as evidence, because the daughter got an abortion after twenty weeks, even though the abortion was performed before *Roe* even fell. Both mother and daughter pled guilty, facing prison time as a result. The federal government hadn't passed laws protecting this kind of data—text or Facebook messages, a Google search history—all of which fall outside of protected confidential medical records statutes, and which could be used by legal authorities in anti-abortion states. In late 2023, Google announced new changes that would roll out in 2024 intended to better secure users' location history, which could potentially help people conceal visits to abortion clinics. Few other cases like the one from Nebraska have emerged. Since abortion bans in general don't criminalize pregnant people, states prosecuting them would

have to rely on other laws, such as homicide or chemical endangerment statutes. And the sheer quantity of consumer data available
online meant that law enforcement officials were often less likely
to pursue a specific case unless they had good reason to believe that
the person had gotten an illegal abortion or helped a friend obtain
one. Still, the fear of becoming the next case, and of going to jail
for seeking medical care, remained potent. Privacy experts warned
that it might take years to see how great a threat unprotected medical information could pose. But many noted that even if the fre-
quency of prosecution was low, the risks if one were caught would
be devastating.

Abortion providers within California were largely incapaci-
tated. In the months leading up to *Dobbs,* doctors had speculated
over whether they might be able to prescribe medication abortion to patients in states that had banned the procedure. Because
California law allowed pills to be mailed without an in-person visit,
some hoped that this could be the answer: abortion medications
were easy to dispense, safe to take at home, and highly effective
up until the second trimester. If mailed across state lines, from a
state where abortion was legal, medication abortions could pose an
"existential threat" to abortion bans, one law professor suggested.
In anticipation, some California doctors got certified in states
like Texas, despite having no intention of moving there, so that,
when the time came, they'd be able to send patients the medications needed to end their pregnancy. But they were relying on an
untested legal theory. If someone lived in California and sent pills
to a patient in Texas, Mississippi, or Oklahoma, which state's laws
would take precedence? Could California really guarantee that doctors would be safe from being prosecuted under another state's
abortion ban?

"It's just complicated," Jody Steinauer, the Bay Area physician,
said with a sigh. "I mean—I'm telling you, if that could be, there'd be
a lot of people available to provide medication abortion. Everyone
wants to do it."

But after *Roe* was overturned, nobody had an answer they
felt good about. Only one state—Massachusetts—immediately
passed a law that explicitly protected doctors who sent abortion
pills to people in other states, even if abortion there had been
outlawed. But even in Massachusetts, few doctors were actually

taking advantage of it. In California, the state's collection of abortion rights advocates had considered including such a protection in their list of priorities for the legislature to pass. But it fell off the list of immediate priorities, in part, some abortion providers said, because many weren't sure if such a protection would actually survive court challenges. Even without a state protection, doctors could theoretically try to prescribe abortion pills to patients in other states. But doing so meant risking legal charges if ever they set foot in the state whose laws they had broken—even a layover at an airport, or a one-night stopover on the way to somewhere else, many worried, could be enough time for them to be arrested. It was a risk few felt able to take, even when a year later the state did in fact pass a law emulating the Massachusetts protection.

After initially feeling so hopeful that they could help, providers soon appeared less certain. Doctors like Kerns and Steinauer could and would continue to volunteer in the Kansas clinics, visiting every four to six weeks, caring for as many patients as they could. But it wasn't a scalable strategy. Border states such as Kansas and Illinois had only so many abortion clinics, and there was only so much physical space for doctors to work in. There simply wasn't room for every willing physician to come from California and volunteer in another state.

And in the longer term, doctors worried that the rise in abortion bans across the country would give far fewer young physicians a chance to properly study providing abortion care—especially the substantial share of those pursuing ob-gyn residencies in states with harsh abortion restrictions. Doctors in states with abortion bans could not learn how to provide this kind of care—not unless they were able to leave the state and find training somewhere else. The concern was great enough that after *Dobbs* fewer medical students applied to residencies in states with abortion bans, with the drop especially noticeable among those pursuing ob-gyn careers. And in a profession that seemed under concerted, unabating attack, the implications for medical trainees added another layer of concern. A few years after the decision, where would all the doctors be who knew how to perform abortions? It was a question with potentially wide-ranging impact. People who pursued residency in a state that banned abortion wouldn't necessarily stay there; close to half of all medical residents end up practicing in another state.

Those who didn't know how to do abortions, the research suggested, would struggle in other ways. The similarity between abortion care and miscarriage management meant that often doctors who hadn't been trained in the former were less proficient in the latter. Without the opportunity to care for patients seeking abortions, residents often don't see enough miscarriage patients to become fully proficient at taking care of them.

This was a question Steinauer agonized over. In just a few short years, she feared, the state abortion bans could do long-lasting damage to the number of trained providers: fewer would be able to care for people in need of either abortions or help managing their miscarriages. It was certainly a problem far bigger than one California hospital could solve. But maybe, she hoped, there was something she could do.

Even before the *Dobbs* ruling, medical residents, and in particular those studying to be ob-gyns, were required to at the very least have access to abortion training. (Residency programs offered in hospitals that didn't provide abortions might have agreements with local clinics, where physicians in training could go to practice abortion care.) Ob-gyn trainees could decline to learn how to provide abortions—a level of flexibility in medical education that is unique to abortion—but in practice few took up that option. Per data Steinauer's team collected in 2020, only 12 percent of ob-gyn residents across the country refused abortion training. In a way, the data weren't that surprising. They simply underscored that, as far as most physicians were concerned—and especially those who cared about providing pregnancy-related care—abortion was considered a standard, core health care service. And after the *Dobbs* decision, the council that accredited medical residency programs reaffirmed that commitment. Whether or not states had banned abortions, the council declared, residency programs training ob-gyns were required to make abortion education available, even if that meant offering to temporarily send residents to another state, where they could legally provide the care. But doctors who worked in medical education worried that the onus of setting up residency partnerships—and the burden on residents of having to travel out of state—would ultimately deter physicians from seeking comprehensive training in abortion.

Steinauer hoped that this was where she might be able to step in. From her perch in San Francisco, she ran a program called the Kenneth J. Ryan Residency, whose mission was to incorporate robust abortion training into ob-gyn programs across the country. Only about one-third of the nation's almost three hundred ob-gyn residencies are part of the program. But it was enough for a start. She could set up exchange programs between hospitals, allowing Ryan programs in Texas, for instance, to send residents to California for abortion training. They'd start small: by 2023, Steinauer's staff had paired every Ryan residency in a state that had abortion restrictions with a program in a state where abortion was still protected. Residents would travel to the other state as part of their training, learning to perform and manage abortions in a setting without legal threats.

Describing the program, Steinauer's voice bubbled with optimism. But at the same time, she acknowledged, it would be at best an uphill battle for programs like hers to fill in the medical training gaps that had emerged. How would they find enough ob-gyn programs that could host all the residents who might be traveling from states with abortion bans? Setting up travel programs would be logistically difficult, and many abortion clinics, overwhelmed by the number of patients they were seeing, might not have the bandwidth to host more trainees. And at least some hospitals, she knew, would be skittish about participating, or at the very least publicizing the option to students, despite the abortion requirements needed to keep an accredited residency. Their leaders would have to decide what was a greater concern: losing certification or risking a possible state prosecution if they sent residents out of state to study abortion—and for many, it wasn't an easy decision. Then there were longer-term worries: Would state lawmakers who had successfully banned abortion start targeting training programs next—perhaps making it illegal (or at the very least incredibly inconvenient) for hospitals to send their residents somewhere else for abortion training?

"Of course, we're all worried this will happen," Steinauer acknowledged. Still, she was resolute. They didn't have the luxury of fretting over hypotheticals. All they could do was keep going, trying to train as many doctors as they could.

Darlene's doctor couldn't find a New York physician willing to see her. He'd trained there and thought it would be an easy connection to make, but it seemed that everyone he spoke to was too terrified to take on a patient from Texas. No one wanted to face the legal risk that might come if they counseled her to get an abortion. Finally, Darlene called San Francisco General, where at last a physician agreed to see her. She'd have to wait nine precious days for her appointment. But if she could hold out that long, she'd know what options—if any—were still available to her. She and her husband booked their flights, including a hotel within walking distance of the hospital.

Already, the prospect of choosing an abortion weighed on her. Because she hadn't been able to get one earlier, the pregnancy was progressing, and she was able to visualize the second child she so badly wanted, the potential sibling for her daughter. After doing her best to avoid the information, she'd accidentally seen the medical record detailing the sex: it looked like another girl. She wished she could erase that knowledge from her memory. But still, Darlene knew that if she carried this pregnancy to term it could end up killing her.

What if I die? she kept thinking. *How do I explain that to my two-year-old? Like I chose this baby over her.* No matter what, she feared making the wrong decision.

———◆———

CHAPTER 6

Just Because It's Legal

Colorado

Things were simpler back when Amanda Carlson started running Colorado's biggest abortion fund, about four and a half years before *Roe*'s overturn. Back then, maybe five people called in for help each day; if things were really busy, the fund might hear from ten people. Most were Colorado residents, Carlson recalled, with maybe one in five coming from another state. The Cobalt Abortion Fund, which had launched in 1984 and was now almost forty years old, served what felt like a critical need: helping people pay for their abortions, a procedure that in Colorado could cost hundreds or even thousands of dollars, and that largely wasn't covered by health insurance.

Money was one of the few barriers to accessing an abortion. Colorado, unlike most states, does not and did not have any laws limiting when in pregnancy someone could get one. There was no mandatory waiting period, no state-required counseling that clinics must provide before patients could end their pregnancies. Getting an abortion was by no means easy: as is true in most states where the procedure is legal, the majority of the state's eighteen clinics were largely clustered near the cities—which, in Colorado, meant Boulder, home to the largest university, and Denver, the biggest city in the state. Still, depending on how far along you were and where in the state you lived, residents could usually find an abor-

tion provider no more than an hour's drive away. For decades, this
state had served as a refuge of sorts, both for patients from within
the United States but also those who had traveled from Canada or
who'd taken day-long flights from parts of Europe. People traveled
to Colorado when they couldn't get abortions elsewhere, often
after learning late in pregnancy of a life-threatening complication
for either the fetus or themselves.

Carlson, a social worker by training, understood just how
meaningful her work was. In 2018, her first full year at Cobalt, the
fund spent close to $130,000, helping maybe 750 patients pay for
their abortions. Each one of those people, she'd remind herself,
was someone who badly needed care and who otherwise might
have been forced to go without, and instead carry an unwanted
pregnancy to term. She knew also that those 750 patients represented a fraction of people who sought an abortion in Colorado, a
state where, per data collected by the Guttmacher Institute, close
to twelve thousand abortions were done per year. The patients she
helped did not represent everyone for whom paying the full cost
of the procedure—at a minimum about five hundred dollars, but
potentially up to thirteen thousand dollars—would mean assuming
other financial hardships, whether that meant skimping on groceries or taking on credit card debt they'd hope to pay off later. What
she didn't understand, what was impossible to fully predict, was
how drastically the need for her fund would grow in just a few short
years.

It started with Texas. When, in the fall of 2021, the state's six-
week abortion ban took effect, Colorado's abortion clinics became
the fallback option for patients who couldn't get an appointment in
Oklahoma, New Mexico, or Kansas. Cobalt, by extension, emerged
as their main source of financial support. With more callers now
traveling to Colorado from out of state, the fund began helping
people pay not just for their abortions but for the other costs they
might incur along the way: a hotel room, meals while traveling, a
last-minute plane ticket that would otherwise have set a patient
back twelve hundred dollars.

And after *Dobbs* the numbers only kept growing. There were
ten to thirty people calling each day for help, desperate not only
for money to pay for the procedure but also for anything that could
alleviate the hefty cost of traveling to Boulder or Denver.

In the last four months of 2021, Cobalt spent $5,000 just helping people travel to Colorado for abortions; that year, the fund gave out $206,511 in total, serving 1,154 people.

After *Dobbs,* the numbers grew exponentially. In all of 2022, Cobalt spent almost $700,000 to help people get abortions, with most of that money supporting people who traveled to Colorado in the months after *Roe* had fallen. It was clear the money wasn't going as far as it used to. The fund disbursed more than 60 percent of the year's funds used to support procedures themselves—as opposed to the logistical costs associated with travel—after June 24. But the money covered only 743 people, less than half of all the patients whose abortions Cobalt subsidized that year. It underscored the truth that clinicians and patients had been learning over and over across the country: because the need to travel farther for care was pushing people later into their pregnancies, abortions themselves had grown more expensive. It was a change with obvious significance for a fund like Cobalt. Without *Roe,* the resources it had typically subsisted on would no longer be enough.

Now most of the people calling Cobalt for help came from outside Colorado, and the majority of those callers were from just one state: of the 640 people who received "practical support" to cover the travel associated with abortion, 435 were from Texas alone. By contrast, only 49 people supported by the fund in 2022 came from Colorado. It was a new source of pressure, and Carlson half joked about just how drastically her job had now changed. In the wake of the decision, running an abortion fund meant being a part-time travel agent, figuring out the best flight deals and hotel bookings for patients traveling from as far away as Georgia. It meant solving the problems nobody else had thought of, making sure nothing stood in the way of people's ability to get care. Some callers didn't have credit cards to use when they checked in at a hotel; Carlson arranged to leave a card from the Cobalt Fund at the front desk when patients needed to register for incidentals. One day, a group of patients' flights back home were canceled because of weather conditions. Carlson's team sent food vouchers so that the patients' children—waiting back in their home states for their moms to return—would have dinner taken care of. They helped make sure every patient had someone at home taking care of their kids.

It was a mammoth responsibility for their tiny team. Cobalt technically had twenty-one full-time employees on staff, but the abortion fund was just one branch of the organization, which also worked to advocate politically for laws that protected abortion rights. Only two full-time staffers worked in the abortion fund, fielding patient calls, booking flights, and ensuring that people who sought funding were actually able to get it. At the same time, Carlson knew, they were increasingly patients' first, last, and only option for aid.

With *Roe* overturned, the number of abortion funds available to help people had fallen dramatically. In Texas, which was once home to a robust network of such funds, the fear of prosecution—specifically, of violating a vague abortion ban that had been passed in 1857, was never repealed, and could now be enforced by the state's attorney general—was particularly acute. Abortion funds there worried that giving someone money to leave the state might constitute "aiding and abetting" them in the termination of a pregnancy; fearful of eliciting criminal penalties, they stopped distributing money for almost three-quarters of a year. One fund, Texas Equal Access, resumed supporting people who traveled for abortions in late March 2023, after a favorable ruling from a federal district court; another, the Lilith Fund, followed suit in early April of that year—though in both cases longer-term uncertainty remained about Texas-based abortion funds. In Oklahoma, where abortion is completely banned, the state's sole abortion fund had also scaled back operations. It gave money to clinics in states where abortion was legal, but it was doing its best to be cautious. "We don't know how vigorously the state will pursue prosecution," one fund member said.

Their hesitation made sense, but it also meant organizations in states like Colorado were now tasked with connecting exponentially more people with abortion appointments. They were some of the only ones available to do the job.

At least immediately, finding the money wasn't difficult. Whenever abortion bans appeared in the news, funds like Carlson's would experience what managers knowingly described as "rage giving"— a sudden influx in donations from people across the country, newly eager to help people access abortions. The summer that *Roe* fell,

Cobalt was among the many abortion funds that saw a dramatic surge in donations. It was enough to keep going; Carlson would note with pride that even as requests for aid grew in the post-*Dobbs* world, Cobalt never had to turn anyone away completely empty-handed. Every person who called the fund would receive some money to help pay for their journey.

But what Carlson also knew was that this kind of support wasn't predictable. She certainly couldn't expect it to be sustained long-term. Already, she worried that what they were giving patients wasn't enough. "We want to be good stewards of this funding, but the need is just so high and everything's so expensive," she said. "It's very hard to set parameters on how much per client we spend. Everybody's situation can be so different." Only a year after the *Dobbs* decision, the wisdom of her caution had become clear: as people became acclimated to a post-*Roe* reality, the level of donations to abortion funds began to fall significantly. But the needs faced by Carlson's organization—as well as others like hers—persisted.

For decades, abortion rights had been a winning issue in Colorado. It was the first state in the country to decriminalize the procedure for people pregnant as a result of rape or incest or for whom giving birth could cause permanent physical harm, doing so in 1967, years before the *Roe* decision came down. More recently, in 2020, voters had overwhelmingly rejected a ballot measure that would have banned abortions for people past twenty-two weeks of pregnancy. Access was something almost taken for granted. When the Supreme Court agreed to hear the *Dobbs* case, reproductive health groups in the state sprang into action: Colorado, they vowed, would be proactive, passing laws to protect abortion explicitly. It wasn't an easy victory, recalled Daneya Esgar, who at the time led the state legislature's Democratic majority and sponsored the Reproductive Health Equity Act. Lawmakers she spoke with were hesitant to prioritize abortion; the right to terminate a pregnancy was hardly under threat in the state, the thinking went, and few grasped right away that national abortion rights might actually be vulnerable. Not until after the high court had heard oral arguments did legislators take seriously the notion that Colorado had to protect abortion rights, she said. "That's what was the urgency here. But when there's not really any urgency, I'm not sure folks are really jumping up to try and work on this."

The bill had the votes to pass. But still, even in Denver, it faced fourteen-hour hearings and a twenty-seven-hour straight floor debate, the longest in the legislature's history. In the spring of 2022, when the governor finally signed it into law, Colorado became only the sixteenth state in the country (not including Washington, D.C.) with clear statutory abortion protections. It was a guarantee that abortion providers would rely on in the coming months and years. Much like with other destination states, the surge in out-of-state patients coming to Colorado was dramatic—by the end of 2022, with *Roe* overturned, the number of people who had traveled to the state for an abortion appeared to have more than doubled, increasing from 1,560 to 3,385. About one in four abortions in Colorado was for someone from out of state. And though most of those people came from Texas, patients were traveling from virtually all over: Georgia, Mississippi, Missouri, Louisiana, Idaho, Ohio. Even an abortion fund like Cobalt wasn't able to help everyone in need. Doctors would show up for work to discover patients who had slept in their cars in the clinic parking lots, because they hadn't been able to scrounge up the money for a hotel. Wait times for an appointment sometimes stretched to twenty-one days, sometimes even thirty—delays long enough that they would drastically change patients' options. Clinics tried expanding their capacity as much as they could, but it was hard to foresee a world where they would be able to meet the demand, especially as it felt like lawmakers in their neighboring states remained determined to further quash access to abortion. "It's very disheartening as a provider, that we're going to have to continue to fight this fight just to keep access for patients," said Dr. Kristina Tocce, the medical director for Planned Parenthood of the Rocky Mountains. Another physician, Dr. Rebecca Cohen, noted that, just like in other safe-haven states, clinicians were seeing people later and later in pregnancy, a by-product of how much harder it was to get an appointment across the United States and within the state, and how much more difficult it had become to make the journey. The shift was obvious in her Denver clinic, a hospital-based health center known for treating people with complex pregnancies, and where someone without insurance might, depending on how far along they were, pay between two thousand and five thousand dollars for an abortion. In the past, the clinic had seen only maybe five patients a week who were later than week thirteen. Now they saw two or three each day. And, even more striking, before Texas's six-week abortion ban took effect, no more than 5 percent of their patients had come from out of state. But now, with total abortion bans in effect across the country, close to one in three had traveled to Colorado from somewhere else.

It was, frankly, too many patients for the state's abortion infrastructure. "We can't possibly see all the patients who want to come here," said Dr. Warren Hern, the leader of a Boulder-based clinic and one of the few physicians in the country equipped and willing to provide abortions to patients in their third trimester. "We have a waiting list. We have to put people off, and that puts them in later in pregnancy." For Hern, in his eighties, that development was especially troubling. He remembered what life was like in the days before *Roe*. Prior to becoming an abortion provider, he had studied the public health implications when people were denied abortions. He saw firsthand just how many people died attempting to end their pregnancies on their own, because it was the 1960s and they didn't know where or how to find a doctor who might help them. Hern recalled too how unequal the burden was: how Black women were significantly more likely to die from illegal attempted abortions than White women, and how wealth dictated who was able to travel to another state or country to access abortion. What he saw post-*Dobbs* offered a brutal reminder of how things were when he was young—the bans spreading across the country, the patients terrified of jail time and unsure where to find an abortion, and the ungodly sums of money needed to cross state lines to reach providers who were operating at their limits. He knew where this was going and just how bad it could be. "It's an unfolding national disaster," Hern worried. Just like before.

With clinics facing heightened demand for abortion, doctors found themselves limiting how often they could provide other kinds of medical care. One physician, whose clinic offered both primary care and abortion services, said that to accommodate all their abortion patients, her practice had to scale back how many days it offered primary care. Another outpost, Boulder Valley Health Center, had previously operated two clinics: one focusing on abortion, and another that emphasized other family planning and contraception services. To fulfill the overwhelming demand for abortion care, the center's leaders shut down their family planning facility. Some health centers that had never before performed abortions began offering the service, too, in what was a direct response to the growing wait times for patients who in the past would have been referred to a local Planned Parenthood. Clinic administrators noticed a new influx of physicians eager to work for them, doctors who hoped they might be able to help serve everyone now in need. And ob-gyns who had previously worked in other parts of the country, providing abortions in states that had now banned the procedure, found themselves moving to Denver and Boulder to offer their support. Here, they imagined, they could make a difference.

That was what compelled Leilah Zahedi-Spung, an ob-gyn specializing in high-risk pregnancies, to move out to Denver. Born and raised in Georgia, Zahedi-Spung had finished her medical education in Missouri and eventually set up shop in Chattanooga, Tennessee, a city with few physicians who had her level of expertise in caring for complex pregnancies. Once a month, she'd drive five hours to Memphis to provide abortions there, too. Her work was a source of pride; as long as she'd wanted to be a doctor, Zahedi-Spung had planned to work in a southern state, to be of service to a community that felt like the place she grew up. And she knew that the need for her kind of skills was particularly acute in Tennessee, a state with one of the highest pregnancy-related death rates in the country.

But it was no longer tenable. The state's abortion ban, she said, had made her work impossible: it often wasn't even safe for her to recommend chemotherapy for a pregnant patient who discovered they had cancer. The fear was that the chemicals could threaten the pregnancy, even induce a miscarriage, and open up the physician to criminal charges as a result. It was a challenge health care providers like her were facing across the country, in any state with a restrictive abortion ban; legal filings from Ohio reported multiple cases of women who had to leave the state for an abortion if they wanted to continue their cancer treatments, because they were past the state's legal limit to end a pregnancy. Cases like those illustrated just how deeply bans on abortion had interfered with patients' ability to access all kinds of lifesaving health care and how medically complex pregnancy can be. Packing her bags in Chattanooga, Zahedi-Spung didn't want to leave—who would care for her patients if she left Tennessee?—but she was no longer able to provide the care that was so desperately needed. It wasn't easy. Moving meant finding a place not only where abortion was legal and available but where her husband, a lawyer, could relocate and stay with his law firm, and where he didn't have to retake the bar exam. Colorado was one of the few viable options. Then there were the other parts of moving: finding a new home, figuring out where her older child would go to school, and hiring someone to take care of her younger kid. Most of her family was back in Georgia, now a plane ride away. Still, when she moved across the country, children and husband in tow, she told herself that the change would be worth it. Here, she'd be able to provide the care her patients needed, instead of coming home each night living in fear that her work could ultimately land her in jail. And who knew? Maybe people from Tennessee would find a way to show up here; maybe she'd be able to treat some of them from Denver.

But in Colorado, too, clinicians knew their work came with inherent risk, even in a state where the right to an abortion was ostensibly sacrosanct. Every few years, the state's anti-abortion movement would launch ballot campaigns attempting to restrict access in Colorado. Now they were getting new support from activists just a few states over, fresh off their victories at home and ready to target the next major state. In Pueblo, a city just two hours south of Denver, Texas-based activists who had fought for abortion restrictions in their home state began lobbying the lawmakers to pass a local ordinance that would ban the procedure within Denver's city limits. The measure failed to pass, with the city council's president arguing that individual municipalities couldn't ban abortion if it was explicitly protected by state law. But the message was clear: if they had any say about it, abortion rights opponents wouldn't let Colorado remain the sanctuary it had become.

These threats came with teeth, and they dated back decades.

Hern, for one, opened his clinic almost immediately after the *Roe* ruling, eager to help reverse the trends he'd studied; soon after he launched his practice, the death threats began. To this day, he lives hyperaware of the risks he faces, of the same man who stalks him every Tuesday morning and the protesters who camp outside his clinic at all hours of the day. George Tiller, whom Hern considered a colleague, was murdered only one state away. Even now, the danger remained omnipresent. In Colorado Springs, less than two hours from his clinic, an anti-abortion extremist had in 2015—not even ten years earlier—instigated a mass shooting at the Planned Parenthood affiliate, killing three people and injuring eight more. Another physician, who opened her own abortion clinic soon after the *Dobbs* decision, worked hard to maintain a low profile. She had seen too many of her colleagues find protesters in their yards, and she lived in fear that they might appear in front of her house while she was playing with her two toddlers. The stigma around providing abortion care affected her work, too, she said. Securing office space for the clinic meant finding a landlord who wouldn't feel nervous about the potential crowds of protesters (or the numerous patients the facility might attract) or, if she tried to buy an office, knowing that her profession could deter someone from selling to her. The subtext: supporting abortion access was easy for most residents in principle. But in practice?

"People are supportive, but once it starts affecting their bottom line—you know, there's protesters out there every day—that's a different situation," the doctor worried.

This was the challenge. Abortion rights in Colorado were generally popular, and politicians campaigning on them could count on voter support. But taking the next step—translating that slogan into actual policies, into expanding access to clinics or investing money to help people get care—was a far harder sell. Abortion was still treated as something separate from ordinary health care. Unless that changed, the right to an abortion could still feel like just that: an abstract right, rather than a concrete reality.

Ashley Acre hadn't been trying to get pregnant when, in late February 2022, she started to sense that something was different. It wasn't anything in particular—no nausea, breast soreness, or any other physical discomfort. Instead, she said, it was more like intuition: she just knew that something was growing inside her.

The week Ashley tested positive was perhaps the happiest she'd felt in a long time. She was twenty-nine, and for a few years she had thought about wanting to be a mother someday. It was the right time for her: she had a good job, she was in a committed, healthy relationship with someone she loved, and she had a great support network in the Detroit suburbs where she lived. And she knew she'd be a good mom. The morning she found out she was pregnant, Ashley told almost no one—confiding in just one close friend until she had a chance to tell her boyfriend, Nick. A few days after taking her pregnancy test, she bought some baby clothes and called him on FaceTime. When she told him the news, she could see it in the way his expression transformed: he was over the moon, just like she was. They were going to start a family together.

Pregnancy wasn't easy for Ashley. Especially in the first few months, she felt regularly drained of energy. And once the nausea began, it seemed like it would never go away. Still, the good parts outweighed the bad. It was surreal to imagine herself as a mom; in the middle of the day, she'd find herself fantasizing about what it would be like to look after her child. Around her second trimester of pregnancy, she and Nick bought a house together. They started planning the life they'd have after she gave birth: picking a room in the house for the nursery, brainstorming potential names for the baby. Since she worked from home, she figured she could find a way to balance breastfeeding and working full-time. When Ashley found out she was expecting a daughter, she tried to picture what the little girl would look like. Maybe, she told herself, the baby would look a bit like her.

Ashley wouldn't find out until five months into her pregnancy—her twenty-week checkup, and by chance also her thirtieth birthday—that things were not going according to plan. It was the first doctor's visit Nick had been able to join; it was supposed to be a good day, a chance to see the emerging silhouette of their future child. In the days leading up to the appointment, the couple couldn't stop talking about it. This was a moment they hoped they'd remember forever.

The scan itself went fine, but afterward things started to feel a little off. Ashley and Nick waited for ten minutes after the scan; the doctor was double-booked, but there was something she'd seen on the image that she wanted to discuss with the couple. Ashley tried her best not to think too hard about what it might mean.

When she finally arrived, the doctor told them she had seen a tiny buildup of liquid inside their baby's lungs. It sounded bad, but it really might be nothing, she told Ashley. There was no need to worry just yet. All the same, she recommended a follow-up visit, one week later at a nearby hospital. There, they'd do a more comprehensive fetal scan and, if needed, any subsequent genetic tests to figure out what, if anything, was wrong. And really, she kept telling them, the odds were on their side: everything was probably fine. Ashley would hold on to those words over the next seven days. There was no sense in panicking just yet, the doctor had suggested, so she wouldn't let herself spend too much time thinking about the alternative. When, the next week, the ultrasounds still didn't give her an answer, Ashley agreed to come back a day later and get follow-up genetic testing, just in case it revealed anything else. Her insurance, Michigan's Medicaid program, would cover it.

Everyone kept telling her not to worry. The baby might be perfectly healthy. Or whatever they found might be minor enough that, with advance notice and planning, Ashley and Nick could manage as parents, still raising a happy, healthy child. But by now the volume of information Ashley was receiving—the tests, the scans, the uncertainty—had begun to feel overwhelming. And she was starting to internalize the part that, until now, nobody had been able to say out loud: her baby might not make it.

As in Colorado, abortion was and is a protected right in Michigan, a guarantee that voters would overwhelmingly affirm in the 2022 midterm elections. But it is legal only up until what's known as fetal viability, the point at which a fetus can live independently outside the womb. That typically occurs between twenty-three and twenty-five weeks of pregnancy, well after most abortions are performed. But Ashley wouldn't hear back about the second set of scans until she hit week twenty-four. The diagnosis came the day before her scheduled baby shower: the fetus had tested positive for Noonan syndrome, a rare chromosomal disorder. At first, it was hard to know what that meant. The condition presents differently from person to person, and there is no way to predict severity before someone is born. The diagnosis could mean very little. But on the flip side, it could result in her daughter being born with life-threatening heart problems. A worst-case scenario, they learned, meant her life would be short and painful.

Ashley and Nick spent three weeks agonizing over their decision, finally settling on termination. By the time she was able to schedule an abortion, the earliest she could be seen was in her thirtieth week of pregnancy, and the only state she could find an appointment in was Colorado. They'd have to book two last-minute plane tickets to travel to Boulder, a roughly three-and-a-half-hour flight away, and then stay in the city for five days, the length of time needed for her procedure and recovery. Given how late she was in pregnancy, the clinic staff told her on the phone, the procedure would cost $12,500. When she heard the number, she almost couldn't believe it. Ashley and Nick both worked, and they would be splitting the cost. But still, they didn't have that kind of money, and her health insurance wouldn't cover an abortion, a common restriction on how publicly funded health insurance programs such as Medicaid work, even in states that ostensibly protect access to the procedure. Her mind started racing through the possibilities. Could they spread the cost of the abortion out over a few credit cards? Maybe in time they'd be able to pay off the debt. It felt like their only option.

Ashley was learning something she'd be reminded of in the months and years to come, a phrase she'd hear repeatedly from staff at the abortion clinic and would quietly reiterate to herself: "Just because something is legal doesn't mean that there's access to it." And just because abortion was legal—in her home state of Michigan and in Colorado, a purported oasis of access—that still didn't mean it was easily available.

The clinic staffer recommended that Ashley make a few calls. Surely, she and Nick would be able to get some help. Cobalt, the Colorado abortion fund, pledged a few thousand dollars. They found another that could contribute a bit more. In the end, they called enough funds that they managed to get the entire cost of the procedure and most of the trip's expenses covered. Other than the rental car they'd pick up in Colorado, Ashley and Nick wouldn't have to pay a single cent out of pocket.

When, in late September, she returned home to Michigan, she

spent the next several months recovering—physically, but perhaps more importantly, emotionally. The care she had received was wonderful, Ashley said; the staff at the clinic were kind, supportive, and excellent at what they did. But a third-trimester abortion is an involved medical procedure. If Ashley wanted to get pregnant again, she'd have to wait at least six months. After appearing in public visibly pregnant, she'd have to return to work with no baby, no pregnancy, and no explanation—not one that she wanted to talk about with coworkers and acquaintances. Pregnant people often start lactating partway through their second trimester, and even after an abortion, their bodies can still produce milk. Now the milk in Ashley's breasts kept coming, a reminder of the pregnancy she'd lost. She started donating what she produced to a milk bank; her baby couldn't benefit from it, but, she hoped, maybe someone else's would.

After her home state voted to protect abortion rights, she mused ruefully on just how little those laws protected her when she needed it.

"Despite the fact that we were retaining the rights that we had, in my eyes, they just still weren't good enough. I was having to travel out of state to get care," she said. "It's just unthinkable to most people—having to make this impossible decision, and on top of that, adding to it the fact that I was going to have to fly halfway across the country to do so."

———————

In Colorado, money was and remains one of the biggest barriers for people seeking an abortion. Forty years ago, in 1984, state residents voted to amend their constitution to prohibit using state funds to pay for the procedure. (The amendment won by fewer than ten thousand votes, an incredibly slim margin.) In the post-*Dobbs* world, the implications of the state ban were more potent than ever. The policy precluded Colorado from taking the kinds of steps seen in other states where abortion was protected—allocating state funds directly to clinics, helping build new clinics, or supporting cash-strapped abortion funds—at a time when resources felt harder to come by than ever. And it had other implications: making abortion even less accessible for people in Colorado who earned less money and for whom the price tag of an abortion already represented a significant barrier.

A ban like Colorado's principally affects two groups of people: those who work for the state and who get their health insurance paid for through those jobs, and those who receive coverage through Medicaid, the government-backed health insurance program for people with low incomes, which is jointly funded by state and federal governments. Because of the ban on using federal money to pay for abortions, with an exception for cases of rape, incest, or if the pregnancy threatens the pregnant person's life, Medicaid will generally cover the procedure only if states choose to set aside money for it, a relatively rare benefit. In 2023, only seventeen states legally set aside money to let their Medicaid programs cover abortion; Colorado's funding ban prohibited the legislature from doing so. In practice, policies like this one amounted to an insurance carveout, and another example of the way the health care system continued to silo abortion away from other forms of medical care. People with Medicaid for their insurance could get most forms of medical treatment covered, but if they needed an abortion they'd have to pay for it themselves, finding hundreds of dollars at a minimum. And because people covered through the program already earned less money, the cost of an abortion represented an even more significant barrier to care. The state's funding restriction helped explain why so many people—including those who lived in Colorado, who didn't have to find a plane ticket or hotel room or last-minute babysitter—had long relied on the Cobalt Fund to help make an abortion attainable. Post-*Dobbs,* with the fund's resources stretched even thinner, the state funding ban had taken on a new level of significance. Every person asking for help covering their abortion costs was another dollar used, at a time when money was badly needed. Practically, the state law had racial implications, too, exacerbating an already stark divide in who was able to afford an abortion and those for whom getting one would represent immense financial hardship.

All across the United States, abortion had always been an issue with unequal racial impact, and the Medicaid restrictions exacerbated that disparity. Government data have long shown that

Black and Hispanic women are more likely than White ones to get abortions. The disparity, health care researchers say, largely stems from systemic economic discrimination and heightened barriers to medical care, including contraception—factors that increase the likelihood of experiencing an unintended pregnancy. That same economic inequality means that, nationwide, Medicaid disproportionately covers Black and Hispanic people. And the data in Colorado are particularly stark. About one in five of the state's residents identifies as Hispanic or Latino, per the U.S. Census Bureau, and about 4.7 percent are Black. But 39 percent of Coloradans on Medicaid identify as Hispanic, and 6.3 percent are Black. In practice, Hispanic, Latino, and Black people in Colorado were substantially more likely than White people to be covered by Medicaid; in turn, they faced greater odds of having health insurance that was explicitly banned from covering abortion. If they wanted or needed to terminate a pregnancy, they'd have to find the money on their own, securing hundreds of dollars at a minimum for an expense that was by definition unplanned. (More broadly speaking, just fewer than one in five people on Medicaid across the country is Black and about three in ten are Hispanic, making up a disproportionate share of the program's beneficiaries.)

All this was on Aurea Bolaños Perea's mind. An organizer at Denver-based COLOR—short for Colorado Organization for Latina Opportunity and Reproductive Rights—Bolaños Perea was particularly attuned to just how deeply people were affected by the state's funding ban and how potent the impact was in her community. COLOR had played a key role in lobbying the statehouse to pass its abortion rights protections in 2022, and she knew better than most how to secure support from the lawmakers likely to promote abortion access. With *Roe* overturned, she was on a new mission. If Colorado was going to protect abortion rights, the state had to make it more than just nominally available. It had to be something people could realistically afford, without the hovering fear of taking on credit card debt, of skipping groceries, or of falling behind on rent to find the money. What Colorado needed, she kept saying, was to get rid of its funding ban. The state had to treat abortion like any other kind of health care and let insurance pay for it.

Bolaños Perea, working in partnership with the team at Cobalt and activists affiliated with Planned Parenthood, would devote herself to that cause; for the next two years, she'd try to convince everyone she knew that legal abortion rights mattered little without a state policy that helped people actually access care. It was a different kind of campaign from what she'd done before. Because Coloradans had voted in favor of the funding ban forty years earlier, the only way to undo the policy was going not through the statehouse but instead directly to the state's millions of voters. They had to convince people that, come the next state election, in the fall of 2024, they should vote to allow the state government to start channeling money specifically toward helping people get abortions. And this, she knew, was going to be a far trickier sell.

In the wake of *Dobbs,* ballot initiatives—campaigns in which people voted directly on whether to protect abortion rights—had gained what felt almost like an aura of invincibility. It began with the Kansas election in August 2022, just a month after the Supreme Court ruling. Then, again, just three months later, voters in California, Kentucky, Michigan, Montana, and Vermont all separately turned out in droves to affirm abortion rights. Those elections felt like more evidence, building on what every public opinion survey had shown: the vast majority of Americans clearly didn't agree with state laws banning abortion or with the Supreme Court's decision to overturn *Roe.* Maybe, the thinking went, this sort of direct democracy offered a silver bullet, an easy way to undercut abortion bans and to expand access. In those early days, it wasn't uncommon to hear pundits suggest that abortion rights should simply be put to an election in every single state—and that, based on all the evidence available, voters would come out in overwhelming numbers both to shut down restrictions on the procedure and to vote in favor of abortion rights protections.

But the truth of it was more complicated. Direct votes aren't an option everywhere: almost half of all states don't allow for citizen-launched ballot initiatives, including Texas, the largest state in the country to outlaw abortion. In the wake of the 2022 elections, Republican state lawmakers instituted a bevy of proposed bills to raise the threshold for voter-initiated measures, requiring 60 or, in some cases, 66 percent approval for voters to amend the constitution. Most of the efforts arose in states where legislatures were already hostile to abortion, but also where public opinion data suggested that voters themselves opposed the wholesale abortion bans favored by state leadership. Those efforts didn't always work—in Idaho and Ohio, conservatives failed in their efforts to raise the threshold for voters to enshrine abortion protections—but they signified just how willing state-level Republicans were to change the rules of their elections if doing so would help in their fight against abortion rights.

Then there was the question of money: a massive campaign to win people over and bring them out to vote would be incredibly expensive. In Kansas, the campaign to protect abortion rights had raised millions of dollars, which organizers used to bankroll TV ads, direct mail, social media messaging, and canvassing across the state, both to bring out voters already likely to vote for abortion rights but also to convince people who might otherwise have been skeptical. It was a similar story in Kentucky, where the state's abortion rights coalition raised close to $5 million for its campaign. And it was true even in states that tilted less red. In purple-state Michigan, with a population roughly twice as big as Kentucky's (or, for that matter, Colorado's), the abortion rights organizing arm raised more than $40 million; Ohio-based abortion rights organizers raised $28 million between August and November 2023 to campaign for a Buckeye State protection that fall—yet another affirmative abortion rights measure that would succeed, and the first to do so in a conservative-led state. These were numbers that even a few years ago would have been unheard-of for state ballot campaigns. At a certain point, some abortion rights advocates worried, it raised different kinds of questions: Was this kind of strategy really scalable? And in a world where every dollar felt precious, what else could this kind of money have gone to?

Even the money was only one part of it. Perhaps trickiest of all was the substance of what message campaigns could transmit to voters, an issue with particular salience in Colorado. "Arguing the details is never especially effective," said Molly Murphy, president at Impact Research, a Democratically aligned public opinion firm in Washington, D.C. Murphy, a pollster for close to twenty years, knew what she was talking about. In the months after *Roe* fell, she ran poll after poll tracking how Americans felt about the decision, watching voters grow increasingly angry as restrictions piled up, and sat in more focus groups than she could count. Americans didn't want more limitations on abortion; that much was clear. Harder to gauge, though, was how they would react to proposals that seemed to expand access beyond the status quo. There was danger in getting too far into the weeds: talking to voters about the nuances of state funding law, of what it took to pay for an abortion and who should cover the cost. People simply didn't respond with the same kind of visceral anger and fear that a straightforward ban evoked. "You have to go back to this core idea that this is a fight between protecting access to abortion and blocking access to abortion," Murphy argued.

It wasn't lost on Bolaños Perea—twenty-eight years old, who got her political science master's while focusing on Latinas in politics—how much it would take to win in the state. Colorado was no stranger to abortion ballot votes, but in the past the state's reproductive rights organizers had always been coming from the other side of things: convincing voters to reject a proposed new restriction, rather than to solidify or expand protections. And they were pushing for a policy more complex than the abortion rights protections voters had enshrined in states like Michigan and Ohio. Her team had to translate the dry complexity of state funding policy into something that felt existential. How the state spent its money, she would have to argue, was an expression of a deeper value: whether individuals could decide for themselves if they needed an abortion, or whether the government deserved to pick and choose, and whether abortion should be treated separately from other forms of health care. It was a complex needle to thread, an argument that would require carefully wording the ballot initiative itself, making public funding seem like a natural extension of preserving the right to an abortion. Arguably, this campaign was one of the hardest that abortion rights advocates had ever run in the state. Convincing this many people would take time, money, and buy-in from every organizer, activist, and lawmaker they could find—from Colorado and from across the country. It meant TV and online ads, but also multilingual canvassing, ideally with people going from door to door to talk to voters. Estimates on what this kind of work would cost ranged widely, but in all likelihood organizers expected to need somewhere between $12 and $14 million if they were going to win.

As time passed, there were signs that their message might find a receptive audience. In the spring of 2023, Colorado lawmakers passed a host of new laws meant to bolster the state's abortion rights protections—including the increasingly popular form of legislation across bluer states, a bill that shielded health care providers from out-of-state prosecutions for procedures they performed in Colorado, and another bill that, among other changes, allowed the state's Medicaid program to cover the cost of transportation to and from an abortion appointment. "We did everything we could with the exception of letting Medicaid pay for the actual procedure," said Meg Froelich, a member of the state legislature and regular sponsor of abortion rights bills. Watching the process unfold, she felt more optimistic. The animosity toward abortion protections, she thought, seemed less powerful, at least in the capitol: in 2023, half as many people testified in opposition to the proposed new protections compared with a year before. The day after the legislature passed its abortion rights bills, only fifty activists showed up to protest outside the statehouse. At the same time, Colorado legislators had tried to broaden the coalition of reproductive rights. Their bill shielding abortion providers from out-of-state penalties also protected medical practitioners who offered other forms of marginalized health care—specifically, those who offered gender-affirming care. Between New Mexico and Colorado, it was a grouping that was growing more common in states whose lawmakers were considering how to protect abortion rights. And it made sense, Froelich said. The right to gender-affirming care and the right to an abortion were both backed by medical science; both forms of care were often lifesaving; the attacks on both were, she argued, grounded in an effort to restrict people's bodily autonomy, rather than any proven health concern. But this kind of grouping wasn't just good policy, she argued. She hoped it could prove smart politics as well.

"I think that's the other thing that helps us going into 2024," Froelich said. "The coalition is really strong, and broader than it was."

Abortion rights, it seemed, were a winning issue; across the country, that had proved to be true again and again. And Coloradans had a track record of winning. But for all the optimism state progressives were feeling, the uncertainty remained. Public opinion—especially on something like public funding of abortion—is tricky at best to gauge. And elections are dynamic; there are all sorts of reasons people do or don't vote, including what other initiatives might be on the ballot, whether there is a presidential race, or if another contested statewide race brings more people out.

Still, this was a campaign that organizers felt distinctly equipped to run. Among other Latino Coloradans, Bolaños Perea did her best to highlight the distinct implications the current state law had in her community. She talked about her mother, a public school teacher who paid taxes in the state of Colorado; if a woman like her ever needed an abortion, she would have to dig deep into her own pockets to find the money. At its core, Bolaños Perea believed, the argument she was making was obvious, and one that voters would take to heart: "It's economic justice," she said. "People shouldn't have to worry about what may happen if they have to choose between rent and [terminating their] pregnancy."

———————

The flight from Dallas to San Francisco is roughly four hours, and Darlene spent the bulk of it quietly weeping. After weeks of uncertainty, Darlene—accompanied by her husband and her young daughter—was on a journey to finally find out whether she could keep her baby or whether staying pregnant would kill her. At the time, even those four hours in the air felt risky. It was her first time flying since the onset of COVID-19; she felt so pregnant and so scared. Her doctor in Texas had told her never to be too far from a hospital. What if her uterus ruptured midflight? Would there be anyone who could help her?

There was a surreal quality to the trip. In a different life, they could have been an ordinary family, out here for vacation, not a desperate mother traveling out of state for a medical procedure that very well might be necessary to keep her alive. When Darlene first came to the San Francisco hospital, the doctors she met weren't sure how dire things might be, and if, as the pictures they'd gotten indicated, Darlene might need her uterus removed entirely. Depending on how bad it looked, she could be bedridden for weeks after, meaning they'd have to push back their return to Texas, extending how long her sister-in-law, who had traveled from Las Vegas to meet them in San Francisco, would help with child-care and how many hundreds or even thousands of dollars they'd spend on their hotel. The money felt in some ways like a secondary concern—Darlene kept remembering that her life was on the line— but it still registered in the background. It was a grim reminder that if she and her husband hadn't been financially secure, she wouldn't have been able to come here at all. Just getting more information about her pregnancy, and learning whether it was even safe to keep, was a privilege she could access only because they had the extra money to fly halfway across the country.

Measuring the gestational age in pregnancy is imprecise at best, and what looks like nineteen weeks to one physician might look more like twenty-one to another. But Darlene was by now around twenty weeks pregnant, still just within the deadline to receive an abortion in California, which, like Michigan, cuts off access at the point of fetal viability. Before coming, she'd told the clinic staff about her condition, that she was fairly sure she would need an abortion, and that she didn't have much time. She couldn't get over how lucky she felt to get here when she did; had she been forced to wait much longer, she wasn't sure which hospital would have been able to take her or where she'd be able to go.

It was Darlene's first doctor's appointment accompanied by her husband, and the clinic here was nothing like what she had expe-rienced at home: the doctors radiated a sense of confidence she hadn't experienced in ages. They had the tools to figure out what was wrong and to assess how dangerous her pregnancy was—even the machines here seemed different, newer and yielding clearer, more detailed pictures. They could figure things out that nobody in Dallas or Houston had been able to. And if Darlene did need an abortion, that was something they could safely, easily provide her. Somehow, she already felt calmer here than she had ever since becoming pregnant; here, she knew, she'd be able to get whatever health care she needed, without worrying that her doctors might be hamstrung by state laws. Before beginning her tests, the staff had also called her insurance to confirm she was covered. The couple might have had to foot the bill for their travel, but they wouldn't have to worry about what her treatment here would cost. It felt like another good omen, and a welcome relief, however small—good news this year had felt so difficult to come by.

After reviewing Darlene's results, the doctor delivered her assessment. Things weren't great, but they weren't nearly as bad as they might be. She'd certainly cared for patients with weaker uteruses than this one—from what she could see, she estimated Darlene had maybe a one in ten chance of hers rupturing during the pregnancy. It wasn't a ringing vote of confidence, but it was hardly the disaster scenario she'd spent all these months fearing.

Still, when they heard the results, Darlene wasn't quite sure what to do. To her husband, the answer seemed obvious: a one in ten chance was far too risky. What if the worst-case scenario did happen? What if this pregnancy did kill Darlene? It was her decision, he said, but if it were up to him he'd say she should terminate the pregnancy.

But the doctor could see it in Darlene's face: she just wasn't ready to decide yet. Jumping in, she offered to get a bit more information. If, eventually, Darlene did decide to have an abortion, she'd have to undergo a proper surgery. The clinicians would need to have more detailed visuals about what things looked like inside her uterus. Why not do an MRI, too? The full-body scan would yield more information—and maybe it might help her make a fully informed decision about what was best for her.

None of this had ever felt like an option in Texas. After all, the subtext had been: Why bother collecting more details, especially if it might suggest the need for an abortion? It wasn't like she'd be able to get one anyway. What good would it do?

After the MRI, the doctor delivered even better news. Based on these pictures, Darlene's uterus looked healthier than she had expected. At this point, the odds of rupture seemed quite low: maybe around 4 or 5 percent. If she didn't want to get an abortion, the physicians here would do everything they could to help with her pregnancy and to make sure she stayed healthy. The doctor wrote down some notes. She recommended Darlene get a follow-up visit every two weeks. Here, in her record, was a set of questions she should ask at each visit. Here were numbers representing what her uterine thickness should look like. As long as things stayed where they were, Darlene shouldn't worry too much. She shouldn't let her doctor convince her to get an early C-section, instead letting her pregnancy progress for as long as possible. And if she had any other questions, everyone in San Francisco would be there for her, no more than a phone call away.

They decided to sleep on it. Darlene and her husband had already scheduled an appointment for an abortion, forty-eight hours later. They had time—or, rather, Darlene had time—to figure out what to do. But in some instinctual part of her, she already knew. When Darlene called the next day to cancel her appointment, explaining that in a twist of good fortune, it looked like she should be able to safely continue her pregnancy, she could hear the smile at the other end of the line. The woman at the clinic sounded so happy for her; she could tell that, when Darlene became a mom again, it would be a choice she'd been able to make for herself.

CHAPTER 7

Even the Best-Laid Plans

New York

It had been decades since Keren Form discovered her own unintended pregnancy, back when she was a college student at New York University and nowhere near ready to be a parent. She'd always understood abortion as essential; it was a medical procedure that she'd needed and that she'd quickly accessed to end her pregnancy. It shouldn't be any more complicated than that. Yet even in New York, access was something she'd never felt could be taken for granted. She told the story often of how her mother had been born in a New York Catholic hospital, where abortions are typically not performed. But abortion is permissible according to her family's Jewish faith, so when his wife was in labor, Form's grandfather had been deliberate in making his point clear: if anything went wrong with the birth, saving her had to be the hospital's first priority, no matter what that meant for the pregnancy. The idea that this was something he even had to ask for offered a lesson that had stayed with Form since she was young.

When Donald Trump was elected in 2016, Form's worries about abortion access grew. The nation had voted for a president who promised he'd overturn *Roe,* and it seemed like only a matter of time before he succeeded. In New York, she knew, Democrats controlled the state government, and they generally supported abortion rights, but she worried about the implications for people who could no longer get an abortion where they lived, who if they were lucky might be able to travel out of state for a procedure, coming to a place like her home city. So six years before the *Dobbs* decision—a lifetime ago, it felt like—Form signed up to volunteer at Choices Women's Medical Center, a reproductive health clinic in Queens whose opening predated 1973. There, she helped escort patients past anti-abortion protesters, getting them safely inside the clinic. It seemed like a way to get involved and to offer what support she could to the people who needed abortions. The work had always felt important, if draining. The clinic was frequently filled with patients who came there because it was the only place within their budget. She heard from the people who were seeking an abortion because they had been raped, because their pregnancy was no longer viable, or because they were struggling already and could not afford another child. Someday, she told herself, the work would be even harder—because someday New York would be the destination.

If any place in the country could absorb the patients seeking abortions post-*Dobbs,* the thinking went, it had to be New York. The state was an early adopter in the effort to legalize abortion, passing a law in 1970—three whole years before *Roe* was decided— that would allow people to terminate a pregnancy if they were earlier than twenty-four weeks along and that didn't require that people live in New York to receive care. It was transformative: in the first two years after the law was passed, more than four hundred thousand abortions were performed in the state, with the majority for people who had traveled to New York from somewhere else. Billboards advertised New York as an abortion hub; magazines printed advertisements noting that this was a state where you could safely and legally terminate a pregnancy.

New York had done it before, and post-*Dobbs* it could do it again. It was arguably an even more prominent access hub today than it had been fifty years ago, now home to more than one hun- dred abortion-focused clinics, with another hundred medical facilities in the state also providing the service. In 2019, three years before the Supreme Court decision, New York had passed its own law strengthening the state's abortion protections. And in 2022, anticipating the looming end of *Roe,* New York's governor implemented new policies meant to further expand abortion rights in the state, including funding grants to support the state's abortion care network and signing legislation that ostensibly protected health care providers if, while in New York, they performed an abortion for someone who had traveled from a state where the procedure was illegal. Between the three major airports in New York City, the train system, and buses, getting to New York—to the city or to another clinic in the state—seemed easier than traveling to lots of other places that had positioned themselves as abortion oases.

It wasn't necessarily that simple. There were still people like Darlene who, despite all their efforts, couldn't find a physician in the state willing to treat them. But the idea of New York as an abortion refuge to many wasn't unreasonable on its face. With *Roe* gone, the state's abortion clinics, like those in other destination states, started seeing a steady increase in the number of patients who had traveled from out of state. Before *Dobbs,* Choices Women's Medical Center reported 3 to 4 percent of patients as from somewhere other than New York. A year later, the proportion had increased about fivefold, with almost 20 percent of abortion patients saying they had traveled to the clinic from another state. Escorts noticed more and more patients coming from farther away, sometimes for their first trip ever to New York, even arriving at the abortion clinic with their luggage in tow.

This pattern was emerging across the country, and in New York, too, it had obvious implications for the state's abortion support network. The New York Abortion Access Fund, the state's largest, was operated almost completely by volunteers, people who donated their time, energy, and money to the cause. NYAAF was pledging more money to abortion-seeking patients than it ever had before, fueled by demand from people traveling to New York, even as, just like abortion funds across the country, NYAAF served only a fraction of the people who traveled to the state for care. The spike in callers was obvious almost right away, said Alia Tejeda, a volunteer who worked exclusively on answering calls from people traveling from out of state. Elizabeth Estrada, who volunteered on the abortion fund's Spanish-language calling service, still mostly found herself advising people from New York City, people for whom an abortion was unaffordable despite the state's laws protecting access. But she too found herself talking more to people who had called from states where new abortion bans had taken effect or where increases in out-of-state patients had made timely care impossible to come by: states such as Georgia, Texas, and North and South Carolina. The people who called were some-times lost as to where to go in the city for a procedure and afraid to seek financial assistance to help cover the costs, almost embar-rassed by having to ask for money. A year after the *Dobbs* decision, with bans looming in more states, NYAAF's executive director had begun to worry that the donations they received couldn't keep up with the increasing need for money; in 2023 alone, the organization expected to allocate close to $2 million for abortion support.

Most people who came to the city traveled there because they had a friend or relative to stay with, but a growing number—those who came simply because it was the cheapest flight or bus or train they could book, home to the only clinic with an appointment in less than six weeks, or the place where somehow an abortion cost the least—started to rely as well on free homestays with strangers, coordinated through a volunteer group called the Haven Coalition, which hosted people who traveled for abortions and helped drive them to and from appointments. The organization had existed for decades, but in the past had largely helped people who came to New York City—sometimes from other states, but often just from elsewhere in New York—because they were in their second trimester already and didn't live near any clinics that provided care that far along. After *Dobbs,* by contrast, people came for homestays from all over the South while they were early in their first trimester, because their home states had made abortions illegal for all or most of pregnancy.

In terms of health care access, calculating the impact of that influx remained difficult. Wait times for appointments fluctuated from week to week, as clinics in different parts of the state struggled to balance surges in patients from out of state. These surges were impossible to predict, varying based on whether a different state's abortion ban had been recently unblocked by the courts, or per-haps whether a clinic in another access state had its only physician go on parental leave, or even if a clinic had to cancel appointments because of a snowstorm. "Any of those things can dramatically shift access," said Georgana Hanson, who headed Planned Parenthood Empire State Acts, the advocacy arm of New York's Planned Parenthood clinics. The impact of those delays in care didn't always fall evenly, worried Estrada, who, separately from her volunteering, worked as a community organizer with the National Latina Institute for Reproductive Justice, which advocates for improved Latina access to reproductive health care of all forms. She had long noted how unequal abortion access already was, especially in the Bronx, where she lived. Frequently, she asked callers if they had Medicaid, which in New York covers the cost of an abortion. Over the years, she had noticed that undocumented New Yorkers, even those with low incomes who would qualify for the benefit, still hesitated to sign up for a government-offered health insurance plan because they were afraid that filling out too many forms could jeopardize their status in the United States. It was a systemic inequality that meant paying for an abortion would still represent an enormous, in some cases insurmountable, hurdle. Post-*Dobbs*, things were even more difficult, and it felt to Estrada like the burden was hitting her community the hardest. She was increasingly hearing from other New Yorkers, largely Spanish speakers, who had tried to schedule an abortion only to be told that there were no slots available for weeks. It was a shift from the old days, she recalled, back when patients could generally count on being seen within seven days.

For those traveling from out of state, if they could make it to New York City and secure an appointment, getting care could feel relatively doable, compared with what patients were used to back home. It still meant counting on a million things going right, which often relied on factors patients couldn't control. Keren Form escorted one patient, a woman from Texas who had traveled to Queens for care only to learn that, actually, she couldn't get her abortion as scheduled. Clinics often advise that people not eat for several hours prior to a surgical abortion, but this woman wasn't aware that she was supposed to fast before her appointment. She had eaten earlier in the day. The clinic couldn't find an opening to reschedule her before her return flight, and she wasn't sure if she'd be able to make the journey back to New York, or to any other state where abortion was legal. She didn't know how she'd be able to take the time off work for another trip, let alone pay for another round-trip plane ticket on a weekend, which she knew would be more expensive. Form tried to help her find an organization that might at least help cover the cost of airfare. But she never heard from the woman again or found out if she'd been able to get her abortion.

If you were one of the lucky ones, though—if every star aligned, if the hotel was within reach and the airfare affordable—people who traveled to New York from states with abortion bans often marveled at how much easier it seemed to access care. It could be isolating and painful, and the fear lingered about facing legal risks or judgment once patients returned home, if anyone found out what they had done. But at the very least, New York's clinics could see patients relatively quickly and had few state-mandated hoops to jump through.

Carla, a twenty-six-year-old woman from Houston, found out she was pregnant just a week before a planned work trip to Manhattan; her period was two days late, and then the cramps and nausea she experienced prompted her to take a pregnancy test. She knew without hesitation that she wanted an abortion, but she didn't want to involve another voice in the decision—she wouldn't tell her boyfriend, with whom she lived, and certainly not her parents, who had immigrated to Texas from Mexico and whose Catholic faith, she knew, formed the basis for their opposition to abortion. Carla had looked online to see if she might be able to order abortion pills to be sent discreetly to her house, but everything she read suggested it could take as long as six weeks for the medication to arrive. At that point, she worried, she'd be thirteen weeks pregnant, too late for medication to reliably end her pregnancy. And there would be no way to conceal the abortion from her boyfriend if she took the pills in their home.

Sneaking the visit into her New York trip was the only real option. Only days before her work trip, Carla found an appointment at Planned Parenthood and rescheduled her flight, choosing the earliest one possible. Unlike with Darlene, her pregnancy was still early and her medical needs uncomplicated—she had no trou-

ble whatsoever finding an appointment in New York City. But putting the trip together was still grueling. Carla landed in New York
at ten a.m., five hours before she had originally planned, giving her
just enough time to drop her bags at the hotel her company had
booked and rush to the appointment she'd been offered, a one p.m.
slot for a surgical abortion at the clinic on Bleecker Street. It was
the only logical choice: they could finish the procedure that afternoon, and she'd leave the clinic knowing with almost absolute
certainty she was no longer pregnant. She wouldn't have to worry
about follow-up symptoms the next day, while she was meeting
with clients, or about coming home to Texas to discover that the
abortion hadn't worked or that she needed more medical care. All
the same, Carla was nervous upon arriving at the clinic. Everyone
around her had someone with them, a significant other or a friend.
It made the contrast feel even more stark. The circumstances under
which she'd been able to come here meant that she was all alone—
she couldn't even accept a sedative during her procedure because
there was no one to help her walk back to the hotel after.

Typically, the clinic would have charged $600 for an abortion at
her stage in pregnancy. But based on her income it was able to pull
from other funds it had reserved for patients in need. Carla would
pay only $150, far less than she'd dared to hope might be possible.
Still, the process was exhausting. Including the financial counseling, the ultrasound, the wait time, and her actual procedure, Carla
spent four hours at the clinic, leaving around five p.m. to wander
back to her hotel. She'd been on the go since three a.m., when she
had woken up to head to the Dallas airport. It was difficult to process just how much she'd been through that day, and even harder
to realize that no one in her life knew what had happened. She'd
walk in to work tomorrow and fly home at the end of the week,
resuming her life with her family with nobody the wiser about her
abortion.

Even in her state of fatigue, Carla couldn't get over how lucky
she'd been. Like Darlene, she kept marveling at the contrast between how available abortions seemed in a bluer state. Everything
in New York was so much easier than it would have been at home,
even before Texas had banned abortion altogether. There were
no waiting periods in New York, no second visits or mandatory

counseling. And it felt like there were clinics all over the city, with appointments available at any time she could have wanted. It felt so unfair—she'd been able to get her abortion only by a stroke of good timing and company resources she knew other people didn't have. All day, she kept asking herself the same questions: *What if I wasn't here? What would I have done?* She couldn't come up with an answer.

The post-*Dobbs* reality and stories like Carla's offered a sense of déjà vu. Now, just like in the pre-*Roe* world from more than fifty years earlier, New York health providers were seeing patients from across the country. And people like Donna Schaper—a Protestant minister in the city—hoped that even in the new world order there was something they might be able to do to help. It wouldn't be the first time. Schaper had been part of the pre-*Roe* network of faith leaders who helped people seeking abortions through the organization known as the Clergy Consultation Service on Abortion, founded in the late 1960s by two ministers who practiced in Greenwich Village. It was a radical proposition, even then, but born of a simple idea: people were dying because they couldn't access safe abortion services. The job of faith leaders was to help their parishioners, and connecting those in need to abortion services fell under that umbrella. After the failure of a 1965 proposal to decriminalize abortion in New York, the network's leaders set themselves to work, learning about abortion from physicians who provided the service and speaking with lawyers about the legal penalties they could face if prosecuted for connecting people with care. One woman, a church employee named Arlene Carmen, even pretended to be pregnant to assess the services of various physicians, including learning what they would charge and how they treated patients. In 1967, *The New York Times* ran a front-page article announcing the existence of the faith-led abortion referral network.

The Clergy Consultation Service worked with pregnant people across the nation. Schaper, then studying to be a minister, worked out of Chicago, helping hundreds of people get abortions and staying in touch to provide support for those who ultimately decided to keep their unplanned pregnancies. The work felt like a natural extension of how she understood religion and of the kind of faith leader she hoped to be—one who, in her words, rejected the notion of a God who just "made women to be baby carriers." In 2023, post-*Dobbs,* she believed fervently there had to be a role religious leaders could play in helping people access abortions again. Already, she knew of a group in New Mexico, the Religious Coalition for Reproductive Choice, a descendant of her organization, that helped people pay for abortions. But New York was no longer the same nexus it had been fifty years ago. When Schaper traveled to Mexico, where she picked up medication abortion pills, she thought that maybe they could stockpile them in the church, distributing them to people in need the way they did for opioid overdose medications. If anyone came to her for help, she would do her best to provide resources. But the need in New York City for a group like hers wasn't the same as it once was—abortion was legal there, and there were clinics and medical services that provided care. People didn't need to come to a church next to Washington Square Park and ask the minister for pills, or even to help them find a doctor who might help. Organizations like hers were far more useful in Texas or New Mexico, where the Religious Coalition for Reproductive Choice worked to help people fly from Dallas to New Mexico for abortion services. And even more challenging was that, in 1967, ministers had felt some level of security advertising their services on the front page of the newspaper—something that was inconceivable in post-*Dobbs* America, reflected Abigail Hastings, one of the church's archivists. "I don't think anybody's safe anymore," Hastings said. "What we're in now is very much of a Big Brother situation, where people are willing to rat out each other. There's no sense of safety or privacy."

What people like Schaper and Hastings would eventually realize was that, even if New York could be an access point, it was unlikely—perhaps impossible—that it would ever be what it once was.

———

After deciding to go through with her pregnancy, Darlene called her oldest sister. Yes, she was still terrified, but she wanted to start sharing the good news. So far, everything looked like it would be okay. The doctors thought she could give birth to her little girl.

Her sister was circumspect. "Well," she told Darlene, "this kid's a fighter." But Darlene could hear the worry in her sister's voice, the fear she would hear from so many friends and loved ones each time she said that she was going to go forward with her pregnancy. They knew this was what she wanted—but if something went wrong, they all seemed to wonder, could she really count on the physicians in her home state to take care of her?

It wasn't just fear for her health, though. Soon after the California trip, Darlene and her family flew up to Washington State, where she had grown up. It was a partial reunion on her side, a chance to celebrate her niece's high school graduation. When her father asked about her visible pregnancy, she told the truth: it was wanted but unplanned, and on the advice of her doctors she had previously looked into whether she could or should terminate it. For now, she was hopeful she could keep her baby, but there was still a chance things could go wrong.

It was a conversation she had practiced in her head more times than she could count. But, still, she couldn't fully prepare herself for his reaction. The risks to her health—or to her baby's—didn't seem to matter to him. Her father couldn't believe she would consider an abortion. He was, in her words, mortified that she even brought it up. How could this be the daughter he had raised? How could she think of doing such a thing?

Darlene hadn't even gotten an abortion, but she could tell that her father would never look at her the same way. Even considering it, even when her life was at risk, was somehow unforgivable.

Every two weeks, Darlene kept going back to the doctor, bringing the same list of questions and the uterine thickness numbers she'd saved from her trip to California. Now that she'd come back home to Texas, the contrast with California was impossible to overlook. In San Francisco, everyone had been eager and excited to help, confident in the care they'd been able to provide and sure they could help her make the right decision. Back home, the doctors seemed hesitant, nervous to offer medical advice and surprised at Darlene's comfort with staying pregnant. At her thirty-six-week checkup, the doctor asked if she was ready to give birth; they could perform a cesarean section that week. She'd no longer be pregnant, and the risk to her life would be over. Why keep pushing it?

It wasn't what Darlene wanted. At that stage in pregnancy, every week can count toward having a healthier baby. And cesarean sections are invasive, high-risk procedures—more dangerous than the abortions Texas had outlawed. Meanwhile, a baby born at thirty-six weeks, though likely to survive, is technically considered premature and can require intensive care upon delivery, sometimes suffering what is known as respiratory distress syndrome or having a low birth weight. Once again, she checked her uterine numbers; when they seemed fine, she asked her doctors if there was any chance they could hold off two more weeks before scheduling a C-section. She'd make it to thirty-eight weeks, giving her little girl a bit more time to grow in utero before she gave birth.

Days before her scheduled delivery, Darlene ran into a friend she hadn't seen in months, a neighbor who worked in health care. In the weeks before Darlene had discovered her pregnancy, they'd sat together and tried to diagnose what might be wrong with her—if perhaps her nausea and fatigue might stem from an illness that she'd contracted sitting in the hot tub one evening. When Darlene learned she was pregnant, her friend had urged her to leave the state for an abortion. Her explanation: *We can't worry about you for the next four or five months.* When she decided against termination, Darlene made it a point not to see her neighbor—she didn't want more people worrying about her than absolutely necessary.

Darlene's pregnancy was obvious when they saw each other again; she could see the tears in her friend's eyes as she realized that Darlene was still pregnant.

"I'm glad you hadn't told me," she told Darlene. "I would have been scared every day."

—•—

The impact of *Dobbs* was and remains complex and multifaceted—and the implications in a large metropolis like New York City naturally looked different from what clinics experienced in other parts of the state. But no matter where one practiced, the changes were impossible to miss. With more abortion bans taking effect, Planned

Parenthood of Central and Western New York, which operated nine clinics largely near Rochester and Buffalo, saw patients from more than twenty different states, estimated Michelle Casey, the health system's CEO. The influx varied, depending on where and when neighboring abortion bans took effect: Ohio, for instance, enforced a six-week ban for almost three months before the law was blocked by state courts; in the period when abortion was outlawed in that state, the number of non–New Yorkers the Planned Parenthood affiliate saw increased threefold. Clinics in New York couldn't adequately plan ahead for when they might see a surge in patients—they depended entirely on decisions made by courts and legislatures hundreds of miles away. And still, the largest share of patients came not from Texas, Ohio, or anywhere else where abortion was at any point outlawed: they traveled from western Pennsylvania, where abortion was legal up until twenty-four weeks, but where, especially farther away from Pittsburgh, there weren't enough clinics to see everyone seeking care. It illustrated just how stretched abortion clinics were and how insufficient the supply was—even in states that didn't have an active ban.

For Casey, an ardent Buffalo Bills fan who had worked for decades in health care administration, the cases she saw now were some of the most harrowing she'd ever known. There were patients who drove more than twenty hours each way from Texas to Buffalo because it was the only way they could afford to travel and the soonest appointment they could come by. One woman flew to New York from Texas the morning of her abortion and was booked on a flight to return home that same night, a tight timeline for completing her procedure. She needed a first-trimester surgical abortion, which is typically simple to perform, but she had what is called a tipped or retroverted uterus; her uterus faced backward, toward her spine, instead of forward. There isn't a meaningful medical risk that comes from a tipped uterus, but it makes the process of doing an abortion more difficult. "It really does cause a lot of unnecessary trauma and expense and just mental anguish to the people who need to go to those extra limits, or extra efforts, to travel for care," Casey said. Because the surges in patient demand were so hard to predict, the clinics relied on their ability to provide multiple termination options—surgical procedures but also, critically, medication abortions, which were faster and simpler for her clinics to provide, and easier to scale up. But much like in California, while the increase in patients was noticeable and a source of strain, it wasn't enough to overwhelm the health systems—at least, not the way it had in states like New Mexico, Kansas, or Colorado. The increase in New York was actually about the same as that in Kansas—in the first six months post-*Dobbs,* the state reported about 207 more patients per month than it had before—but New York State had far more abortion providers to absorb that increase. There was still time and space to see everyone. When things got particularly bad, abortion providers added an extra clinic day each week.

If anything, some providers in New York believed they should be even more on the front lines—just like they had been in the early 1970s. There were physicians like Dr. Linda Prine, a doctor at Mount Sinai who had been providing abortions since the 1990s and was licensed to practice both in New Mexico and in New York. When she wasn't in the clinic, Prine staffed what was known as the Miscarriage and Abortion Hotline, an anonymous phone service she'd helped launch in 2019, through which physicians helped guide people through either medical process. The hotline didn't provide pills or prescriptions, but it had all the same become a lifeline for people who had ordered medication online and wanted to self-manage their abortions at home. Since starting the hotline, Prine had found herself talking to people from all over the country who had for whatever reason chosen to end their pregnancies on their own and who needed medical support. But the phone calls she received now troubled her in a new way. More often, people were attempting to self-manage their abortions later in pregnancy, seeing if pills might still work for them when they were at week fifteen or week twenty. It was a testament to just how difficult it had grown for people to access medication abortions—the demand was such that people were waiting weeks for their package to arrive, pushing their pregnancies to the point where pills simply aren't as effective, and with no other realistic options for getting an abortion. Now, rather than passing large blood clots, as is normal in a first-trimester medication abortion, patients were calling to say they were attempting to expel a small fetus into their home bathtubs. Others were worried because, as a result of attempting a medication abortion so late, their placentas had gotten stuck, and they weren't sure how to complete the process.

Prine and her colleagues had developed solutions for these types of questions. If patients had extra doses of misoprostol, the second medication typically taken, that could help them complete the abortion. They could use their fingertips to gently massage their uterus, leveraging the pressure to push out the remaining tissue. And if things didn't resolve, she'd recommend they go to the hospital and tell the clinicians on duty that they were having a spontaneous miscarriage—which many patients, terrified of being caught in a lie, were often hesitant to do.

Prine had made a new argument to New York lawmakers. Getting to the state was still too difficult for many people who needed an abortion. The desperation she heard from callers highlighted to her that the most meaningful thing the state's doctors could do was help send more medications to patients in states where abortion was illegal. In her mind, the state should pass a law that protected New York doctors, making sure they weren't vulnerable to criminal charges from another state. She pointed to the law passed in Massachusetts and found an ally in Albany who pushed a telemedicine shield bill through the state legislature. The state's Democratic governor signed that bill into law just before June 24, 2023—one full year after *Dobbs*. California, too, would follow in New York's footsteps a few months later, passing a similar shield law.

But the arguments for whether such a law would actually work divided abortion rights supporters, including in New York. The New York Civil Liberties Union, an affiliate of the national ACLU, had been worried for months about the inherent limitations of laws passed by its own state government. Its lawyers did their best, trying to advise state legislators on potential loopholes or weaknesses in the state's shield bill, hoping to make it as bulletproof as possible. Still, "no state can protect its folks beyond its borders from the laws of another state," worried Donna Lieberman, the NYCLU's executive director, who'd founded its reproductive rights initiative. "What it can do is protect them from state consequences—from New York consequences." There was no way, she argued, New York could guarantee that it would protect doctors from being prosecuted under Texas or Oklahoma or Alabama state law.

Certainly, laws like this would make some difference. As shield laws like New York's had begun to take effect in a handful of states across the country, Aid Access, the European service through which Americans could order pills, began working with American physicians, tasking doctors in protected states with prescribing and mailing the medication abortion regimen to people in states with bans. In three weeks, more than 3,500 people in states with abortion bans mail-ordered pills from a handful of health care providers in other American states who were willing to take the risk that untested shield laws would in fact protect them. In theory, physicians like Prine hoped, this could shorten the wait time patients faced when ordering pills; she hoped more doctors in states with such laws would join her ranks in mailing medications. But although this service was and remained meaningful, making abortion pills available to many who otherwise couldn't access them, there was no way it could reach every person in need. It certainly wouldn't benefit people like Carla, Angela, or Darlene, none of whom would have been able to rely on pills mailed to their homes. It couldn't have helped someone like Tiff, who didn't have a private online bank account or credit card she could use to pay. And even with laws like New York's in place, not all health care providers would be as willing to endanger their professions, their licenses, and their livelihoods to try to mail medication abortion pills across state lines. Arguably, most wouldn't. Prine, for one, couldn't predict how many pills they would be able to mail to people in states with abortion bans over the course of a single year, let alone years to come, or whether their model was financially sustainable, or—despite the interest she heard expressed by more than a hundred other doctors—whether a team like hers would have the manpower to supply pills to everyone in need. "It's like a video game where things are coming at you from the top and the side and the bottom," she said. "You have to figure out which you need to hit, and it's too hard to figure out."

Jen Kerns, the California physician, wasn't sure what she would do when given the option—despite being the type of doctor who was more willing to stretch the limits of abortion restrictions, she worried about jeopardizing her Kansas license if law enforcement there discovered she had prescribed abortion pills to someone in a state that banned access. And the idea that this kind of prescription would be widely adopted? It was too much to ask.

"You're talking about people's livelihoods and careers. That could be in jeopardy for doing something like this," Kerns said. "It's a tricky and unfair thing to expect of people."

———•———

Even without taking on the risk of prescribing out of state, providers in New York already faced substantial dangers for simply doing their jobs. As far back as the state's history as an abortion haven went, so went its history as one where providers faced stigma, harassment, and even violence. In 1981, a clinic on Staten Island had actually shut down, citing the threatening phone calls, graffiti, and efforts by anti-abortion activists to track down patients' families and reveal that they were at an abortion clinic. More recently, a few weeks after *Dobbs,* a man from the Bronx attempted to stop a clinic in Hempstead, New York, from seeing patients, supergluing chains and locks to the facility's gate. A month later, abortion opponents had attempted to infiltrate a Planned Parenthood in Brooklyn, pretending that they were patients. While threats and infiltration can be prosecuted under the law, verbal protests—the kinds prevalent outside clinics in every borough of New York City—are considered protected free speech. In Queens, the escorts recognized the people who showed up each weekend, and they noticed patterns emerge: protesters were careful to tailor their words to individuals and occasions, perhaps tying their remarks to Mother's Day, speaking in Spanish if they thought that was a patient's native language, or yelling at people who they thought were Black or Hispanic that the doctors inside the abortion clinic were promoting a racial genocide. If they thought someone was Jewish, they would reference the Holocaust. This kind of targeted harassment didn't technically stop people from accessing abortion. But it fostered the sense that there was something for patients to be ashamed of in coming to the clinic—whether for an abortion, to manage a miscarriage for a wanted pregnancy, or because this clinic was simply the most affordable place to get a pap smear.

That culture of stigma spurred a perpetual fear of violence against abortion providers, with arguably greater consequences outside New York City, where care was already harder to find. In 1998, a doctor near Buffalo who performed abortions had been killed by a sniper, an attack that providers at the time noted resembled other attacks on abortion-providing physicians in the area. It was the kind of traumatizing incident people didn't forget. Even decades later, many providers in the community were hesitant to talk too loudly about their work providing abortions.

And the threats and stigma were still just one facet; in New York, like so many states even with abortion-friendly leadership, abortion clinics had long struggled to make ends meet. Part of the challenge here came from the state's Medicaid program, which, unlike in Colorado, generally covers people's abortions, and not just in cases of rape, incest, or life endangerment. But the benefit was still limited, a function of how Medicaid works. Research shows that in states with Medicaid coverage, more people are able to access abortions than in those that lack the benefit—but it still came with complications. As with any other covered service, the state government sets a limit for what the program will pay, and again like with any other service, what Medicaid pays is often far lower than the cost of actually providing the service. That means that even when a clinic is paid it still can actually lose money on providing an abortion. The payment gap is meaningful for procedures at all stages, said Tracy Weitz, a sociology professor at American University who studies abortion financing, but it's particularly acute for abortions performed in the second trimester—which is one of the reasons that many clinics choose not to offer that service. Nuances in how health system contracts are negotiated and regulated mean that it's incredibly difficult to find data illustrating what Medicaid actually pays clinics for abortions, and it depends in part on the type of Medicaid plan someone has. Still, one study found that, on average, many state programs cover less than half the costs of actually providing abortion care; that paper, one of its authors said, likely underestimated the scope of the loss. From an economics standpoint, those kinds of deficits were and are hard to sustain, and it's even more challenging for providers that don't see a large volume of patients—those that serve smaller communities or where people have to drive farther for care—and that still have to pay for things like clinic space, employee salaries, malpractice insurance, and medical equipment. The low reimbursement rate also meant that some clinics didn't even bother accepting Medicaid; they couldn't make the numbers work.

There is, some health finance researchers say, an obvious solution: states could choose to increase what Medicaid will pay for abortion services. But in reality that happens rarely—again, often a result of the stigma against abortion and, Weitz argued, a sense that people place a lower value on the procedure because they don't believe they would ever need it. In New York, the state's Medicaid reimbursement rate for abortions hadn't been increased in more than a decade. There had been other short-term initiatives by the state to invest money in abortion clinics, notably the tens of millions of dollars distributed in response to *Dobbs*. This kind of money was helpful, though on its own couldn't close the funding gap that had only grown larger over the years. What little research existed suggested that New York's Medicaid payment rates had for years lagged behind that of comparable states: someone providing an abortion in Massachusetts, for instance, was likely to earn more than someone in New York. The stagnant payment rates meant that providers who were paid through Medicaid had long operated on incredibly slim margins and often struggled to recruit staff. It wasn't surprising; on top of the threats and harassment people would face, why take a lower-paying job in abortion care when you could earn far more in virtually any other medical field? In 2023, the state's governor, Democrat Kathy Hochul, approved a budget that would finally increase how much money the state's Medicaid program paid for surgical abortions by 30 percent, a proposal that the legislature would approve later that spring. It didn't increase reimbursement at all for medication abortions. Providers hailed the increase as badly needed, even if they had hoped for more— but it still couldn't rebuild an underfunded system overnight, one that over the years had felt as if it were held together by metaphorical duct tape, and that they feared would face even greater strains when more states passed abortion bans in the months and years to come.

The history of financial neglect had visible implications across the state. Eleven abortion clinics provided care within roughly an hour's drive of Albany—but only four of those sites provided in-clinic surgical abortion procedures in addition to medication abortions or were able to provide abortions for anyone in their second trimester. From Syracuse, farther west, there were only four abortion clinics you could drive to in an hour. Past twenty weeks, it was almost impossible to find an abortion provider without traveling a minimum of two hours—by finding care in New York City or its immediate suburbs, or by leaving the state entirely. "People have been traveling for years," said Katharine Bodde, a reproductive rights–focused lawyer at the NYCLU. The fragility of abortion access upstate was easy to see in New York City as well; whenever a new pressure point emerged farther north, more patients turned to the city for care. There was a story that Karen Duda, the woman who coordinated New York City's abortion homestay program, liked to tell from several years before *Roe* was overturned. Back then, most people who used the program were largely from farther upstate who simply needed a faster appointment than what they could get where they lived. For a few weeks, she had started noticing a pattern of people consistently coming from a single town. When she finally asked one of the visitors for an explanation, she almost couldn't believe the answer. Only one doctor in the town did abortions, but she had broken her hand. The abortion care network for a whole community rested on a single person, and it wasn't enough. Although *Dobbs* hadn't created that precarity, it exacerbated the situation. Longer term, if and as more states passed abortion bans, it was hard to see how New York's clinics—in the city or outside it—could continue to meet the need.

This, of course, was assuming that New York's state laws would keep abortion access safe—that they were strong enough in the post-*Dobbs* world to withstand an anti-abortion movement newly energized by a victory fifty years in the making. And that, it turned out, might be too big an assumption to make.

In the spring of 2023, Michelle Casey had been watching the news for weeks, checking her phone nervously for whenever the decision would come. Across the state from her Buffalo clinic, lawmakers in Albany had been debating new legislation that would ostensibly increase New York's protections, creating what they hoped would be an even safer haven for abortion. But arguably what mattered more were the threats coming from farther south—ones the state seemed powerless to stop.

Amarillo, Texas, is fifteen hundred miles away from Buffalo; it's seventeen hundred miles from New York City and almost eighteen hundred from Albany. There are no direct flights from New York to Amarillo, a city in the Panhandle almost six hours northwest of Dallas, home to about two hundred thousand people and without a single abortion clinic for hundreds of miles. In a normal world, it would have been difficult to imagine what could happen in Amarillo that might affect an abortion provider in New York—let alone what might fundamentally undercut the state's entire abortion access network. But after *Dobbs* the world was no longer normal. And as abortion providers like Casey had long understood, overturning *Roe* had, for a large share of the anti-abortion movement, represented not an end goal but the beginning of a new phase in the quest to end access entirely. Enter Amarillo, home to a branch of the federal courts assigned to Texas's Northern District—a court that by spring 2023 would become the center of the next great legal battle over abortion rights.

The case involved mifepristone, the first of the two drugs used in medication abortions. Approved by the federal Food and Drug Administration in 2000, the drug has an incredibly low rate of complications and an even lower rate of death; taken in the first trimester, the mifepristone-misoprostol regimen is almost 100 percent effective in terminating a pregnancy. And yet just as the drug had become a mainstay for patients and providers trying to secure access to abortion, even under duress, mifepristone—and the two-drug regimen it was part of—had become a target for abortion rights opponents. In states with conservative legislatures, abortion opponents pushed for legislation that might ban medication abortion pills. In the Amarillo federal court, they believed they'd finally found a man who could help them achieve something even bigger: halting the distribution of the drug across the entire country. An anti-abortion organization founded three months after the *Dobbs* decision—one that affiliated itself with groups such as the Christian Medical and Dental Associations and the American Association of Pro-Life Obstetricians and Gynecologists—filed a lawsuit in November 2022 arguing that the FDA's approval of mifepristone should be completely overturned, claiming that the drug had been rushed to market and its safety never adequately studied. (The federal government had in fact taken four years to approve the application that put mifepristone on the market, and its safety is well established.) If they succeeded, they argued, the ruling judge had the power to block distribution of mifepristone, rendering it unavailable across the country.

There was no precedent for a federal judge effectively blocking an FDA-approved drug like this, and the lawsuit's arguments faced robust criticism from legal experts across the political spectrum. Still, the judge who would hear this case, Matthew Kacsmaryk, was known for his anti-abortion views and for issuing rulings that reflected those beliefs. Arguments in the case took place in mid-March; that day, the judge said he would issue a ruling "as soon as possible"—and seemed open to arguments that mifepristone's approval should be revoked and the drug no longer be distributed for use. No one knew when that decision would come, and the federal government had indicated it would appeal such a ruling, potentially bringing the case back through a judiciary that had already shown itself to be hostile to abortion protections. The implications of a ruling that might block mifepristone distribution were far from settled; some legal scholars argued that federal courts did not actually have the authority to revoke the FDA's approval, and that even if a judge tried to halt mifepristone distribution the government agency could choose not to enforce his ruling. Some abortion providers, including Prine, said that they would continue to distribute mifepristone as long as they could, no matter what the courts said. In Washington State, the governor announced that his administration would buy enough of the drug to last between three and four years, to continue providing it to people in the state who needed care; his government led a coalition of seventeen states plus the District of Columbia to sue in a different federal court, arguing that instead of restricting access to mifepristone the FDA should expand its availability. (Those states all had Democratic leaders; New York was not one of those plaintiffs.) But, with so little legal clarity at this stage, clinicians across the country had begun preparing to halt use of the drug at a moment's notice, no matter what their state's abortion protections said or how their government leaned.

The Texas-based case made clear that with *Roe* gone anti-abortion activists were more emboldened than ever. They had found a novel way to impose and expand abortion restrictions, and if they could succeed in eliminating mifepristone across the country, it seemed like only a matter of time before they found their next target. (Some abortion rights advocates anticipated that even intrauterine devices, which many abortion opponents view as an "abortifacient"—a perspective that is firmly contradicted by all medical expertise and evidence—could also someday be vulnerable to a similar legal strategy.)

On a practical level, medication abortions can still be done without mifepristone; the alternative is the same regimen Emma had attempted in Texas, trying to expel a pregnancy using only the second drug, misoprostol. That approach is fairly common in many other countries, where mifepristone can be prohibitively expensive, and in most cases people can successfully end a first-trimester pregnancy using just the one drug. But the evidence is clear that using only misoprostol is still less effective than the two-drug regimen: the risk of failure is higher, more misoprostol is needed, and the pain patients experience is often greater without mifepristone.

Almost two thousand miles from Amarillo, back in Buffalo, the mechanics of the legal back-and-forth mattered, but only somewhat. More important was what they foreshadowed: despite being located in a state that protected abortion rights, clinics like the ones Casey managed were in a precarious position and now deeply vulnerable to federal attacks on the services they provided. All her clinics offered abortion, but at about half of those outposts medication abortion was the only option they had the staff and training to provide. Even when clinics did offer procedural abortions, those services were far less frequently available—surgeries took place maybe one day a week, while medication-based terminations, which were easier and took fewer resources to administer, were offered daily. Patients also seemed to prefer the option, she'd noticed: in the post-*Dobbs* world, more than half of all the abortions her clinics now performed used mifepristone and misoprostol.

Casey knew that any day now her clinics might not be able to use one of the drugs their patients so clearly relied on, a dictate from somewhere else, by judges from outside her state, that they could realistically do nothing to affect. In the weeks that she—along with many other abortion providers across the country—spent waiting for a decision, she kept herself busy, making sure physicians on staff were comfortable providing abortions using only misoprostol, a regimen that many had never had to prescribe. And she kept thinking about her patients. She could not predict how many of them would no longer feel comfortable taking medication, worried about higher failure rates or heightened pain, and would instead opt for a surgical abortion instead. How would her system withstand that kind of strain, and how would they make sure they had enough doctors and appointments? If the wait times were bad now, if the system felt under-resourced already, things were about to get so much worse.

Hardest to ignore was the unfairness of it all: they had a medical treatment that was clearly safer and more effective, but they soon might not be able to offer it. If it were any other medical service, if they provided cardiac care or diabetes treatment, she knew, this kind of case would never be tolerated. The issue at stake—her patients' reproductive autonomy, their ability to choose whether to have children—made the injustice even more deeply felt. Casey understood what a commitment parenthood meant, psychologically, physically, and financially; her own son had just turned eighteen. She had chosen to become a parent on her own terms, and still it wasn't easy. How could people continue to deny her patients the right to make that choice for themselves?

"It actually seems really ridiculous, right?" Casey said. "There seems to be a different set of rules when it comes to sexual and reproductive health care."

———◆———

When the ruling came down, on April 7, 2023, Casey had known what to expect. But, reading the words, she still couldn't quite believe it. In his decision, Kacsmaryk had ignored all the science, all the medical facts, and ruled—in writing steeped with anti-abortion buzzwords and that frequently referred to fetuses as "unborn humans"—that mifepristone had to come off the market within one week. Language in the ruling even appeared to endorse a fringe legal theory that some experts worried could be used by a

Republican presidential administration to enforce a national abortion ban.

The weeklong delay meant there was time for the federal government, the case's defendants, to appeal before any changes might occur, potentially getting a higher court to block the ruling. But it also meant that Casey was working on a strict deadline, trying to figure out what she would do if the drug's approval was revoked. She got on the phone with the clinic's legal and policy advisers that same night. What would it mean if the ruling took effect? Could any laws specific to New York somehow protect access to the drug? Was there any way to make sure her patients weren't affected?

That month was a blur. Days after the Texas decision, New York's governor announced plans to buy a five-year supply of misoprostol, even though access to that drug wasn't under threat, to ensure that at least some kind of medication abortion would be available. Casey's team was in talks with state leaders too, trying to figure out what New York could do to let them keep using mifepristone if the ruling took effect. The short answer, as far as she could tell, was nothing.

Things only grew more uncertain. On April 12, the Wednesday after the Texas ruling had been delivered, the relevant appeals court—the conservative Fifth Circuit, the same court that had upheld Texas's six-week abortion ban so long ago—weighed in as well, attempting to moderate what the Amarillo judge had suggested. For the duration of the case, the Fifth Circuit said, mifepristone actually could stay on the market, but only under strict new limitations. It would be approved for use only in the first seven weeks of pregnancy. Patients using mifepristone would potentially need to make three in-person visits to a doctor. And efforts to prescribe and provide the drug virtually would have to stop. The change, they said, would still take effect by the end of the week, the morning of Saturday, April 15, 2023. Once again, Casey had to go back to the drawing board, trying her best to figure out a whole new plan of action. Given how many people in the northern part of the state struggled to get care, her clinics had been hoping to soon start providing medication abortions via telemedicine. Doing so, Casey figured, could allow them to see more New Yorkers who lived too far from an abortion clinic to travel for in-person care, and, she hoped, it might expand the number of people they would be able to treat. But if the Fifth Circuit's proposed change took effect they'd have to scrap those plans, or at least seriously revise them. And then there were all the other abortion providers in the area, which she knew relied on telemedicine and focused largely on medication abortions. If they had to stop doing that, if they had to adapt their schedules to see each patient in person three separate times, then as a result they would have to see fewer patients—meaning, she knew, that more people would come to her affiliates. Anything that affected one abortion provider would affect them all.

It was striking just how much the situation resembled that of Senate Bill 8 in Texas: there was the uncertainty over what kind of care clinicians would be allowed to provide within a matter of days, the desperate hope that some other court might intervene, and, of course, the sense of how ludicrously unprecedented the whole situation was—how obviously outside the realm of normal law it felt, in a way that seemed reserved for reproductive health care, and for abortion specifically. The difference was that in this case abortion care across the entire country could be affected immediately. The national impact would be impossible to ignore. This was the world *Roe*'s overturn had created; this was the world Senate Bill 8 had foreshadowed.

Just like there had been for Texas, there remained one last avenue of recourse: the Supreme Court, which had time and time again ruled against abortion rights. The federal government had asked them to block any changes to how mifepristone was dispensed, at least while this case played out. Maybe, Casey kept hoping, this case would be too extreme even for the court that had overturned *Roe*. She never let herself get too far from her phone. And on April 14, the day before the new mifepristone restrictions were set to take effect, the high court finally stepped in. They didn't issue a decision right away, but they bought abortion providers more time, declaring that any changes in mifepristone's legality couldn't take effect until the nine justices had a chance to weigh in. The news was a spot of relief, but it still felt temporary. Over the next several days, Casey kept watching the news, kept checking her email, all the while trying to brainstorm what her clinics might be able to do in the seemingly infinite scenarios they might soon operate under. If the court started to impose a three-visit requirement for anyone getting mifepristone, that could derail patient visits her clinics already had scheduled, making it legally impossible to provide care under the new regulations. And that wasn't even the worst scenario she could think of. What if the court decided to block mifepristone distribution after all? If so, she hoped, maybe they'd say so with language that could let her staff at least use up what remaining medication they had on hand—but there was no way to know without seeing the actual text of the ruling.

Friday, April 21, was unseasonably warm for Buffalo, with just a few scattered clouds. After work, Casey headed over to the local pickleball court; maybe moving around a bit would help calm her now-frayed nerves. But it was impossible to focus for too long, and between each game she kept checking her phone. An update from the Supreme Court should come out at any minute. If it didn't, the Fifth Circuit's decision—including its prohibition on virtual care and on using mifepristone past seven weeks—would take effect the next morning. They had patients on the schedule starting at eight a.m., most of whom were getting medication abortions. Nobody knew what kind of care they'd be allowed to provide. Casey had told the staff to be on the lookout for news. If the Supreme Court didn't block the ruling, they'd meet before the clinic opened to discuss what options were on the table. Every patient scheduled for a medication abortion had agreed to the medication regimen of mifepristone first, misoprostol later. If they had to revise that with no warning, she wasn't sure how many patients would change their minds—asking at the last minute to get a surgery instead, potentially needing more in-clinic resources and more of her staff's time. How was she supposed to prepare for all this? *It just feels like we're waiting for a bomb to drop,* she kept thinking.

It was just after six thirty p.m. when the answer came: for once, shockingly, the news she and abortion providers across the country had been hoping for. In a brief order, the court had said that, as long as this case progressed through the courts, access to mifepristone would remain unchanged. At least for some time, clinics like Casey's could keep prescribing it as they had been for years. She could move forward to institute a virtual care program—especially if more states were planning to ban abortion, she knew clinics like hers absolutely needed to expand their capacity. Already, it felt like they weren't big enough. There was no sigh in the world potent enough to express her relief that, for now, Casey's clinics could keep serving their patients.

Still, the reprieve was temporary. Mifepristone would remain available only while this case—still unprecedented and still an existential threat to providing evidence-based abortion care—worked its way through the federal court system. The Fifth Circuit properly heard this case in May 2023, and a majority of the judges reasserted their view that virtual provision of the drug should be halted, despite reams of evidence showing the practice to be safe and effective. The April 21 decision meant that this ruling would take effect only under two scenarios: if upheld by the Supreme Court or if the high court declined to hear the mifepristone case at all. And so, with no other options left, the federal government went back to the Supreme Court, hoping the majority that overturned *Roe* might this time rule in its favor. Even entering 2024, uncertainty lingered. In December 2023, the Supreme Court finally agreed to take up the mifepristone case once more, promising to weigh in not on the drug's 2000 approval but instead on whether the anti-abortion doctors from Texas had the right to file this kind of lawsuit, and whether the Fifth Circuit's May ruling should take effect. Legal scholars alike suggested that the narrow scope of questions being considered was a positive sign for access to the drug—an indication of the justices' unwillingness to curb access, at least at this time.

All the same, providers like Casey couldn't be certain. Once again they were forced to wait for the court to tell them what kind of care they were allowed to provide, despite no change in the medical consensus.

In the interim, everything in New York would be, if not fine, then unchanged. But the episode had made even more obvious what *Dobbs* had signified and what providers even in safe states had long feared. With *Roe* gone, anti-abortion advocates were eager to shape policy and limit access across the entire country—not just in states with Republican leadership. Eventually, if one of those efforts succeeded, states like New York or California or Washington or Massachusetts wouldn't be immune. "This is an attack nationally. It's not and will not be the last attack," Casey said. "And honestly, New York's not its own sovereign nation."

———

The day of her cesarean, Darlene was not quite praying, but quietly pleading as she drove to the hospital. *Please,* she kept thinking. *Please let her be healthy.* She wasn't worried about herself—she felt good, walking four miles a day and feeling confident that she could safely give birth. But the doctors were still worried that after she was born her daughter might require extra attention in the neonatal intensive care unit, or NICU. And Darlene kept flashing back to her first trimester, when she hadn't realized she was pregnant. What if the anesthesia she'd undergone at the time, back when she got her myomectomy, somehow affected her baby's health? Everyone told her it would be fine, but the nagging possibility wouldn't leave her mind.

After the surgery, Darlene met her new daughter, an eight-pound baby girl. She was, Darlene would say forever after, absolutely perfect: healthy, beautiful, and a quick learner. Still, in the weeks and months that followed, Darlene couldn't forget what it had taken to bring her second girl into the world; there was nobody else with whom she'd gone through quite as much. Sometimes, gazing idly at her daughter, the memories of her pregnancy would flood back, causing her heart to beat faster.

Darlene would try to imagine what it might look like to raise her two girls in Texas, a state that she no longer felt confident could protect them. Someday, either of them could need an abortion, just like she almost had. Maybe, she decided, when they were old enough for their first gynecological visits, she'd start planning regular trips with them to California: a back-to-school-season checkup, in a state where she knew they could see doctors who felt safe providing them proper health care. Perhaps it seemed drastic, but, as a mother, she wasn't sure how else she was supposed to care for her girls and make sure they never went through what she had.

PART IV

Jasper

THE FIGHT FOR THE FUTURE

CHAPTER 8

The Center That Couldn't Hold

Florida

Jasper never even considered that he might be pregnant. There was little reason to think he should be. He'd begun testosterone therapy, a form of gender-affirming care, in December 2021, about six months earlier. It had taken ages to get his father and stepmother fully on board—though eighteen years old at the time, Jasper, a budding artist, lived with and relied on them for support. But now, looking in the rearview mirror, he knew that treatment was one of the best things he'd ever done for himself. Feeling the scratchy peach fuzz grow on his face, hearing his voice deepen, noticing as his jawline shifted and his eyebrows grew darker—it was the first time in his life that he felt truly at home in his body. The treatment made him look and feel like himself; it also meant that he barely menstruated. That wasn't a big deal, though. Ever since hitting puberty, he had never had regular periods. Their absence now didn't even register.

Jasper's health saga began in June 2022, on a trip with his boyfriend's family. He caught COVID-19 while traveling, and between the viral symptoms and his newfound back soreness it became, through no fault of his hosts, one of the most miserable vacations he'd ever taken. When he returned to Orlando, Jasper kept waiting for the pain to get better. Instead, it persisted. So at the end of the month he visited a doctor, who ran a host of blood and urine tests on him. They couldn't figure out what was wrong. And nobody thought to check for pregnancy.

Maybe, Jasper thought, there was something wrong with his kidneys. He kept feeling pain around that area, and the doctors had mentioned something "abnormal" about his urine, though nobody told him what, precisely, that meant. In his free time, he googled his symptoms, trying to figure out what might be wrong with him and doing his best to keep his growing anxiety at bay.

Then the nausea began, followed by mysterious new stomach pains. Every morning after eating, Jasper immediately wanted to vomit, and he constantly felt bloated. After enduring another month of discomfort—hoping he might get answers or that it might just go away—he scheduled another doctor's visit. Maybe, they told him, he had an autoimmune condition; perhaps it was rheumatoid arthritis, which ran in his family. But the stomach pains still posed a mystery. The answer, they said, was more tests: they referred him for an ultrasound. Jasper scheduled yet another doctor's visit, choosing a Saturday so he wouldn't need to take time off work.

The day of Jasper's checkup was typical of August in Orlando: wet, sweltering, preferably spent inside with a fan. He was excited. This, he told himself, was the moment that they would figure out his mystery ailment and prescribe him some medication regimen that would make it all better. Finally, his peculiar medical journey would end.

Jasper was lying on the table and chatting with the nurse when she broke the news. Her voice was sweet, even chipper. "Well," she said. "Of course, you know that you're pregnant, right?"

Jasper sat up. "You're joking."

In retrospect, it should have been obvious. The nausea, the pain, the fatigue—the telltale symptoms he'd struggled to place were actually something so simple. He was *pregnant*. Still, Jasper couldn't quite believe it. How could this have happened? *When* did this happen?

She showed him the screen. "I'm surprised nobody told you," she said, "because you're so far along."

From her reading of the ultrasound, it looked like Jasper was about twelve weeks pregnant, already through his first trimester. Just looking at the screen, he felt his stomach and chest almost hollow out.

Abortion in Florida was legal at this point, but he didn't know to what extent. He'd heard about *Roe v. Wade* being overturned but hadn't yet learned what that meant in his home state—that as of July 2022 the state had begun enforcing a law that prohibited the procedure for anyone past fifteen weeks of pregnancy.

"Are there still options?" he asked, almost afraid to hear the answer.

When the nurse told him about this deadline, it sank in just how little time he had.

If Jasper wanted an abortion, he had three weeks to make up his mind, to raise the money, and to schedule not one appointment but two. Earlier that spring, the state courts had upheld a law mandating that anyone seeking an abortion needed to make two visits to the clinic, the first for counseling and the second—at least twenty-four hours later—for the abortion itself. He had no idea how difficult it would be to get an appointment here, how long he might have to wait to be seen by a doctor. All he knew was that he had to move quickly.

It was pouring—a typical Florida summer rainstorm—when Jasper left the clinic to call his boyfriend from the car. The phone kept ringing, finally going to voicemail. Jasper called back. It went to voicemail yet again. Amid all this, he'd started sobbing.

Well, Jasper figured, they'd just have to discuss things in person later. But for now he had another call to make. He found himself shaking as he picked up his phone once more, looking up the number for Planned Parenthood. He found two different phone numbers and alternated dialing the two of them. It took him maybe five or six tries before someone answered.

When he heard a woman's voice on the other end, he told her that he had just found out he was already twelve weeks pregnant. He always thought he'd want an abortion, but now, facing the decision, he was no longer sure what he wanted to do. All the same, he needed to know his options. How quickly could they see him?

Despite being decades in the making, *Roe*'s undoing caught many abortion opponents by surprise—particularly elected Republican officials who had long campaigned on vows to outlaw the procedure as soon as they could. Abortion bans were and remain unpopular with the vast majority of American voters, including voters in Florida. But restrictions were a way to maintain favor with influential hard-line groups, particularly the conservative religious organizations that championed total bans. It had become a rite of passage in conservative-led statehouses to pass law after law restricting access to the procedure, with the underlying assumption that lawmakers would never have to face the actual consequences of an abortion ban.

After the *Dobbs* decision, this sort of trick became far more difficult to pull off; passing an abortion ban meant actually dealing with the real-life human costs. And in Florida, a once-purple state now tilting red, that tension was even more potent. Already, the state's Republican Party had struggled to cater to both constituencies. There was no meaningful abortion limit it could pass that the state's residents actively supported. All it could hope for was that it could pass a restriction that people might tolerate or not consider when voting.

In the months before *Roe* fell, the Republican-run state legislature, urged on by ultraconservative governor Ron DeSantis, had passed the state's fifteen-week abortion ban. The state was one of three in the country to settle on this approach in the lead-up to *Roe*'s overturn. (The legislatures in Arizona and West Virginia passed similar laws.) The policy was one that poll after poll showed most people in Florida opposed, and one that represented a stark shift both in what was permitted and in how comfortable lawmakers seemed with pushing for abortion restrictions. Just a year earlier, when Republican state legislators had attempted to pass a ban on abortions for anyone past twenty weeks, the bill had failed to even get out of committee. The right to an abortion was supposed to be sacrosanct in Florida. In 1989, the state's supreme court had found that it was protected in Florida's constitution, an extension of Floridians' explicit privacy rights. Until now, the state had allowed abortions for people up to twenty-four weeks of pregnancy.

Yet the fifteen-week ban's supporters attempted to frame the law as a middle ground, noting that most abortions do occur within the first trimester. And in Florida specifically, only 6 percent of all abortions done in 2021 happened after twelve weeks of pregnancy. (The state's data didn't specify how many were done after fifteen weeks.) If those people—who still represented almost five thousand Floridians—wanted abortions, the argument went, they should simply have gotten them done sooner. It was an argument that conservatives across the country had attempted to make; even the Supreme Court's chief justice, John Roberts, had articulated a variation of it while hearing arguments over whether to overturn *Roe*.

But that argument failed to consider just who might be affected by a fifteen-week ban, a law almost uniformly criticized by medical providers, who noted that there is no health-based reason to deny someone an abortion at that specific point. Historically, the people who sought abortions later in pregnancy have often been those who could not afford to get to a clinic earlier—for whom pulling together money, time off work, and childcare to make an appointment represented tremendous obstacles that required substantial planning, or waiting at least until they'd already paid rent for the month and gotten another paycheck. There were people like Ashley Acre, the Michigan woman who did not learn until far later about the risks to her pregnancy because doctors themselves couldn't detect them yet. And there were those like Jasper, who did not realize they were pregnant until later on, for whom a fifteen-week deadline meant almost no time to decide what to do. One physician, ob-gyn Herman Miller, remembered the countless patients—usually children—who had not realized they were pregnant because they weren't old enough to have regular periods. By the time they knew what was happening, they were often past fifteen weeks. The youngest patient he'd ever seen was an eleven-year-old girl, one who was still figuring out what a menstrual cycle even meant. Others, who were just a few years older than that when they got pregnant, had delayed getting an abortion because they were too scared to tell their parents. (In Florida, parental consent is required for minors seeking an abortion, unless a judge is willing to override that requirement, a process that can take weeks.)

Even before *Roe*'s overturn, before the fifteen-week ban took effect, clinics in Florida reported seeing more and more patients later in pregnancy. It wasn't entirely surprising. Some were Texans traveling across multiple state lines, finally landing in the Sunshine State. Then there were people from other nearby states who could no longer get a timely appointment at home because their state's fragile abortion infrastructure didn't have the capacity to account for all the out-of-state travelers. And even Floridians themselves were taking longer to come in for abortions—a product, according to one employee at the Jacksonville-based clinic A Woman's Choice, of just how much harder it had become to get an abortion, even when *Roe* was still intact. In the spring of 2022, the state had begun to implement a law requiring patients make two visits to the clinic in person, separated by twenty-four hours, if they wanted to terminate a pregnancy. That necessitated more time off for working people seeking an abortion, more childcare for parents, and an extra night in a hotel if someone had traveled. The change came just as it felt like everything was becoming more expensive: escalating price tags for gas, rent, and childcare meant that saving up the money for an abortion was more challenging than ever.

After *Dobbs,* the state's fifteen-week ban took on another layer of meaning. Florida had become a destination for more than just Texans. It was one of the only options for people living in Louisiana, Georgia, Arkansas, Mississippi, and Alabama. Only four states in the southeast allowed abortion at all: Florida, North Carolina, South Carolina, and Virginia. In South Carolina, this was because the state courts blocked and eventually ruled unconstitutional a state law that would have banned abortion for people past six weeks of pregnancy. Of the southernmost three, Florida easily had the most options. Only thirteen abortion clinics operated in North Carolina. In South Carolina, there were only three, and none offered care past fourteen weeks of pregnancy. Florida, the third most populous state in the country, had more than sixty.

The number of abortions done in Florida went up immediately after the *Dobbs* ruling; researchers tracked a 10 percent spike between April and August 2022. In 2022 alone, Florida recorded more than 6,700 abortions for people from out of state, a 38 percent increase from the previous year. Nine months after *Dobbs,* Florida recorded 12,460 more abortions than the state's medical providers otherwise would have performed—an average increase of almost 1,400 more abortions per month, and the largest jump of any state in the entire country. And one full year out from the decision, the same analysis found an excess of 20,460 abortions in Florida compared with what the state would have recorded a year prior. The growth was clearly visible to the workers at Florida Access Network, an abortion fund that in 2022 supported 750 people in paying for their abortions, donating an average of $305 per person to help with the cost of care and travel. It was an astronomical change. The year before, they'd helped fewer than half that many people, providing 290 patients with assistance. Demand was so intense—from Floridians seeking help leaving the state, thanks to the fifteen-week ban, and from people out of state trying to come there—that in 2023 the abortion fund stopped supporting anyone who didn't already live in Florida. It was a painful decision to make, acknowledged Alyx Carrasquel, one of the fund's employees. But, much as they wanted to give money to anyone in need, they felt a sense of duty to aid Floridians first—people in other states could find other organizations to support them. Without drawing a line somewhere, they wouldn't be able to keep going; there were simply too many people, and the aid networks that existed were too small. "Just because I hate it doesn't mean we don't have to do it," she said. Whenever Florida passed and then enforced its six-week law, she feared, there was no way they'd have the resources to help everyone who needed to leave the state.

By the start of 2023, Florida was arguably the nation's most important abortion sanctuary—just as the procedure was becoming much harder to come by. With abortions after fifteen weeks outlawed, in the months after *Dobbs,* appointments for abortions quadrupled across the state's Planned Parenthood affiliates. Staff at the Jacksonville clinic, not even an hour from the Georgia border, began caring for twice as many patients as they used to. The contrast was night and day, clinic employees said. Before *Dobbs,* a busy day might mean forty people, largely from within the city. But without *Roe*'s protections the influx of out-of-state patients meant they regularly saw eighty, even ninety people each day; the waiting rooms were always full, with children playing in the small toy area near the door, waiting for their parents' hours-long visits to be done. Jessica Wannemacher, the clinic manager, regularly popped out into the lobby, simultaneously no-nonsense and apologetic. With immaculate makeup and an accent hinting at her Tennessee roots, she promised they'd see everyone who came. It just might take them some time. There were just so many people to care for, and only so many physicians, nurses, and exam rooms.

The majority of people there were from out of state, coming to Duval County, sprawling and studded with pear and pecan trees, from all over the South. The clinic was so busy that those who were earlier in pregnancy and who lived nearby might have to wait weeks for an appointment. Staff regularly worked past closing hours, sometimes not leaving the building until midnight; nobody wanted to be the one to say no to someone who had traveled across state lines to come there for care. Jacksonville was a refuge, and it was a responsibility that clinic staff, exhausted as they were, took seriously. Even after someone came for their first visit—the newly required pre-abortion consult—there was no guarantee they could be scheduled for a procedure twenty-four hours later. The appointments often weren't available. So instead, patients would have to wait days, even a week, before the clinic could see them again to do the actual abortion. If patients were pushing the fifteen-week limit, and no appointments in Jacksonville were available, the staff would try to book them in Tallahassee instead, more than 150 miles away. It wasn't ideal, but it was the best they could do.

Under the fifteen-week regime, most people who made it to the clinic would be able to get an abortion there, though more and more were pushing up against the state's cutoff. Data from the state would ultimately illustrate the ever-growing share of people affected: whereas in 2021, 6 percent of abortions in Florida were for people past the first trimester, data from 2022 showed an increase to 8 percent. The percentage only kept growing. Halfway through 2023, one in ten abortions in Florida was for people past the twelve-week mark—people for whom running up against the new ban represented a real and substantial concern.

There was Shayla, a twenty-six-year-old mother with two kids at home in Georgia, where abortion was banned after six weeks of pregnancy—or, in terms that mattered to her, only two days after she'd found out she was pregnant again. Her morning sickness was so intense that she missed her first appointment at Planned Parenthood, which she'd booked for a Saturday morning so she wouldn't have to take off work. When she woke up that morning, she simply hadn't been able to drive the two and a half hours needed to get there. By the time Shayla finally made it to the clinic, calling in sick at work and waking up at six a.m. Wednesday to make the trek to Jacksonville, she was already twelve weeks and five days into her pregnancy. The clinic staff would rearrange their calendars to squeeze her in the following Saturday. It was the only way she'd be able to get her abortion done in time. Shayla was too far along to get a medication abortion, which meant she would require a surgical procedure, ideally performed with sedation, either lidocaine applied locally to her cervix or Valium or intravenous medication if she was worried about pain or anxiety. If she were to opt for one of the latter two pain management options, she wouldn't be allowed to drive herself home from the clinic. Shayla didn't have anyone who could drive her back to Georgia after the procedure; her family didn't approve of abortion, and her boyfriend had to stay home to watch the kids—which left her little choice about the level of pain she would have to experience. Still, she was determined. Her job didn't pay much, and she couldn't afford another pregnancy, let alone another child.

If Shayla hadn't made it to Jacksonville in time—if Florida hadn't been an option—she didn't know what she would have done. There was no way she could make it to North Carolina, let alone another state even farther north. The thought filled her with rage.

"What if I was raped? You can't take away someone's right."

She was one of the lucky ones. For every twenty people who came to the clinic, staff said, there was always a patient further along than they had thought—who hadn't realized they were already past fifteen weeks and who, after coming all the way there, would have to go somewhere else. One girl, only fourteen years old, had come to Jacksonville with her grandmother, traveling from out of state to get an abortion in Florida. Her pregnancy was the result of incest. But because she was past the state's deadline there was nothing the staff at the clinic could do for her. All they could offer was to help her set up an appointment and find a way to get to a clinic somewhere else. From Jacksonville, the closest options were in North Carolina, and then Virginia, Washington, D.C., and Illinois. That meant making a six-and-a-half-hour drive to Charlotte or hopping on a plane to get to the next nearest clinic. The share of people making that journey only continued to grow: about halfway through 2023, 15 percent of people getting support from the Florida Access Network, the abortion fund, were using the money to leave the state for care—a substantial increase from years prior.

In addition to patients often not knowing how far along they were, many hadn't heard about the new abortion restrictions, said one clinic employee, ultrasound technician Kedisha Madison. "It sucks that I just can't help," she said. "If you have kids at home? Or are supposed to take off work again?" While the clinic would help people go to other states—setting up appointments, covering the cost of airfare, connecting patients with abortion funds for extra support—it still didn't feel like enough. Helping everyone who needed an abortion leave the state was simply too big an ask for a single clinic to fulfill.

The fifteen-week deadline was, objectively, far more forgiving than any new bans the state might pass; still, it made abortions impossible for many in the state to access.

Amber, a twenty-eight-year-old woman in Orlando, had begun to suspect that she might be pregnant. But she kept brushing the idea away. Thinking about pregnancy was difficult for her, to put it mildly. A decade ago, as a college student, Amber had been raped and became pregnant as a result. When she had sought an abortion that time, she discovered she had already miscarried; the doctors just needed to give her medication to expel the fetus. Just thinking about the possibility of pregnancy transported her back to that awful time, to that painful memory of having a physical reminder of how deeply she'd been violated. For a moment, it was as if she were eighteen years old again and being told that, actually, her body wasn't hers, that her autonomy didn't matter.

Amber waited as long as she could until finally, shortly after Christmas 2022, a friend convinced her to take a test. The next day, she raced to an emergency room to confirm it. It wasn't just that she was pregnant, she learned. She was already at twenty-three weeks; she had probably conceived sometime after July 4. Even the nurse was shocked that she was so far along. Amber was barely showing, and the ultrasound showed a far smaller fetus than would have been expected at this point in pregnancy.

Amber had been drinking and smoking heavily up until then. And at the ER she learned that she had what's called a "short cervix"—the pressure of pregnancy had prematurely shortened the lower end of her uterus, and it was likely that, if she stayed pregnant, she'd go into labor before thirty-six weeks. It was a pregnancy dangerous for herself and for the fetus growing inside her.

She needed an abortion, and nobody in Florida could legally provide one. Because medication abortions wouldn't be as effective at her stage of pregnancy, the options were few and far between. Finally, she found two places that might provide abortions at as far along as she was: one health center in New Jersey and another in Washington, D.C. But when she heard the price—about $6,500 in New Jersey and near $8,800 in D.C., she was told—she felt that familiar sting of defeat sink in. That wasn't the kind of money she had lying around. Amber worked in a restaurant, and her boyfriend had some money saved up. Still, she estimated, they'd need to find a couple thousand dollars to pay for the abortion. And that didn't even account for the plane tickets they'd have to buy, the two nights in a hotel near the clinic, or the money she'd lose from missing work.

Amber got lucky. Someone told her about a few abortion funds to try; when she called the New Jersey clinic, the Cherry Hill Women's Center, they referred her to another organization, the Brigid Alliance, which focused on helping cover travel costs for people seeking abortions past fifteen weeks of pregnancy. She and her boyfriend made phone call after phone call until eventually they found enough funds to cover everything but their plane tickets. And if they flew a budget airline from Orlando to Philadelphia—bringing no carry-ons beyond their backpacks—the travel would cost them just a few hundred dollars. She scheduled an appointment for a Thursday in mid-January, taking the requisite four days off work. Somehow, her good luck continued. Amber and her boyfriend had booked a flight for that Wednesday morning. They took off from Florida without a hitch, only to hear about how, hours later, a series of other flights out of Orlando had been canceled. For weeks after, she couldn't stop thinking about what would have happened if they'd been on a different flight, if they'd missed her appointment and had to go through this process all over again. When they made it to New Jersey, almost everything about getting her abortion was easy, the only exception being the pain she felt during the procedure itself. It was in direct contrast to how difficult things were back home—and a constant reminder of how it didn't have to be this way. Every barrier she'd faced was the result of choices politicians had made, choices they'd made with little to no regard for how they would affect someone like her.

Upon returning, Amber told few people about where she'd been. She knew that she hadn't broken any laws, but she still lived in fear of what might happen next—whether her state might in the future pass a law criminalizing even the act of traveling somewhere else for an abortion. Could they someday come after her? She kept telling herself how lucky she was to live in a state where abortion was allowed in some form, even though she'd still had to leave the state to get care. But at the same time she felt sure that the state's fifteen-week ban was only the beginning.

———

Stories like Amber's drove home what felt like an increasingly obvious truth. Conservatives touted the state's fifteen-week prohibition as a middle-of-the-road compromise. But even that law represented a meaningful, tangible shift in abortion rights and a loss in access for thousands of pregnant people.

Even more obvious was how soon things would change. *Roe* was gone, but technically abortion bans were still considered unconstitutional in Florida, thanks to the 1989 ruling from the state's supreme court, which found that the state's constitution guaranteed the right to an abortion. But the court's makeup had shifted significantly in recent years, tilting to become more conservative. When Florida abortion providers filed suit challenging the state's fifteen-week ban, the high court refused to block the law while the case was pending—a decision many took as a hint that, when the time came to rule, the justices would eliminate Florida's abortion rights guarantee.

In 2022, just months after the *Dobbs* decision and the institution of the fifteen-week ban, Florida Republicans won a supermajority in the state's legislature, and DeSantis easily won reelection. The state's residents may have opposed the abortion restriction in theory, but it wasn't enough to turn them against the Republican Party. Lori Berman, a Democratic state senator from Palm Beach County, won reelection that cycle and even campaigned on abortion rights—but the issue hardly seemed to resonate with her constituents. It made sense in a way: voters in 2022 prioritized abortion when they perceived it to be under threat, and Floridians, it seemed, hadn't understood how meaningful an impact the fifteen-week ban had had. In their minds, there was no reason to vote based on that issue.

After the election, the pressure from the state's anti-abortion lobby was immediate, and it was fierce. Chief among them was the state's largest anti-abortion organization, the Florida Family Policy Council, a right-wing, Christian-affiliated registered nonprofit that took in hundreds of thousands of dollars per year and similarly opposed marriage equality. The group had a long history of proudly campaigning against abortion, pushing in 2020 for the state's new law that restricted minors' ability to access the procedure and organizing anti-abortion rallies in the state capital; as governor, DeSantis had even spoken at the organization's legislative prayer breakfast. In the months after the governor's reelection, and in the days leading up to the 2023 legislative session, the Florida Family Policy Council's leader, John Stemberger, spoke publicly about his support for a six-week abortion ban. Andrew Shirvell, the leader of another anti-abortion group called Florida Voice for the Unborn, made similar remarks; he had already criticized the state for settling for a fifteen-week ban, calling it an insufficient compromise. In the weeks after the *Dobbs* leak, he expressed disappointment and frustration that the governor had not swiftly called for a special legislative session specifically to ban abortion in the state. And then there was the mounting attention from national anti-abortion groups, such as Students for Life and SBA Pro-Life America. Founded in 1993, SBA Pro-Life America was established to serve as a counterweight to the abortion rights political group known as EMILY's List; the choice of name, a reference to Susan B. Anthony, was meant to position the organization as one that supported women's rights and is a reference to the pioneering suffragist's alleged anti-abortion views, though historians note that in actuality there is little evidence to suggest that Anthony opposed abortion rights. Both Students for Life and SBA Pro-Life America frequently identified Florida as a priority state in the post-*Dobbs* world, one where it seemed that the timing was right to push for a harsher abortion ban. Given the state's large population and geographic significance, they assessed correctly that Florida-specific restrictions would have outsized importance.

No anti-abortion groups would be satisfied with a status quo allowing abortions up to fifteen weeks of pregnancy. If the GOP wanted to hold on to their support, it would have to push for more extreme measures.

In the weeks before the Florida legislature reconvened, lawmakers speculated about all kinds of new limits. Some said they'd heard that Republicans would push for a twelve-week ban with exceptions for people pregnant as a result of rape or incest, a policy floated by their senate majority leader in an effort to appear more moderate. Others talked about an eight-week ban, or a six-week one. The governor, at that point frequently discussed as a likely presidential candidate, remained noncommittal whenever asked about the issue, saying only that he would sign "great life legislation," a vague phrase open to far-ranging interpretation.

Given carte blanche to restrict access, the nation's anti-abortion movement had grown ever more fractured. In state-houses across the country, a cohort of elected Republicans—seeing firsthand voters' anger at *Roe*'s overturn, an anger Democrats had successfully harnessed in the 2022 midterms—had become skittish about the political ramifications of abortion restrictions, even though it was a policy many had previously supported unequivocally. (Florida remained the outlier in this level of voter backlash.) Doctors pointed out that bans on the procedure, with exceptions that were poorly worded at best, consistently prevented them from providing lifesaving care—such as miscarriage management, an abortion to end a pregnancy that was likely to result in hemorrhaging, or treatment for placental abruption—until patients were at death's door. Joined by two frustrated ob-gyns, a collection of more than a dozen women in Texas sued the state for clarity surrounding its medical exceptions, noting that in the absence of clear guidance doctors had been unable to end their pregnancies, despite knowing that without an abortion the women were at risk of dying. All these doctors had been able to do was wait for their patients' conditions to deteriorate or encourage them to seek care out of state.

Meanwhile, poll after poll showed voters' strong opposition to bans that, like Florida's fifteen-week law, did not have exceptions for people pregnant as a result of rape or incest. In states with abortion bans, some lawmakers began to talk about amending their laws to incorporate some kinds of nominal exceptions for people pregnant as a result of rape or incest, or to add some ostensibly clarifying language to theoretically allow for limited access if patients experienced a miscarriage, an ectopic pregnancy, or another medically dangerous scenario. But doctors and other experts said the impact of such exceptions would be limited at best. Sexual violence researchers frequently noted that statutory exceptions for rape and incest survivors almost never translated into access; in states whose bans allowed for abortions in such cases, virtually nobody was able to actually utilize them. Miller, the Jacksonville doctor, never even asked why his patients sought an abortion—as he saw it, it wasn't his business. That omission, common among the physicians who provided abortions, meant they were less likely to know if a patient was seeking an abortion as a result of rape or incest. And in some states patients had to file a police report before qualifying for a rape or incest exception—a stipulation that often made the exception functionally useless, since most sexual assaults are never reported. These revisions to state abortion bans were, clinicians said, superficial at best; they did not and would not allow people to access abortions, but if passed they might allow anti-abortion politicians to minimize pushback from voters. And still, in most states with anti-abortion leadership, efforts at adding in rape and incest exceptions largely didn't gain traction—they were too difficult for staunch abortion opponents to swallow. Idaho, the rare state that did add these exceptions, still allowed abortion under those circumstances only during the first trimester of pregnancy;

the state also amended its abortion ban to specify that it did not prohibit treating people with ectopic pregnancies, though it did not address other life- or health-threatening concerns. North Dakota's new rape and incest exceptions applied only for the first six weeks of pregnancy; Tennessee added exceptions to its ban only for cases of ectopic or molar pregnancies, both of which are life-threatening and neither of which is viable. Texas ultimately did pass a law allowing for abortions only in cases of ectopic pregnancy and cases where patients' water broke prematurely, but even that would require doctors to hire a lawyer, go to court, and defend their decision. And it addressed only two out of the countless dangerous complications pregnant Texans could face.

Pressure had grown to add some kinds of exceptions, though the rare abortion-ban revisions remained narrow at best. And simultaneously, a collection of hard-line state lawmakers had grown more and more frustrated by people's ability to access abortions even when they lived in states with bans in place—by traveling out of state or by obtaining medication abortion pills. In the early days of 2023, Texas lawmakers debated new bills that would discourage businesses from helping their employees travel out of state for an abortion, though the state's top Republicans showed little eagerness to revisit the subject. State legislators in Oklahoma, Arkansas, Georgia, Kentucky, and South Carolina introduced bills that would make it a crime to get an abortion—a drastic escalation from previous bans, which had largely focused on punishing health care providers rather than patients themselves. In South Carolina, where self-managed abortion was already illegal, the new bill would treat abortion as homicide and apply the death penalty as punishment. It wasn't the first time a state had considered such legislation—a similar bill in Louisiana in the summer of 2022 had ardently divided the state's anti-abortion movement and ultimately failed to make it out of committee—and in South Carolina, too, the homicide bill quickly lost support from Republican lawmakers in the wake of national media attention. A number of legislators suggested they didn't realize what the bill would actually have done.

Major anti-abortion lobbies sought to distance themselves from those types of legislation, arguing that they didn't truly reflect the "pro-life" movement. Though abortion is a safe and simple procedure, those organizations had for years sought to cast abortion restrictions as policies that protected the pregnant person from unscrupulous physicians; criminalizing people who chose to end their own pregnancies would undercut that carefully crafted argument. Without support from the largest anti-abortion organizations, policies that explicitly and overtly criminalized pregnant people could not in the near term gain traction. But it had become clear that there remained a vocal faction of lawmakers who were ready to take this approach, if the political window to do so ever opened. And, historians of abortion politics suggested, if enough time finally passed that voters seemed less concerned about the implications of abortion bans, even the more established anti-abortion organizations might eventually jump on board, even if it took years. Meanwhile, some abortion opponents continued to look for ways to cut people off from support in traveling out of state for care. Counties in Texas, for instance, attempted to outlaw driving someone through their jurisdiction if one person was helping another get an abortion. The Alabama attorney general, Steve Marshall, threatened to prosecute state residents who helped people leave Alabama for an abortion, using the state's criminal conspiracy laws. But it remained difficult to see how these types of restrictions or efforts could actually be enforced or leveraged to deny people access. And the mainstream anti-abortion movement remained hesitant to support such approaches.

The largest priority of the mainstream anti-abortion movement remained banning the procedure in states where restrictions hadn't yet passed—and where the politics suggested that doing so was possible. And in Florida in particular the demand for new abortion restrictions was building. Leaders at SBA Pro-Life America had indicated they believed the state was ripe for a new, even more restrictive law. Students for Life, which opposes abortions in all forms as well as most forms of contraception, was planning to go door-to-door, speaking to people who lived in the district represented by Kathleen Passidomo, the president of the state's senate who had indicated early on that she preferred a twelve-week ban with rape and incest exceptions. Anti-abortion organizers found that message troubling. In their view, a twelve-week ban was nowhere near enough; it barely seemed like progress from fifteen.

The legislature, they argued, had to go further—at the very least, push for a six-week or eight-week ban. And they would do all they could to let her know that anything less would mean losing their backing. Then there was the question of DeSantis. The governor, at the time a darling of national conservative media, had made headlines for his attacks on transgender Floridians and his efforts to ban discussion of sexual orientation and gender identity in schools. He was clearly eyeing a campaign for the White House. Why hadn't he directed his energy toward abortion?

"He has not led on this issue," Kristan Hawkins, president of Students for Life, said in early 2023. "It's a real missed leadership opportunity for him."

———————

Jasper's boyfriend called him back while he was still on the phone with Planned Parenthood. For the moment, he pressed decline, texting that he'd call back later. He'd finally gotten through to someone who could help him schedule an abortion consultation, and his window to decide was rapidly closing.

The woman on the phone told him that she didn't see any appointments open for the next few weeks. Things had been hectic all summer; with *Roe* overturned, patients from all over the South had been flocking to their Orlando clinic, just a mile away from the University of Central Florida campus where Jasper attended school. By the time they could find an opening for Jasper's first appointment—just the consultation, not even the procedure itself—it would probably be after the state's fifteen-week deadline. But she was going to keep looking, just in case she was wrong.

Even as he listened, Jasper began thinking ahead. Maybe they'd have to travel out of state. He didn't want to tell his family about any of this. They had struggled to accept his transition and hesitated to support him starting testosterone therapy, relenting only after the urging of multiple therapists. He'd recently begun rebuilding his relationship with them—his father and stepmother, at least—but things still felt fragile. And he knew that his stepmother, raised Catholic, deeply opposed abortion on principle. But if Jasper had to leave Florida, maybe they could tell his boyfriend's family. They had relatives in Las Vegas, where abortion was legal up to twenty-four weeks. It wasn't the closest place to fly to, but at least if the young couple went there they'd have a place to stay and a reasonable cover story for why they were leaving the state. He ran the numbers in his head, and he was pretty sure he could find them each round-trip tickets for two hundred dollars through budget airlines—money he'd rather not spend, but still doable, if that was what it came to.

"Wait." The woman on the phone broke through his train of thought. "We just had a cancellation."

The opening for the first visit, the pre-abortion consultation, was in four days. There, Jasper would get an ultrasound, go through his state-mandated counseling, and decide what he wanted to do about his pregnancy. Without thinking, he took the appointment. Then, still crying, Jasper called his boyfriend back to deliver the news.

"Can you get off work?" Jasper asked.

"I'm doing that right now," he answered.

The two of them met at Jasper's boyfriend's family home, a twenty-minute drive from the imaging center. It was the middle of the day still, and nobody else was in the house. The two of them spent the rest of the afternoon lying in bed together, holding each other and only occasionally speaking. There wasn't much to say. Jasper kept thinking about the past few weeks and months: the day he'd tried psychedelic mushrooms for the first time, the times he'd smoked marijuana, the occasional drinks he'd had. He couldn't shake the feeling of guilt, that one of those drugs must have harmed the pregnancy—even though, as he kept reminding himself, he'd had no idea he was pregnant.

Another thought flickered through his mind: if he had been born a cis male, he never would've had to deal with worrying about becoming pregnant or figuring out how to get an abortion. This was yet another way his body didn't fully feel like his own, and another way it felt as if Florida—which had also recently passed a law outlawing gender-affirming care for people younger than eighteen—was attempting to deny him basic physical autonomy. He'd keep coming back to that feeling in the weeks and months ahead.

When Jasper went home to his dad's house, he put on a stoic

face, doing his best to conceal what had happened that day. In four days, he knew, he'd once again be confronted with the decision about whether he really did want to end his pregnancy, or if there was any way he could envision a life for himself where he became a parent now. He hardly felt prepared to make this decision—it wasn't something he'd ever expected to have to decide at this age. But for now all he could do was shove the thought away, as something to be dealt with later.

—◆—

The week before Florida lawmakers returned to govern, Students for Life held a rally in Naples, where Passidomo lived. They planned another in March 2023 in Tallahassee, to coincide with the first day that the Florida legislature came back into session—the deadline for lawmakers to introduce new bills that year. There, the group planned to call on the state to outlaw abortion entirely. The news came that same morning: on the last possible day, Florida's Republican lawmakers had responded to the growing pressure by introducing a new proposal for an abortion ban. This bill would prohibit the procedure for anyone past six weeks of pregnancy, set to take effect thirty days after any state supreme court ruling that eliminated Florida's abortion rights protections. It wasn't a total ban, but it ended access early enough that people would functionally lose the ability to get abortions, as experience in Texas and Oklahoma and so many other states had shown. The bill forbade the use of state dollars to help people leave the state for an abortion, and—unlike abortion legislation in most other GOP-led states—it did in fact introduce new exceptions for people who had become pregnant as a result of rape or incest. Still, even those applied only up to fifteen weeks of pregnancy and only if people could produce documents such as police reports, restraining orders, or court orders certifying that they had in fact become pregnant as a result of rape or incest. It was enough to win over holdouts like Passidomo, who endorsed the legislation soon after it was introduced.

Democratic lawmakers, of whom there were scarcely any left, knew they couldn't stop the ban. They would put up a fight, they said, and they knew that public opinion was on their side: Polling from the Public Religion Research Institute, conducted after *Roe* fell, showed that almost two-thirds of Floridians believed abortion should be legal in most or all cases. Another survey, conducted just a week before lawmakers rolled out their proposal for a six-week ban, found that 75 percent of registered voters did not support such a restriction, with 62 percent characterizing their opposition as "strong" (though that poll described a ban with no exceptions for rape or incest). The distaste was bipartisan: a majority of Republicans in the poll said they wouldn't back a six-week abortion ban.

And yet lawmakers also knew that what constituents wanted didn't matter. State Republicans had the votes to pass a six-week ban, and they had the backing of a governor who knew that fifteen weeks wasn't enough to satisfy anti-abortion groups. Frankly, even a six-week ban wasn't enough for some abortion opponents—Hawkins, of Students for Life, criticized the proposal as insufficient and full of "loopholes." If the momentum continued in this direction, abortion could be completely outlawed in Florida in a few short years. It was a shocking shift from the state Democrats, abortion rights advocates, and health care providers had known even two years earlier, a change they all struggled to process.

"They're never going to be satisfied until there's a full ban," Florida Access Network employee Carrasquel said.

A six-week ban wasn't the total prohibition that state and national anti-abortion groups had sought, but it was a massive victory for them, and a sign of where things were headed beyond just Florida. Even under the best of circumstances, six weeks was a tight turnaround. Carrasquel herself had become pregnant in early 2023, noticing symptoms as soon as her period was late. She got an abortion quickly and easily—the local clinic could see her promptly, her work paid for the procedure, and her partner canceled a trip so he could drive her home after. Even with all those advantages, by the time she got her abortion she was four days past six weeks. Under the new Florida law, she would have been too far along. And if six weeks was tight for locals, it was impossible for people coming from out of state. If the bill passed, it would end Florida's status as an abortion haven.

And beyond the tangible implications and human impact, the legislation had tremendous symbolic value: a six-week prohibition put an end to the notion that a Republican-led state could dare to attempt to "compromise" on abortion, especially if the party leader had higher political ambitions. Put simply, there was no way to remain in good standing with the anti-abortion movement—whose support for the GOP had been unflinching for decades—without going all in to end abortion. The era of Republicans compromising on abortion would end here in Florida, if it had ever existed at all.

Florida also represented something broader. Right after *Dobbs,* thirteen states had succeeded in banning abortion almost completely; Georgia's active six-week ban brought the number up to fourteen states where the procedure was mostly unavailable. But those were just the early adopters. Post-*Dobbs,* anti-abortion advocates at last had the time and energy to turn their attention to the next states: the ones that didn't outlaw abortion right away, but would incrementally limit access such that, in a few more years, the procedure would become largely unavailable. These were places like Nebraska and North Carolina, which by the summer of 2023 had both enacted twelve-week abortion bans—in North Carolina, overriding the Democratic governor's veto to do so—and states such as South Carolina, where changes in the makeup of the state supreme court would by August 2023 finally allow the conservative government to enforce its six-week ban. In North Carolina, Republican lawmakers hinted that if they were able to win the governor's mansion, a six-week or total ban on the procedure would likely follow. Indiana's legislature had passed an abortion ban almost immediately after the *Dobbs* decision; in the summer of 2023, the state's supreme court would finally rule that that state too could enforce its prohibition.

It would take years to see the full impact of losing federal abortion rights, but in time the effects would be seismic, with close to half of all the states in the country seeing the procedure heavily restricted or totally outlawed. Access in both the South and the Midwest would be wiped out almost entirely, with abortion permitted in at most a handful of states. For someone living in Miami, the closest option to get an abortion in America would soon be Virginia or Illinois, a distance unfathomable for most forms of medical care.

As for what would happen to people like Shayla, the woman from

Georgia who drove hours to get an abortion in Jacksonville? In time, every realistic option for her to get an abortion would disappear.

The burden of abortion bans like Florida's wouldn't fall equally; such laws rarely do. Just as is true nationally, Black and Hispanic Floridians were more likely to get abortions and therefore more likely to be denied care under a ban. The cost of travel posed a greater burden for them; institutional inequities in pay, combined with what's called "occupational segregation"—social forces pushing people of particular demographics into certain professions—meant Black women and Latinas earned less than almost any other income group. Then there were those who couldn't travel, even if they wanted to: Florida is home to nine hundred thousand undocumented people, the third-largest number in the country, and undocumented Floridians make up nearly 6 percent of the state's population of women between the ages of fifteen and forty-four, a demographic considered "reproductive aged." Per state law, those residents are ineligible for a driver's license. While pushing for abortion restrictions, DeSantis has also campaigned to make Florida one of the states most hostile to immigrants, touting legislation that would, among other changes, make it illegal to house undocumented people or to help them travel, and that would nullify driver's licenses they might have gotten out of state. Those kinds of policies made it incredibly dangerous to ever consider leaving for an abortion. "People don't feel comfortable traveling outside of the state to access care," said Aurelie Colon Larrauri, who worked at the Florida branch of the Latina Institute. "They could be easily pulled over and detained because they don't have a license."

Unspoken but equally true: there was little, if anything, providers could do to help. In abortion clinics like Jacksonville's, there was a sense of, if not helplessness, then looming defeat. The reason staff had worked as hard as they could for so many months was because they didn't know how much longer they had left. They'd already been told to plan for the possibility that, by the end of the year, they would be able to offer abortions only to people within the first six weeks of pregnancy; when that ban passed, it was a confirmation of their worst fears. The clinic's employees worried about all the patients who would never make it to them, for whom an abortion was too difficult to obtain. The people who had been coming there would have nowhere else to go. Some, they hoped, might make it to North Carolina and then, when that state's ban took effect, to Virginia. But for many the trip was too far and too expensive, and abortion clinics too few to care for all the people about to lose access at home. In time, people seeking abortions would have to travel even farther for care: to clinics in Washington, D.C., and states like New York and Illinois, or to take whatever the cheapest flight was to wherever they could find an appointment.

The Floridian "compromise" would barely last. Florida's six-week ban, introduced at the start of March, reached the governor's desk by April 13—it hadn't taken even six weeks to become law. In time, clinicians knew, they would likely have to stop providing the vast majority of abortions—the only question was when. The law offered a preview of what residents could expect in any other state where anti-abortion lawmakers claimed to endorse a moderate path, including those states like Nebraska and North Carolina, where lawmakers had settled on a twelve-week ban. The so-called center wouldn't hold. In time, restrictions on abortion would only become more onerous, more prohibitive.

All Florida's clinicians could offer was to see as many patients as possible until their time was up. After that, they would pivot to something else: providing gender-affirming care in the state as long as that remained legal, offering abortions up to six weeks, helping people get to other states, and perhaps focusing on other kinds of pregnancy-related health services. But it was hard to see a long-term future there. Even Wannemacher, who'd taken to her adopted hometown with fervor, screaming her lungs out at home games for the Jacksonville Jaguars, was starting to think about what might come next—and specifically about which state she would eventually have to relocate to so she could raise her young daughter and son knowing they had equal rights, and where she could keep doing the work that she knew she was meant to do.

She sighed one afternoon, saying, "If my kids ask me—ten, twenty years from now—at least I can tell them I tried."

CHAPTER 9

Neither Living nor Dead

Arizona

After *Roe* was overturned, Dr. Jill Gibson could hardly keep track of what she was allowed to do anymore. The rules kept changing, sometimes every other week.

She was caught off guard the Friday morning of the *Dobbs* decision. Intellectually, she'd known it was possible that a ruling might come, but Gibson, who by nature tended toward baseline optimism, had been holding out hope the court wouldn't say anything until the following Monday, giving her enough time to see even a few more patients. As the medical director for Planned Parenthood Arizona, the state's largest abortion provider, she had scheduled extra staff to come in, with the plan that they'd work Friday, Saturday, and Sunday, providing as many abortions as possible. Clinicians drove the two hours from Flagstaff to Phoenix; a doctor she was friends with flew in the night before from California to lend an extra pair of hands, just to help them get through the weekend.

Then, at seven a.m. Friday, June 24, 2022, sitting at her computer before the workday had even begun, Gibson saw the news. *Roe* was gone, and in Arizona nobody had a clue what that meant. Was she allowed to see any of her patients? Would treating them break state law? Despite months of warning that this day would come, it was impossible to know what was actually legal—and it was a disaster everyone had seen coming from miles away. The problem was simple: Arizona had too many abortion bans on the books, some working in direct competition with one another. The state had never repealed its old ban on the procedure, a law passed in 1864 (decades before Arizona even became a state) that forbade abortions unless they were needed to save a pregnant person's life. Violators faced imprisonment for two to five years. The 1864 law hadn't been enforced since 1973, but lawmakers hadn't ever repealed it. Arguably, they'd never had the votes to do so. Democrats had occasionally won the governor's seat, and only a third of Arizona's voters are registered as Republican—the party typically more likely to support abortion restrictions—but since 1973 the legislature had largely been dominated by conservatives who opposed abortion rights. At their core, statewide politics had long favored Republicans: in 2020, Joe Biden became the first and only Democratic candidate for president in the twenty-first century to win Arizona, doing so by only about ten thousand votes. Given that reality and with *Roe* intact, some in Phoenix said, it seemed like there were other priorities to focus on, rather than spending political capital on repealing a law they never expected to have an impact.

Little changed until the 2010s, when the state's leadership started to prioritize passing new abortion restrictions. There was a twenty-week ban in 2012 (it was ultimately blocked by federal courts), and, in the years that followed, lawmakers prohibited doctors from using telemedicine to provide medication abortion, added new regulations on how clinics could operate, banned abortion on the basis of sex selection, and limited the cases in which state-backed insurance plans could cover abortion. Still, abortion never emerged as the principal target it had become in other conservative-led states—lawmakers never passed a six-week ban, a trigger law, or any new policies that could cut off access to the procedure completely if *Roe* fell.

Things changed in 2021, the year before *Dobbs,* when the state passed what was then one of its most meaningful restrictions: a law that prohibited abortion in cases of a genetic anomaly in the fetus. Such "reasons bans" were a popular restriction in the lead-up to *Dobbs,* and one that arguably violated the *Roe* guarantee, albeit less blatantly than a straightforward gestational limit. But buried in Arizona's law was another legal change: language arguing that a fetus had the same rights as a person, a provision that, if enforced, could be used to ban abortion, in vitro fertilization, and even some methods of birth control—and could treat those actions as murder. Abortion providers swiftly challenged the law, but a federal judge, while striking down the state's reasons prohibition, declined to block the fetal personhood provision. Practically, that part of the law had no real impact anyway, as long as *Roe* existed. Then, in 2022, with anticipation building that the 1973 case might be overturned or at the very least weakened, Arizona's Republican-led government settled on a new law, prohibiting abortions after fifteen weeks. That ban would take effect in the late summer of 2022, ostensibly well after the Supreme Court would rule. It was a deliberate choice; a Republican lawmaker had introduced other, harsher abortion bans, including one that would have revised Arizona's pre-*Roe* ban to treat abortion as a felony and another that would have replicated Texas's six-week abortion ban. But instead, lawmakers had settled on what seemed more moderate, more likely to survive court challenges, and less likely to engender backlash in a state where most people supported at least some access to abortion.

The bevy of laws over the past decade carried clear implications, abortion rights lawyers would argue: when Arizona's own lawmakers planned for a post-*Roe* future, they had assumed their pre-statehood ban didn't apply. There was no reason it should ever take effect. But tacit repeal of a law doesn't have the same impact as actually undoing it. And in the months leading up to the Supreme Court's decision, legal experts and abortion providers alike had tried desperately to figure out what the law in Arizona might be—whether a total ban or fifteen-week one would take precedence when *Roe* fell, and who, if anyone, would be able to access an abortion in the state. Lawmakers gave conflicting answers. The governor at the time, Republican Doug Ducey, said that the newest law trumped all others: if the *Dobbs* decision came before the new fifteen-week ban took effect—slated for the end of summer 2022—abortions would still be available up to the point a fetus could live on its own outside the womb, and eventually the state would enforce its fifteen-week restriction. But some legislators suggested the exact opposite, arguing that if *Roe* disappeared there was no reason the 1864 ban shouldn't take effect. With nobody able to confirm what would happen, clinicians would simply have to wait and see what they would be allowed to do if *Roe* fell.

On June 24, 2022, with the federal right to an abortion gone, that theoretical question had become a painful reality. Physicians across the state were on their own, trying to figure out if they could provide basic, in some cases lifesaving, health care, and the wrong guess could put them in prison. Steeling herself, Gibson called the clinic to make sure her staff knew: with the risks being what they were, they couldn't provide abortions this weekend, and she'd be on her way in soon to start breaking the news to patients. To end their pregnancies, people would have to look for appointments somewhere else, perhaps in California, Nevada, or New Mexico.

Gibson's clinic wasn't the only one to send patients home that day, forced to halt abortion care with no real warning. Just three miles east, Dr. Gabrielle Goodrick, who ran the independent clinic Camelback Family Planning, began her morning convinced they'd be able to care for everyone on the schedule. The fifteen-week ban didn't take effect for months, and she told herself there was no way lawmakers would enforce a law whose passage predated Arizona even being a state. It wasn't until lunch, halfway through the day, when the clinic's lawyers told her otherwise. Things weren't as clear-cut as they'd hoped, and they couldn't say for sure if abortion was still legal. Goodrick could finish up any patients whose abortions had begun. But the rest—the ten people scheduled for Friday afternoon, plus anyone with an abortion on the books for the following Saturday, Monday, or Tuesday—were out of luck. Goodrick sent them home. "It was safer that way," she said. But, months later, the anger stayed with her. "I wish we could have seen those patients."

Clinicians in other states with abortion bans were having similar conversations, doing their best to offer patients advice on where they could find care, if they could afford the trip. But in Arizona the shock providers felt was tinged by something else: a potent blend of regret, frustration, and confusion. It wasn't just that people didn't know what their rights were. It also felt like all of this could have been avoided—there had been half a century for the state to clarify what Arizona's laws actually were. Statehouse lobbyists in Phoenix had been trying for years to get the state's pre-*Roe* ban undone, but the bills they pushed never seemed to go anywhere. The lack of urgency wasn't unusual. Even in states whose leaders ardently supported abortion rights, governments had only in the past few years begun to undo pre-*Roe* bans; winning lawmakers over in a state like Arizona was a far tougher sell.

After *Dobbs,* Arizonans had to resign themselves to months of back-and-forth; clinics and doctors would change what kind of care they offered on a moment's notice, based on the latest rulings from the state's judges. Gibson described those months as a "roller coaster." Even when it seemed like the uncertainty might be over, the fear lingered that—in a place where abortion rights had long taken a back seat and whose politics still remained somewhat unpredictable—the state was always just one election away from another sudden loss of the full spectrum of reproductive health care. Physicians caring for high-risk patients—including those with wanted pregnancies now facing complications—had no idea what care, if any, they were allowed to provide. Dr. Laura Mercer, an ob-gyn, recalled working the night shift *Dobbs* weekend, when, as far as she could understand, abortion had been completely outlawed. The patient she was caring for had a pregnancy that, because of severe chromosomal abnormalities in the fetus, neonatal specialists had described as "incompatible with life." But when the woman went into labor just before the end of the second trimester, Mercer had no idea what she was supposed to do. Usually in a situation like this where the fetus had no chance of living, she would recommend helping the patient deliver early. Now, though, she wasn't sure if that was even allowed. Did Mercer have an obligation to somehow stop the patient's labor from progressing? Medically, who was her primary responsibility: the pregnant woman lying here in her hospital room, or the fetus with minimal chance of living, but that did, at that stage, have a beating heart?

Days after *Dobbs,* Arizona's Republican attorney general issued a statement saying that, per his office's legal review, the state's 1864 abortion ban could take effect and that his office would swiftly begin enforcing it. Still, it wasn't clear how soon providers were required to comply—especially if the governor had long argued the exact opposite. (Both the attorney general and governor would be replaced by Democrats in the 2022 elections.) Two weeks later, a federal court in Arizona issued a decision blocking the state's other major abortion ban, the 2021 fetal personhood law. It felt like a green light. Abortion providers in the state resumed their work the next day, providing abortions up until viability, around twenty-four weeks—only to hear, while in the literal midst of seeing patients, that the attorney general's office had filed a lawsuit in state court to reinstate Arizona's pre-*Roe* abortion ban. Once again, they were waiting for news telling them whether they could keep caring for patients. But nobody knew when they might get a decision or how long it might take to go into effect. It seemed like lawyers were giving conflicting information, Goodrick said; she had to take her best guess as to whether they were even allowed to stay open. And she had to convey that uncertainty to her employees, who relied on her to know whether doing their jobs could put them in prison.

At Planned Parenthood, the staff had been handing out flyers to patients, doing their best to explain what was currently allowed. Before the *Dobbs* decision, the flyers warned patients that abortion could soon be outlawed in the state and that they should plan accordingly. Soon after, they had to revise the sheets again, to tell patients that abortion was unavailable here and letting them know where they could travel, as well as what kinds of requirements other states had for people seeking abortions. After the judge ruled, Gibson once again had her team update their flyers: Yes, they were pretty sure abortion here was legal. No, they had no idea how long that would last. If patients wanted to terminate a pregnancy, they had to move quickly—but they should also know that there was a good chance their appointment would be canceled and they would have to go somewhere else. The Tucson Abortion Support Collective, a small abortion fund, held a community teach-in focused on trying to help everyone simply understand when abortion had been legal in the state and when it had not been. Just tracking it all on one calendar felt like a Herculean task, said Sarah Tarver-Wahlquist, one of the collective's members. Everyone seemed confused by the whiplash over such a simple question: What basic rights were they entitled to?

Across the country, uncertainty reigned when it came to this category of law: decades-old bans that had never been repealed. There was no real precedent for how to address pre-*Roe* bans, which typically had almost no exceptions and exacted harsh penalties for those who violated them. Instead, the question of access initially came down to how individual governors, attorneys general, and even county prosecutors interpreted laws that in some cases predated their state's founding. After *Dobbs,* abortion providers filed lawsuit after lawsuit challenging states' pre-*Roe* bans. The final decision on each law would lie with individual state court systems, and rulings would vary across the country, meaning that clinicians often could not predict with any real certainty whether they had even a shot of prevailing.

Often, these bans—sometimes called "zombie laws," seemingly back from the dead—served as a stopgap, a bridge to block abortion access until a newer law could take effect. In West Virginia, the threat of violating a pre-*Roe* ban forced the state's sole abortion clinic to halt terminations for several weeks, even though, as in Arizona, the state had far more recently passed a less restrictive ban— one that would have kept abortion legal up until fifteen weeks. The threat of violating West Virginia's old law ended access to abortion until a state court stepped in; months later, the state legislature passed a new near-total prohibition.

In Texas and Alabama, where lawmakers had passed more recent abortion bans, and with governments run entirely by abortion-opposing Republicans, these older laws allowed lawmakers to block abortion access as soon as *Roe* fell; their newer trigger bans couldn't have an impact at least until the Supreme Court's decision had been certified by state government. Alabama's zombie law was in effect for only hours before the state could begin to enforce its post-*Dobbs* trigger law. Texas's trigger law took longer: it became active two months after the Supreme Court's decision. Until then, its 1857 abortion ban, which was passed before Texas seceded to join the Civil War Confederacy, empowered the attorney general to deny patients access much sooner. The impact was immediately devastating. Andrea Gallegos, then still operating a clinic out of San Antonio, sent twenty-five patients home the Friday *Roe* fell—the threat of violating the state's zombie law was too great. Three days later, the following Tuesday, a state judge blocked the pre-*Roe* ban, meaning that abortion was once again available in the state up until six weeks of pregnancy. Gallegos called every patient she had sent home; of the twenty-five, only ten—fewer than half—came back to her clinic. Those who could make the trip back sobbed with joy on the phone. But there were others she wouldn't see again: a handful of patients didn't pick up, some had already made appointments in New Mexico, and others had, over the weekend, crossed the six-week threshold. Those were the most devastating cases; Gallegos knew that enforcing the zombie law for even a few days had made abortion impossible to access in their home state. All she could do was hope they might find an appointment somewhere else.

Even in other states, where new bans had no chance at passing—because of divided government or because of the political risk—the zombie laws gave conservative lawmakers a chance to block abortion access without having to navigate the political fallout. Wisconsin's abortion providers, fearful of violating the state's 1849 ban, halted services once *Roe* was overturned. Hillary McLaren, a doctor in Illinois, got a call literally that day from a colleague in Wisconsin, whose patient, much like Laura Mercer's, was carrying a pregnancy with fetal abnormalities deemed incompatible with life. She could not give birth to a healthy baby, but the threat of the pre-*Roe* ban had tied her doctors' hands. They had no choice but to send her—alone, without her partner or children or support system of any kind—to see McLaren in Chicago. Wisconsin's attorney general and governor had challenged their state law in court and indicated they had no desire to enforce it, and the governor, a Democrat up for reelection, even promised clemency to anyone who was found by a court to have broken the state's law. But it wasn't enough to guarantee security; governors can change, the Republican-run state legislature largely opposed abortion rights, and at the time the state's supreme court had a narrow conservative majority, who many providers feared would ultimately uphold the ban. The ban stayed active for more than a year—abortions in Wisconsin did not resume until September 2023, following a state court ruling—and the Wisconsin judiciary was so influential that abortion rights groups campaigned that same year at an unprecedented level in elections for the state supreme court, making it the most expensive judicial election in American history. (The candidate in favor of abortion protections, Judge Janet Protasiewicz, won handily.)

Across the lake in Michigan, a similar pre-*Roe* law remained on the books—but with different outcomes. Throughout the state, clinicians largely continued to offer care, buoyed by a series of early court rulings blocking the ban, by the support of a governor who staunchly supported abortion rights, and ultimately by a state vote explicitly adding abortion protections to the state's constitution. (One Michigan court ruling did temporarily allow individual prosecutors to charge clinicians under the zombie law, though the decision did little to stop abortion providers from offering services or to stop patients from seeking them.) After the 2022 elections, Michigan's government, run completely by Democrats, repealed its zombie law.

The uncertainty was arguably most palpable in Arizona; in no other state had elected officials of the same party taken directly opposing stances about which abortion ban to enforce. Flip-flopping court decisions would repeatedly change the state's laws back and forth for months. The whiplash in states like Arizona had implications beyond state borders; across the country, polling showed that Americans did not know whether abortion was legal in their state and whether they could access care. (Public opinion data from early 2023 showed that one in ten Americans in states with legal abortion incorrectly believed mifepristone was illegal in their states, and only 44 percent knew they could legally get an abortion.) The confusion often felt, if not deliberate, certainly effective: it convinced people that they could not receive health care to which they were in fact legally entitled. The implications—on clinicians' ability to offer care, as well as patients' ability to seek it or knowledge of its legality—would radiate with no obvious resolution in sight.

Providers across Arizona began to report challenges in holding on to staff, a product of the unending uncertainty. Some staffers left the state altogether, moving to places where they knew they could continue to do their work unencumbered. Others stayed local but simply found jobs elsewhere, leaving the reproductive health care field. Gibson could hardly blame them. The fear of a new ban taking effect and not knowing when it might happen had a direct impact on clinics' revenues. And there remained the lingering fear that at some point the state might force them to shut things down altogether. How could you ask someone to stay, to keep providing care, when they didn't know how much longer their job might even exist?

Despite the tenuous access, Arizona clinics were, whenever their total ban was blocked, seeing patients who had come from states enforcing even more punitive abortion restrictions—largely people from Texas and Oklahoma who hadn't been able to get an appointment anywhere else. The demand came on top of the crunch in staff. Arizona, like most states in the country, allows only physicians to administer abortions, a restriction criticized by many reproductive health care providers and researchers, who frequently note that nurse practitioners and physicians' assistants—of whom there are often far more—can also be trained to provide this kind of care. That state law meant that, at Planned Parenthood, Gibson was often the only provider available to perform abortions. Arizona's telemedicine prohibition meant that doctors had to see patients in person, even though medication abortion can safely be offered through the mail with a virtual consult. And, much like in Florida, patients were required to make two in-person visits to an abortion clinic, separated by at least twenty-four hours.

The strain stretched wait times for an abortion to three or four weeks; at the same time, finding new physicians to join abortion clinics grew more difficult. Beyond the worry that clinics could shut down again with little to no notice, providers felt like there was a new level of vitriol and harassment directed their way—it seemed as if the *Dobbs* decision had emboldened abortion opponents. For someone like Gibson, the loss of staff meant more responsibilities fell on her. Yes, she was often the only person in the building who could provide abortions, but there was so much more she had to do: she was also the only one who could insert or remove intrauterine devices, who could perform colposcopies for patients with abnormal pap smears, or who could do procedures that required sedation. As abortion took up more of her time, she couldn't find room to schedule patients for those other complex gynecological procedures. Just as had been the case in so many other states, patients' ability to access reproductive health care suffered across the board.

Even when abortion was legal, patients were deterred by how long it would take for them to be seen, and they made appointments in California instead, if they could afford it and if it was safe for them to travel. It's difficult to track how many undocumented people live in any single state, but about 250,000 live in Arizona, the thirteenth-largest share in the country and 3.4 percent of the state's population, according to estimates from the Pew Research Center. (About 4.4 percent of reproductive-aged women in Arizona are undocumented, per those same estimates.) People traveling out of state, and specifically driving from Phoenix the five hours to San Diego or the five and a half hours to Los Angeles, were likely to run into an immigration checkpoint; that threat alone was reason enough for people to stay away from the California border. Those who lived farther south in Arizona, in a town like Patagonia, not even twenty miles from the Mexican border, had no way to travel north without risking a stop by immigration officials; they certainly couldn't travel south of the border. Eloisa Lopez, who ran the Abortion Fund of Arizona, found herself referring people who were undocumented to clinics in Las Vegas whenever she could. If they traveled that way, they were less likely to be stopped by authorities. But, even with that caveat, not everyone felt comfortable traveling. She knew through the grapevine that some patients who couldn't leave the state were finding abortion pills through other, extralegal back channels, getting them online or from friends and taking them at home, sometimes without medical supervision. They didn't have any other options.

When, in September 2022, the clinic's lawyers told Gibson the news—another judge had ruled, and once again abortion was banned in Arizona—she almost resented that she felt surprised. After everything she and other providers had gone through, she really shouldn't have been expecting stability, let alone any longer-term relief. But instead Gibson had been holding out hope that they'd finally get some clarity, maybe even a promise that Arizona would allow abortions to remain legal. Now she'd once again have to cancel any procedures they had scheduled. She knew what that meant. Every time a patient lost an appointment, the challenge of finding a new one—tracking down a clinic and making sure it had a timely appointment available, finding the money and making the arrangements to travel out of state—could prove to be too much. Some of her patients would be able to reschedule their abortions elsewhere. But for others it would be impossible. The hardest part was knowing that, if only they'd been scheduled a few days earlier, they would have been able to get care with no problem. It was a matter of bad timing, of the worst possible luck.

Two weeks later, in early October 2022, yet another court ruled differently, this time reversing the decision to let Arizona ban abortion. That court, just one tier below Arizona's state supreme court, had a higher level of authority. For at least a few months, the decision promised, the state would allow abortions to continue. But the same day, the state's other ban—the newer law, which prohibited abortion for anyone past fifteen weeks of pregnancy—would now take effect. Clinics across the state started hearing back from patients who had lost their appointments and now wanted another chance to get an abortion. Planned Parenthood booked two weeks of abortion appointments within forty-eight hours; Gibson spent all the time she could trying to recruit more physicians to join her in providing care. Still, it was clear that not everyone who had lost their abortion appointment would be able to get a new one—for some, it was impossible to plan another trip to Phoenix or Tucson or Flagstaff, the other cities where abortion clinics operated. Others simply never learned about the latest change in the law.

For patients, just keeping track of their rights seemed virtually impossible. Lopez constantly found herself receiving calls from people with no idea as to whether they could get an abortion. Even a short-lived loss in access could be enough to throw people off; after hearing that their appointment had been canceled or catching a story on the news about abortion being banned, many would never hear about its reversal and what that meant for them. As long as multiple abortion bans remained on the books, the risk remained that the state would again boomerang between competing laws. At any point, different judges or lawmakers could step in to change what bans were enforced and how—returning the state with little warning to a place where abortion was once again outlawed. In early fall 2023, the state supreme court—whose members were all appointed by Arizona's Republican governors, including one justice who had once accused Planned Parenthood of "the greatest genocide known to man"—finally agreed to weigh in on the state's abortion laws. They heard the case that December, a full year and a half since *Roe* had been overturned and Arizona's legislative chaos had begun. Once again, abortion providers were forced to simply hold their breath and wait.

———

With days left before his initial appointment at Planned Parenthood, Jasper kept playing the scenarios out in his mind. An open, friendly person by nature, he loved children deeply, and he knew that he was good with them. He'd even thought about someday, once he had his college degree, teaching kindergarten full-time. But there was a difference between working well with kids and being a good dad, and when it came to the latter, he definitely didn't think he was up to the task—maybe not ever, but certainly not now. He was still a teenager, still figuring out what his life was going to look like, and still living with his parents so that he could stretch his thin paychecks a bit further each month.

Jasper and his boyfriend had talked about abortion before; if he ever got pregnant, they'd long established that this was the path they would take. And, intellectually, the more Jasper thought about the past few weeks, the more he internalized the risks to the fetus growing inside him. He still didn't think his body would be able to give birth to a healthy child. He didn't have the money to raise a baby or a stable enough home life. Getting an abortion was the right thing to do.

Still, no one had warned him how hard this would feel and how ardently he would wish for more time to figure out what he wanted to do. His boyfriend kept talking about it logically: They'd get an abortion, and after that everything would be taken care of. They'd never have to talk about any of this again. But, much as Jasper knew his boyfriend was right, none of this felt that simple. By the stage of pregnancy he'd hit, a fetus is not viable and cannot live outside the uterus. Still, it felt as if on some level he was experiencing a primal instinct: his body wanted to protect the being growing inside him, which he'd begun to think of as a baby, and it felt as if nobody else could truly understand what he was going through. He'd spend the next few days pretending to himself that he was going to keep the pregnancy, imagining that he would give birth to a healthy baby, that he'd be able to do a good job being a dad. But he knew it wasn't real.

Jasper's first appointment was August 10, four days after that imaging appointment that had initially revealed his pregnancy. There, he learned that the nurse's read wasn't quite correct; instead of twelve weeks, he was closer to fourteen weeks along, days away from the state deadline. The clinic, following Florida law, provided him with an ultrasound and government-crafted counseling—materials meant to dissuade him from seeking an abortion. They ran his lab tests, including a urine sample to confirm his pregnancy, and the doctor told him what, precisely, the procedure would entail. In total, getting an abortion would cost him about $785, an expense the couple could split, though it did mean canceling a vacation to Chicago they'd long been planning. Chicago, he told himself, would always be there. But if he didn't get an abortion now, he'd soon have the choice made for him. Even at the clinic, Jasper couldn't shake a sense of frustration. It made no sense to him to separate this visit from the day of his actual abortion; all the waiting period did was push him closer and closer to the state's legal limit.

Sitting there that day, Jasper knew the right decision for him. Clearly, he couldn't stay pregnant. He was too young, and he didn't have the money or the career or the stability to give a child the life he would want to. In three days—Saturday morning, exactly a week after learning he was pregnant—he'd come back to the clinic for his abortion.

That night, Jasper slept at his boyfriend's before going home to his father and stepmother the next day, neither of whom knew he was pregnant. He wasn't showing, and he hadn't told them. Still, he felt the symptoms of panic coming on: the thumping heart, the way everything sounded a little bit louder, and the hint of dizziness. Could they see it on his face? Would they figure out what he had done—or what he was about to do?

Jasper inhaled deliberately, eventually feeling his heart rate slow down. He needed to get ahold of himself. Rationally, he knew they couldn't have figured out what was going on. And once his abortion was over, there was no need for them to ever find out. He just had to make it a few more days. Maybe after Saturday, he could finally put all this behind him.

Arizona represented a state in the midst of political transition: once red, now slowly trending purple. It was the kind of switch that progressive activists across the country looked to as a model, and one that had taken more than a decade to pull off, due in part to deliberate grassroots organizing but also thanks to substantial changes in the state's demographics. The changes underway had helped Democrats win repeated statewide elections, and even the legislature—run by Republicans for decades—was within only a few seats of shifting parties by 2023.

Still, it hadn't yet changed how people talked about abortion. Abortion funds, some of Arizona's biggest local advocates for abortion rights, were fairly new to the state: the Abortion Fund of Arizona launched in 2017, the same year as Tucson Abortion Support Collective. NARAL, the national abortion rights advocacy group, had a small presence in the state until 2019.

Doctors like Gibson weren't used to having to lobby on behalf of their patients or for the ability to keep providing care. They hadn't ever thought lawmakers "would go there," she said—by which she meant pass laws that literally stopped them from practicing medicine the way they were trained. "This has been a wake-up call," she said. "I'm not trying to become a politician. But you have to, if you're interested and engaged and don't want to have the practice of medicine taken away from those who have studied to do it." Mercer described it as a form of complacency: "I, like many of my colleagues and many of the women in the United States, sort of took *Roe* for granted," she reflected. Historically, many doctors had been hesitant to take a strong stance on abortion rights; the American Medical Association, which never even filed an amicus brief in the original *Roe v. Wade* case, began assertively challenging abortion bans only in the late 2010s, just a few years before the Supreme Court overturned *Roe*.

Part of it was that sense of abortion exceptionalism—the idea that abortion was somehow separate from other forms of health care and that it wasn't worth arguing on behalf of access. "It was just easier to not have to take a position on something that can be so politically or individually divisive," Mercer said. Only in recent years had that hesitancy shifted, as threats to abortion became even more apparent and as even more epidemiological research illustrated the medical harms of denying people access. "That has made it less about an individual's personal feelings about abortion and more about the overall idea that abortion is health care. And when it comes to health care, we've got to do what's right for our patients." It wasn't an issue unique to medical spaces, either. Lopez, from the abortion fund, said she frequently felt unwelcome in the state's progressive coalitions, getting a sense from them that because her group focused explicitly and specifically on paying for people's abortions, it was seen as too polarizing.

Advocates for abortion rights had worked in the state for decades, but it seemed like the issue often hadn't been treated as the existential concern it soon would become. Polling didn't necessarily suggest that abortion was a winning issue, even among voters who were sympathetic to other causes that liberals typically supported. Progressive organizers, who hoped they could mobilize state residents to oppose voting restrictions or to come out in favor of immigrant rights, noticed something similar: voters who seemed persuadable on those issues still were squeamish about abortion, or at the very least didn't want to prioritize it. The energy shifted, said Jenny Guzman, a community organizer in Phoenix who largely focused on reproductive rights, only after Trump's election and then the decision to hear *Dobbs*. Polling in the months leading up to June 2022 showed that Arizonans opposed the total ban that the state retained on the books and that, without *Roe*, could actually take effect. But by then it was too late.

Likewise, nationally, losing *Roe* created what some analysts suggested could be a political realignment of sorts—voters changing their political parties and preferences specifically because of the abortion rights issue. In Arizona, it seemed that this could be the moment progressives had been waiting for. But the challenge was figuring out what to actually do next.

Some had been arguing for a ballot initiative, though even what the measure would achieve remained a source of debate. The week after a draft of the *Dobbs* opinion leaked, a group called Arizonans for Reproductive Freedom sprang into action, filing a petition to have the state vote that fall on whether to codify abortion rights.

The measure would have preserved what was then the status quo in Arizona, protecting abortion rights up until the point of fetal viability. But the effort was doomed to fail. Other abortion rights organizations in the state, including Planned Parenthood, the Abortion Fund of Arizona, Arizona List, and NARAL, weren't involved in the campaign (or, representatives said, even consulted before it launched). And there wasn't enough time. To make the November 2022 ballot, a citizen-initiated referendum in Arizona needed close to 384,000 signatures by July; Arizonans for Reproductive Freedom didn't even come close to that. Still, the momentum and interest in preserving abortion rights seemed clear: within just sixty-one days, 175,000 Arizonans had put their names to the ballot proposal. That energy was a sign, argued people like Amy Fitch-Heacock, the head of Arizonans for Reproductive Freedom. Clearly, the state would come out in favor of abortion rights if given the chance—and the next election, 2024, was two years away. They had time to raise money, get signatures, and figure out what measure might have the best chance of success. It was an approach gaining favor even in states with a more conservative lean. A similar effort launched in Florida after the passage of its six-week ban, with abortion rights advocates pushing for a 2024 vote to amend the state constitution to explicitly protect abortion rights up to fetal viability. (If enacted, such an amendment could nullify both a six-week and fifteen-week abortion ban.)

But a ballot campaign wasn't the only way to preserve abortion rights in Arizona—and some worried it wasn't necessarily the best way. The state legislature was two members away from being Democratically controlled. Perhaps, said Lopez, it would be easier to focus on winning control of the capitol and ensuring that lawmakers could then repeal the state's abortion bans. (Efforts to win control of the legislature failed in 2022.) Ballot initiatives are expensive to run and typically require years of preparation to pull off. Unlike a state like Colorado, Arizona had virtually no history of organizing direct votes on abortion rights, and losing this kind of race could seriously weaken long-term prospects for the state's abortion rights movement. There was also the question of what Arizonans might vote for and what was most likely to actually win. Reverting to the pre-*Dobbs* status quo would represent a massive gain in terms of abortion access in Arizona. But was it really enough? There was a common refrain in abortion rights circles, one that had grown more prominent since June 2022: *Roe,* some activists argued, had never been sufficient. If the plan was to devote resources to an expensive ballot measure, they said, the initiative should seek to expand access to the procedure, allowing abortion at any point in pregnancy, like Colorado did, rather than cutting off access at around twenty-five weeks.

A little more than a year out from the 2024 election, abortion rights organizers discussing a ballot initiative hadn't settled on whether a more expansive abortion protection was workable and whether it could win in Arizona. The polling still wasn't done, and neither were the focus groups. The state's abortion rights coalition was divided on whether to even pursue a constitutional amendment—harder to pull off, but considered a more secure protection—or to simply leverage direct democracy to pass a law repealing Arizona's existing abortion restrictions. Arguably, a well-crafted ballot initiative could increase the chances of flipping the legislature as well, driving turnout among voters who cared specifically about abortion rights. But this kind of electoral effort takes intense planning, and as late as the spring of 2023, Brittany Fonteno, president of Planned Parenthood Arizona, said the state's abortion rights coalition was still in its "exploratory phase" to figure out what exactly might work. "We can't get on the same page," Lopez worried. Only by the end of summer 2023 did the state's abortion rights coalition settle on an initiative that would amend the state's constitution to protect abortion rights up until around twenty-five weeks. Still, it would be difficult at best to secure the signatures needed to get that measure on the state's 2024 ballot; it would also take substantial fundraising to convince voters this was a right worth affirming come Election Day. When in the fall of 2023 Ohio voters turned out in substantial numbers to amend their constitution to protect abortion rights—enshrining an affirmative protection even in a conservative state—it offered a glimmer of hope for comparable efforts in Arizona and Florida. Still, that effort was hard-won, the result of tens of millions of dollars spent by out-of-state groups.

Until something changed in Arizona, the state, with a newly

elected Democratic governor and Democratic attorney general, would stay in a state of indefinite uncertainty. The legislature was still run by Republicans, including those who had advanced the state's fifteen-week ban. But the new governor, Katie Hobbs, who had highlighted abortion rights in her campaign, wouldn't sign off on any new bans and continued to tout herself as someone who supported abortion rights. The new attorney general, Kris Mayes, wouldn't support efforts to reenforce the state's pre-*Roe* abortion ban. Practically, the divide in government meant there was almost no chance of new laws being passed in either direction. With Republicans entrenched in the statehouse, restrictions on abortion such as Arizona's prohibition on telemedicine and its continued twenty-four-hour waiting period requirement would not be undone. The government certainly would not reverse its fifteen-week ban. And the legislature, with its conservative makeup, would also never vote to repeal the state's pre-*Roe* ban, despite representing a state whose residents supported at least some level of abortion access.

What was perhaps most striking was how deeply one single election had mattered. In states like Michigan and Minnesota, where Democrats had sailed into higher office at every level, pre-*Roe* bans were repealed, and lawmakers pushed to codify abortion rights explicitly. In Arizona, that wasn't possible. Instead, Republican lawmakers pushed for bills that might stigmatize abortion and leave open a path to bring back heightened restrictions. In 2023, legislators attempted to pass a bill that would require any "infant who is born alive," including during the course of an abortion for a nonviable pregnancy, be given all forms of lifesaving care possible. Physicians worried that such legislation—which failed to pass— would force them to provide needless care to newborns with no chance of survival, rather than letting parents even briefly hold their babies before they died. And there was another concern, too: while having no medical benefit, and instead causing demonstrable harm, such bills would continue to stigmatize abortion, even though a case of a live birth resulting after an attempted abortion is, per all government data, exceptionally rare. Then there was a slew of bills that would expand the rights of fetuses, making pregnant people eligible for child support payments and child tax credits even before giving birth, or to increase legal penalties against those who assaulted pregnant people. On their face, those types of bills sounded like the type of legislation that might benefit pregnant Arizonans, a "softer" form of the bills being pushed in other states to endow fetuses with the same rights as people, noted Mary Ziegler, an abortion historian who studied fetal personhood legislation. But they had the same logical endpoint, she said: creating a legal framework that, down the line, would allow the state to treat abortion as murder. With a Democrat in the governor's mansion, none of these restrictions became law, but they offered a window into how abortion opponents would try to further limit access even in a state where their stance on the issue was unpopular at best. Meanwhile, the governor did what she could, issuing executive orders meant to block any low-level public prosecutors from enforcing any abortion restriction more stringent than the state's fifteen-week ban. But expanding access beyond the status quo remained impossible.

For providers, the stalemate meant the fear lingered. Even if they could provide abortions for now, albeit in a limited form, a more stringent ban remained on the books. Arizona's constitution did not guarantee the right to an abortion, and there were no state laws protecting access, either. More than a year and a half after the *Dobbs* ruling, there was still no guarantee that the zombie law wouldn't someday take effect again: there was only the pending lawsuit regarding the constitutionality of the state's pre-*Roe* abortion ban. And, even beyond that, the makeup of the courts could change, someone could file a new lawsuit, or the whims of the government could shift toward an administration eager to enforce a total ban. Clinicians could once again find themselves scrambling with no notice to tell people that they'd learned they could no longer provide abortions. In the interim, a fifteen-week limitation was the best they could hope for. It was the law that was supposed to be a compromise—a partial victory for providers and patients in states where passing a six-week restriction or near-total ban was too politically risky.

Still, clinicians were reminded regularly that, though a fifteen-week ban offered a reprieve from the state's zombie law, it too represented a dramatic loss in access. Even though most patients receive abortions earlier in pregnancy, the strains on the state's abortion clinic network meant more and more patients had to wait longer for appointments, getting pushed closer to the fifteen-week mark. For those who couldn't get care in time, leaving the state often wasn't possible.

Gibson received a phone call one afternoon from another doctor at a local hospital, where a woman was being treated for renal failure, requiring dialysis just to function. Her hemoglobin levels were dangerously low, and she was pregnant, a condition that could put extra stress on her kidneys. The pregnancy—which she didn't want—would be at best a high-risk delivery; at worst, it could be fatal. The doctor at the hospital estimated she was just one day past fifteen weeks pregnant. She already had a child at home, a son with congenital heart disease, and she barely made enough to take care of him. She didn't even own a phone. The doctor asked Gibson: Was there anything she could do? Was there some exception that would allow her to provide an abortion?

Technically, Arizona's law allowed abortion when necessary to save the pregnant person's life. But the wording was vague enough, allowing termination only in a "medical emergency," that Gibson, like the state's other physicians, hardly knew what qualified. A case like this might not be dire enough. She told the doctor at the hospital that there was nothing she could do, at least not in Arizona. If the woman followed up with her, maybe Gibson could refer her to a clinic somewhere else. But even as she made the offer, she knew that it was futile. She never got another phone call; she would never find out what happened, if that woman got an abortion or if she gave birth—and if the latter, if she survived doing so. This kind of conversation was hardly uncommon, said Dr. Shelly Tien, a physician who traveled between Florida, Kansas, and Arizona to care for patients. In Arizona, she focused on maternal-fetal medicine, caring for high-risk pregnant patients for whom abortion was often the best option. She frequently found herself speaking with other ob-gyns, trying to navigate the state's narrow medical exception law. What if a patient developed a preterm premature membrane rupture, which increases the risk of infection and can be treated only by ending the pregnancy—by an abortion? If a patient was past fifteen weeks, it was often impossible to know for sure if these cases qualified as a medical emergency, without delaying care to consult with the hospital's board of advisers or attorneys. "It's real," Tien said. "These are common, everyday discussions we have when we're caring for women that have high-risk pregnancies."

"We know what to do, but what's happening is we're all stopping or pausing. We're hesitating because we're afraid that anything that we do could end up causing us legal ramifications," Mercer said. She forced herself to become an expert in what was allowed and what wasn't—no small feat, given how frequently laws changed—and she found herself constantly fielding calls from other doctors across the state. Each week, she would without fail hear from another doctor uncertain about what kind of care they were allowed to provide, worried about their patient's health deteriorating. The questions began to sound familiar: *"Is this still legal?" "Am I allowed to help?"*

The challenges weren't just in providing care. Though Arizona's total ban had been blocked since October, the number of patients getting abortions never truly rebounded; by the end of 2022, the state was tallying close to 850 abortions per month. (By contrast, in the lead-up to *Dobbs,* about 1,500 abortions took place in the state each month.) With abortions banned after fifteen weeks, clinics that had specialized in second-trimester procedures could barely afford to stay in business. The math wasn't complicated for Desert Star Family Planning, a Phoenix-based outpost that was known in particular for offering second-trimester abortions. Abortion clinics typically operate on thin margins, and patients pay less for first-trimester abortions than they do for second-trimester ones. Before the law took effect, Desert Star primarily cared for patients after twelve weeks of pregnancy. With the fifteen-week ban in place, they had lost a critical revenue stream, and one that, no matter how many more patients they saw earlier in their pregnancies, they couldn't make up. "I can't work enough hours in a day or weeks in a month to meet my own basic financial needs," worried Dr. DeShawn Taylor, the physician who ran the clinic. She'd do her best to keep going, but it was hard to promise that they would have the resources to continue. And losing even one clinic could have drastic ramifications; only seven brick-and-mortar facilities offered abortion in Arizona, in a state where close to fourteen thousand abortions occurred per year. Each provider lost meant fewer appointment slots, longer wait times, and more patients forced to leave the state—that is, if they could.

———————

Allowing access up to fifteen weeks was objectively a reprieve after a near-total abortion ban, no matter how brief. But, compared with the viability standard that had once been the norm, fifteen weeks was still a tremendous loss. The challenge was communicating that to the majority of Arizonans. In Arizona, public polling generally failed to ask about a fifteen-week limit specifically, and little independent public opinion data existed that captured whether Arizonans would back limitations on abortion in the second trimester compared with those in the first. Most people hadn't considered what it meant to ban abortion at that point in pregnancy and who would be affected. They'd never had to.

This was how Jen, a twenty-six-year-old in Phoenix, had always thought about it. Abortion, especially so late, was wrong—it was the kind of thing irresponsible girls did: the ones who were careless, who had sex unthinkingly, who didn't consider the consequences. It was a view she'd inherited from her parents. They were Christians, ones who believed that abortion was a sin. And they'd always expected her to be their version of a "good" girl, who had sex only with her husband, who used birth control and didn't get pregnant too early. Jen, a petite young woman on the shyer side, hadn't inherited her parents' faith, but she'd internalized their beliefs about abortion. Someone like her, who followed all the rules and who did her best not to get into trouble, wouldn't ever need to worry about abortion.

And it wasn't just that abortion was wrong. It felt like an abstract issue, one barely relevant to her. Growing up in South Korea, Jen hadn't ever seen abortion as a real option for people she knew—not through legal means, anyway. The practice there was outlawed and became decriminalized only in 2021. By then, Jen had already left Korea to live in the United States for the better half of a decade. She'd immigrated to Arizona when she was just sixteen years old.

Now twenty-six and living near Phoenix, Jen had what felt to her like an ordinary life. Her husband worked in IT, and she was an artist, finding gigs on a freelance basis. Between the two of them, it felt like they had enough money to just about get by. She didn't care for politics and hardly noticed when *Roe v. Wade* was overturned. When she heard in passing that Arizona was enforcing a fifteen-week abortion ban, she didn't think much of it. How could someone not know they were pregnant by then? If they ever wanted an abortion, fifteen weeks sounded like plenty of time. And, frankly, she wouldn't ever need one—she used birth control, and she would have known if she was pregnant.

Jen experienced intense depression, for which she took medication, and the side effects included exhaustion so intense that it was often hard for her to get out of bed. Lately, her fatigue had begun to worsen. It was a deeper kind of malaise that persisted for months, to the point that she was too exhausted to work and had to nap repeatedly to make it through the day. The couple began to rely solely on her husband's earnings to make ends meet. Maybe, she thought, she'd developed a persistent flu. That could explain her chronic tiredness and even the bouts of nausea she'd recently begun to experience. Her body began to change, her scrawny frame looking a bit like it had filled out more. But, if anything, that seemed like good news. Jen had long worried about being underweight, and any change that helped her stay above a hundred pounds must be for the better.

Jen probably wouldn't have taken a pregnancy test at all if not for her husband. He was the one who urged her to do so, convinced that her fatigue must mean something bigger. She didn't believe it when the test was positive; how could she be pregnant when she took birth control? The next morning, Jen took another test just to be sure. Only after the second positive did she make an appointment at an abortion clinic. Much like with Jasper, the mystery ailments she'd battled for months had been no mystery at all—in retrospect, pregnancy was the simplest, most obvious answer.

Having a child just wasn't an option for Jen: the specific type of antidepressants she took each day weren't recommended for pregnant people, and neither was the medication she took for her

ADHD. She'd have to either change her medication or continue with a treatment that worked for her but that she feared could jeopardize the baby's health. They weren't financially ready to support another person, and her mental health wasn't stable enough for her to become a parent. Looking at the positive test, she knew she could not stay in this condition. Even before she had conceived, Jen's depression had often felt debilitating. How could she be present for a baby, someone who needed her unconditional love and full-time support? She knew what the alternative looked like: Jen's mother, whom she had stopped talking to years ago, had told her often as a child that she had never wanted to give birth to her and that she wished it would have been possible to abort her—an ironic sentiment, given how Jen's parents vocally opposed abortion. It was an awful thing to hear. And it solidified for Jen that when she became a mom she wanted to be ready, and to be the kind of parent who could love her child unreservedly, without hesitation or resentment.

When the staff at the clinic looked at her ultrasound, it seemed as if they couldn't quite believe how far along she was. Jen was barely showing; her stomach looked a bit bloated, as if maybe she'd eaten something that disagreed with her. In fact, she was in her second trimester already—it turned out that she had been pregnant for five months, or about twenty weeks. By the time she'd even thought to take her first pregnancy test, she'd already been well past the state's fifteen-week limit. And now, if she wanted an abortion, she'd have no choice but to leave the state. The doctor told her that her best bet would be traveling to California or Las Vegas. If the price was too high, she recommended Jen try a few abortion funds to help manage the cost.

The procedure would take three days at a clinic in Las Vegas. The staff estimated an abortion at her stage of pregnancy would cost about $2,500—less than what she'd been told by the California providers—and the clinic had a patient assistance fund that would cut the price in half. Still, when you added in the gas money and the nights that they'd have to stay at a Vegas hotel, it was well more than Jen and her husband could afford. She started calling and emailing any abortion fund she could find online, unsure of what she was doing. When she didn't hear back, she would panic, researching and emailing and calling more groups. Finally, they got a reply from the Abortion Fund of Arizona. Then they heard from a few more funds. Between all the donations they received, Jen and her husband would have to pay no more than six hundred dollars for their whole trip. Without that help, she knew, there was no way they could have afforded it.

Jen and her husband drove to Las Vegas on a Sunday night. Her appointment was the next morning, nine thirty sharp at the clinic. She went inside the facility while her husband waited in the car, working on his laptop from the driver's seat so that he wouldn't have to take three days off. The clinic staff were wonderful, she said—kind, thoughtful, and so eager to help her any way they could. Still, much as Jen thought she had researched what an abortion would be like, nobody had warned her just how it would feel: the physical pain of the procedure, which was far worse than anything she'd ever experienced, or the harassment she faced each day from the protesters who lined the streets outside the clinic, yelling at her not to harm her baby. *They care so much about "life,"* she thought. *But they don't care anything about people like me*—someone who mentally, physically, and financially could not responsibly bring a child into the world. If these people cared so much about protecting babies, she kept asking, why didn't they want to help the people who were already parents?

Jen never told anyone about her abortion; she and her parents had hardly any relationship now, and even if they did, she knew they wouldn't understand. But the experience changed her. She wanted more people to understand what she hadn't, to understand just how essential abortion was and how punitive a ban at fifteen weeks felt. She couldn't be the only person with a story like hers— someone who didn't figure out they were pregnant until it was too late, and who knew they wouldn't be able to give a child the life they deserved.

This, of course, was the challenge Arizona's organizers had to navigate if they hoped to restore access to abortion, let alone expand it. There were so many people like Jen who hadn't thought or cared about abortion, or who even in the wake of losing *Roe* didn't consider that a fifteen-week ban might affect them. Now they had to convince those people otherwise.

Back in Florida, fourteen weeks and five days pregnant, Jasper woke up at seven a.m. on Saturday, aiming to be at Planned Parenthood right when it opened forty-five minutes later. The clinic was still quiet when he and his boyfriend arrived, but slowly, as the morning progressed, more and more patients started showing up. He couldn't stop watching the others: some who looked like they were there for birth control or pap smears, others who he deduced must be in a situation like his. There was one girl he kept glancing at. She was clutching the pictures from her ultrasound. Seeing the fear, confusion, and sorrow on her face, he felt like he was looking in a mirror. Maybe, he thought, he should go talk to her; he could try his best to commiserate with her, or at the very least offer her a hug. But he couldn't muster the courage to walk over to her—it didn't feel like his place, and besides, he wasn't good at starting conversations like that.

The two young men sat in the waiting room for hours before it was Jasper's turn. Because he was in his second trimester, he couldn't get a medication abortion. Instead, Jasper had what's called a dilation and evacuation procedure: he received a mild sedative and then medication to help open up his cervix, followed by a simple surgery to remove the fetus from inside him. It was a safe, effective, easy procedure—and what Jasper could remember of it was immensely painful, enough to reduce him to tears before the sedation kicked in. But when he awoke, it was over. He was no longer pregnant, and the mystery symptoms that had plagued him all summer disappeared almost immediately. They left the clinic by early afternoon.

Jasper's boyfriend had picked up dinner for the two of them—pho from a restaurant they both loved—and the couple watched TV in bed all evening. He still couldn't process what they'd been through the past week. In just seven days, he'd learned he was pregnant, processed the news, scheduled an abortion, and, over two visits to a clinic, been able to terminate his pregnancy. He didn't regret his decision. But the feeling stayed with him—a nagging, insistent voice asking him, *What if?* What if he'd been able to remain pregnant, give birth, and maybe put the child up for adoption? Would the baby have been healthy? Physically, would he have been able to handle the pregnancy? Could he have figured out his life enough to maybe become a parent, young as he was? They were questions he'd never been given a chance to fully ask himself, let alone to consider the answer.

He just kept wishing that he'd had more time to decide. But he knew that was magical thinking. Where he lived, time was a luxury nobody could afford.

———

CHAPTER 10

How Far Will This Go?

Washington, D.C.

Barbara Lee hadn't thought this was a story she'd ever tell. Frankly, it wasn't one she thought she should ever have to.

It had been close to sixty years since that day when, at just fifteen years old, Lee had boarded a plane from California to El Paso, looking for someone who would help end her pregnancy. In the 1960s, abortion still wasn't legal anywhere in the United States; *Roe* wouldn't be decided for more than ten years, and back then the only way to get an abortion was to know someone who knew someone—and to have the means to travel to wherever that someone might work. For Lee, a cheerleader at San Fernando High School, that somewhere was Juárez, Mexico, just across the border from El Paso. That someone was a doctor whom her mother's friend from Texas had recommended to them soon after Lee's missing period confirmed that she was pregnant.

Now, at seventy-five years old, Lee was a fixture in Washington, D.C., a congresswoman from California for close to twenty-five years. But she could still vividly recall that teenage odyssey. There was the doctor who treated her in a dimly lit clinic, a small building situated in an alley in Juárez. Her mother's friend had told them not to worry, that this doctor knew what he was doing, words she kept repeating to herself. But still, she knew the statistics of all the other

Americans—especially young Black women like herself—who had died after contracting sepsis from their surreptitious illegal abortions, a disparity that would only take on heightened significance in the post-*Dobbs* world. Per data collected by the Pew Research Center, close to 50 percent of Black Americans lived in states that, by the end of 2023, had abortion bans cutting off access sometime before the second trimester began; most of those bans almost totally outlawed the procedure. Sitting at the clinic in Juárez, Lee had prayed silently that things would go better for her. Even after the procedure, after returning home to San Fernando, it took ages to overcome the fear of being caught. She'd broken the law, hadn't she? What if someone found out? Would they send her to jail for her abortion? It was, of course, a perfect parallel to the silent worries that would plague pregnant Americans decades later, those who, like Lee, missed the window of *Roe*'s protections.

For sixty years, Lee told nobody what had happened, discussing her abortion only with her mother. But the experience fueled her career. In 1998, upon beginning her first term on Capitol Hill, Lee immersed herself in abortion rights work, helping spearhead a campaign to repeal the Hyde Amendment, the federal policy that prevented government-funded health insurance programs from covering the procedure. Even more than twenty years after *Roe,* "abortion" still felt like a dirty word in Washington. Any lawmaker who prioritized abortion access—let alone called the procedure by its name—was treated as an extremist. And for all her work on abortion rights, Lee hoped she would never have to share her story. It was, she'd say later, nobody's business but her own.

But by September 2021 the situation had become dire. Texas had begun to enforce its six-week ban, and Lee had realized that *Roe*'s protections wouldn't last more than a few months at best. If they didn't do something, she began to fear, the world she so vividly remembered—where you could get an abortion only if you had the right contacts, and where countless young girls like herself risked their lives to attain reproductive autonomy—would be a reality once more. Someone had to make Congress understand what was about to happen and what it actually meant to live without the promise of abortion access. The country had to know just how common abortion was. Everyone, no matter their status in American society, would lose something essential if *Roe* was overturned.

Telling her story, Lee, in a black-and-white suit, appeared poised, by turns angry and thoughtful. It was a mask, just like the sparkly fabric face covering she wore that day, concealing just how scared she felt. Lee had joined a tiny club, becoming one of just a handful of sitting elected officials to share her story of getting an abortion.

It could have been a turning point. Afterward, Lee remembered politician after politician approaching her, men telling her about the abortions that their wives and girlfriends had received. Two other Democrats, Missouri's Cori Bush and Washington's Pramila Jayapal, shared their own stories of abortion as well—Bush's from a pregnancy after she was raped as a teenager, Jayapal's from when, still recovering from debilitating postpartum depression, she learned that a new pregnancy faced serious medical complications. By sharing their experiences, Lee hoped, the three of them might break down the stigma that still surrounded abortion. But in a practical sense it didn't change much. Nine months later, the Supreme Court overturned *Roe*. Instead of a warning, Lee's story would function as a preview of what kind of country the United States would soon become. And it would offer yet another reminder that, in defiance of all those who had long feared *Roe*'s fall, the federal government had done nothing to prepare.

The modern Democratic Party supported abortion rights, but sometimes it had seemed like that support didn't extend beyond rhetoric. Between 1989 and 2007, a handful of Democratic lawmakers repeatedly introduced a bill they called the Freedom of Choice Act. On the heels of the 1992 *Casey* decision that many had thought could lead to *Roe*'s overturn, it seemed for a moment like the time was ripe for abortion rights to finally pass. Democrats controlled the White House and both chambers of Congress. Even then, the politics around abortion were tricky. Bill Clinton had campaigned on keeping abortion "safe, legal, and rare"; his bill deeply divided abortion rights supporters. The National Organization for Women criticized its provisions that would allow states to continue restricting minors' ability to access abortions and to keep their laws banning the use of public funds (including Medicaid) to pay for health insurance that covered the procedure—making abortion a right, certainly, but leaving it inaccessible for many. The bill died after losing support from Senator Carol Moseley Braun, the first Black woman elected to the Senate, who said at the time that it "discriminate[d] against young and poor women" and traded their rights to protect wealthy Americans' access.

In subsequent years, Democrats introduced new versions of the Freedom of Choice Act, which by 2004 had dropped both of those restrictions, but they never made it out of committee—and under Clinton's conservative successor, President George W. Bush, they stood no chance of becoming law. (Bush actually signed a law, the Partial-Birth Abortion Ban Act, that prohibited doctors from using "dilation and extraction" abortions, a medically safe procedure that had been used primarily to terminate pregnancies past twenty weeks' gestation.) After Bush came Barack Obama, who as a candidate in 2007 had promised that one of the first actions he'd take would be to sign the Freedom of Choice Act. Two months after being sworn in, Obama said the bill wasn't his "highest legislative priority," dropping any pursuit of passing abortion protections. Though Democrats held substantial majorities in the House and Senate, many still opposed abortion rights. Others said they were hesitant to prioritize the issue. Abortion was so polarizing that even efforts to make private insurance plans cover the procedure—using their own money, not federal funds—almost derailed the passage of the Affordable Care Act, thanks to a cohort of anti-abortion Democrats in the House of Representatives. Rachel Rebouché, a legal scholar who worked then for the Washington-based Women's Legal Defense Fund (later renamed the National Partnership for Women and Families), recalled pushback when advocating for the law to include even the most basic reproductive health care benefits: access to affordable birth control. It just reminded her how uphill the battle would be to codify *Roe*. "Covering contraceptives in a well-woman's plan was controversial," she said. "That's all you need to know."

In the years that followed, Democrats who voted against abortion rights became rarer, with most losing their seats or switching parties. By 2023, only two anti-abortion Democrats would remain in Congress: Senator Joe Manchin of West Virginia and Texas congressman Henry Cuellar. On the flip side, only two Republican senators, Lisa Murkowski of Alaska and Susan Collins of Maine, said they supported abortion rights. In 2013, almost a decade before *Dobbs,* and spurred by the surge of anti-abortion bills passing in statehouses across the country, Democratic lawmakers introduced the bill they called the Women's Health Protection Act, legislation meant to codify federal abortion rights. But that bill had no chance of passage. After the 2010 elections, Democrats wouldn't regain simultaneous control of Congress and the White House until 2021, as anti-abortion fervor continued to bloom in state legislatures and remained an organizing principle of the Republican Party. The inertia that characterized Washington posed a stark contrast to Republican-led statehouses across the country. All the while, the onslaught of state-level abortion restrictions meant that clinics continued to shut down; the Supreme Court, which had continued its drift to the right, kept issuing decisions that seemed to weaken not only *Roe*'s protections but access to reproductive health care in general, undercutting even the contraceptive benefits people like Rebouché had fought for.

Even after Donald Trump had left office, it didn't seem to fully register in the capital how vulnerable *Roe*'s protections were. The Supreme Court agreed to hear *Dobbs* on May 17, 2021. Abortion rights lawyers quickly and correctly interpreted the decision as a sign that the conservative majority was ready to overturn federal abortion protections, but the same concern didn't emerge en masse on Capitol Hill. Few lawmakers put out a statement acknowledging the case; neither did President Joe Biden, whose position on abortion had changed over the years. In 1973, the first-year senator said he believed that *Roe v. Wade* was wrongly decided, and in 1981, he supported a proposed constitutional amendment that would have let states ban abortion (he opposed the same measure a year later); by the 2020 campaign, Biden the presidential candidate vowed to protect access if elected to the White House. When asked that day about the case, Biden's press secretary said she didn't have a comment specific to *Dobbs* but said that "the president and the vice president are devoted to ensuring that every American has access to health care, including reproductive health care, regardless of their income, ZIP Code, race, health insurance status, or immigration status." Part of that commitment was a desire to pass a law codifying *Roe*. Still, that vague remark was as close as the administration would come to addressing the case; given how profoundly it would soon shape national politics, it was striking how little *Dobbs* seemed to infiltrate Washington discourse—and how few lawmakers seemed to anticipate what was coming. (Many legal analysts too expressed skepticism that the Supreme Court would actually overturn *Roe*.)

Some Democrats had begun to talk about abortion differently. In September 2021, a week before Lee's speech, the House of Representatives finally passed the Women's Health Protection Act. But it was hard to see how any bill expanding access would survive the Senate, where Democrats didn't have the votes to overcome a procedural mechanism known as the filibuster, which essentially required that any bill get at least sixty votes to pass. When the Senate considered codifying abortion rights, the Women's Health Protection Act couldn't even get fifty votes. Only months before the *Dobbs* decision, when Biden gave his annual State of the Union address, it took him roughly one hour, thirteen minutes, and thirty seconds before he mentioned *Roe*. Even then, the president was careful to avoid using the word "abortion," instead obliquely referring to "the constitutional right affirmed by *Roe v. Wade*" and "a woman's right to choose."

Observers could argue over whether an urgency was lacking or whether it was simply impossible for lawmakers to do anything. What mattered, though, was that on the night of May 2, 2022, when a leak of the draft *Dobbs* opinion was published, Democrats didn't have a real plan in place.

That May—one of those perfect late spring evenings in D.C., when the air was still crisp and the summer humidity hadn't yet settled in—Tina Smith, a former Planned Parenthood executive turned junior senator from Minnesota, was at dinner in Capitol Hill's Barracks Row neighborhood. When she discovered the leak from a news alert that one of her staffers showed her, she was shocked. Intellectually, she'd known perhaps better than most just how at risk *Roe* was; Smith, sixty-four at the time, had made a career focusing on protecting access to care and fighting back against efforts to restrict abortion rights. And she'd seen the Supreme Court listen with sympathy to Mississippi's arguments for striking down federal abortion protections. But seeing the news felt different. She spent the night rereading the leaked draft decision, struggling to breathe properly, her emotions transitioning from disbelief to fury. It was, she'd say later, impossible to fully grasp what this would mean. Still, she knew that if this took effect the impact would be seismic.

It was clear even then how little was known about the legal and human impacts of undoing *Roe*. Would the Hyde Amendment prohibit the government from covering people's other abortion-related costs? What lengths would states with abortion bans go to to find out if someone had sought to terminate a pregnancy? And was there anything at all the White House could do to help people navigate the looming chaos? There were even more unanswered questions when it came to the issue of digital surveillance; period trackers or geolocation services tracked on a phone, for instance, are not bound by medical privacy laws, and some experts worried that the data stored in them could, under certain circumstances, be subpoenaed to determine if someone had gotten an illegal abortion. (Even though most abortion bans don't target pregnant people themselves, that data could be relevant if a prosecutor sought to charge someone who got an abortion with murder or if the state explicitly criminalized self-managed abortion.) There were new medical privacy questions, too. Standard practice requires documenting patients' health care in an electronic record, which should be accessible in other hospitals and doctor's offices, too—that way, it's part of someone's medical history no matter where they go and can be factored in when assessing their health. But what if someone's abortion, legal in one state, was viewed by a provider in a state that outlawed the practice? Could existing health privacy laws protect them? Or, if law enforcement asked for those records, would they find out that people had left the state for abortions?

For Smith and her colleagues—the largely female Democratic lawmakers who were vocal in their support for abortion rights—the weeks that followed felt frenetic. The Senate held another vote on the Women's Health Protection Act, despite still not having the votes to pass it. Democrats including Smith, Washington senator Patty Murray, and Massachusetts's Elizabeth Warren all pressed the president to issue some kind of executive order, calling for what they often described as a "whole-of-government response." Biden's administration, they suggested in a letter to the president, could try to expand access to medication abortion pills or could investigate the possibility of helping pay for people's childcare and travel costs if they might have to leave the state for an abortion. Perhaps it could explore if existing privacy laws—maybe the Health Insurance Portability and Accountability Act, also known as HIPAA—might be used to protect people's reproductive health information, so that it would be harder for a state to track if they tried to travel elsewhere for an abortion. "These proposals are only starting points," the senators wrote. Smith visited her state's abortion clinics, trying to get a sense of just how severely they would be affected. It quickly hit her: the burden *Dobbs* would place on them would be tremendous, and Minnesota certainly wouldn't be able to support every person coming from a neighboring state where abortion bans might soon take effect. Some scholars suggested that the administration consider opening abortion clinics on federal lands or arguing in court that states couldn't ban medication abortion, since it was approved by the Food and Drug Administration. But everyone understood that these were all untested strategies and might not survive legal scrutiny.

By the day the Supreme Court ruled—Friday, June 24, about seven weeks after the leak—Washington radiated with urgency. Thousands gathered to protest in front of the court, some bringing their children with them. The White House directed its Department of Health and Human Services to figure out whether it could protect access to medication abortion pills. The attorney general argued that states lacked the legal power to ban mifepristone "based on disagreement with the FDA's expert judgment about its safety and efficacy," and in his own remarks Biden vowed to ensure that Americans retained at the very least the right to travel out of state for an abortion.

But as time would show, there was little the federal government could do.

———

After his abortion, Jasper kept waiting to feel some kind of relief. He knew that he had made the right decision—he was still a teenager, still trying to work and finish school, still figuring out what his life might look like someday. It felt like everything in the state was getting more expensive, and he knew, intellectually, that he didn't have the money to support another person. It wasn't that long ago that Jasper had been sleeping in his car—back when his roommates had moved out of the house they'd shared, he couldn't make rent on his own, and he'd felt unsure if he could move back in with his father. Things had gotten better only because Jasper's boyfriend had insisted he patch things up with his dad: "You can't live like this," he'd told him. If Jasper hadn't mended fences and moved back in with his family, he wasn't sure how he'd be making ends meet. And there were other questions beyond the finances. Watching Florida become more conservative, with the state prohibiting schools from discussing queer identity and even limiting what books kids could read, he'd come to the realization that he didn't want to raise a child here—he needed to earn enough money to move out of the state so that he could become a parent somewhere a family like his would feel safer.

But all the same, he couldn't stop thinking about the life he'd chosen and, alternatively, the one he'd rejected. His boyfriend seemed able to move on right away, almost pretending that none of this had ever happened. It wasn't so easy for Jasper. Not even a week after his abortion, he had noticed that something felt off around his chest, the part of his body he probably hated the most. He raced to the bathroom and gingerly squeezed. It was milk; because Jasper's abortion was performed after he had entered his second trimester, he'd started lactating.

Jasper had read online that this was entirely possible. He had just hoped it wouldn't happen to him. He didn't want any reason to think about his chest, to see how it might have changed because of the pregnancy. Now, hands wet from milk, he had no idea what he was supposed to do. Did he have to pump out everything inside him? Could he just ignore it and leave his chest alone? He couldn't find a clear answer until he called Planned Parenthood, where someone kindly told him he could let it dry up, and everything would be fine.

Jasper couldn't predict when his chest would leak, and sometimes the dripping sensation would wake him up in the middle of the night. The chest binder he wore during the day developed a thin crust of dried milk; it felt like he couldn't escape the smell or all the reminders it brought with it—of the abortion he'd chosen to have and the way his body still felt out of his control. On the worst days, it felt like he was less of a man, too.

Even when the milk stopped, it felt like he couldn't escape what had happened. He'd started working at a childcare center, and sometimes, looking at the kids, he'd think once more about the decision he'd made not to have one of his own, wondering once again, *What if?* Every now and then, looking at them made him feel almost guilty for choosing not to become a parent just yet, despite all the reasons he'd factored in when making his decision. It didn't help that the university campus Jasper attended was so close to Planned Parenthood that he couldn't go to class without passing the building; whenever he did, his mind flashed back to that Saturday morning.

Those memories would soon become more frequent. Months after the abortion, Jasper's health had finally recovered enough that he was able to resume testosterone therapy, which he'd paused when his health had taken that confusing turn the previous summer. He was planning to get his care at Planned Parenthood, where his health insurance would cover the costs. Much as Jasper couldn't wait to resume treatment—to see his facial hair grow back and to know that he was doing everything he could to make his body feel more like his own—there was a part of him that felt apprehensive about going back to Planned Parenthood, where he couldn't help but relive that week of his life when he'd felt like he barely had any chance to make a choice for himself. Still, he tried to focus on the good parts. It was great that he could soon resume getting testosterone, even if it meant going back to a place full of fraught memories. Maybe when he went back he'd see the clinic employee who'd been so sweet when they had waited there for his abortion, and who'd offered them homemade peanut brittle and cracked jokes with them.

Someday, he hoped, he'd be able to put all this behind him. And even if he couldn't forget, maybe the memories would be easier to bear.

—◆—

In its own words, *Dobbs* gave the power to regulate or outlaw abortion to "the people and their elected representatives"—that is, to individual state governments. The federal powerlessness was the point: Washington was supposed to be irrelevant.

It was a myth. Of course federal authorities—especially the nation's courts—would still have the power to influence what abortion access could look like. Furthermore, the federal-state dichotomy neglected to consider those who lived in the city of Washington, D.C., which is home to about 700,000 people, or the Washington, D.C., metropolitan area, which includes parts of Maryland and Virginia and at the time counted close to 6.4 million residents. Though the national government that was based in Washington could no longer control abortion policy, the hundreds of thousands of people who lived in the area would not escape the decision's impact. Almost overnight, the so-called DMV—short for "D.C., Maryland, and Virginia"—became a center of access on the East Coast, especially as D.C. remained the rare statelike entity to allow abortion at any point in pregnancy. Historically, the city had always reported a large share of out-of-state patients in its abortion clinics. Post-*Dobbs*, though, people had begun to flock to the city in far larger numbers, a pattern that would only continue.

The DC Abortion Fund, the biggest in the United States, started receiving calls from patients across the country. There were people coming from states like Texas and Mississippi, where abortion was completely outlawed. But even more came from a handful of states—North Carolina, South Carolina, and Florida—where abortion remained legal for the first year after *Dobbs,* but where clinics had become overwhelmed by out-of-state patient demand and appointments either were no longer available or, by the time a doctor could see patients, past the state's gestational limit. Jade Hurley, who worked at the D.C. fund, referred to it as a sort of "second migration": the district was the place to go for those who had been displaced, not by a ban in their own state, but by the national shrinking of abortion options. This too was only temporary. The 2023 institution of abortion bans in the Carolinas, along with the looming prospect of Florida's six-week cutoff, meant that, for Americans living in the South, Virginia and D.C. were among the closest and only options for care. Some people would travel farther north, finding care in states like Illinois and New York. But in the capital, the second migration would eventually collapse into the first. People would be forced to travel to the D.C. area from all over the South because there was nowhere closer to go.

Hurley worried that the continuing increase in patients seeking aid in D.C. couldn't be sustainable. Even in 2022, with *Roe* intact for half the year, the fund had disbursed $2.3 million, funding 7,065 people's procedures. In 2023, those numbers kept growing. A year after *Dobbs,* Hurley could tell that if the demand continued to rise at this rate the fund eventually wouldn't have enough money to help everyone who called. Already, the increase in donations they had seen after the decision had begun to disappear—it seemed as if people thought the money was no longer needed. Partway through the year, the fund, like so many around the country, found itself capping how much money it could disburse in a single week or month; it was the only way to make their budget work, but it meant that patients traveling from the South to the greater D.C. area could no longer count on receiving as much aid as they once could.

An added challenge was that the greater D.C. area was and still is an access point for people later in pregnancy, being home to multiple clinics that offer abortions in all trimesters. As Ashley Acre had learned when traveling to Colorado from Michigan after discovering complications in her pregnancy, and as pregnant people were continuing to learn across the country, those abortions are not only harder to find appointments for, but they are also incredibly expensive. Consequently the DC Abortion Fund could not cover the costs of people's plane or bus tickets, gas, food, or hotel when they made it to the DMV—it didn't have the resources. Given how late in pregnancy many people traveling to the city were, abortions in the D.C. area could cost as much as $20,000. All the fund's resources had to go toward helping defray the cost of the procedure itself. Even then, employees knew there was no way they were meeting the needs of everyone who called, let alone people who lived in or traveled to D.C. and didn't even know the fund existed.

It's a cliché to describe places as "just miles from the White House," but DuPont Clinic, an all-trimester abortion clinic in an office building in downtown D.C., truly is only blocks away. It was a location born of necessity: when the clinic launched in 2017, that building was the only place it could find that was willing to rent it space for a procedure as stigmatized as abortion, especially an abortion done in the third trimester. Much like the Boulder clinic, DuPont Clinic was somewhat of a landmark in the abortion world, a place known for its excellent doctors and technical skill in performing complex abortions. It helped turn the city into a destination for people later in pregnancy, and close to 75 percent of the patients who came to the clinic were from somewhere other than D.C., Maryland, or Virginia. Without *Roe,* the clinic had seen itself become a nexus for people in the South who had no other places to turn—a year out from the decision, its largest share of patients came from Florida, North Carolina, Texas, and Georgia, states with large populations and where abortions, particularly after twenty weeks, were increasingly impossible to come by.

DuPont Clinic was a lifeline for women like Tiffani, a twenty-two-year-old single mother in Texas. Tiffani was thrilled to discover she was pregnant again—and this time expecting identical twins. Her daughter, almost two years old, would finally get to have siblings. Her relationship with the man who'd gotten her pregnant wasn't solid, but she still wasn't worried. She had a supportive extended family who would help her take care of the kids.

But the pregnancy soon became more complicated than she could have imagined. At around ten weeks, Tiffani learned that the twins shared a placenta—not necessarily bad news on its own, but a development that increased the risk of complications and that in turn made it far more difficult to find an ob-gyn who felt comfortable caring for her through her pregnancy. Even once she found a physician who was qualified, it felt like the bad news kept coming. Her pregnancy had a rare condition called "twin-to-twin transfusion syndrome," in which one twin essentially receives more blood than the other; as a result, one twin can become severely undernourished, with low blood volume and weak kidneys and bladder. The other can suffer heart complications, including possibly heart failure. At eighteen weeks, just as Tiffani was procuring new car seats and setting up the nursery, she underwent a surgery that her doctor hoped would save her pregnancy. When, twenty weeks pregnant, she returned for a follow-up visit, Tiffani learned that things had only gotten worse. One of the babies had stopped growing, and in addition to the previous complications, it looked like they had holes in their hearts. The doctor suspected a chromosomal disorder known as trisomy 18, or Edwards syndrome, the consequences of which include heart and kidney disease, low birth weight, and trouble breathing. Infants born with trisomy 18 rarely make it past age one.

Tiffani's doctor never suggested termination, which was illegal in Texas even for a case like hers. But she couldn't fathom giving birth to babies who would die so quickly, or going through the pain of giving birth and subsequently grieving while being a present and active mother to the daughter she already had. By week twenty-four, she had made up her mind: she would have to leave the state and get an abortion. Tiffani called every clinic in New Mexico, the closest state to her with legal abortion, and every clinic in Colorado. DuPont Clinic in D.C. was the rare place she found that saw patients as far along in pregnancy as she was and that had openings within two weeks for the three-day procedure she would need. The staff told her that the procedure would cost $8,600—money she didn't have—but that if she called a list of abortion funds, some might be able to help defray the cost of the procedure, her travel, and a hotel in Washington. They were right: in total, she paid about $1,600 for her entire trip to D.C. It was still money that Tiffani, who had quit her job as a barista to care for her daughter, didn't have to spare, but her mother and grandmother could shoulder the significantly reduced cost for now, and she would pay them back later.

Tiffani's father agreed to care for her daughter over the week, and the three women traveled together, the first time any of them had ever been to the East Coast, and the first time Tiffani had ever boarded a plane. The prospect of a three-hour flight had terrified her to the extent that she briefly considered driving the twenty hours to D.C., rather than traveling from the frenzied Dallas airport. But when she made it to Washington, things were better, as much as they could be. The clinic was clean and soothing, painted in gentle purple hues and adorned with orchids, and the staff were far kinder than the brusque physician she'd been seeing in Texas. Her mother and grandmother did their best to keep her spirits up.

Maybe, her grandmother suggested, the three of them could go see the Washington Monument while they were there. It was a nice idea, even if nothing more. The trip was too short, too busy, and too draining to realistically fit in any tourist attractions. Everything Tiffani knew about the capital—the landmarks, the museums, the White House—existed in a different reality from the version of D.C. she experienced, one far removed from the city that, to her, was first and foremost the only place in the country that could offer her health care in her time of need.

It was easy to forget that these were the same city, and that less than a mile from DuPont Clinic lived and worked people who might have had the power to alleviate the crisis they faced. "I feel like we're working in a different world," said Dr. Matt Reeves, the clinic's founder. After *Dobbs,* as national Democrats scrambled for ways to tout their support for abortion rights, not a single federal official—from the White House or Congress—had ever reached out to the staff at DuPont Clinic, either to ask what policies might help them meet the increase in demand post-*Dobbs* or just to visit the facility and learn more about the care they provided. Karishma Oza, the clinic's director of care coordination, walked past government buildings on her way to and from work, and she registered internally the irony of living so near the people who seemed unable to do anything. The clinic staff weren't naïve about the challenges of passing federal abortion protections; when considering what they would hope to see from their government, they were careful to frame everything in the realm of possibility—even just taking steps to ensure that Medicaid actually covered people's abortions when they were pregnant as a result of rape or incest, or when staying pregnant posed a health risk. That was something the program was already required by law to do; proper enforcement wouldn't require the Herculean task of somehow finding enough senators to support abortion rights. But even asking for so little somehow seemed like too much.

The focus on Washington extended beyond just specialty clinics like DuPont. Months after the decision, Dr. Anne Banfield, an ob-gyn in southern Maryland, received a call from a woman in Texas who had discovered that her pregnancy wasn't viable. She had relatives in the county and wanted her termination done at

Banfield's hospital, in a tiny town called Leonardtown. Maryland, home to another one of the nation's third-trimester abortion clinics, is one of the friendlier states to abortion in the country; still, Banfield's semirural hospital alone didn't have the resources or staff to care for the woman. Before coming to Leonardtown, the woman would have to get preliminary care at the complex family planning unit at its sister facility, a hospital in D.C., before traveling south to Maryland to complete her procedure and then recover with her family. Banfield hadn't expected *Dobbs* to send out-of-state patients to her Maryland hospital, but in retrospect, she realized, it shouldn't have been a surprise. In time, she knew, seeing these patients would become a regular part of her job—an entirely predictable consequence of other states outlawing abortion.

When Erika, a young mother in Missouri, decided she was ready to try for a second child, it had been close to four years since she had given birth to her son—a difficult delivery after which he spent three days in intensive care—and almost two years since she'd lost a second pregnancy to miscarriage. She'd spent that time in therapy, discussing her anxieties over the difficulty of getting and staying pregnant, to say nothing of giving birth to a healthy baby. Since then, they'd moved to a bigger house, and her husband had found a new job, one that paid well enough that they felt like they could comfortably raise a second child. When she learned she was pregnant—only weeks after returning from a long-overdue vacation with her husband—Erika was still nervous about what the coming months might entail. But more than anything she was overjoyed. Despite her fears, she desperately wanted another child, a baby sibling for her young boy.

This pregnancy wasn't easy. Erika quickly lost her taste for all the foods she lived on: peanut butter, eggs, sausages. Her stomach felt incessantly bloated. Worst of all, she kept having flashbacks to the day she gave birth to her son, the feeling of lying in the hospital as they took her baby away. She resumed seeing a therapist, trying to develop the tools she would need to stay psychologically well over the next several months. But by the time she reached twelve weeks, everything looked good. Her second boy would be big and healthy—just like her first. Slowly, they started telling family and friends about the pregnancy, ordering furniture for a new nursery. They settled on a name: Easton.

Erika and her son were cleaning his playroom together when she told him that in a few months he'd be a big brother. She watched as he picked up a collection of toys—things he'd outgrown and that, in theory, they should now give away. "I don't want to get rid of these," he announced solemnly. "I want to keep these for baby brother."

Despite her anxiety over giving birth, Erika hadn't thought about what might happen if things went awry. She knew that when it came to abortion her home state of Missouri was about as hostile as possible, enforcing its near-total ban within hours of *Roe*'s overturn. It was something that angered her in the abstract, but that she never imagined could affect her life. That is, until Erika's anatomy scan at around her twentieth week of pregnancy.

Everything looked good at the start. The ultrasound technician showed how healthy Easton's heart looked and how much his brain had grown. But then Erika's doctor came in. Something, she told them, was wrong—she was referring them to a specialist right away. Erika began to sob, listening as the doctor explained: her baby boy had developed what was called lower urinary tract obstruction. His bladder couldn't empty itself, a condition that damaged both his bladder and his kidneys. His lungs weren't developing properly. If Erika chose to continue her pregnancy, the best-case scenario meant undergoing surgery targeted at the fetus, followed by kidney transplants once her baby was born. More likely, though, he would die soon after being born.

They had three options: they could let the pregnancy progress and wait for the fetus to die in utero; Erika could leave the state for an abortion—though even if she went to neighboring Kansas the doctors didn't think she would make it before the state's twenty-two-week cutoff; or she could get multiple fetal surgeries, give birth, and pray for the best, knowing that if they were lucky they'd have an infant in need of dialysis, followed by a kidney transplant at age two and another when he turned twenty. Even still, there was virtually no chance Erika's son would outlive her. As they discussed how to proceed, Erika had noticed that her doctor began calling her from her personal phone—the only way that they could speak freely, without worrying that the hospital or a medical practice might record their conversations. It underscored another truth: being honest about the appropriate medical options meant Erika's doctor was risking jail time.

When Erika decided to terminate her pregnancy, she learned there were only a handful of places she could travel to where doctors would help her get an abortion at this point. She chose D.C.—about a two-and-a-half-hour flight from the Kansas City area—and her ob-gyn gave her the phone number for a physician at one of the city's hospitals. Erika scheduled her appointment, opting to get an injection that would stop Easton's heart. Once she received the shot, the doctors told her she could come home and complete the abortion in Missouri, telling anyone who asked that she had experienced another miscarriage. A friend used airline miles to book plane tickets for Erika and her husband. They planned to fly out to Baltimore, drive into D.C. for the procedure, and fly home the same night. They wouldn't tell their son what had happened.

It was Erika's first trip to D.C. since she was a teenager, and this journey was so rushed that she barely saw anything other than highways and hospital grounds. She hardly noticed she was in another city. All that mattered to her in this moment was that it was one of the few places where comprehensive medical care was still possible. Driving to the airport at two in the morning, with almost no one else outside, Erika couldn't shake the same feeling that so many others like her had described: that strange sense of illicitness, the heavy reminder that, though she was perfectly within her rights to travel to D.C. for medical care, what she was doing would have been illegal in her home state. It was as if she'd gone through a black market for basic health care. Now, instead of driving fifteen minutes to get the treatment her doctors agreed was best, she spent twenty-one hours in transit, only daring to tell her family and close friends the truth, but otherwise keeping the story a secret. *It's barbaric,* she'd think later. *It's evil. Inhumane.* No matter what someone's reason, she kept thinking, this was a decision people should be able to make on their own. It didn't matter if it was a case like hers, where the abortion ended a pregnancy because of medical complications, or if it was because someone

knew that they simply weren't in a place where they could care for
a baby.

"It's not my choice for someone else, and I shouldn't be able
to force them to not have an abortion," she said. "Trust people to
make the best decision for them."

When Erika returned to Missouri, driving less than twenty
minutes to go to the hospital across the border in Kansas, she didn't
tell the nurse on duty that she'd gotten an abortion. All she said was
the truth: "We can't find his heartbeat." The tears she cried were
real.

Everything Erika navigated—the discreet calls with her doctor,
the airport trip in the dead of the night, the lie by omission when
checking into her hospital at home—was part of a larger story. In
post-*Dobbs* America, it was impossible to live in a ban state and seek
abortion care without the looming fear of being caught. Much like
what Barbara Lee had learned more than half a century ago, the
only way to get care was now to rely on secret informal networks—
knowing someone who knew someone and trusting that they could
keep a secret. In the weeks and months following the end of *Roe*,
legal experts and privacy researchers worried about the extent
to which Americans seeking abortions might be tracked on their
phones, by Google Maps storing and selling the information that
they had visited an abortion clinic, or Facebook messages or search
engine histories being turned over to law enforcement. Surveillance remains a real and looming concern. But the more immediate
threat, it turned out, was more old-fashioned: the biggest risk to an
abortion patient who surreptitiously traveled out of state for care
was someone else overhearing or otherwise finding out what they
had done and sharing that information with the authorities. There
was no law or regulation that could protect people from that kind
of scrutiny.

———◆———

D.C. had emerged as an essential access point, both for Americans
in the South watching the eradication of their abortion rights and
for people across the country who needed care later in pregnancy.
But access in D.C. is still tenuous in its own way. That's because,

although the city's residents pay federal taxes, the district, an incredibly liberal area with a population larger than that of Vermont or Wyoming, is not a state. Its single delegate in the House cannot participate in floor votes, it has no senators, and the federal government—composed of people elected to represent other states, with other interests and no electoral accountability to the people who live in the district—can overrule laws passed by the D.C. city council and mayor. This, local activists have long argued, has obvious civil rights implications: if granted statehood, the district would have a larger share of Black residents than any other state, and denying D.C. statehood thus disproportionately disenfranchised Black Americans.

It was equal parts infuriating and astounding to Vee, a college junior in the city. Vee had learned she was pregnant as early as possible, testing positive when she was only four weeks along. She was able to get an abortion via telemedicine, after a consult with a local abortion provider; when the cost was too much for Vee, a full-time student on financial aid, who already worked part-time to pay for school, the DC Abortion Fund stepped in to help. The clinic mailed her the pills she needed, and she took them safely at home. When, at a follow-up, she found out the abortion hadn't fully worked—the misoprostol hadn't successfully emptied out her uterus—she was able to get more medication that helped complete it. Vee was surrounded by supportive family and friends, in a city full of resources that enabled her to get an abortion. Her college campus had a literal vending machine that dispensed emergency contraception pills. This was the kind of system her city supported; it reflected the will of the people who lived here. But the larger political system that shaped her country—the White House that was just a few blocks over, the Capitol Building that was maybe a fifteen-minute Metro ride away—would not be influenced by the people who lived in D.C. "The people who are in power in D.C., in Congress, have a lot of skewed perceptions around abortion," she said. "If D.C. were to be made a state, to be considered for electoral votes, I think that it would create a massive difference in the political landscape in the United States, especially surrounding health care and how we manage the reproductive rights of people with uteruses."

In fact, D.C.'s unique political status makes it even more vulnerable. Congress can pass laws that would never be approved by

D.C. residents, but that will intimately affect their lives. Already, Medicaid in the capital cannot cover abortions, even using the city's local taxes, thanks to a Congress-backed restriction known as the Dornan Amendment, which was most recently authorized under the Obama administration, one of the tradeoffs made back in 2011 to keep the government funded. Post-*Dobbs,* no matter how many abortion rights protections D.C.'s government passed—joining lawsuits designed to protect access to mifepristone, or passing laws protecting the right to self-manage an abortion—it remained obvious that, the next time Republicans gained simultaneous control of Congress and the White House, they could easily pass a law banning abortion in the capital, or at the very least making it far more difficult to obtain. "It's such a state-by-state game, and D.C. has done an amazing job, but D.C. only has so much power," said Jade Hurley, from the city's abortion fund. "We've lost. We have lost so brutally. I just don't know what the plan is. I don't think anybody knows what the plan is."

———

In the wake of the *Dobbs* decision, federal officials tried to take even some action, while still acknowledging that they had little power to undercut the decision's immediate and dramatic impact. Biden instructed the Department of Health and Human Services to expand access to mifepristone and to use existing medical privacy laws to ensure that health professionals not disclose information to law enforcement about patients' abortions. The administration tried to at least minimize the odds of people dying: HHS told medical providers across the country that, under federal laws protecting the right to emergency medical care, ERs were obligated to give patients abortions if doing so would appropriately address a health crisis, and the Department of Justice sued Idaho, arguing that its abortion ban violated those same federal laws. Idaho, the government argued, had to grant abortions to people who needed them because of medical emergencies. The Department of Veterans Affairs, meanwhile, began covering abortion for veterans who were pregnant as a result of rape or incest, or if staying pregnant threatened their lives—and the policy applied even in states where abortions were banned. In early 2023, the Department of Defense began offering three weeks of leave for military members who had to travel from where they were stationed to another state where they might access an abortion or other reproductive health care. And, in what could have been among the most consequential policy shifts the administration would attempt, the Food and Drug Administration issued long-promised regulations that would allow mifepristone—which had for years been stocked only in specialty pharmacies—to be dispensed in typical retail pharmacy chains, as long as they underwent government certification. CVS and Walgreens, the nation's two biggest such chains, both announced they would seek to dispense mifepristone in states where abortion remained legal. It was a big deal: putting medication abortion pills in more pharmacies would make it far easier for people in those states to get abortions, alleviating some of the strain clinics were facing.

Meanwhile, the concern that states with abortion bans might criminalize people who sought procedures had become even more potent, with thousands of Americans traveling out of state for abortions and still more ordering medication abortion pills online. Doctors remained worried about the legal risks to their patients, especially those who traveled from a state with an abortion ban to get care in a state with fewer restrictions. In April 2023, the Biden administration finally issued a proposed new federal rule that would ensure HIPAA prevented medical providers—including those in states with abortion bans—from disclosing information to law enforcement about legal abortions that patients had sought out of state or about abortion care they had gotten in their home state that wasn't explicitly prohibited. (The latter provision, some suggested, could protect people who self-managed abortions.) But the process of federal rulemaking is incredibly long—proposed rules must typically be available for public comment for thirty to sixty days; the government then has to consider the feedback it has received before publishing a final policy. Given that timeline, an abortion rights privacy rule proposed in the spring of 2023 might not take effect until sometime in 2024 or later—meaning that until then patients and providers would have to keep hoping their medical information was in fact safe, but with little real guarantee.

None of these individual efforts to preserve access could undo the seismic impact *Dobbs* had and would continue to have. But Democrats' attempts at reversing some of the decision's effects—and, critically, talking about it—still felt like a sea change in how the party approached abortion. Polling showed widespread opposition to the bans Republican-led states were enforcing. And voters cared more about the issue now than they had before. In the past, Democrats fighting for abortion rights had been, as Tina Smith of Minnesota put it, campaigning against a sort of death by a thousand cuts, battling countless efforts to winnow away access. Post-*Dobbs,* the message was more existential: they were arguing for a basic guarantee of reproductive autonomy, which had been stripped away. Smith, who'd assumed office in 2018, was a relative newcomer to Washington, but the shift was still obvious to her. Most lawmakers in Congress are men. Some had in the past felt willing to speak about abortion, but they were a minority; before *Dobbs,* abortion had been an issue that was prioritized by primarily women in politics. "For the men in the Senate, I think there has been some expansion of their understanding, absolutely. Because they can see how upset their constituents are," Smith said. Mazie Hirono, a Democratic senator from Hawaii, described it wryly: "They use the word now."

It began to seem like a real possibility that finally lawmakers might pass a bill enshrining abortion rights. Democrats would need to win control of the White House and Congress, electing senators who not only supported abortion rights but who also would be willing to scrap the sixty-vote requirement to pass legislation. And although that hadn't felt doable in the past, the loss of abortion rights had changed things, Smith believed. Still, none of this would be easy, and all of it would take time. And should Washington Democrats eventually have the power to do anything, Smith knew, who could say how many people would have suffered, or even died?

For what felt like every policy initiative the Biden administration put forth, Republican lawmakers had a response. Texas's attorney general challenged the HHS regulations clarifying that abortion qualified as legally essential emergency medical care, resulting in a district court blocking that policy from taking effect in Texas. The lawsuit the administration had filed against Idaho, arguing over that same question, had by the beginning of 2024 made its way to the Supreme Court, the same entity that had not even two years prior overturned *Roe*. While the case was litigated, the court held, Idaho—like Texas—could continue to outlaw abortions, even in cases where the procedure would save a patient's life.

As soon as the administration had tried to expand who could carry mifepristone, Republican state attorneys general began putting pressure on pharmacies not to stock the pill. It worked. In Alaska, Kansas, Iowa, and Montana—all states where abortion in general, and medication abortion in particular, remained legal—Walgreens agreed not to dispense mifepristone. The threat was too much: of what could be costly litigation, and of potentially putting their employees at risk of harassment and violence. And when the Biden administration tried to protect patients' medical data, a group of more than a dozen Republican attorneys general sought to block the proposal, arguing that they had the right to access records showing if someone had traveled out of state for an abortion—exactly what patient after patient had feared would happen.

It was impossible to ignore what a target abortion remained and how inextricable it felt from a growing attack on bodily autonomy. Republican state legislatures—especially those that had successfully banned abortion—turned their energy to curbing access to gender-affirming care, such as the hormone therapy Jasper had relied on. In 2023, more than four hundred bills targeting trans people had been introduced in statehouses across the country, one analysis found; the successful restrictions focused on preventing minors from accessing care. The parallels to the anti-abortion movement were striking. Republicans claimed these laws were meant to protect children, vilifying doctors who offered to care for them. And these bans weren't the only way they sought to limit access to care. Some states had barred Medicaid from covering gender-affirming treatment, curbing access for minors and adults alike in a policy mirroring the Hyde Amendment. Florida pushed legislation limiting what kinds of medical providers were allowed to provide gender-affirming care, similar to the way states permitted only doctors to perform even medication abortions, even though nurse practitioners can also provide such care with training. The Department of Justice could challenge specific bans on care, but—as with abortion—there weren't enough votes in Congress to pass any laws protecting access. Unlike with abortion, it wasn't yet clear how many lawmakers had realized the urgency of doing something, or who viewed the issues as inherently linked. States were working to restrict access to medical care that was not only in some cases lifesaving, but that was crucial to gender equity and a person's sense of bodily autonomy.

Existential threats to abortion rights themselves remained, too. The mifepristone case from Amarillo offered a reminder of the anti-abortion movement's energy. Anti-abortion lobbyists had made clear they would not support any candidate for president who did not endorse, at a minimum, a national law banning abortion for anyone after fifteen weeks. And legal scholars had begun to suspect that abortion opponents might find a new mechanism to ban abortion, even without passing a law. Buried in the lower court rulings from the Amarillo case, conservative judges had weighed in on the long-dormant Comstock Act, the 1873 anti-obscenity law that hadn't been enforced in decades but that remained on the books. They'd zeroed in specifically on the act's prohibitions on mailing anything that facilitated "the prevention of conception or an unlawful abortion"—arguing that in fact the text prohibited mailing anything that could conceivably be used to help someone terminate a pregnancy. That could mean abortion pills, but it could also mean any medical supplies that might be used to provide a surgical abortion. Interpreted in this way, the Gilded Age law, used in its heyday to ban works by authors like Walt Whitman and James Joyce, could end legal abortion entirely. It was a theory that people like Mary Ziegler, the abortion historian, couldn't stop thinking about. If anyone understood the anti-abortion movement, it was someone like her, who had spent her career watching and researching how activists had diligently worked to undo *Roe*. Now all it would take was the right case, a Supreme Court with a majority that opposed abortion enough to buy this interpretation, and a president willing to enforce it. "You can't dismiss it," Ziegler said. "This is a path to a national ban that affects people all around the country." It was one she feared could take effect even if Republicans couldn't get the votes to pass an explicit prohibition on abortion, unless Democrats gained the votes in Congress to repeal the law.

This was the kind of question that terrified Alyssa, a thirty-one-year-old mother from Iowa who had traveled to D.C. for her abortion. Much like Tiffani and Erika, her second pregnancy had faced dangerous complications—in her case, developmental problems with the fetus's brain so severe that the doctors weren't sure he'd ever be able to feed himself or speak. It wasn't a life they wanted to give their child. But by the time she received a diagnosis, Alyssa was well past her home state's twenty-week limit. Washington, D.C., was the only place where she could find a doctor who would help. The trip, the hotel, and the procedure at DuPont Clinic cost Alyssa and her husband roughly $20,000. It was money they had been putting away for years, living frugally and hoping to someday use their savings to build a dream home. The abortion was one of the hardest decisions Alyssa had ever had to make. She hid her tears from her three-year-old as she explained that the baby wasn't coming after all; when she came home after the abortion, her doctor prescribed antidepressants. She started to attend grief counseling. The only thing that helped, she said, was getting the abortion in a place where the doctors and nurses understood what she had been through, and where they didn't seem to judge her for doing what she knew was best for her family.

"We've never traveled out of the country. We don't even have passports," she said. "Looking into going to, like, Canada or something wouldn't have been an option."

If D.C. hadn't been there—if there wasn't someplace in the country where she could find a legal abortion—Alyssa didn't know what her family would have done.

Jasper was feeling down, and it wasn't just from thinking about his pregnancy. Lately, it felt like something bigger was troubling him—like Florida, the state he loved and where his whole family lived, no longer treated him like a whole person.

He'd been stunned when Florida had outlawed abortion past six weeks; if he'd faced that kind of prohibition, he knew it would have been impossible for him to get care in Orlando. Already, the fifteen-week limit he'd worked under hadn't felt like enough time, and he couldn't imagine what it would feel like for people with even less leeway than he'd had. But even beyond the state's abortion ban, it felt like the attacks hadn't let up. Florida had also passed a new law banning gender-affirming care for minors; he was old enough that it wouldn't affect him, but he was worried about his younger sister, who was fifteen and had only just come out. Some things, he knew, would be better for her than they had been for him—their father was more accepting now than he had been with Jasper and so was their stepmother. But he'd been able to get health care that allowed him to feel at home in his own body. By the time she needed that, he feared, Florida would already have moved backward.

Between the abortion ban and the bills explicitly targeting trans people, it felt like every facet of Jasper's identity was under attack. His state didn't trust him to decide his own health care— here at least, he didn't have ownership over his own body. *All these factors are just pushing against me,* he kept thinking. *I have no idea what I'm supposed to do.*

Maybe I should just leave, Jasper had begun to think. He'd fantasize about getting a van and leaving Florida, relocating to Boston or Washington or Canada—anywhere else where he knew he'd be able to get reliable health care and where it didn't feel like his very personhood was under constant attack. But it wasn't more than an idle daydream. He hadn't thought about how he'd say goodbye to his stepmom, whom he loved, or to his dad. Then there was school and his job and his friends. He wasn't the kind of person who got homesick, he'd say, but actually moving was still another level. It wasn't something he'd ever really had to consider before.

For now, he figured, all he could do was try to make the best of things. For every person at work who got his gender wrong or who seemed consistently incapable of addressing him by his name, there was someone like his boyfriend, who loved Jasper without question and who made him feel like a person who mattered, even planning a trip for the two of them to Disney World, where they could wander the Magic Kingdom, gazing up at the spires of the Cinderella Castle and holding hands as they watched the fireworks. Jasper had never really loved his birthday, but that year he planned a big twentieth birthday celebration, traveling to a vacation rental with his closest friends. Eating strawberry cake, he told himself that it was a miracle he'd made it two whole decades. And now that he had, this was going to be the best phase of his life. He had to believe that.

Someday, Jasper kept hoping, he might feel like a person who deserved to be here, whose bodily autonomy was worth not only preserving but also celebrating. He couldn't say how long it would take. Often, it was hard to believe he'd ever get past the way he still felt now: like someone whose every sense of control over his body was slowly being chipped away.

But if he couldn't let himself even imagine a brighter future, what else did he have?

———◆———

The World After *Dobbs*

Texas

Tiff had started working at Little Caesars. Mateo was four months old; she'd left high school, taken and passed her GED exam, and figured it was finally time to start earning some money.

She stuck it out for a month before she found full-time work at a cell phone store next door. It was ten dollars an hour, close to fifty hours a week, and her mom watched Mateo while she was working. He was so much bigger now, and he'd started to giggle at the sight of water. The birth hadn't been that long ago, but she still couldn't believe that he was her son, and that she, somehow, was a mom.

The initial postpartum period had been so difficult. It felt like she'd become a shell of herself, with little purpose beyond feeding her baby. Those first few months, she'd wake up, feed Mateo, maybe eat a snack, and try to sneak in a bit of sleep if she could before the baby got hungry again. She'd discovered the movie *Titanic* on Netflix, which she'd somehow never seen. Whenever she couldn't sleep, she would just press play. Months later, she swore she could still recite the entire movie: she'd memorized every word spoken by Leonardo DiCaprio as an artist and Kate Winslet as a society lady, along with every lyric Celine Dion had sung. It was like a sharp burst of clarity amid a feverish nightmare.

Things were slowly getting better. Tiff was trying to save up money for an emergency medical technician course, and a few months into her new job she estimated she was halfway there. Once she got the money, and once she turned eighteen, she'd find the time to enroll in a local program, get certified, and start working as an EMT. As long as her parents kept helping her, she hoped, she could stick to her plan. Eventually, she'd become a paramedic. It was good work, and she could make double what she earned now at the cell phone shop. (Per the Bureau of Labor Statistics, the average annual salary for a Texas paramedic is about $50,700.) She didn't know if it would be enough money to raise Mateo somewhere other than her small hometown—she'd nodded in rueful agreement when a friend recently described it as nothing more than "gas stations, vapes, weed, and eighteen-wheelers"—but she'd begun to fantasize about eventually moving with him to Houston. Maybe five years or ten years from now, she'd be in a serious relationship with someone who wanted to be involved in raising her son—not like the boys she met online who freaked out whenever she mentioned that she already had a child. She'd be working full-time, earning enough to give Mateo a good life.

It felt so strange to start outlining her own future in such detail this early, but she felt like she had no choice. Tiff was still a child, sure, but to Mateo she was the most important grown-up in the world. If she wasn't there, who would take care of him? She had to plan for his future—her parents wouldn't be around forever, and he needed her. She wasn't even eighteen, but she didn't have time to be a kid anymore.

And thank God she'd had a boy. Mateo would never have to endure what she'd gone through. He'd never wake up one morning, learn he was pregnant, and see his whole life turn upside down. He'd get to do whatever he wanted—not have his future outlined in such clear, defined terms before he was old enough to even vote. His life would be one full of possibility, so much more than hers.

———

Across the country, *Dobbs* had changed everything. In just a few short years, the loss of federal abortion rights had brought into sharp relief every shortcoming of the reproductive health care infrastructure. It had opened up question after question about the future of gender equality in the United States and about the ability to access simple, basic medical care. And it had brought few answers about what all this would mean for years and even decades to come, and how drastically it could reshape the nation.

Nowhere was the seismic impact more obvious than Texas, the first state to undo *Roe,* the largest state to ban abortion, and one of the most diverse states in the entire country. Senate Bill 8 had given Texas a head start. Texas offered a preview of what other abortion-ban states would face, and its neighboring states would illustrate how limiting access to a common medical service could stretch entire medical ecosystems to their breaking points.

An analysis by the Society of Family Planning suggested that in the first year after *Dobbs* the number of abortions held approximately steady in the United States—that states with legal abortion saw an increase as a result of patients traveling for care, while numbers plummeted in states with bans. In Texas alone, abortions fell by about 36,970. It was an underestimate, since the numbers didn't fully reflect that Senate Bill 8's implementation meant that the number of abortions had already been falling, well before *Roe*'s official end, and that in the years leading up to *Dobbs* the national abortion tally had been increasing significantly. In time, researchers believed, abortions across the country would decline dramatically. And for individuals the implications would be life-changing—they already were. One study conducted by a group of scholars at Johns Hopkins University found that in the nine months after Senate Bill 8 took effect, when abortion was banned in Texas for anyone past six weeks, the state recorded ten thousand more births than it otherwise would have. It was as clear a sign as any that, when access to abortion went away, people would be forced to have children they weren't prepared for or that they didn't intend to have. Young girls like Tiffany would be forced into the physically draining state of pregnancy and the lifelong commitment of parenthood before they were ready. Abortion bans in Texas—and soon across the country—would irrevocably alter the contours, possibilities, and ultimately outcomes of individual lives.

After *Dobbs,* the stories began to emerge—across the country, but especially in Texas—of the people for whom abortion wasn't only a matter of reproductive autonomy but also a medical emergency.

There were the patients whom Shelly Tien and Laura Mercer saw in their Arizona hospitals, or the ones who traveled to Kansas with their ectopic pregnancies, where the option of abortion could literally be lifesaving. There were patients like the one Dr. Leilah Zahedi-Spung had left behind when she moved away from Tennessee to Colorado, who would need an abortion to continue cancer treatment, but who couldn't legally get one in their home state; if they didn't have the means to travel, they had no way of accessing chemotherapy. More than a dozen women from across the state of Texas filed suit, arguing that the state's abortion bans had forced them to wait until the onset of a medical crisis or to flee the state for care when their wanted pregnancies had become potentially fatal. In many cases, a person could not receive an abortion in Texas until they developed sepsis—the life-threatening infection that Ginger Tiger, from Oklahoma, had seen in patient after patient in the wake of Senate Bill 8. Even after their patients recovered, doctors worried they might not be able to have children again, a devastating outcome that was entirely preventable.

Polling from KFF, a national health research organization, found that in states with abortion bans almost half of all ob-gyns said they had personally struggled to provide appropriate care for patients experiencing miscarriages or other pregnancy-related emergencies. The data offered some of the starkest evidence of how widespread the health crisis was—how many people could not count on receiving needed medical care because of their states' abortion bans. And even from inside hospitals, medical professionals continued to report seeing patients suffer the consequences of attempting to terminate their pregnancies on their own.

It was visible everywhere you looked. After Texas banned abortion, Kam, a twenty-five-year-old nurse in San Antonio, had begun seeing a new kind of patient in the ward where they worked: hospital wound reconstruction. Historically, the people who needed Kam's care were those who'd sustained severe burns or older patients with bedsores. Young patients were a rarity. But, with legal abortion gone, young girls—some barely eighteen—had begun to travel to the hospital from South Texas with burns and lacerations on their genitalia, resulting in massive, nonstop bleeding. The wounds appeared self-inflicted. After a few such patients, Kam realized what was happening. These girls had become pregnant but had no idea how to access an abortion—but maybe, they thought, this kind of self-harm would do the job. They were willing to risk their lives to end their pregnancies. For every such patient who checked into the hospital, there were, Kam worried, others who had taken the same approach. How many hadn't been able to come here? How many more had died in the process? And how many more would?

Lauren Miller, one of the women who sued the State of Texas when she couldn't get an abortion, despite learning that one of the twins she was carrying likely wouldn't survive, put it starkly and simply. Complications like the ones she and the women around her had faced weren't rare, and, at worst, they could be life-threatening. She had been lucky to have the resources and support networks to leave the state for care. "We're not the only ones like this," she said, sun pouring down outside the Texas capitol. "There are others in our situation, and they're not all coming out of this with their lives."

That people would die as a result of abortion bans was undeniable. Preliminary data in Texas showed that by 2022, a year after Senate Bill 8 had taken effect, the state's infant mortality rate had increased by an entire 11.5 percent, likely the result, doctors believed, of Texans being forced to carry to term pregnancies that medical professionals knew were not viable. National data showed a 3 percent increase in infant mortality across the country between 2021 and 2022, the first time in about twenty years that infant deaths had risen, with much of the growth coming from states such as Texas, Missouri, and Georgia, states where abortion was almost completely outlawed or significantly restricted. People were being forced to give birth—to endure the physical burden of pregnancy and labor—only to have babies who they knew would die, in some cases after just hours of life. For Samantha Casiano, another of the women to sue Texas, the trauma was plainly visible: reflecting on the birth and immediate loss of her young child caused a visceral reaction as she vomited from the witness stand, testifying about what she had suffered under Texas's abortion law. She said that she hoped testimony like hers would help other people, preventing more Texans from going through what she had. But the Texas lawsuit, which directly tackled the question of what kinds of medical exceptions the state's abortion ban permitted, would take more than a year to resolve. Even if the women suing Texas succeeded, their case could address medical exceptions only in one state, albeit the largest one to ban abortion. Pregnant people in other parts of the country would continue to suffer.

And in time more people would die: infants, and those who couldn't access legal abortions. In America, it would be difficult to track, even though from the moment the *Dobbs* decision came down health researchers said they expected pregnancy-related deaths to climb. But measuring by just how much and who were the people affected would be at best a Herculean endeavor and at worst impossible. Data tracking pregnancy-related deaths are largely collected by individual states and can lag by several years. In states with abortion bans, records of a pregnancy-related death wouldn't necessarily note whether the patient might have benefited from the option of termination. In 2024, *The New Yorker* published the story of Yeniifer Alvarez, who died in July 2022 after complications resulting from her high-risk pregnancy—a death that four outside experts told the magazine could have been prevented had someone offered her an abortion.

Rochelle Garza, a civil rights attorney in Brownsville, Texas, could tell more stories than she could count: There were the pregnant people who waited in the hospital for days until their miscarriages developed sufficient complications that medical providers would be forced to intervene, physicians who didn't even mention abortion as an option, despite knowing it was the best response to someone's medical situation. There were new mothers who gave birth to their babies only to watch them die. For these people, the best-case scenario meant experiencing unshakable trauma, while potentially suffering long-term health complications that could have been avoided. The worst-case scenario could mean a shortened lifespan—a quicker death. Still, many of these cases weren't labeled as direct consequences of Texas's abortion ban—at least, not in any state records.

Evidence from around the world had made it obvious what would happen next. You could point to Ireland, where in 2012, before the country legalized abortion, a thirty-one-year-old woman died from an infection after doctors denied her an abortion. Her water had broken when she was only seventeen weeks pregnant—

but, they insisted, the fetus's heartbeat prevented them from doing anything. In 2023, a woman in Poland—where abortion is entirely illegal—died of sepsis after a hospital refused to provide her an abortion, even when it was clear her pregnancy was no longer viable. It wasn't the first such case in the country's recent memory: another woman in a similar situation had died in 2021, only two years earlier. Even in Texas, there was history, names and faces people still remembered of those who were lost because they couldn't access abortion, even when it was legal. In McAllen, there was Rosie Jimenez. She had died in 1977, four years after *Roe* was decided and months after the Hyde Amendment had taken effect. Without insurance coverage, Rosie couldn't afford an abortion through legal means. Instead, she went to a midwife who charged far less, but who, unbeknownst to Rosie, hadn't sterilized any of the equipment she would use. Rosie contracted an infection from the abortion; in just over a week, she was dead. It was naïveté at best and willful denial at worst to imagine that similar fatalities wouldn't occur after *Roe* fell. Health care professionals consistently declined to speak on the record about the issue, citing legal concerns, but it was becoming what felt like an open secret. Doctors and nurses were hesitant to say it out loud, perhaps, but many feared that already people had died because they couldn't access legal abortion.

"These things have happened already. We won't hear about them," insisted Cait, an intensive care nurse in Virginia. Even in her home state, where the procedure was legal, she had cared for a young woman who had attempted to self-manage an abortion, incorrectly taking pills and landing in the ICU as a result. Cait's team was lucky: the young woman lived. But in almost twenty years of nursing she had never seen a case like this—a patient almost dying because she couldn't access such a normal, routine course of medical care. It was entirely preventable. Cait's employer warned her not to speak publicly about the issue, she said, but she couldn't forget what she had seen and what she knew she would see again. One day, she feared, she'd see a girl who didn't survive. In Texas, similar dangers had existed for even longer. Dr. Alireza Shamshirsaz, who used to practice in Houston, still remembered the woman he treated whose twin pregnancy developed complications when one fetus's amniotic sac ruptured. She wasn't eligible for an abortion because her life wasn't in imminent danger, and by the time she could receive care her sepsis had advanced to the point that she needed two weeks of intensive care treatment and her kidney was permanently damaged. Within a year, she would need an organ transplant. Her health was irreversibly worse, and her life expectancy would be diminished. She would suffer long-term health complications that on the surface might not appear to result from being denied an abortion, but that in practice were the direct product of bans on care.

Horrific as these stories were, many of them were somehow the best-case scenarios, the ones people felt comfortable describing even in vague terms, without putting themselves in legal danger.

———

Before *Roe* fell, McAllen had been home to the last abortion clinic in Texas's Rio Grande Valley, and Becky, a lifelong Texan and young college student, knew the place by sight. It was where the other girls at school used to go whenever they needed help, just by city hall, next to a church, and a short drive from an H-E-B supermarket. It was easy to find. There was a mural on the outside of brightly painted women standing in a field, holding what looked like balls of light, gazing up at the sun. The words hovered above them: "DIG-NITY." "EMPOWERMENT." Few places were harder hit by *Roe*'s fall than the Rio Grande Valley, which lies south of San Antonio and abuts the state's border with Mexico. Even before 2021, reproductive health care in the region had been difficult to come by—and abortion, while technically available, was only barely so in practice. Minutes from the border, the clinic, a tiny Whole Woman's Health outpost, had long been the only abortion provider for thousands of miles. In the fall of 2021, when the state's six-week ban took effect, visits to the clinic fell precipitously, with the majority of Texans seeking abortions unable to make it there under that tight deadline. But abortions still happened. At least some people in the Valley were still able to get clinic-based care in the state, even if that meant driving for hours each way, testing themselves daily from the moment their periods seemed late. Even the $650 for an early abortion represented a tremendous expense; one woman recalled using some of the money she'd been saving to buy a home. People prayed to some higher power that they were still early enough in pregnancy to qualify.

After *Dobbs,* though, even that sliver of an opportunity disappeared. Abortion in Texas was outlawed completely, and clinics like McAllen's shut down. Farther north, Texans with means could conceivably drive to Kansas or New Mexico; they could book a flight to Colorado, California, or New York. For a brief time, they could go to Florida or North Carolina. But in the Valley? The drive to any one of those states felt like an absurd proposition. The region's southernmost cities, places like McAllen and Harlingen, were a good twelve-hour drive from the closest New Mexico clinic, and Wichita was even farther. Flying out of the tiny local airport was an option in theory, but it meant having the money to pay for a plane ticket. In 2021, per U.S. Census data, the median household income in the area remained less than fifty thousand dollars, about twenty thousand dollars below the national average and the lowest for major urban areas in the country. Scraping together the money for air travel was a luxury under the best of circumstances. And that was to say nothing of those who, regardless of the cost, simply could not safely leave the area. About 136,000 undocumented people lived in the Valley's two largest counties. It was virtually impossible to drive north without hitting an immigration checkpoint, and without papers flying also wasn't an option—not without risking deportation.

In the Valley, if you wanted an abortion, the options had already been limited. After *Dobbs,* they were virtually nonexistent. Local activists who worked in abortion rights—community organizers, abortion fund volunteers—frequently noted how ridiculous it seemed to suggest people travel north or west for an abortion. So many people who lived in this region had never left before; Albuquerque or Denver might as well be Mars.

It was yet another reminder—as if there hadn't been enough—that, although the end of abortion rights would eventually hit Americans of all stripes, some would suffer more than others. This was the American way.

Nobody had ever taught Becky about birth control. It never came up in school, and her parents, who had both emigrated from Mexico when they were young, didn't tell her about the pill or even condoms. When her mom talked to her about pregnancy, it was in that looming, terrifying way. "You'd better not get pregnant," she'd tell her. "If you do, you'll have to raise the baby." Neither of her parents believed in abortion, and Becky was hesitant to even broach the subject with them. Everything she knew, she'd learned from her friends and from whatever she could find online.

She'd had sex before, but now, at age nineteen, she had finally met her first ever real boyfriend. Luis was the first person she'd loved and the first she considered to be a true partner in every sense of the word. They'd talked about what they'd do if she got pregnant, even if only in the abstract. And for them the answer was clear: it had to be abortion. Becky lived with her parents, worked part-time at McDonald's, and was still a student at the nearby university. She knew she needed to finish school before she had a child; she'd promised herself forever that she wouldn't become a mom until she was at least twenty, though ideally a bit older. And she knew she didn't have the money to feed another person. Her boyfriend, who lived with friends, didn't even have parents to turn to for help. As for Becky, her mother, a school nurse, made as little as she did. Her father, whose immigration status was tenuous, earned even less.

Even adoption, often touted by abortion opponents, was something they wouldn't consider. Becky's boyfriend had entered the state's foster care system when he was nine years old, moving from family to family. Yes, he'd had food to eat and clothes on his back, but he'd never truly felt cared for by anyone who raised him, never received treatment for the asthma that had plagued him since childhood, and never really felt like he'd had a family that wanted him. It was an experience he still struggled to talk about, but it had instilled in Becky an unwavering belief: nobody should give birth to a child they weren't prepared to raise themselves.

In that regard, she was different from her parents. Like them, she believed in God—but unlike them, she didn't think that belief negated her right to get an abortion if she ever needed one. Her religion, she said, was the kind where you didn't judge people for the choices they made about their own bodies.

Still, the day Becky's pregnancy test came back positive, she couldn't quite believe it. She'd been feeling sick for a few days, nursing a more painful version of the cramps and fatigue she usually associated with her period. Finally, at a baby shower for a friend, she snapped, leaving the party to pick up three pregnancy tests from a nearby store. Hiding in the bathroom at her friend's home, she watched each test come back positive. Three double-pink strips, three confirmations.

Becky didn't trust any doctor to help her figure out how she might be able to terminate her pregnancy. She knew about the anti-abortion centers—the places that offered free if often inaccurate ultrasounds, along with diapers and parenting classes. In states like Texas, with abortion outlawed and clinics disappearing, pregnant people had started relying on those facilities, which largely aren't regulated under the same standards as health clinics, at the very least to find out even roughly how far along they were and to learn what kinds of abortions they might be able to access in other states. But for Becky, who had no way of traveling north anyway, there was little point. And the risk of someone learning she was pregnant was too great. She had no idea whom they would tell or what lengths they'd take to make sure she kept it.

Weeks earlier, Becky had seen a post on Instagram from the New York congresswoman Alexandria Ocasio-Cortez touting the potential of misoprostol for people who no longer had access to legal abortion. The image came back to her now. If there was a way Becky could find misoprostol, and if she took enough on her own at home, she reasoned, maybe that could terminate her pregnancy. The fact that a government figure had recommended it—someone with far more authority or knowledge than she assumed any of her friends might have—gave her a shred of confidence. She learned that another friend, someone who had recently had an abortion, still had a few pills of misoprostol at home and was willing to share them. Becky picked up the two pills and prayed.

This was what it had come to: whisper networks and borrowing people's leftover medicine, counting on someone to know a little more than you did, and hoping for good luck.

The Valley offered a picture of the future, a preview of what it looked like to live in a country where legal abortion simply wasn't readily available.

Post-*Dobbs,* abortion rights organizers in communities like this one did what they could to help people access care. The Frontera Fund, an abortion fund serving the Valley, eventually started helping people leave the state for an abortion—if, of course, they could legally and safely travel for care, without worrying about immigration hurdles or the need to keep a trip secret. Another organization, South Texans for Reproductive Justice, pivoted from helping Texans access abortions to educating them on their options post-*Dobbs,* telling them which states still had legal abortion and what it would take to get there. They could steer them away from anti-abortion centers and distribute free Plan B pills to Texans hoping to avoid an unwanted pregnancy. And if people became pregnant, they could help them find medical clinics that offered affordable prenatal care, that might at least help them have as healthy a birth as possible.

All of this, they hoped, would help. But it could never be enough.

For people seeking abortion, it often felt like the only realistic option was to find someone who could help people get pills, from an organization like the European Aid Access or the Mexico-based Las Libreas from a friend who had extras. For those who had access to a car, and the freedom to leave the state, there was another option: scrounging up the cash, driving across the border to Mexico, and finding a pharmacy that might sell misoprostol. If you bought enough pills, and understood how to use them, that could do the trick.

The story of abortion access is and always has been a story of health care, something that other nations have deemed a basic human right but that in much of the United States is still treated as something available only to those with enough money. In Texas, home to the most uninsured people in the country, where one in four people lacked coverage, the ramifications of that valuation had long been clear. Texans—especially those in the Valley, half of whom lacked health insurance—had been forced for years to treat health care as a luxury. As Nancy Cárdenas Peña, a local abortion rights activist, put it, "A lot of the conversations that people have here are either paying for their utility bill or going to their health care appointment." The implications, too, were stark: pregnancy-related deaths, on the rise across the country, had already been far more common in Texas compared with the national average. High-quality data are very difficult to come by, but a state report released in 2022 found that in 2019, the most recent year for which it had data, at least 118 Texas women died in part because of pregnancy; 72.7 people per 10,000 hospital-based deliveries suffered severe health complications. Texas, per one analysis, is home to one in seven pregnancy-related deaths in the entire country, even though only one in ten people lives there. The situation was, and remains, one unfathomable in many other countries.

Once the Valley's only abortion clinic had shut down, there were fewer reproductive health specialists in the area. Almost immediately after Senate Bill 8, Dr. Tony Ogburn, an ob-gyn at the University of Texas Rio Grande Valley—the same university Becky attended—began to see colleagues leave the state because they knew they could no longer provide comprehensive reproductive health care in Texas. The pattern continued after *Dobbs*. He knew it wouldn't stop—and that with each doctor who left, robust health care would get more impossible to come by.

When Whole Woman's Health left Texas, abortion rights organizers in the Valley thought for a moment they might be able to buy the building that had once housed the region's only clinic. They could turn it into a center for reproductive health care, a place where people could learn how to access contraception and how to stay healthy if they found themselves pregnant. It would, they hoped, help people retain at least a modicum of control over their reproductive destinies, an act of resistance against their state's new legal reality.

Instead, the clinic's owners sold the building to an organization they believed to be a collection of doctors, but they would soon realize that they had been misled. The group that purchased the Valley's last abortion clinic quickly sold the building to a local anti-abortion center. The transition—from a health care clinic staffed by actual doctors, where people could learn about their medical options, to one that actively sought to deny people any reproductive choice—encapsulated within one building just what it meant to ban abortion.

· · ·

When the leftover pills from Becky's friend didn't work, she remembered that she still had one other option. Born in the United States, she had the luxury of being able to drive across the border to Mexico—she made the trip every now and then, usually to go shopping at the flea markets. There, she knew, she might be able to find a pharmacy that would sell her more pills. If she took enough misoprostol, she reassured herself, she'd eventually be able to terminate her pregnancy. She'd heard from friends that pills would cost maybe twenty-five dollars, cheaper than an abortion clinic, but still money she didn't exactly have to spare. Doing the math for the cost of the trip, she quickly realized that the only way to cover the cost would be to take on extra shifts at McDonald's and hope that by the time she'd saved up enough money she wouldn't be too late in her pregnancy for the medication to work. Every day that she waited, she grew increasingly nervous.

It was a trip many Texans had made before her, even before *Roe* fell; the border between Texas and Mexico is incredibly porous for those legally able to leave the country, and abortion pills in Mexico are far cheaper than the $650 or so that one might pay in a clinic. For some, it was a safer, more discreet option—you could pretend this was just a normal shopping trip, rather than risk being seen going in and out of the abortion clinic. Back then, though, it had still been somewhat of a choice, even if one option felt much more affordable than the other. You could go to Mexico, or, if you preferred, you could go to the health center in McAllen. You could get medications across the border, and, if for whatever reason they didn't work, you could try getting pills or a surgical procedure at the clinic instead.

But if this trip didn't work for Becky, she wouldn't have any other options. There was no clinic she could go to—she'd have to keep the baby. The rest of her life, it felt like, was riding on whatever happened on this trip and how she made it through the days that followed.

The day she and her boyfriend crossed the border was another sticky summer morning, and Becky kept reminding herself how lucky she was to even make it this far. Abortion in Texas had been functionally outlawed for so long. She'd known other girls who hadn't been able to get an abortion at the clinic and whose immigration status prevented them from safely leaving the country. There was one girl she kept remembering, a friend from school who wanted to wait a few more years before having a kid, but who was undocumented. She couldn't go to Mexico for pills—even driving up north where she might pass an immigration checkpoint was far too risky. Instead, she'd had a baby at seventeen, even younger than Becky was now.

Once in Reynosa, the city on the other side of the border, Becky and her boyfriend went from pharmacy to pharmacy with a sense of purpose. They'd agreed to stick to areas well trafficked by tourists, hoping that there the odds were better of finding medication that was safe to use. Although generally the pills people got by crossing the border *were* safe, there were instances where people got the wrong kind, didn't know how to take them properly, or, for whatever reason, found that the abortion didn't work. Becky had never done something like this before—leaving the country to get health care or taking her reproductive health so directly into her own hands. Her Spanish wasn't good enough to converse naturally with the men who worked at the pharmacy, some who sold misoprostol for well above the twenty-five dollars she had brought with her. Those, she knew instinctively, must be tourist prices. The men were trying to overcharge her because it was obvious even to them how little she knew what she was doing and how desperate she was. Becky kept pulling out her phone, using internet translators to double-check the ingredients listed on the box and ensure it was in fact misoprostol. Still, a voice kept nagging at her. *If I get this wrong . . . ,* she worried. She couldn't let herself complete the sentence.

Late in the day, they bought a twenty-four-pack of pills. It was enough, she hoped, to terminate her pregnancy and to maybe keep a few extra in case a friend might need them in the future, paying it forward the way others had tried to do for her. From everything she'd found on the internet, she figured ten to twelve pills would do the trick. She just hoped it wouldn't be too much; she didn't know if it was possible to overdose on the drug or what would happen if she took too many.

Becky had to wait another three days—her next scheduled time off from work—before she could take the pills. She waited until her parents had left the house, gagging slightly as she swallowed the medication. She wouldn't tell even her brother what she had done. It wasn't worth the risk of him telling her parents, which she knew he might if they ever got into a fight.

The aftereffects were just as miserable as she'd imagined. For the next two weeks, it felt like Becky couldn't stop bleeding; she kept running out to the store to buy extra menstrual pads—more money she would have preferred not to spend—and hoping that eventually the blood would stop. In time, she kept telling herself, she'd know incontrovertibly that the medication had worked its magic. But the only proof she could count on was a negative pregnancy test.

It felt like such a big thing to hide, and she couldn't always tell how well she was even keeping the secret. Only days after she took the pills, Becky's mother began asking her when she'd go to the gynecologist—had she been tested recently for sexually transmitted infections? She really ought to go soon. Becky couldn't tell if her mother suspected something, had noticed the blood, the pads, and Becky's general fatigue over the past few weeks and put two and two together. But she wouldn't risk asking her mother what she thought was going on. A week after taking her pills, Becky finally made a doctor's appointment. By now, Becky hoped, the medication had done the trick—even if she was still bleeding, the doctor could mistake it for a period. If she was lucky, nobody would know she'd ever been pregnant. A part of her was still nervous that what she had done might somehow be against the law. Abortion was illegal in Texas, after all. If anyone found out she'd been pregnant, or figured out that she'd tried to get an abortion, would she go to jail? Or what about her boyfriend, who'd helped her cross the border and get the pills? What would happen to him?

It made sense she was afraid. Post-*Dobbs,* women like Becky represented a final frontier for the anti-abortion movement. They'd found a way to circumvent their states' bans and to cling on to their own reproductive autonomy. Eventually, abortion opponents hoped to find a way to outlaw purchases like the one she had made. They just hadn't yet figured out the best way to do it: whether they wanted to pass a new law, or whether they should attempt to prosecute people who self-managed their abortions under existing murder laws. The latter was something anti-abortion law enforcement officers had even attempted to do before *Roe* was overturned, typically targeting women of color, especially Black women and Latinas. It remains an open question how far the movement will go.

If the medication abortion had worked, it would take close to a month for Becky's hormone levels to change, meaning that in the days and weeks after taking the medication a pregnancy test would still show up positive. When she went to the gynecologist, ostensibly just for STI testing, the doctor took one look at her bloodwork and scheduled a prenatal visit. She never mentioned abortion, never asked Becky if she wanted a baby. For weeks, Becky kept hoping that the doctor had been wrong, that the hormone levels were just residual. She couldn't let herself think about the alternative.

At her first prenatal visit, Becky finally got the news she'd been waiting for: confirmation she was no longer pregnant. The doctor never asked any questions then, either. She just assumed that Becky must have experienced a miscarriage—she told her she was sorry.

Only while driving home from the doctor's office did Becky at last let her relief show. At least for now, she could continue her life as a young woman in South Texas with no idea of what the future might hold for her, but with no constraints on what she could imagine. For now, she still had the freedom to decide for herself the life she wanted to live.

———————

By the end of 2023, close to half the country had outlawed or severely restricted abortion. And as a result, the strongest recourse people living in abortion-ban states had now was one another's support. They just had to hope that mutual aid—coupled with creativity, know-how, and good luck—could be enough. Still, whatever they could accomplish together wouldn't suffice to reverse the medical harm these laws inflicted.

In Texas, there would be young girls like Tiff whose lives would be forever changed by the abortions they could not get. There would be women like Angela who used every resource they had to flee the state for care, keeping their abortions as secret as possible. Women like Darlene would discover the hard way that abortion was a vital medical option, without which they could die. And there would be people like Jasper, trans men who sought abortions and who would be forced to stomach the dehumanizing feeling of navigating law after law that told them they didn't have the right to make their own medical decisions.

Tiff, Angela, Darlene, and Jasper had done whatever it took to secure some kind of reproductive autonomy. Success wasn't always possible. And the process had been by turns devastating, insulting, and life-threatening. They'd never be able to forget this feeling, or the fact that these barriers were deliberately created by their own political leaders. In the post-*Dobbs* world, there would be so many more people like them: navigating the same kinds of crises, going outside their states, outside the law, outside the country if they had to, in order to access medical care.

And yet even in the most difficult circumstances, those who found care—and even those who couldn't—continued to imagine that a better future might exist, even if just for their own families.

Tiffany still held out hope that someday she'd have another child, on her own terms, when she was ready. She told herself that her dreams remained within reach, if only she worked as hard as possible. She'd be the kind of mom her son could rely on, an adult who knew how to take care of herself and him. And, she promised, Mateo would never want for anything. She was still so young—there was so much possibility ahead.

The abortion behind her, Angela was overjoyed when Nigel proposed. She'd never been to a wedding before, but she let herself daydream about what hers might look like and what it would mean to plan a celebration meant to honor their family of three. She watched with pride as Nigel did well in school. Slowly, as she worked at a new job and saved money at every opportunity, she watched her bank balance grow. The couple moved into a new home, with a bedroom just for their son. And Angela started making plans to go back to school—the local community college had a great nursing program. Nobody would ever have to know about her abortion if she didn't want to tell them. Someday, she hoped, it could simply be a setback on the road to building a better life for her son, but one they had overcome—and one that had opened up doors for her and her family to live and even thrive on their own terms.

Darlene would always remember the year of her pregnancy as one of the worst she'd ever lived through. After the delivery, she had her tubes tied; she never again wanted to risk the danger of being pregnant in Texas. But she never lost sight of how grateful she was. She was healthy and, more importantly, so were her two wonderful girls. Nothing mattered as much as making sure they were okay. Even in Texas, a state where she felt less and less sure of their rights, she would do everything in her power to protect them, to make sure they grew up healthy and happy.

As for Jasper? Close to a year after his abortion, he and his boyfriend ended their relationship. Jasper knew he'd made the right choice for himself—that he couldn't become a parent at this juncture in his life—yet he still found himself thinking about his pregnancy and what might have been. But he would do his best to look forward, to focus on what he loved: the kids he taught, his younger sister, his friends who kept supporting him. It was hard to imagine what it would take to live in a state where he felt equal, where he was treated as a full citizen. But he would keep going—and keep hoping things would someday get better.

Afterword

This book is ostensibly about a world without *Roe v. Wade,* but in practice it is about so much more. As the past several years have reminded me—and as I hope these stories have conveyed—the loss of *Roe,* fragile and loophole laden as it was, has ushered in a new era of American politics, one in which gender is more than ever one of the fundamental dividing lines in how we can exist in society.

For many of us who could get pregnant, *Roe* promised a world in which we were equal. If we did not want to be pregnant, if we did not ever want to give birth or become parents, we did not have to. Or if we did decide we wanted children, we could determine when that happened; rather than circumstances forcing us into parenthood, it was a phase of our lives we could opt in to. If the timing was wrong, and if we did not feel prepared to work while raising a child—if we wanted to pursue college degrees, build a career, choose a partner and co-parent whom we actively wanted to commit to, or even just save up a bit more money—we could do all those things first. Our bodily autonomy was ours; the state of pregnancy, with the irreversible physical burdens and serious risks it brings, was something we entered only willingly.

When the leak of the decision overturning *Roe* was published the evening of May 2, 2022, the news was simultaneously shocking and unsurprising. It felt like a moment we had seen coming for months, if not years. The only question was what it would mean in practice. Two months later, the Supreme Court overturned *Roe* on Friday, June 24. In the days after the decision came out, I spent hours on the phone with abortion providers and medical experts across the country. What were they seeing in clinics? What were they telling patients? How did they break the news to someone that their desperately needed medical appointment was no longer legal? And what were they going to do tomorrow, or the day after? How did they intend to live in this world?

Every person I spoke to sounded tired and scared. None of them knew what the future would bring. They had foreseen this moment, sure, and even spent months planning how they would adjust to the post-*Roe* world. They were trying to think about whether and how to send people seeking abortions to states where the procedure remained legal, a list that would only shrink in the months to come. But, for all the anticipation, living in this new world felt completely different. Nothing, each one told me, could have prepared them for something like this.

At the end of each interview, I'd steel myself for the final, highest-stakes question—the one to which we knew the answer but that still felt essential to say out loud.

"Are people going to die?"

Each time I asked, the uncertainty that had been so evident in their voices before melted away. There was so much we didn't know about what it would mean to overturn *Roe v. Wade,* but this was something we could see clearly. All the evidence was in front of us. This was a story of health care denied; there was only one natural outcome. Every time I asked this question, clinic staffers, doctors, and reproductive health researchers offered the same unequivocal answer: Yes. People would lose their lives because abortion rights were gone.

We knew that abortion bans would change the course of people's lives in myriad ways, denying them the freedom to build the lives they had wanted, forcing people with unwanted pregnancies to push through unimaginable circumstances in search of a clinician who could help them. We also knew that the abortion bans set to take effect would kill people, directly or indirectly. The only question was how many—and how many of those cases we would never even learn about.

Abortion is an issue that touches all our lives, whether we know

it or not. In the hours, days, and weeks that followed *Roe*'s fall, I
heard from people in my own life about their experiences with
abortion and pregnancy. One had her abortion late in her second
trimester, about thirty years ago. She had no choice; the pregnancy
was unviable and, if continued, could have prevented her from having future children. Still, the abortion pushed up against the limit of
what was legal in her state. I thought often about how I'd for years
kept a stash of pregnancy tests in my medicine cabinet, looked up
Planned Parenthood appointment schedules when my period had
come late—just in case—and counted on knowing that, no matter
what, my body wasn't going to be forced through pregnancy when
I didn't want it to be. Even friends with wanted pregnancies confided in me about the physical pain of carrying another being inside
of you. It was a heavy burden, and one they could not fathom forcing upon someone against their will.

There are still many questions about what it means to live in
a nation without abortion protections. Some truths, however, are
already clear. Reporting this book, I have heard people express
the same emotions over and over again: fear, anger, and a sense
of betrayal. Many of them had not thought much about abortion
until they had to—it was something that they had never worried
they would need, until the moment that access became essential. I cannot count how many people have broken down in tears,
recounting what they had to endure to seek health care, and their
sense of injustice at how needlessly difficult the process was. The
bans and barriers they faced in accessing care have given them the
same message: the country they live in does not trust them to make
their own decisions about their lives. They are less of a person than
someone who could not get pregnant. Many of them believe that
America does not care if they live or die. After hearing their stories,
I cannot blame them.

Why *Roe* fell is unavoidably a story of politics. But, more importantly, it is one of human rights—of what it means to live in a country
where people of all genders are truly created equal, and of what it
means to live in one where they are not. Dissenting from the *Dobbs*
opinion, the three liberal Supreme Court justices described what
Roe promised—even if that commitment was never fully actualized—
writing that, under *Roe*'s protections, "the government could not

control a woman's body or the course of a woman's life: It could not determine what the woman's future would be." Furthermore, they added, "respecting a woman as an autonomous being, and granting her full equality, meant giving her substantial choice over this most personal and most consequential of all life decisions." The power to determine when and how one becomes pregnant is exactly that: one of the most personal and most consequential choices someone will ever make. In many cases, it is hardly even a choice; it is a medical necessity.

Yet the promise of equality those justices described no longer exists—if, of course, it ever truly did. We live in a country where patients are afraid to admit that they have even sought an abortion, let alone received one. Abortion rights advocates speak often about a future America that will restore *Roe*'s protections, but few believe it will happen soon. In the interim, countless lives will be disrupted and endangered. In this new world order, gender has become even more of a dividing line in American society, one that has amplified existing inequalities and created new ones. Gender determines whether people have the right to make their own medical decisions. More than ever, it shapes something even more foundational: people's right to decide how and on what terms they wish to live.

Sourcing Note

Due to the stigma around seeking abortion in the United States—and in some cases fear of criminal or civil prosecution for seeking abortion care—the vast majority of patients who spoke with me requested that I withhold their last names from publication. Four patients requested the use of pseudonyms, fearing that publishing even their distinctive first names would make their story easily identifiable. The names used for their stories—"Angela," "Amber," "Jen," and "Vee"—are pseudonyms they requested. I also used a pseudonym in relaying the experiences of "Anna" because of particular details in her experience seeking care. In reconstructing patients' stories of accessing abortion-related care, I relied on their detailed recollections and contemporaneous writing, such as journal entries, calendars, text exchanges, medical records, and social media posts.

The majority of physicians who spoke with me felt comfortable sharing their full names. One physician, citing threats of harassment and violence toward abortion providers in her community, requested that I use only her last initial; she is referenced in this work's endnotes as "Dr. S." Kam, a nurse quoted in the epilogue, feared professional repercussions for speaking out about what they had seen. Cait, another nurse quoted in the epilogue, also asked for her identifying information to be withheld, citing concerns about legal risks.

Acknowledgments

This book was reported, researched, and written over the past three years, but its origins date back a decade. Every person who has spoken to me over the years about their experiences seeking an abortion or providing care—those whose stories are in these pages and the countless others whose are not—I owe you a debt I can never repay. Your bravery and honesty in sharing your experiences, reliving episodes that many of you wish you never had to endure, will help us build a better, more equal country. Your trust has meant the world to me, and it was an honor to listen to and work with you.

This book wouldn't exist without the countless people who believed in it and whose voice, influence, and expertise shaped my reporting and writing. Working with the Robbins Office and the trifecta of Kathy Robbins, David Halpern, and Janet Oshiro is such a privilege. I am so grateful for how their insights have shaped and finessed this book, from initial vision to final product. The editing team at Doubleday has invested so much in this project, and I cannot say enough in particular about Cara Reilly. Her passion, knowledge, and care were unparalleled, and everything I am proud of in the final product is because of her. Janet and Cara especially, thank you both for continuing to cheer for this book and for your incredible ability to make it better. You made every session of edits and brainstorming an activity to savor and a source of true joy, and I don't understand how I was so lucky to be on the same team as the two of you. I'm also so grateful for Bill Thomas and Kris Puopolo at Doubleday, who have offered so much support and so many constructive ideas in fleshing out this text. Kathleen Cook, Lily Dondoshansky, Anne Jaconette, and Michael Goldsmith played crucial roles in getting this book to the finish line; it was such a privilege to work on the same team as all four of them.

There are so many others to thank. Jonathan Cohn was one of this project's earliest champions, someone who believed in it from the first phone call and who encouraged me to pursue a book before I ever thought I could. Chabeli Carrazana read the initial pages that became chapter 1 and understood immediately what it could be. I've spent so much time brainstorming and discussing this project with my colleagues at *The 19th*, especially Jennifer Gerson, Lance Dixon, Errin Haines, Terri Rupar, Jessica Kutz, and Orion Rummler—your insights have meant so much to me, and I'm inspired daily by the work that all of you do. Mel Leonor Barclay and Grace Panetta, some of the most generous and smartest collaborators in the industry, it's a special privilege to be on this beat with you. For all the challenges of our profession, working with all of you reminds me daily why journalism remains the best job on earth. The incredible Grace Segers was one of the first people to read a full manuscript of this work, and I could not have asked for a more generous pair of eyes; I cannot wait to read her own books someday very soon. Madeline Conway, Collin Doyle, and Victoria Knight—some of the smartest people I know—offered invaluable feedback. Your edits, ideas, and regular conversations about the state of abortion post-*Dobbs* helped me so much in refining the themes of this project; thank you for always pushing me to ask more questions. And I'm so unspeakably grateful for the friendship of Caroline Kitchener and Rachel Cohen, two journalists whose work covering abortion I deeply admire and who have offered me inspiration, support, and the encouragement that kept me going. It is a privilege to know both of you, and the world is a brighter, better place because of the journalism you do.

A special form of thanks goes to my accomplished, brilliant, and incredibly generous group of college friends: Stacy Bartlett, Elizabeth Carr, Chelsea Feuchs, Kayla Rosen, Kimberly Takahata, and Sienna Zeillinger. I think often of eating falafel in New York with you while first fantasizing about the possibility of writing something like this. (I try to think far less about the Celtics' performance against the Warriors that night.) This book exists because of your accountability texts and the time many of you spent reading my preliminary drafts—offering so much of your various professional and personal expertise to make this book the best it can be—and because of the enthusiasm you've shared at every milestone I hit. I am so lucky to have benefited from your support, not only these past few years, but ever since we met several lifetimes ago in the first-floor Keeney dorms, the Blue Room, the Writing Center, 195 Angell, and (of course) the GCB. Thank you for your belief in me and in this work, and for helping me survive the particular insanity of 2021 through 2023. I love you all and rely on you more than I can say.

I would be lost without the editors whose generosity, time, and patience have turned me into the reporter I am now. Nicole Friedman taught me years ago that powerful journalism relies on moral clarity, honesty, accountability, and, above all, nuance. Sydney Ember pushed me to apply for an internship at *The Texas Tribune,* a job that changed my life and put me on the path to covering health and reproductive health full-time. Rebecca Ballhaus continues to make me a more thoughtful, better-informed student of journalism. When I read through these pages, I hear the voice of Stephanie Stapleton, who taught me so much of what I know about writing and whose editorial instincts and knowledge of health policy have shaped my work. Diane Webber has constantly reminded me in word and deed of all the ways in which empathy makes us better journalists. Andrea Valdez, Damon Darlin, Jay Hancock, Julie Rovner, John Hillkirk, Susan Weiss, and Kelly Johnson have been so generous with their time and mentorship; I am a better reporter because I have had the privilege of watching and working with each of them. And I'm especially grateful for Elisabeth Rosenthal, whose faith in me pushed me to become a more confident reporter and whose knack for constructing a compelling, clear, human-anchored narrative remains unparalleled.

I could write an entire volume just about Abby Johnston, who has pushed me since I joined *The 19th* to pursue the story of abortion with compassion, rigor, and honesty. Abby, you are both an exceptional editor and a dear friend, and there is nobody else on earth

I could run eight miles with on a Friday morning while discussing the details of abortion policy, with only occasional digressions about our favorite books and music. I hope I have done you proud. Emily Ramshaw, the editor who saw something in a twenty-year-old intern and who believed in me more than anyone ever has, none of this would have happened without you. As much as any single person can be, you are the reason I'm a journalist. Thank you for everything, always.

My mother taught me that a teacher is second only to God, and this book wouldn't exist without the instructors who have nurtured and challenged me over the years. My high school journalism adviser, Michael Moul, taught me the value of empathy, clarity, and persistence, both in reporting and in life. Galen Rosenberg transformed how I approach both reading and writing, separate crafts that each require their own skill sets. And I learned so much from my brilliant college professors, including James Egan, Deak Nabers, and Michael Tesler. Being your student was an honor, and I am a better writer and sharper thinker because of the time you spent on me.

There are several voices whose expertise I have constantly relied on, in this work and in my reporting over the years: Elizabeth Nash, Rachel Rebouché, Mary Ziegler, Laurie Sobel, and Ashley Kirzinger. Thank you for always making the time to help me understand what is going on and, more importantly, what it means for people's real lives. The world is so much better and smarter because of the work you do. And, researching this book, I have also been regularly in awe of the exceptional work done by so many journalists who have devoted themselves to covering this moment in our nation's history. There are far too many of you to name, but I am so grateful and honored to be doing this work alongside you.

While writing this book has been incredibly rewarding, living in this world for the past several years—hearing people relive some of the most painful, often traumatic moments of their lives—has been harder than I could have imagined. I am so lucky to have a rich support network in D.C. and beyond: Madison Mundy, Nick Sueppel, Isabelle Fisher, Gayatri Mehra, Andrea Mirviss, Eliza Relman, Hannah Norman, Maura Carey, Rachel Bluth, Alex Arduino, Sydney Lupkin, Todd Harris, Katherine Xiong, Michelle Hackman, Zac Krislov, Eli Okun, Eugénie Boury, Adam Gilbert, Gray Barrett, Caroline Herre, Katie Saviano, Nina Russell, Colin Diersing, Adam Waters, Shubh Agrawal, Uday Agrawal, Julie Diamond, Adam Kemerer, Maggie Tennis, Joe Van Wye, Isabella Levy, and Andrew August. It is such a joy to count on your friendship. Thank you for taking me rock climbing, attending Julien Baker and Thom Yorke concerts with me, planning horror movie nights, Red Derby trips, FaceTimes, ice cream outings, dance parties, and weekend getaways. And thank you for listening to me talk endlessly about these stories. Your time and listening ears and, critically, your willingness to provide infinite distractions have meant more to me than I can say. I am so, so grateful to have you all in my life.

My in-laws, Janet and Lewis Buzzell, have given me so much to love, including the state of Florida, where they hosted me multiple times as I reported this book, nursing me through journalism-induced stomach bugs, showing me the best running paths in Jacksonville, and always making sure to equip me with a travel-friendly Pub Sub. It is such a joy to be a part of your family, and I cannot thank you enough for all you did to make this reporting possible.

The Mehta, Lakhan-Pal, and Ambady families feel as close to me as my own, and I'm so thankful for your love and care, extending well beyond these past few years. Shreya, Kunal, Arushi, Nihaal, Nandi, Nanu, Maya, and Leena are the extra siblings I never had, the ones who taught me how to wear makeup, watched Amanda Bynes movies and *Kuch Kuch Hota Hai* on repeat, and filmed all those embarrassing home videos together. Anju Aunty, Mehul Uncle, Nilita Aunty, and Vivek Uncle, you are my other sets of parents; I cannot say enough how much your lifetime of support has meant to me, whether that involved taking me to dance classes, teaching me how to make the perfect Thanksgiving cocktail, or sharing my reporting with your group texts. And in writing this book I thought often of Raj Uncle and Nalini Aunty, mentors and role models who encouraged me to pursue journalism even when I feared I didn't have what it takes. I miss you both.

Nobody has teased or supported me as devotedly as Sahil and Nikhil Luthra. The two of you make me funnier, more thoughtful, and a better cook and baker. You are the best brothers and cheerleaders I could have hoped for. The only people who can compare are our parents, Nalini and Sanjiv Luthra, who have taken more joy in my reporting than even I do and who helped carry extra loads for me when I wasn't sure if I could finish this book. I don't know where to begin in thanking each of you, but I do know that everything I have ever done—well beyond this book—is a testament to you, the care with which you've raised all three of us, and the values of fairness, equality, and empathy that you have always instilled in us. (And, Mom, we all know that my sense of humor comes from you.) I hope I've done all of you proud.

Finally, Logan. I don't know how I could have made it through the past several years without your support. I am a better person because of you and, I know, a better journalist. Thank you for reading everything I write, for living through this process with me, and for caring about these stories as much as I do. This final work exists in no small part because of all the dinners you've cooked and dishes you washed, the movie breaks and walks you scheduled between drafts and edits, and the ice cream celebrations you made sure we honored. Thank you for helping me trust myself enough to tell this story. And, most importantly, thank you for continuing to believe that it can do good.

Notes

INTRODUCTION

xi In 1973: "US States Have Enacted 1,381 Abortion Restrictions Since *Roe v. Wade* Was Decided in 1973," Guttmacher Institute, June 21, 2022.

xi In 1976: Julie Rovner, "Abortion Funding Ban Has Evolved Over the Years," NPR, December 14, 2009.

xii Then came 2016: Brian Naylor, "Trump Backtracks on Comments About Abortion and 'Punishment' for Women," NPR, March 30, 2016.

xiii The right to end a pregnancy: Jessica Ravitz, "The Surprising History of Abortion in the United States," CNN, June 27, 2016.

xiii Historians have written at length: Brandon Baker, "The History of Abortion Access in the U.S.," *Penn Today,* November 1, 2022.

xiii One of the era's: Nicola Beisel and Tamara Kay, "Abortion, Race and Gender in Nineteenth-Century America," *American Sociological Review,* August 2004, https://doi.org/10.1177/000312240406900402.

xiii Through the Great Depression: Annalies Winny, "A Brief History of Abortion in the U.S.," *Hopkins Bloomberg Public Health Magazine,* October 26, 2022.

xiii A small number: Leslie J. Reagan, *When Abortion Was a Crime* (Berkeley: University of California Press, 1997).

xiii But illegal abortions remained: Rachel Benson Gold, "Lessons from Before *Roe*: Will Past Be Prologue?," Guttmacher Institute, March 1, 2003.

xiii Religious leaders wrote frequently: Kate Hoeting, "Abortion, Eugenics, and Civilization: Catholic Anti-Abortion Arguments During the Great Depression," Harvard Divinity School, May 10, 2021.

xiv When in the late 1950s: Daniel K. Williams, *Defenders of the Unborn: The Pro-Life Movement Before* Roe v. Wade (New York: Oxford University Press, 2016).

xiv The same people: Gillian Frank and Neil J. Young, "What Everyone Gets Wrong About Evangelicals and Abortion," *The Washington Post,* May 16, 2022.

xv There were cases in which: Lisa Rosenbaum, "Perilous Politics— Morbidity and Mortality in the Pre-*Roe* Era," *The New England Journal of Medicine,* September 5, 2019, https://doi:10.1056/NEJMp1910010.

xv One doctor recalled: Shefali Luthra, "'You Never Forget It': These Are the Stories of Life Before *Roe v. Wade* Transformed America," *The 19th,* January 20, 2022.

xvi Data collected over the first year: Shefali Luthra, "Florida's Proposed Six-Week Abortion Ban Could Cut Access in Half," *The 19th,* October 26, 2023.

xvii Even before *Roe* fell: Eugene Declerq, Ruby Barnard-Mayers, Laurie Zephyrin, and Kay Johnson, "The U.S. Maternal Health Divide: The Limited Maternal Health Services and Worse Outcomes of States Proposing New Abortion Restrictions," Commonwealth Fund, December 14, 2022.

xvii We know that more people: "Abortion," World Health Organization, November 25, 2021.

xvii Even in countries: Tanika Godbole, "India: Why Are So Many Women Seeking Unsafe Abortions?," DW, April 13, 2022.

xvii Now the United States represents: "U.S. Abortion Laws in a Global Context," Center for Reproductive Rights, September 20, 2022.

CHAPTER I WHERE IT STARTED, WHERE IT ENDS

3 By Texas standards, it had been: Tiff, interviewed by Shefali Luthra, August 17, 2022.

5 Anyone caught "aiding or abetting": "SB8," Texas Legislature Online History, 2021.

5 If the law took effect: "2020 Induced Terminations of Pregnancies for Texas Residents," Texas Health and Human Services.

6 And the judge: "President Obama Nominates Four to Serve on the United States District Courts," The White House, President Barack Obama, June 26, 2014.

6 *Roe* said: *Roe v. Wade,* Justia U.S. Supreme Court.

6 But they couldn't outright ban them: *Planned Parenthood v. Casey,* Justia U.S. Supreme Court.

7 A higher authority: Shefali Luthra, "Texas' Six-Week Abortion Ban Could Create Abortion Vigilantes," *The 19th,* August 30, 2021.

7 at the second: "Counseling and Waiting Periods for Abortion," Guttmacher Institute, August 1, 2022.

7 So, early in the morning: Marva Sadler, interviewed by Shefali Luthra, August 26, 2022.

8   Norma McCorvey: Joshua Prager, "The *Roe* Baby," *The Atlantic*, September 9, 2021.

8   Sarah Weddington: Katharine Q. Seelye, "Sarah Weddington, Who Successfully Argued *Roe v. Wade*, Dies at 76," *The New York Times*, December 27, 2021.

9   Her family minister: Donna Howard, interviewed by Shefali Luthra, March 28, 2023.

9   underground church support: Gillian Frank, "The Religious Network That Made Abortion Safe When It Was Illegal," *The Gender Policy Report*, August 17, 2022.

10   "There was a strong sense": Donna Howard, interviewed by Shefali Luthra, August 29, 2022.

10   In 2003: "H.B. No. 15," Texas Legislature Online History, 2003.

10   less than 5 percent: Rachel K. Jones, Elizabeth Nash, Lauren Cross, et al., "Medication Abortion Now Accounts for More Than Half of All US Abortions," Guttmacher Institute, February 2022.

10   Two years later: "S.B. No. 1150," Texas Legislature Online History, 2005.

10   In 2011: "H.B. No. 15," Texas Legislature Online History, 2011.

10   And in 2013: Becca Aaronson, Ryan Murphy, and Shefali Luthra, "Interactive: How Texas' Proposed Abortion Restrictions Stack Up," *The Texas Tribune* (archive), July 3, 2013.

10   The bill sparked: Julián Aguilar, Becca Aaronson, Jay Root, and Shefali Luthra, "Liveblog: Abortion Bill Fails Amid Midnight Chaos After Filibuster," *The Texas Tribune*, June 26, 2013.

11   Weeks later: Shefali Luthra, "Perry Signs Omnibus Abortion Bill into Law," *The Texas Tribune*, July 18, 2013.

11   The restrictions: "Opposition to Requirements for Hospital Admitting Privileges and Transfer Agreements for Abortion Providers," American Public Health Association, November 3, 2015.

11   One study found that: Elizabeth Raymond and David Grimes, "The Comparative Safety of Legal Abortion and Childbirth in the United States," *Obstetrics and Gynecology*, February 2012, https://doi:10.1097/AOG.0b013e31823fe923.

11   Only once the bill was blocked: Marva Sadler, interviewed by Shefali Luthra, August 26, 2022.

11   the case reaffirmed: *Whole Woman's Health et al. v. Hellerstedt*, Supreme Court of the United States, June 27, 2016.

12   It was a promise: "Political and Religious Identities and Views on Abortion," Public Religion Research Institute, April 8, 2022.

13   By the time someone knows: Abby Johnston and Shefali Luthra, "Texas' Governor Got a Basic Fact About Pregnancy Wrong," *The 19th*, September 7, 2021.

14   When the update finally came: Abby Johnston and Shefali Luthra, "The Supreme Court Refused to Block Texas' Abortion Ban. Sonia Sotomayor

Says Majority 'Opted to Bury Their Heads in the Sand,'" *The 19th,* September 2, 2021.

14 A week later: Candice Norwood, "Department of Justice Sues Texas over Abortion Ban," *The 19th,* September 9, 2021.

14 Tiff was realizing: Tiff, interviewed by Shefali Luthra, August 17, 2022.

16 The story made: *The New York Times,* front page from September 2, 2021; *The Washington Post,* home page from September 1, 2021.

17 Howard never received: Donna Howard, interviewed by Shefali Luthra, August 29, 2022.

17 hardly anybody was concerned: *The New York Times,* front pages from September 10, September 21, and October 21, 2021.

17 All they would weigh in on: Shefali Luthra and Candice Norwood, "The Supreme Court Will Hear Arguments on Texas' Abortion Law. Here's What You Need to Know," *The 19th,* November 1, 2021.

18 the conservative justices said: Shefali Luthra, "Supreme Court Ruling Doesn't Change Anything for Texas Abortion Providers," *The 19th,* December 10, 2021.

18 one appeals judge mused: Shefali Luthra, "Texas' Abortion Law Could Stay in Effect for Months, Appeals Court Suggests," *The 19th,* January 7, 2021.

19 Tiff's inability: Shefali Luthra, "Medication Abortion Is Recognized as Safe—Even Without a Doctor—but Do Enough People Know About It?," *The 19th,* May 17, 2022.

19 Legally, the answer was no: Tiff, interviewed by Shefali Luthra, August 17, 2022.

20 the perinatal period: "Improving Mental Health Care for Pregnant and Postpartum Women," American Hospital Association, May 21, 2021.

21 the number of clinics offering: Alexa Ura, Ryan Murphy, Annie Daniel, and Lindsay Carbonell, "Here Are the Abortion Clinics That Have Closed Since 2013," *The Texas Tribune,* June 28, 2016.

21 People who lost: "Impact of Clinic Closures on Women Obtaining Abortion Services After Implementation of a Restrictive Law in Texas," *American Journal of Public Health,* April 6, 2016, https://doi:10.2105/AJPH .2016.303134.

21 Limited access had meant: Kari White, Sarah E. Baum, Kristine Hopkins, et al., "Change in Second-Trimester Abortion After Implementation of a Restrictive State Law," *Obstetrics and Gynecology,* April 2019, https://doi:10.1097/AOG.0000000000003183.

21 Patients even had a hard time: Rochelle Garza, interviewed by Shefali Luthra, September 22, 2021.

21 Prior to the six-week ban: "ITOP Statistics," Texas Health and Human Services.

21 Between 2018 and 2021: "Maternal Deaths and Mortality Rates per 100,000 Live Births," KFF.

21 in Texas, as is true nationally: "Texas Maternal Mortality and Morbidity Review Committee and Department of State Health Services Joint Biennial Report 2022," Texas Health and Human Services, December 2022.

22 Patients would have to wait: Andrea Gallegos, interviewed by Shefali Luthra, September 20, 2022.

23 When it was finally her turn: Shefali Luthra, "After New Law, a Look Inside One of South Texas' Last Abortion Clinics," *The 19th,* September 27, 2021.

23 The medication had worked: Karla, interviewed by Shefali Luthra, September 24, 2021.

23 "We pride ourselves": Marva Sadler, interviewed by Shefali Luthra, August 26, 2022.

24 Even while battling morning sickness: Kari White, Asha Dane'el, Elsa Vizcarra, et al., "Out-of-State Travel for Abortion Following Implementation of Texas Senate Bill 8," Texas Policy Evaluation Project Research Brief, March 2022.

24 And though Senate Bill 8: Orion Rummler, "*The 19th* Explains: What to Know About Texas' Abortion Law," *The 19th,* September 1, 2021.

26 "It is a thing you can do": Emma, interviewed by Shefali Luthra, May 11, 2022.

26 In April 2023, a woman named Kaleigh: Kaleigh, interviewed by Shefali Luthra, August 22, 2022.

29 Republican lawmakers were openly: Ariana Garcia, "Texas Republicans Aim to Further Restrict Abortions—Here's How They Might Do It," *The Houston Chronicle,* July 8, 2022.

CHAPTER 2 "IT SHOULDN'T BE THIS HARD"

31 When they made the appointment: "Mandatory Waiting Periods for Women Seeking Abortions," KFF, May 1, 2022.

32 When the abortion ban's effects: Ginger Tiger, interviewed by Shefali Luthra, September 16, 2022.

32 It was a trend: Rachel Benson Gold, "Lessons from Before *Roe*: Will Past Be Prologue?," Guttmacher Institute, March 1, 2003.

33 Research would ultimately show: Kari White, Asha Dane'el, Elsa Vizcarra, et al., "Out-of-State Travel for Abortion Following Implementation of Texas Senate Bill 8," Texas Policy Evaluation Project Research Brief, March 2022.

33 In both 2020 and 2021: "Induced Termination of Pregnancy," Oklahoma State Department of Health, September 2022.

34 Tiger, a veteran: Shefali Luthra, "At Oklahoma Abortion Clinics, Each Day Could Be the Last for Patient Care as New Laws Loom," *The 19th,* April 25, 2022.

35   What did Tiger suggest: Ginger Tiger, interviewed by Shefali Luthra, September 16, 2022.

35   In Oklahoma City: Shefali Luthra, "Texas' Six-Week Abortion Ban Is Still Causing More Than Twice as Many Patients at Clinics in Nearby States," *The 19th*, February 11, 2022.

35   It felt like: Alan Braid, "Why I Violated Texas's Extreme Abortion Ban," *The Washington Post*, September 18, 2022.

38   She didn't know what: Andrea Gallegos, interviewed by Shefali Luthra, September 20, 2022.

38   When Kelly's pregnancy test: Kelly, interviewed by Shefali Luthra, September 16, 2022.

41   It wouldn't: Ginger Tiger, interviewed by Shefali Luthra, September 16, 2022.

42   Said another lawmaker: "March 10, Session 1," Oklahoma Senate, https://sg001-harmony.sliq.net/00282/Harmony/en/PowerBrowser /PowerBrowserV2/20231018/-1/53770.

43   She saw tears: Ginger Tiger, interviewed by Shefali Luthra, September 16, 2022.

43   Simply the fear: Shefali Luthra, "At Oklahoma Abortion Clinics, Each Day Could Be the Last for Patient Care as New Laws Loom," *The 19th*, April 25, 2022.

43   Monica Martinez, thirty-seven, had known: Monica Martinez, interviewed by Shefali Luthra, September 17, 2022.

45   They knew that: "Abortion Bans in 13 States Defy Public Opinion," Public Religion Research Institute, June 24, 2022.

49   "It feels like": Shefali Luthra, "Many States Are Bracing for a Post-*Roe* World. In Oklahoma, It's Practically Arrived," *The 19th*, May 12, 2022.

50   Such policies would be devastating: Lindsey Dawson, Jennifer Kates, and MaryBeth Musumeci, "Youth Access to Gender Affirming Care: The Federal and State Policy Landscape," KFF, June 1, 2022.

50   "If you can understand why": Kailey Voellinger, interviewed by Shefali Luthra, December 2, 2022.

53   Even prior to 2022: Munira Z. Gunja, Evan D. Gumas, and Reginald D. Williams II, "The U.S. Maternal Mortality Crisis Continues to Worsen: An International Comparison," Commonwealth Fund, December 1, 2022.

53   In large swaths of the country: Shefali Luthra, "Medicaid Is Rural America's Financial Midwife," KFF Health News, March 12, 2018.

53   Tiff assumed that treatment: Tiff, interviewed by Shefali Luthra, September 16, 2022.

54   In particular, physicians: "Key Findings—A Closer Look at the Link Between Specific SSRIs and Birth Defects," Centers for Disease Control and Prevention, July 16, 2020.

54   Newer research: Maureen Salamon, "Expectant Mothers Can Rest Eas-

ier About Taking Antidepressants," *Harvard Women's Health Watch,* January 1, 2023.

55   By Tuesday, August 9: Tiff, interviewed by Shefali Luthra, August 17, 2022.

56   For hours, she waited: "Biophysical profile," Cleveland Clinic.

CHAPTER 3   NOT STRONG ENOUGH

61   On a normal day: Chelsea Souder, interviewed by Shefali Luthra, June 27, 2022.

63   "We're not going to be able": Chelsea Souder, interviewed by Shefali Luthra, July 5, 2022.

64   The problem: Eve Espey, interviewed by Shefali Luthra, September 29, 2022.

65   There were no new laws: Megan Jeyifo, interviewed by Shefali Luthra, September 30, 2022.

65   In Chicago: "Mayor Lightfoot and the Chicago Department of Public Health Announce Delegate Agencies for 'Justice for All' Initiative," Office of the Mayor, August 31, 2022.

65   Never before had a state: "Executive Order 2022-123," State of New Mexico, August 31, 2022.

66   Espey, an adviser on the project: Eve Espey, interviewed by Shefali Luthra, September 29, 2022.

66   The best evidence available: Diana Greene Foster, *The Turnaway Study* (New York: Simon and Schuster, 2020).

66   Because of decades of discrimination: Chabeli Carrazana, "How Abortion Restrictions Like Texas' Push Pregnant People into Poverty," *The 19th,* September 7, 2021.

66   This wasn't a story that Angela: Angela, interviewed by Shefali Luthra, October 30, 2022.

68   In that regard: "Abortion Surveillance—United States, 2020," Centers for Disease Control and Prevention, November 25, 2022.

69   National data: "National Foster Care Month 2023: Key Facts and Statistics," Office of Administration for Children and Families, May 2023.

69   And Texas's foster care system: Sneha Dey, "Texas Lawmakers Move to Close Foster Care Hiring Loopholes," *The Texas Tribune,* March 2, 2023; Paul Flahive, "Texas 'Washing Hands' of Runaway and Missing Foster Kids," Houston Public Media, March 20, 2023.

70   major anti-abortion groups: Texas Alliance for Life, https://texasalliance forlife.org; Diocese of Austin, https://austindiocese.org.

70   It's a view out of step: "Political and Religious Activation and Polarization in the Wake of the *Roe v. Wade* Overturn," Public Religion Research Institute, July 7, 2022.

70   Across the country, the judgment: Abigail S. Cutler, Lisbet S. Lundsberg,

Marney A. White, et al., "Characterizing Community-Level Abortion Stigma in the United States," *Contraception,* March 28, 2021, https://doi: 10.1016/j.contraception.2021.03.021.

70   The threat of abortion stigma: M. Antonia Biggs, Katherine Brown, and Diana Greene Foster, "Perceived Abortion Stigma and Psychological Well-Being Over Five Years After Receiving or Being Denied an Abortion," *PLOS One,* January 29, 2020, https://doi.org/10.1371/journal.pone .0226417.

71   The only exception: Shefali Luthra, "State Abortion Bans Are Preventing Cancer Patients from Getting Chemotherapy," *The 19th,* October 7, 2022.

72   Some clinics in the state: "Post-*Roe* Abortion Bans Threaten Women's Lives," Office of Senator Elizabeth Warren, October 2022.

72   She knew that over the long term: Eve Espey, interviewed by Shefali Luthra, March 30, 2023.

72   Per federal health data from 2020: "Abortion Surveillance—United States, 2020," Centers for Disease Control and Prevention, November 25, 2022.

74   despite the state's: I Need an A, https://www.ineedana.com/.

74   "It's so awful": Eve Espey, interviewed by Shefali Luthra, September 29, 2022.

74   Back in San Antonio: Angela, interviewed by Shefali Luthra, November 15, 2022.

75   In theory, Angela and Nigel: Angela, interviewed by Shefali Luthra, September 24, 2022.

80   Unlike employees at the clinics: Caroline Kitchener, "A Post-*Roe* Surge Could Reshape This Illinois Steel Mill Town," *The Washington Post,* July 14, 2022.

80   Granite City: 2020 General Election Official Results, Madison County, Illinois, November 3, 2020.

81   And what did: Patricia A. Lohr, Jennifer E. Starling, James G. Scott, Abigail R. A. Aiken, "Simultaneous Compared with Interval Medical Abortion Regimens Where Home Use Is Restricted," *Obstetrics and Gynecology,* April 2018, https://doi.org/10.1097/AOG.0000000000 002536.

81   "It comes down to": Julie Burkhart, interviewed by Shefali Luthra, September 29, 2022.

82   Anti-abortion centers had already existed: Shefali Luthra, "A Slew of Abortion Clinics Are Opening in New Mexico. Crisis Pregnancy Centers Are, Too," *The 19th,* July 20, 2022.

82   The move was in some ways: Brad Brooks, "New Frontline of U.S. Abortion Battle Opens in New Mexico," Reuters, October 26, 2022.

82   In March 2023: "Governor Signs House Bill 7, Reproductive and Gender-

Affirming Health Act," Office of the Governor Michelle Lujan Grisham, March 16, 2023.

83 the town didn't have any abortion clinics: Brian Munoz, "An Illinois Town Is Becoming an Abortion Hub. Some Locals Are Opposed to New Clinics," NPR, August 11, 2022.

84 Opening a new abortion clinic: Andrea Gallegos, interviewed by Shefali Luthra, November 16, 2022.

86 In New Mexico, Angela had just: Angela, interviewed by Shefali Luthra, September 24, 2022.

CHAPTER 4 A HAVEN, FOR NOW

89 Melissa really hadn't been: Melissa, interviewed by Shefali Luthra, September 26, 2022.

91 Now the state was putting: Shefali Luthra, "Kansas Has Become a Beacon for Abortion Access. Next Year, That Could Disappear," *The 19th*, October 13, 2021.

91 To Melissa, though: Melissa, interviewed by Shefali Luthra, September 26, 2022.

92 Just before nine p.m.: Shefali Luthra, "Kansas Voters Reject Effort to Eliminate State Abortion Protections," *The 19th*, August 2, 2022.

94 in November 2022: Shefali Luthra, "Election 2022 Results: Abortion Initiatives on the Ballot," *The 19th*, November 12, 2022.

94 across the country, in Kentucky, Michigan: Shefali Luthra, "Kansas, a Critical Abortion Access Point, Will Soon Vote on Whether to Protect the Procedure," *The 19th*, July 27, 2022.

94 But in February 2023: "Opinion of the Court by Justice Lambert," Supreme Court of Kentucky, No. 22-CI-003225, February 16, 2023.

95 Per one study: Alison Norris and Ushma Upadhyay, "#WeCount Report," Society of Family Planning, October 28, 2022.

95 In 2022, Kansas recorded: "Abortions in Kansas 2022: Preliminary Report," Kansas Department of Health and Environment, June 2023.

95 Few expected her: Shefali Luthra, "Why Kansas' Democratic Governor Isn't Talking About Abortion on the Campaign Trail," *The 19th*, September 20, 2022.

96 It marked a small: "About," Aria Medical, https://www.ariamedical.org /about.

96 So many people were calling: Zachary Gingrich-Gaylord, interviewed by Shefali Luthra, July 25, 2022.

96 She knew there were few places: Selina Sandoval, interviewed by Shefali Luthra, September 26, 2022.

97 And without Kansas: Jody Steinauer, interviewed by Shefali Luthra, October 25, 2022.

97   When Anna, a seventeen-year-old: Anna, interviewed by Shefali Luthra, September 24, 2022.

101 And in Kansas: "Value Them Both Association," Kansas Governmental Ethics Commission, July 18, 2022.

102 research has consistently shown: "Political and Religious Activation and Polarization in the Wake of the *Roe v. Wade* Overturn," Public Religion Research Institute, July 7, 2022.

102 two local nuns: Sister Angela Fitzpatrick and Sister Michele Morek, "To Many Catholics, Social Justice Demands a No Vote on Kansas Constitution Amendment," *The Kansas City Star,* July 27, 2022.

102 polling from the Associated Press: "Midterms Reinforce Christian Voter Trends on Abortion, GOP," AP News, November 11, 2022.

103 On a widespread policy level: Melissa Deckman, interviewed by Shefali Luthra, December 15, 2022.

104 A little over six hours: Jennifer Kerns, interviewed by Shefali Luthra, December 12, 2022.

104 And in a month: Stormi, interviewed by Shefali Luthra, December 13, 2022.

104 By the end of the year: Madison Gresham, interviewed by Shefali Luthra, December 12, 2022.

104 It could make a trip: Ashley Brink, interviewed by Shefali Luthra, December 12, 2022.

105 And she would have gone: Natalie, interviewed by Shefali Luthra, December 12, 2022.

105 Telling patients that they would be able: Stormi, interviewed by Shefali Luthra, December 13, 2022.

106 In the spring of 2023: Kansas 2023–2024 Legislative Sessions, "HB 2264," May 29, 2023.

106 A few Democratic legislators: Kansas 2023–2024 Legislative Sessions, "HB 2313," April 26, 2023.

106 one that would have banned: Kansas 2023–2024 Legislative Sessions, "SB 5," May 29, 2023.

107 The only option: Jennifer Kerns, interviewed by Shefali Luthra, December 13, 2022.

107 After Angela and Nigel returned: Angela, interviewed by Shefali Luthra, November 15, 2022.

108 Angela didn't regret her abortion: Angela, interviewed by Shefali Luthra, April 5, 2023.

109 a strong cultural stigma: "Rising Share of Americans See Women Raising Children on Their Own, Cohabitation as Bad for Society," Pew Research Center, March 11, 2022.

110 The situation had finally improved: Angela, interviewed by Shefali Luthra, April 4, 2023.

110   In the days and weeks following: Angela, interviewed by Shefali Luthra, October 30, 2022.

CHAPTER 5   THE PROMISED OASIS

113   Darlene Schneider recognized: Darlene Schneider, interviewed by Shefali Luthra, October 13, 2022.

115   Ob-gyn residency programs: Jody Steinauer, Jema Turk, Tail Pomerantz, et al., "Abortion Training in U.S. Obstetrics and Gynecology Residency Programs," *American Journal of Obstetrics and Gynecology,* July 2018, https://doi:10.1016/j.ajog.2018.04.011.

116   In the post-*Dobbs* world: Jody Steinauer, interviewed by Shefali Luthra, October 25, 2022.

116   even in places like New York: Jennifer Kerns, interviewed by Shefali Luthra, May 9, 2022.

117   In some states: Kelcie Moseley-Morris, "Idaho Hospital to Stop Delivering Babies. One Reason? 'Bills That Criminalize Physicians,'" *The Idaho Statesman,* March 17, 2023.

117   Providing ob-gyn care outside dense: Shefali Luthra, "Medicaid Is Rural America's Financial Midwife," KFF Health News, March 12, 2018.

118   Her doctor told her: Jennifer Kerns, interviewed by Shefali Luthra, September 26, 2022.

118   she had started building: Jennifer Kerns, interviewed by Shefali Luthra, December 13, 2022.

119   This, more than anything else: Eleanor Drey, interviewed by Shefali Luthra, December 8, 2022.

119   After *Dobbs,* the volume: Eleanor Drey, interviewed by Shefali Luthra, December 8, 2022.

120   The staff in San Francisco: "San Francisco District Attorney Boudin Announces Multiple Charges Against Leader of Anti-Choice Group for Stalking a Doctor Who Provided Abortions," San Francisco District Attorney, May 19, 2022.

120   The episode left employees: Eleanor Drey, interviewed by Shefali Luthra, December 8, 2022.

120   the threat of physical violence: Jennifer Kerns, interviewed by Shefali Luthra, September 26, 2022.

120   Darlene's doctor had an update: Darlene Schneider, interviewed by Shefali Luthra, October 13, 2022.

122   One estimate: Shefali Luthra, "Abortion Bans Could Add Hundreds of Miles of Travel to Those Seeking the Procedure, Analysis Shows," *The 19th,* October 28, 2021.

123   In September 2022: Lara Korte, "Gavin Newsom Promotes California as Abortion Sanctuary on Red-State Billboards," *Politico,* September 15, 2022.

123   The state also passed new laws: "New Protections for People Who Need Abortion Care and Birth Control," Office of Governor Gavin Newsom, September 27, 2022.

123   In Los Angeles County: "Los Angeles County Abortion Safe Haven Grant Program," Essential Access Health.

123   And Dr. Susie Baldwin: Susie Baldwin, interviewed by Shefali Luthra, April 5, 2023.

124   The only statutory restriction: "State Facts About Abortion: California," Guttmacher Institute, June 2022.

124   The state, the largest: Alison Norris and Ushma Upadhyay, "#WeCount Report," Society of Family Planning, October 28, 2022.

124   And already some people traveled: Stacy Cross, "If *Roe* Is Overturned, California Will Become an Abortion Refuge. We Aren't Ready," *San Francisco Chronicle,* December 3, 2021.

124   That figure still constituted: Kristen Hwang, "California Doesn't Collect Basic Abortion Data—Even as It Invites an Out-of-State Influx," CalMatters, June 28, 2022.

124   estimates from Guttmacher: Rachel K. Jones, Jesse Philbin, Marielle Kirstein, et al., "Long-Term Decline in U.S. Abortions Reverses, Showing Rising Need for Abortion as Supreme Court Is Poised to Overturn *Roe v. Wade,*" Guttmacher Institute, June 15, 2022.

124   "It's not realistic": Eleanor Drey, interviewed by Shefali Luthra, December 8, 2022.

124   It wasn't the first time: Shannon Connolly, interviewed by Shefali Luthra, October 10, 2022.

125   Pratima Gupta, an ob-gyn: Pratima Gupta, interviewed by Shefali Luthra, October 26, 2022.

125   the people in immediate need: Quita Tinsley Peterson, interviewed by Shefali Luthra, October 24, 2022.

126   Abortions in California: Alison Norris and Ushma Upadhyay, "#WeCount Report," Society of Family Planning, October 28, 2022.

126   a year after *Dobbs*: Alison Norris and Ushma Upadhyay, "#WeCount Report," Society of Family Planning, October 24, 2023.

126   Many abortion providers: Shannon Connolly, interviewed by Shefali Luthra, October 10, 2022.

126   By the beginning of 2023: Abby Johnston, Shefali Luthra, and Jasmine Mithani, "What Abortion Looks Like in Every State—Right Now," *The 19th,* May 25, 2022.

126   The patients in health centers: Jennifer Kerns, interviewed by Shefali Luthra, September 26, 2022.

127   The fear of criminalization: Pratima Gupta, interviewed by Shefali Luthra, October 26, 2022.

127   In late 2023, Google announced: Chris Velazco, "Google Is Rolling Out

New Protections for Our Location Data," *The Washington Post,* December 14, 2023.

128   And the sheer quantity of consumer data: Erik Perakslis, interviewed by Shefali Luthra, October 31, 2022; Raman Khanna, interviewed by Shefali Luthra, November 15, 2022.

128   If mailed across state lines: Shefali Luthra, "Is Medication Abortion an 'Existential Threat' to Abortion Restrictions?," *The 19th,* March 22, 2022.

128   In anticipation, some California doctors: Rachel Bluth, "Doctors Trying to Prescribe Abortion Pills Across State Lines Stymied by Legislation," KFF Health News, April 6, 2022.

128   "Everyone wants to do it": Jody Steinauer, interviewed by Shefali Luthra, October 25, 2022.

129   But it fell off the list: Michele Gomez, interviewed by Shefali Luthra, October 24, 2022.

129   And in the longer term: Kavita Vinekar, Aishwarya Karlapudi, Lauren Nathan, et al., "Projected Implications of Overturning *Roe v. Wade* on Abortion Training in U.S. Obstetrics and Gynecology Residency Programs," *Obstetrics and Gynecology,* August 2022, https://doi:10.1097/AOG.0000000000004832.

129   The concern was great enough: Shefali Luthra, "Bans on Abortion and Gender-Affirming Care Are Driving Doctors from Texas," *The 19th,* June 21, 2023.

129   People who pursued residency: "Report on Residents," Association of American Medical Colleges, https://www.aamc.org/data-reports/students-residents/report/report-residents.

130   Without the opportunity: Sarah Horvath, Jema Turk, Jody Steinauer, et al., "Increase in Obstetrics and Gynecology Resident Self-Assessed Competence in Early Pregnancy Loss Management with Routine Abortion Care Training," *Obstetrics and Gynecology,* January 1, 2022, https://doi:10.1097/AOG.0000000000004628.

130   Even before the *Dobbs* ruling: "ACGME Program Requirements for Graduate Medical Education in Obstetrics and Gynecology," Accreditation Council for Graduate and Medical Education, September 17, 2022.

130   Per data Steinauer's team collected: Jody Steinauer, interviewed by Shefali Luthra, December 12, 2022.

130   But doctors who worked: "ACGME Program Requirements for Graduate Medical Education in Obstetrics and Gynecology," Accreditation Council for Graduate and Medical Education, September 17, 2022.

131   She could set up exchange programs: Jody Steinauer, interviewed by Shefali Luthra, October 25, 2022.

131   Their leaders would have to decide: Jan Hoffman, "OB-GYN Residency Programs Face Tough Choice on Abortion Training," *The New York Times,* October 27, 2022.

131   All they could do: Jody Steinauer, interviewed by Shefali Luthra, December 9, 2022.

132   Darlene's doctor couldn't find: Darlene Schneider, interviewed by Shefali Luthra, October 13, 2022.

CHAPTER 6   JUST BECAUSE IT'S LEGAL

133   The Cobalt Abortion Fund: Amanda Carlson, interviewed by Shefali Luthra, November 18, 2022.

134   People traveled to Colorado: Warren Hern, interviewed by Shefali Luthra, November 21, 2022.

134   She knew also that: "State Facts About Abortion: Colorado," Guttmacher Institute, June 2022.

134   With more callers: Jaki Lawrence, interviewed by Shefali Luthra, June 22, 2022.

135   In the last four months of 2021: Amanda Carlson, interviewed by Shefali Luthra, June 30, 2022.

135   the numbers grew exponentially: Laura Chapin, interviewed by Shefali Luthra, January 23, 2023.

135   Some callers didn't: Amanda Carlson, interviewed by Shefali Luthra, November 18, 2022.

135   They helped make sure: Christie Burkhart, interviewed by Shefali Luthra, December 19, 2022.

136   Abortion funds there: Kamyan Connor, interviewed by Shefali Luthra, December 8, 2022.

136   "We don't know how vigorously": Janice Massey, interviewed by Shefali Luthra, January 18, 2022.

137   "Everybody's situation": Amanda Carlson, interviewed by Shefali Luthra, November 18, 2022.

137   It was the first state: "House Bill 22-1279," Colorado Legislature, April 4, 2022.

137   More recently, in 2020: Shefali Luthra, "Initiatives to Restrict Abortion Access Fail in Colorado, but Pass in Louisiana," *The 19th,* November 4, 2020.

137   It wasn't an easy victory: Daneya Esgar, interviewed by Shefali Luthra, December 22, 2022.

138   In the spring of 2022: "After *Roe* Fell: Abortion Laws by State: Colorado," Center for Reproductive Rights.

138   Much like with other destination states: Leigh Paterson, "Out-of-State Abortions in Colorado More Than Doubled in 2022," KUNC, March 22, 2023.

138   Wait times for an appointment: Kristina Tocce, interviewed by Shefali Luthra, February 6, 2023.

138   Another physician: Rebecca Cohen, interviewed by Shefali Luthra, November 22, 2022.

139   "We have a waiting list": Warren Hern, interviewed by Shefali Luthra, November 21, 2022.

139   Hern recalled too: Willard Cates Jr., "Legal Abortion: Are American Black Women Healthier Because of It?," *Phylon*, 1977, https://doi.org/10 .2307/274589.

139   Just like before: Warren Hern, interviewed by Shefali Luthra, November 21, 2022.

139   One physician: Dr. S, interviewed by Shefali Luthra, December 19, 2022.

140   To fulfill the overwhelming: Christie Burkhart, interviewed by Shefali Luthra, December 19, 2022.

140   Some health centers: Claire Cleveland, "Kaiser Permanente to Offer Abortion Services in Response to Long Planned Parenthood Wait Times," CPR News, November 28, 2022.

140   That was what compelled: Leilah Zahedi-Spung, interviewed by Shefali Luthra, January 8, 2023.

140   And she knew that: "Maternal Deaths and Mortality Rates by State for 2018–2020," Centers for Disease Control and Prevention; "Maternal Mortality in Tennessee 2017–2020," Tennessee Department of Health, April 13, 2022.

140   It was a challenge: Shefali Luthra, "State Abortion Bans Are Preventing Cancer Patients from Getting Chemotherapy," *The 19th*, October 7, 2022.

141   Packing her bags in Chattanooga: Leilah Zahedi-Spung, interviewed by Shefali Luthra, October 5, 2022.

141   if they had any say about it: Andrea Chalfin, "Pueblo City Council Tables Anti-Abortion Ordinance Following Controversy Around Potential New Abortion Clinic," KRCC, December 13, 2022.

142   In Colorado Springs: "Robert Dear Indicted by Federal Grand Jury for 2015 Planned Parenthood Shooting," U.S. Department of Justice, December 9, 2019.

142   Another physician: Dr. S, interviewed by Shefali Luthra, December 19, 2022.

142   Ashley Acre hadn't been trying: Ashley Acre, interviewed by Shefali Luthra, December 6, 2022.

144   the fetus had tested positive: "Noonan Syndrome," National Health Service; "Noonan Syndrome," Mayo Clinic.

146   Forty years ago: P. Donovan, "The People Vote on Abortion Funding: Colorado and Washington," Family Planning Perspectives, July 1985, https://pubmed.ncbi.nlm.nih.gov/3842805/; "Colorado Amendment No 3, Public Funds for Abortion Initiative (1984)," Ballotpedia.

146   The policy precluded Colorado: Elizabeth Nash, interviewed by Shefali Luthra, December 16, 2022.

147 In 2023, only seventeen states: Alina Salganicoff, Laurie Sobel, and Amrutha Ramaswamy, "The Hyde Amendment and Coverage for Abortion Services," KFF, March 5, 2021.

147 Government data have long shown: "Abortion Surveillance—United States, 2020," Centers for Disease Control and Prevention, November 25, 2022.

148 The disparity: Liza Fuentes, "Inequity in US Abortion Rights and Access: The End of *Roe* Is Deepening Existing Divides," Guttmacher Institute, January 17, 2023.

148 About one in five: "QuickFacts Colorado," U.S. Census Bureau, July 2022.

148 But 39 percent: "Distribution of the Nonelderly on Medicaid by Race/Ethnicity," KFF.

149 Direct votes aren't an option: "States Without Initiative or Referendum," Ballotpedia.

150 Most of the efforts: Kelly Hall, interviewed by Shefali Luthra, November 28, 2022.

150 In Kansas, the campaign: Shefali Luthra, "Kansas, a Critical Abortion Access Point, Will Soon Vote on Whether to Protect the Procedure," *The 19th,* July 27, 2022.

150 It was a similar story in Kentucky: "Issue Committee for Protect Kentucky Access," Kentucky Registry of Election Finance, October 26, 2022.

150 And it was true: Yue Stella Yu, "Proposal 3 Abortion Measure Generates $57M in Michigan Campaign Donations," *Bridge Michigan,* October 28, 2022.

150 Ohio-based abortion rights organizers: Grace Panetta, "Money Pours into Ohio in Final Push on Issue 1 Abortion Ballot Measure," *The 19th,* November 2, 2023.

150 "Arguing the details": Molly Murphy, interviewed by Shefali Luthra, January 6, 2023.

150 In the months after *Roe* fell: Shefali Luthra, "The End of *Roe* Could Be Changing People's Minds About Abortion Bans," *The 19th,* September 19, 2022.

151 Convincing this many people: Aurea Bolaños Perea, interviewed by Shefali Luthra, December 15, 2022.

151 Estimates on what this kind of work: Karen Middleton, interviewed by Shefali Luthra, April 5, 2023.

152 "We did everything": Meg Froelich, interviewed by Shefali Luthra, April 3, 2023.

153 Among other Latino Coloradans: Aurea Bolaños Perea, interviewed by Shefali Luthra, December 15, 2022.

153 The flight from Dallas to San Francisco: Darlene Schneider, interviewed by Shefali Luthra, October 13, 2022, and October 11, 2023.

CHAPTER 7   EVEN THE BEST-LAID PLANS

158   Someday, she told herself: Keren Form, interviewed by Shefali Luthra, February 16, 2023.

158   The state was an early adopter: "Abortion in New York State: Know Your Rights," New York State.

158   It was transformative: J. Parter, D. O'Hare, F. Nelson, and M. Svigir, "Two Years' Experience in New York City with the Liberalized Abortion Law—Progress and Problems," *American Journal of Public Health,* 1973, https://doi.org/10.2105/AJPH.63.6.524.

158   now home to: "State Facts About Abortion: New York," Guttmacher Institute, 2022.

158   In 2019: "Bill No. A00021," New York Assembly, 2019.

158   And in 2022: "Governor Hochul Announces $13.4 Million Awarded in the Second Round of Abortion Provider Support Fund," New York State, October 12, 2022.

159   and signing legislation: "Governor Hochul Signs Nation-Leading Legislative Package to Protect Abortion and Reproductive Rights for All," New York State, June 13, 2022.

159   A year later: Merle Hoffman, interviewed by Shefali Luthra, February 17, 2023.

159   NYAAF was pledging more money: Claire Lampen, "No Matter Where You Live, New Yorkers Can Help You Get an Abortion (And We'll Pay for It, Too)," *The Cut,* December 5, 2022.

159   The spike in callers: Alia Tejeda, interviewed by Shefali Luthra, March 13, 2023.

160   A year after the *Dobbs* decision: Chelsea Williams-Diggs, press conference, interviewed by Shefali Luthra, June 16, 2023.

160   After *Dobbs,* by contrast: Karen Duda, interviewed by Shefali Luthra, February 28, 2023.

160   "Any of those things": Georgana Hanson, interviewed by Shefali Luthra, March 14, 2023.

161   It was a shift: Elizabeth Estrada, interviewed by Shefali Luthra, February 16, 2023.

161   She didn't know how: Keren Form, interviewed by Shefali Luthra, February 28, 2023.

162   Carla, a twenty-six-year-old woman: Carla, interviewed by Shefali Luthra, February 24, 2023.

164   the Clergy Consultation Service on Abortion: "Even Before *Roe*: RCRC's Legacy of Bold Clergy Activism," Religious Coalition for Reproductive Choice.

164   One woman, a church employee: Howard Moody, *A Voice in the Village* (Bloomington, IN: Xlibris, 2009).

165   People didn't need to come: Donna Schaper, interviewed by Shefali
       Luthra, June 16, 2023.

165   Organizations like hers: Heather Beasley Doyle, "Dallas Congrega-
       tion Supports People Seeking Abortions," *UU World Magazine,* May 10,
       2023.

165   "There's no sense of safety": Abigail Hastings, interviewed by Shefali
       Luthra, June 26, 2023.

167   And cesarean sections: Elizabeth G. Raymond and David A. Grimes,
       "The Comparative Safety of Legal Induced Abortion and Childbirth in
       the United States," *Obstetrics and Gynecology,* February 2012, http://doi:10
       .1097/AOG.0b013e31823fe923.

167   Meanwhile, a baby born: Chaunie Brusie, "Will Babies Born at 36 Weeks
       Be Healthy?," Healthline, January 10, 2018.

168   Because the surges: Michelle Casey, interviewed by Shefali Luthra, Feb-
       ruary 2, 2023.

169   The increase in New York: Alison Norris and Ushma Upadhyay,
       "#WeCount Report," Society of Family Planning, April 11, 2023.

170   In her mind: Linda Prine, interviewed by Shefali Luthra, February 21,
       2023.

170   She pointed to the law: "Senate Bill S1066A," New York Senate, 2023.

171   Aid Access, the European service: Linda Prine, interviewed by Shefali
       Luthra, July 21, 2023.

171   not all health care providers: Donna Lieberman, interviewed by Shefali
       Luthra, February 27, 2023.

172   "It's a tricky and unfair thing": Jen Kerns, interviewed by Shefali Luthra,
       July 20, 2023.

172   In 1981: "Abortion Unit on S.I. Closes After Threats," *The New York
       Times,* October 6, 1981.

172   More recently: "Recent Cases on Violence Against Reproductive Health
       Care Providers," U.S. Department of Justice, October 18, 2022.

172   A month later: Liam Quigley and Rocco Parascandola, "Brooklyn Pro-
       Life Protesters Slip Inside Planned Parenthood Office with Shout of
       'You're Killing Babies!,'" *New York Daily News,* August 19, 2022.

172   In Queens, the escorts recognized: Keren Form and Karen Trudeau,
       interviewed by Shefali Luthra, February 28, 2023.

172   In 1998: Michael A. Fletcher, "Sniper Kills Abortion Doctor Near Buf-
       falo," *The Washington Post,* October 25, 1998.

173   As with any other covered service: Tracy Weitz, interviewed by Shefali
       Luthra, March 29, 2023.

173   it's incredibly difficult: Yves-Yvette Young, Terri-Ann Thompson,
       David S. Cohen, and Kelly Blanchard, "Contextualizing Medicaid Reim-
       bursement Rates for Abortion Procedures," *Contraception,* September
       2020, https://doi.org/10.1016/j.contraception.2020.03.004.

173 some health finance researchers say: Tracy Weitz, interviewed by Shefali Luthra, March 29, 2023.

174 the state's Medicaid reimbursement rate: Cadence Acquaviva, interviewed by Shefali Luthra, April 7, 2023.

174 This kind of money was helpful: Katharine Bodde, interviewed by Shefali Luthra, February 27, 2023.

174 What little research: Terri-Ann Thompson, interviewed by Shefali Luthra, April 3, 2023.

174 Eleven abortion clinics: I Need an A, https://www.ineedana.com.

175 "People have been traveling": Katharine Bodde, interviewed by Shefali Luthra, February 27, 2023.

175 The abortion care network: Karen Duda, interviewed by Shefali Luthra, February 28, 2023.

176 Approved by the federal: Laurie Sobel, Alina Salganicoff, and Mabel Felix, "Legal Challenges to the FDA Approval of Medication Abortion Pills," KFF, March 13, 2023.

176 In the Amarillo federal court: Shefali Luthra, "A Federal Judge Could Soon Block Access to Mifepristone. Here's What That Means," *The 19th,* February 7, 2023.

176 filed a lawsuit: Oriana González, "Anti-Abortion Group Sues FDA to Challenge Approval of Abortion Pills," *Axios,* November 18, 2022.

177 Arguments in the case: Sarah McCammon, "Read the Transcript Here: What Happened Inside the Federal Hearing on Abortion Pills," NPR, March 17, 2023.

177 The implications of a ruling: David S. Cohen, Greer Donley, and Rachel Rebouché, "Abortion Pills," University of Pittsburgh Legal Studies Research Paper No. 2023-12, February 1, 2023, *Stanford Law Review* (forthcoming 2024), https://dx.doi.org/10.2139/ssrn.4335735.

177 In Washington State: "Governor Jay Inslee Media Availability," TVW, April 4, 2023.

177 his government led: *State of Washington v. United States Food and Drug Administration,* CourtListener, February 23, 2023.

178 Some abortion rights advocates: Kirsten Moore, interviewed by Shefali Luthra, February 3, 2022.

178 But the evidence: Shefali Luthra, "A Federal Judge Could Soon Block Access to Mifepristone. Here's What That Means," *The 19th,* February 7, 2023.

179 "It actually seems really ridiculous": Michelle Casey, interviewed by Shefali Luthra, February 2, 2023.

184 "And honestly": Michelle Casey, interviewed by Shefali Luthra, April 24, 2023.

184 The day of her cesarean: Darlene Schneider, interviewed by Shefali Luthra, October 13, 2022, and October 11, 2023.

CHAPTER 8   THE CENTER THAT COULDN'T HOLD

187   Jasper never even considered: Jasper, interviewed by Shefali Luthra, January 8, 2023.

190   In the months before *Roe* fell: Shefali Luthra, "*The 19th* Explains: 15-Week Abortion Bans May Become Law in Three States. What Does That Mean?," *The 19th*, February 22, 2022.

190   The policy was one that: "New UNF Poll Shows Opposition to Florida Abortion Bill," UNF Public Opinion Research Lab, February 22, 2022.

190   Just a year earlier: Elizabeth Nash and Jonathan Bearak, "Florida's Proposed 20-Week Abortion Ban Would Force Pregnant People to Travel More Than 30 Times as Far for Care," Guttmacher Institute, March 2021.

191   The state's data: "Reported Induced Terminations of Pregnancy by Reason, by Trimester—2021," Florida Agency for Health Care Administration, May 9, 2022.

191   It was an argument: Shefali Luthra, "Supreme Court Indicates It Could Eliminate a Core Element of *Roe v. Wade*," *The 19th*, December 1, 2021.

191   Others, who were just: Herman Miller, interviewed by Shefali Luthra, May 25, 2022.

192   In the spring of 2022: "Florida's 24-Hour Abortion Waiting Period Law Can Go into Effect, Says Judge," WFSU, April 12, 2022.

192   The change came just as: Terry Salas Merritt, interviewed by Shefali Luthra, May 25, 2022.

192   The number of abortions done in Florida: Alison Norris and Ushma Upadhyay, "#WeCount Report," Society of Family Planning, October 28, 2022.

192   In 2022 alone: "Reported Induced Terminations of Pregnancy," Florida Agency for Health Care Administration, February 3, 2023.

193   the largest jump of any state: Alison Norris and Ushma Upadhyay, "#WeCount Report," Society of Family Planning, June 15, 2023.

193   And one full year out: Alison Norris and Ushma Upadhyay, "#WeCount Report," Society of Family Planning, October 23, 2023.

193   Whenever Florida passed: Alyx Carrasquel, interviewed by Shefali Luthra, February 21, 2023.

194   The majority of people: Jessica Wannemacher, interviewed by Shefali Luthra, February 22, 2023.

194   Staff regularly worked past: Clinic staff, interviewed by Shefali Luthra, February 22, 2023.

194   Data from the state: "Reported Induced Terminations of Pregnancy by Reason, by Trimester," Florida Agency for Health Care Administration, 2021, 2022, and 2023 reports.

195   "What if I was raped?": Shayla, interviewed by Shefali Luthra, February 22, 2023.

196   That meant making: Clinic staff, interviewed by Shefali Luthra, February 22, 2023.

196   The share of people making that journey: Stephanie Lorraine, interviewed by Shefali Luthra, August 22, 2023.

196   In addition to patients often not knowing: Kedisha Madison, interviewed by Shefali Luthra, February 22, 2023.

196   Amber, a twenty-eight-year-old woman: Amber, interviewed by Shefali Luthra, January 23, 2023.

198   When Florida abortion providers: Matt Dixon, "Florida Supreme Court Agrees to Hear Challenge to 15-Week Abortion Law," *Politico*, January 23, 2023.

199   It made sense in a way: Lori Berman, interviewed by Shefali Luthra, January 26, 2023.

199   After the election: Michael Moline, "Abortion Foes Press DeSantis for Quick Action on Additional Abortion Restrictions," *Florida Phoenix*, November 10, 2022.

199   Chief among them: "Florida Family Policy Council Inc.," Nonprofit Explorer, ProPublica, 2023.

199   The group had a long history: "Governor Ron DeSantis Addresses Eighth Annual Legislative Prayer Breakfast," Florida Family Policy Council, March 19, 2021; "Accomplishments," *2022 Year in Review*, Florida Family Policy Council.

199   In the months after: Mary Ellen Klas, "Florida Lawmakers Say Further Abortion Restrictions Likely," *Tampa Bay Times*, November 11, 2022; Mel Leonor Barclay and Shefali Luthra, "What Ron DeSantis' Budding Presidential Campaign Could Mean for Florida Abortion Laws," *The 19th*, March 3, 2023.

199   In the weeks after: Shefali Luthra, "Florida Could Be a Critical Access Point for Abortion, but the State's Own Battle Is Just Starting," *The 19th*, June 8, 2022.

199   the choice of name: Shefali Luthra and Barbara Rodriguez, "Trump Pardons Susan B. Anthony, a Pioneering Suffragist with a Complicated Legacy," *The 19th*, August 18, 2020.

200   Given the state's large population: Mel Leonor Barclay and Shefali Luthra, "What Ron DeSantis' Budding Presidential Campaign Could Mean for Florida Abortion Laws," *The 19th*, March 3, 2023; Shefali Luthra, "Here's How States Plan to Limit Abortion—Even Where It Is Already Banned," *The 19th*, December 5, 2022.

200   The governor, at that point: Zac Anderson, "DeSantis Dodges 'Heartbeat' Abortion Bill Question, Says He's 'Ready' for Gun Bill," *Sarasota Herald-Tribune*, December 15, 2022.

201 All these doctors: Shefali Luthra, "Texas Denied Abortions to These Women When Their Lives Were in Danger. Now, They're Suing the State," *The 19th,* March 7, 2023.

201 Sexual violence researchers: Shefali Luthra, "Abortion Bans Like Lindsey Graham's Say They Have Rape and Incest Exceptions—in Practice, They Don't Work," *The 19th,* September 14, 2022.

201 Miller, the Jacksonville doctor: Herman Miller, interviewed by Shefali Luthra, May 25, 2022.

201 And in some states: Megan Messerly, "In States That Allow Abortion for Rape and Incest, Finding a Doctor May Prove Impossible," *Politico,* June 27, 2022.

202 And it addressed only: "House Bill 3058, Session 88(R)," Texas Legislature Online, June 16, 2023.

202 In the early days of 2023: Eleanor Klibanoff, "In Texas' First Post-*Roe* Legislative Session, There's a New Political Power Dynamic on Abortion," *The Texas Tribune,* January 23, 2023.

202 State legislators in Oklahoma: Shefali Luthra, "Abortion Bans Don't Prosecute Pregnant People. That May Be About to Change," *The 19th,* January 13, 2023; "Georgia House Bill 496," Georgia General Assembly, February 23, 2023; "Kentucky House Bill 300," Kentucky General Assembly, February 14, 2023; "South Carolina House Bill 3549," South Carolina General Assembly, 125th Session, May 9, 2023.

202 It wasn't the first time: Zoe Richards, "9 Republicans Pull Support from South Carolina Bill Allowing the Death Penalty for Abortion," NBC News, March 18, 2023.

203 Meanwhile, some abortion opponents: Shefali Luthra, "Abortion Opponents Are Trying to Deter People from Traveling Out of State for Care," *The 19th,* October 12, 2023.

204 And they would do all: Kristan Hawkins, interviewed by Shefali Luthra, February 17, 2023.

204 The governor, at the time a darling: Andrew Atterbury, "DeSantis Targets Trans Health Care in Florida Universities," *Politico,* January 18, 2023.

204 and his efforts: Laurel Wamsley, "What's in the So-Called Don't Say Gay Bill That Could Impact the Whole Country," NPR, October 21, 2022.

204 "It's a real missed leadership opportunity": Kristan Hawkins, interviewed by Shefali Luthra, February 17, 2023.

206 But for now all he could do: Jasper, interviewed by Shefali Luthra, January 26, 2023.

206 There, the group planned: Kristan Hawkins, interviewed by Shefali Luthra, February 17, 2023.

206 It wasn't a total ban, but: Shefali Luthra, "A Proposed Six-Week Abortion Ban in Florida Could Threaten Access for the Entire South," *The 19th,* March 7, 2023.

206 Still, even those applied only: "House Bill 7," Florida House of Representatives, 2023.

206 It was enough to win over: Rachel Roubein, "How Public Health Officials Got Figuratively Handcuffed," *The Washington Post,* March 8, 2023.

206 Polling from the Public Religion Research Institute: "Abortion Attitudes in a Post-*Roe* World: Findings from the 50-State 2022 American Values Atlas," Public Religion Research Institute, February 23, 2023.

207 The distaste was bipartisan: "UNF Poll: DeSantis Ahead in Florida for Republican Presidential Primary," University of North Florida Public Opinion Research Lab, March 9, 2023.

207 Even with all those advantages: Alyx Carrasquel, interviewed by Shefali Luthra, February 21, 2023.

208 Post-*Dobbs,* anti-abortion advocates: Shefali Luthra, "Three GOP-led States Are Set to Vote on New Abortion Bans Today," *The 19th,* May 16, 2023.

209 Just as is true nationally: "Abortion Surveillance—United States, 2020," Centers for Disease Control and Prevention, November 25, 2022.

209 The cost of travel posed a greater burden: Chabeli Carrazana and Jasmine Mithani, "Happy Equal Pay Day? Here Are 6 Charts Showing Why It's Not Much of a Celebration," *The 19th,* March 14, 2023.

209 Then there were those who couldn't travel: Jeffrey Passel, "Estimated Unauthorized Immigration Population for the U.S. and Selected States, 2021," unpublished from Pew Research Center, interviewed by Shefali Luthra, August 3, 2023.

209 While pushing for abortion restrictions: Miriam Jordan, "DeSantis Pushes Toughest Immigration Crackdown in the Nation," *The New York Times,* April 10, 2023.

209 "They could be easily pulled over": Aurelie Colon Larrauri, interviewed by Shefali Luthra, February 17, 2023.

210 Even Wannemacher: Jessica Wannemacher, interviewed by Shefali Luthra, February 22, 2023.

CHAPTER 9   NEITHER LIVING NOR DEAD

211 After *Roe* was overturned, Dr. Jill Gibson: Jill Gibson, interviewed by Shefali Luthra, February 16, 2023.

212 Violators faced imprisonment: "Arizona Revised Statutes, 13-3603," Arizona Legislature, 2023.

212 and with *Roe* intact: Jodi Liggett, interviewed by Shefali Luthra, April 12, 2023.

213 Practically, that part of the law: "Key Part of Arizona Genetic Abnormality Law Blocked," Associated Press, September 28, 2021.

213 It was a deliberate choice: "55th Legislature, Second Regular Session, SB

1464," State of Arizona, 2022; "55th Legislature, Second Regular Session, SB 1339," State of Arizona, 2022.

213   But instead, lawmakers had settled: Elizabeth Nash, interviewed by Shefali Luthra, March 14, 2023.

213   But some legislators: Andrew Oxford, "Arizona After *Roe*," Arizona Public Media, May 10, 2022.

214   To end their pregnancies: Jill Gibson, interviewed by Shefali Luthra, February 16, 2023.

214   But, months later: Gabrielle Goodrick, interviewed by Shefali Luthra, January 6, 2023.

214   Statehouse lobbyists: Caroline Mello Roberson, interviewed by Shefali Luthra, April 5, 2023.

215   Even in states: Elizabeth Nash, interviewed by Shefali Luthra, March 14, 2023.

215   Physicians caring for high-risk patients: Laura Mercer, interviewed by Shefali Luthra, March 13, 2023.

215   Days after *Dobbs*: Andrew Oxford, "Arizona AG Will Ask Court to Lift Injunction on State Abortion Ban," Arizona Public Media, June 29, 2022.

216   Once again, they were waiting: Elizabeth Nash, interviewed by Shefali Luthra, January 5, 2023.

216   And she had to convey: Gabrielle Goodrick, interviewed by Shefali Luthra, October 13, 2022.

216   If patients wanted to terminate: Jill Gibson, interviewed by Shefali Luthra, February 16, 2023.

216   Everyone seemed confused: Sarah Tarver-Wahlquist, interviewed by Shefali Luthra, March 13, 2023.

217   The threat of violating: Elizabeth Nash, interviewed by Shefali Luthra, January 5, 2022.

217   Until then, its 1857 abortion ban: Eleanor Klibanoff, "Not 1925: Texas' Law Banning Abortion Dates to Before the Civil War," *The Texas Tribune*, August 17, 2022.

217   empowered the attorney general: Shefali Luthra, "Pre-*Roe* Abortion Bans Are Cutting Off Access—Even Laws That Aren't Supposed to Be in Effect," *The 19th*, July 6, 2022.

217   Andrea Gallegos: Chabeli Carrazana and Shefali Luthra, "'How Soon Do You Need Me to Be There?': For a Short Window, These Three States That Banned Abortions Can Resume Services," *The 19th*, June 30, 2022.

218   They had no choice: Hillary McLaren, interviewed by Shefali Luthra, June 28, 2022.

218   But it wasn't enough: Corrinne Hess, "Wisconsin DOJ Replaces Republicans with Local District Attorneys in Abortion Lawsuit," *Milwaukee Journal-Sentinel*, September 16, 2022.

218 The ban stayed active: Grace Panetta, "Janet Protasiewicz and Daniel Kelly Will Face Off for Crucial Wisconsin Supreme Court Seat," *The 19th,* February 21, 2023.

219 Across the lake: Elizabeth Nash, interviewed by Shefali Luthra, January 5, 2022.

219 The confusion often felt: Shefali Luthra, "Americans Don't Know If Abortion Is Legal in Their State, New Poll Shows," *The 19th,* February 1, 2023.

220 Just as had been the case: Jill Gibson, interviewed by Shefali Luthra, February 16, 2023.

221 It's difficult to track: Jeffrey Passel, "Estimated Unauthorized Immigration Population for the U.S. and Selected States, 2021," unpublished from Pew Research Center, interviewed by Shefali Luthra, August 3, 2023.

221 They didn't have any other options: Eloisa Lopez, interviewed by Shefali Luthra, February 16, 2023.

222 Others simply never: Jill Gibson, interviewed by Shefali Luthra, October 13, 2022.

222 Lopez constantly found herself: Eloisa Lopez, interviewed by Shefali Luthra, February 16, 2023.

222 At any point, different judges: Mary Ziegler, interviewed by Shefali Luthra, March 14, 2023.

222 In early fall 2023: Shefali Luthra, "An Arizona Supreme Court Justice Openly Opposes Abortion. He'll Hear a Case Deciding Legality Anyway," *The 19th,* October 19, 2023.

224 The clinic, following Florida law: "State Facts About Abortion: Florida," Guttmacher Institute, June 2022.

224 Maybe after Saturday: Jasper, interviewed by Shefali Luthra, January 8 and 26, 2023.

225 The changes underway had helped: Elizabeth Nash, interviewed by Shefali Luthra, March 14, 2023.

225 Abortion funds: Sarah Tarver-Wahlquist, interviewed by Shefali Luthra, March 13, 2023.

225 "But you have to": Jill Gibson, interviewed by Shefali Luthra, February 16, 2023.

225 Mercer described it: Laura Mercer, interviewed by Shefali Luthra, March 13, 2023.

225 Historically, many doctors: Julie Rovner, "American Medical Association Wades into Abortion Debate with Lawsuit," NPR, July 2, 2019.

226 "And when it comes to health care": Laura Mercer, interviewed by Shefali Luthra, March 13, 2023.

226 she frequently felt unwelcome: Eloisa Lopez, interviewed by Shefali Luthra, April 6, 2023.

226   Polling didn't necessarily suggest: "Views About Abortion by State," Pew Research Center, 2014.

226   Progressive organizers: Araceli Villezcas, interviewed by Shefali Luthra, March 30, 2023.

226   The energy shifted: Jenny Guzman, interviewed by Shefali Luthra, April 4, 2023.

226   Polling in the months: Katherine Davis-Young, "Poll: Most Arizonans Want Abortion to Remain Legal," KJZZ, May 26, 2022.

226   The week after a draft: Amy Fitch-Heacock, interviewed by Shefali Luthra, March 13, 2023.

227   Other abortion rights organizations: Brittany Fonteno, interviewed by Shefali Luthra, April 6, 2023; Eloisa Lopez, interviewed by Shefali Luthra, April 6, 2023; Caroline Mello Roberson, interviewed by Shefali Luthra, April 5, 2023.

227   To make the November 2022 ballot: Anna V. Smith, "In a Post-*Roe* West, Abortion Is on the Ballot," *High Country News,* September 30, 2022.

227   That energy was a sign: Amy Fitch-Heacock, interviewed by Shefali Luthra, March 13, 2023.

227   Perhaps, said Lopez: Eloisa Lopez, interviewed by Shefali Luthra, April 6, 2013.

228   The state's abortion rights coalition was divided: Jodi Liggett, interviewed by Shefali Luthra, April 12, 2023.

228   as late as the spring of 2023: Brittany Fonteno, interviewed by Shefali Luthra, April 6, 2023.

228   "We can't get on the same page": Eloisa Lopez, interviewed by Shefali Luthra, February 16, 2023.

229   But the new governor: Jack Healy and Jazmine Ulloa, "In Tight Arizona Governor's Race, a Democrat Looks to Abortion to Win," *The New York Times,* September 29, 2022.

229   And the legislature: "Abortion Attitudes in a Post-*Roe* World: Findings from the 50-State 2022 American Values Atlas," Public Religion Research Institute, February 2, 2023.

229   And there was another concern: Mel Leonor Barclay and Shefali Luthra, "A 'Born Alive' Measure Is One of the House GOP's Priorities. Here's What It Would Actually Do," *The 19th,* January 6, 2023.

230   the same logical endpoint: Mary Ziegler, interviewed by Shefali Luthra, March 14, 2023.

230   Meanwhile, the governor: "Executive Order 2023-11: Protecting Reproductive Freedom and Healthcare in Arizona," Arizona Memory Project, June 23, 2023.

230   there was only the pending lawsuit: CV-23-0005-PR: *Planned Parenthood et al. v. Kristin Mayes/Hazelrigg,* Arizona Supreme Court, January 12, 2023.

231   But the wording was vague: "55th Legislature, Second Regular Session, SB 1164," State of Arizona, 2022.

231   She never got another phone call: Jill Gibson, interviewed by Shefali Luthra, February 16, 2023.

232   "These are common": Shelly Tien, interviewed by Shefali Luthra, February 23, 2023.

232   The questions began: Laura Mercer, interviewed by Shefali Luthra, March 13, 2023.

232   Though Arizona's total ban: Alison Norris and Ushma Upadhyay, "#WeCount Survey," Society of Family Planning, April 11, 2023.

232   She'd do her best: DeShawn Taylor, interviewed by Shefali Luthra, November 28, 2022.

232   And losing even one clinic: "Abortions in Arizona, 2021 Abortion Report," Arizona Department of Health Services, December 31, 2022.

233   They'd never had to: Eloisa Lopez, interviewed by Shefali Luthra, February 16, 2023; Amy Fitch-Heacock, interviewed by Shefali Luthra, March 13, 2023.

233   This was how Jen: Jen, interviewed by Shefali Luthra, February 14, 2023.

237   Back in Florida, fourteen weeks: Jasper, interviewed by Shefali Luthra, January 8 and 26, 2023.

CHAPTER 10   HOW FAR WILL THIS GO?

240   Per data collected: Mohadam Moslimani, Christine Tamir, Abby Budiman, et al., "Facts About the U.S. Black Population," Pew Research Center, March 2, 2023.

241   The bill died: Kevin Merida, "Senator Drops Support for Abortion Rights Bill," *The Washington Post,* July 10, 1993.

242   Bush actually signed a law: Julie Rovner, "'Partial-Birth Abortion': Separating Facts from Spin," NPR, February 21, 2006.

242   dropping any pursuit: Molly Moorhead, "Obamameter: Sign the Freedom of Choice Act," PolitiFact, June 1, 2009.

242   efforts to make private insurance plans: Jonathan Cohn, *The Ten-Year War* (New York: St. Martin's Press, 2021).

242   "Covering contraceptives": Rachel Rebouché, interviewed by Shefali Luthra, April 12, 2023.

243   In 1973, the first-year senator: Heidi Przybyla, "Joe Biden's Long Evolution on Abortion Rights Still Holds Surprises," NBC News, June 5, 2019.

243   When asked that day: "Press Briefing by Press Secretary Jen Psaki, May 17, 2021," The White House, May 17, 2021.

244   it was striking how little *Dobbs*: Tara Palmeri, Rachael Bade, Ryan Lizza, and Eugene Daniels, "Politico Playbook: The Curious Case of Stephen Miller and Andrew Yang," *Politico,* May 18, 2021.

244   When the Senate: Amanda Becker and Shefali Luthra, "Collins, Murkowski Introduce Alternative Senate Bill to Codify Abortion Rights," *The 19th,* February 28, 2022.

244 it took him roughly one hour: "State of the Union Address," The White House, March 1, 2022.

245 It was, she'd say later: Tina Smith, interviewed by Shefali Luthra, April 17, 2023.

245 period trackers: Hannah Norman and Victoria Knight, "Should You Worry About Data from Your Period-Tracking App Being Used Against You?," KFF Health News/PolitiFact, May 13, 2022.

246 "These proposals are only starting points": "Murray, Warren Lead Over 20 Senators Urging President Biden to Issue Executive Order to Defend Americans' Right to an Abortion," U.S. Senate Committee on Health, Education, Labor and Pensions, June 8, 2022.

246 Some scholars suggested: Shefali Luthra and Amanda Becker, "Medication Abortion and Clinics on Federal Land: Here Are Democrats' Ideas to Protect Abortion Access," The 19th, June 15, 2022.

246 Thousands gathered to protest: Lydia Chebbine, "'This Day Really Is About Her Future': Why So Many Parents and Their Children Are Rallying for Abortion Rights," The 19th, July 1, 2022.

246 The White House directed: Shefali Luthra, "The Biden Administration Just Hinted at How It Could Protect Access to Medication Abortion," The 19th, June 24, 2022.

246 and in his own remarks: "Remarks by President Joe Biden on the Supreme Court Decision to Overturn Roe v. Wade," The White House, June 24, 2022.

246 After his abortion, Jasper kept waiting: Jasper, interviewed by Shefali Luthra, April 6, 2023.

250 Partway through the year: Jade Hurley, interviewed by Shefali Luthra, November 6, 2023.

251 It was a location born of necessity: Matt Reeves, interviewed by Shefali Luthra, March 24, 2023.

251 close to 75 percent: Karishma Oza, interviewed by Shefali Luthra, March 23, 2023.

251 Her pregnancy had a rare condition: "Twin-to-Twin Transfusion Syndrome," Johns Hopkins Medicine, April 2023.

253 Everything Tiffani knew about the capital: Tiffani, interviewed by Shefali Luthra, March 27, 2023.

253 "I feel like we're working": Matt Reeves, interviewed by Shefali Luthra, March 24, 2023.

253 she registered internally: Karishma Oza, interviewed by Shefali Luthra, March 24, 2023.

253 Months after the decision: Anne Banfield, interviewed by Shefali Luthra, March 30, 2023.

258 "If D.C. were to be made a state": Vee, interviewed by Shefali Luthra, March 27, 2023.

259 Medicaid in the capital: "The D.C. Medicaid Abortion Ban: Disastrous Policy for Low-Income D.C. Residents," National Partnership for Women and Families, June 2019.

259 the next time Republicans: Meagan Flynn, "Officials Worry About Legal Abortion in D.C. if GOP Takes Control of Congress," *The Washington Post*, May 3, 2022.

259 "I don't think anybody knows": Jade Hurley, interviewed by Shefali Luthra, March 28, 2023.

259 Biden instructed: Shefali Luthra, "Biden Signs Executive Order on Abortion Access and Legal Backing," *The 19th*, July 8, 2022.

259 The administration tried: Candice Norwood, "Biden Administration Clarifies That Pregnant People Can Receive Abortions for Emergency Care," *The 19th*, July 11, 2022.

259 the Department of Justice sued: Mariel Padilla, "After Slow Response, Biden Administration Ramps Up Abortion Access Protections," *The 19th*, August 5, 2022.

259 The Department of Veterans Affairs: Mariel Padilla, "*The 19th* Explains: How Pregnant Veterans May Access Abortions Despite State Restrictions," *The 19th*, September 8, 2022.

259 In early 2023, the Department of Defense: Haley Britzky and Oren Liebermann, "U.S. Military Says It Will Grant Service Members Up to 3 Weeks Leave to Travel for Abortions," CNN, February 16, 2023.

260 CVS and Walgreens: Shefali Luthra, "Two Major Pharmacies Say They Plan to Offer Medication Abortions. Here's What That Could Mean," *The 19th*, January 5, 2023.

260 The latter provision: Cobun Zweifel-Keegan, interviewed by Shefali Luthra, April 25, 2023.

261 "some expansion of their understanding": Tina Smith, interviewed by Shefali Luthra, April 17, 2023.

261 "They use the word now": Mazie Hirono, interviewed by Shefali Luthra, April 21, 2023.

261 Texas's attorney general: 5:22-cv-00185-H: *State of Texas et al. v. Xavier Becerra*, U.S. District Court Northern District of Texas, Lubbock Division, August 23, 2022.

262 In Alaska, Kansas: Alice Miranda Ollstein, "Walgreens Won't Distribute Abortion Pills in States Where GOP AGs Object," *Politico*, March 2, 2023.

262 The threat was too much: Rachel Cohen, "The Sole US Supplier of a Major Abortion Pill Said It Would Not Distribute the Drug in 31 States," *Vox*, March 17, 2023.

262 And when the Biden administration: Alice Miranda Ollstein, "Biden's HIPAA Expansion for Abortion Draws Criticism, Lawsuit Threats," *Politico*, July 18, 2023.

262   In 2023, more than four hundred bills: Annys Shin, N. Kirkpatrick, and Anne Branigin, "Anti-Trans Bills Have Doubled Since 2022. Our Map Shows Where States Stand," *The Washington Post*, April 17, 2023.

263   It was one she feared: Mary Ziegler, interviewed by Shefali Luthra, April 17, 2023.

264   This was the kind of question: Alyssa, interviewed by Shefali Luthra, May 14, 2023.

266   But if he couldn't let himself: Jasper, interviewed by Shefali Luthra, April 6, 2023.

EPILOGUE   THE WORLD AFTER *DOBBS*

267   Tiff had started working at Little Caesars: Tiff, interviewed by Shefali Luthra, April 16, 2023.

268   Per the Bureau of Labor Statistics: "Occupational Employment and Wage Statistics," U.S. Bureau of Labor Statistics, May 2022.

269   across the country would decline dramatically: Alison Norris and Ushma Upadhyay, "#WeCount Report," Society of Family Planning, October 24, 2023.

269   in the nine months after Senate Bill 8: Suzanne O. Bell, Elizabeth A. Stuart, and Alison Gemmill, "Texas' 2021 Ban on Abortions in Early Pregnancy and Changes in Live Births," *JAMA*, June 29, 2023, https://doi:10 .1001/jama.2023.12034.

270   The data offered some: Brittni Frederiksen, Usha Ranji, Ivette Gomez, and Alina Salganicoff, "A National Survey of OBGYNs' Experiences After *Dobbs*," KFF, June 21, 2023.

271   How many more had died: Kam, interviewed by Shefali Luthra, June 4, 2023.

271   Lauren Miller: Shefali Luthra, "Texas Denied Abortions to These Women When Their Lives Were in Danger. Now, They're Suing the State," *The 19th*, March 7, 2023.

271   Preliminary data in Texas: Isabelle Chapman, "Nearly Two Years After Texas' Six-Week Abortion Ban, More Infants Are Dying," CNN, July 30, 2023.

271   National data showed: Danielle M. Ely and Anne K. Driscoll, "Infant Mortality in the United States: Provisional Data from the 2022 Period Linked Birth/Infant Death File," NVSS Vital Statistics Rapid Release, November 1, 2023.

271   For Samantha Casiano: *Zurawski v. State of Texas*, hearing on July 19, 2023.

272   In states with abortion bans: Kavitha Surana, "Maternal Deaths Are Expected to Rise Under Abortion Bans, but the Increase May Be Hard to Measure," ProPublica, July 27, 2023.

272   In 2024, *The New Yorker* published: Stephania Taladrid, "Did an Abor-

tion Ban Cost a Young Texas Woman Her Life?," *The New Yorker,* January 8, 2024.

272   Rochelle Garza, a civil rights attorney: Rochelle Garza, interviewed by Shefali Luthra, August 7, 2023.

272   You could point to Ireland: Krishnadev Calamur, "Pregnant Woman's Death Sparks Abortion Debate in Ireland," NPR, November 15, 2012.

273   In 2023, a woman in Poland: Weronika Strzyzynska, "'All Pregnant Women Are in Danger': Protests in Poland After Expectant Mother Dies in Hospital," *The Guardian,* June 14, 2023.

273   the first such case: Anna Wlodarczka-Semczuk and Kacper Pempel, "Death of Pregnant Woman Ignites Debate About Abortion in Poland," Reuters, November 5, 2021.

273   Rosie contracted an infection: Alexa Garcia-Ditta, "Reckoning with Rosie," *The Texas Observer,* November 3, 2015.

273   "These things have happened already": Cait, interviewed by Shefali Luthra, January 19, 2023.

274   She would suffer: Shefali Luthra, "Bans on Abortion and Gender-Affirming Care Are Driving Doctors from Texas," *The 19th,* June 21, 2023.

275   In 2021, per U.S. Census data: "Quick Facts: Harlingen city, Texas; McAllen city, Texas; Rio Grande City city, Texas; Laredo city, Texas," U.S. Census Bureau, April 2023.

275   About 136,000 undocumented people: Shefali Luthra, "After New Law, a Look Inside One of South Texas' Last Abortion Clinics," *The 19th,* September 27, 2021.

275   Nobody had ever taught Becky: Becky, interviewed by Shefali Luthra, May 15, 2023.

278   Texans—especially those in the Valley: "Texas Has Highest Uninsured Rate, Rio Grande Valley Highest in State," ValleyCentral.com, November 21, 2017.

278   "A lot of the conversations": Nancy Cárdenas Peña, interviewed by Shefali Luthra, April 18, 2023.

279   High-quality data: "Texas Maternal Mortality and Morbidity Report Review Committee and Department of State Health Services Joint Biennial Report 2022," Texas Health and Human Services Department, December 2022.

279   Texas, per one analysis: "The State of Reproductive Health in the United States," Gender Equity Policy Institute, January 19, 2023.

279   He knew it wouldn't stop: Shefali Luthra, "Bans on Abortion and Gender-Affirming Care Are Driving Doctors from Texas," *The 19th,* June 21, 2023.

279   When Whole Woman's Health left: Noemi Pratt, interviewed by Shefali Luthra, April 5, 2023.

279   the clinic's owners sold the building: Eleanor Klibanoff, "Rio Grande

Valley Abortion Clinic Bought by Anti-Abortion Pregnancy Center," *The Texas Tribune,* November 4, 2022.

280   When the leftover pills: Becky, interviewed by Shefali Luthra, May 15, 2023.

283   The latter was something: "Abortion Bans Don't Prosecute Pregnant People. That May Be About to Change," *The 19th,* January 13, 2023.

AFTERWORD

290   "respecting a woman": *Dobbs v. Jackson Women's Health Organization,* Supreme Court of the United States, June 24, 2022.

Index

ABOUT THE AUTHOR

Shefali Luthra has covered national health policy for the past decade, most recently at *The 19th*. She was previously a correspondent for Kaiser Health News, where her work received multiple awards, including a Batten Medal and Headliner Award. Luthra's writing has appeared in *The New York Times* and *The Washington Post,* on NPR, and elsewhere. She lives in Washington, D.C.

A NOTE ON THE TYPE

This book was set in Hoefler Text, a family of fonts designed by Jonathan Hoefler, who was born in 1970. First designed in 1991, Hoefler Text was intended as an advancement on existing desktop computer typography, including as it does an exponentially larger number of glyphs than previous fonts. In form, Hoefler Text looks to the old-style fonts of the seventeenth century, but it is wholly of its time, employing a precision and sophistication only available to the late twentieth century.

Typeset by Scribe,
Philadelphia, Pennsylvania

Printed and bound by Berryville Graphics,
Berryville, Virginia